D1590452

BUILDING THE SOUTH SIDE

HISTORICAL STUDIES OF URBAN AMERICA

Edited by Kathleen N. Conzen, Timothy J. Gilfoyle, and James R. Grossman

ALSO IN THE SERIES

Parish Boundaries: The Catholic Encounter with Race in the Twentieth-Century Urban North
by John T. McGreevy

Modern Housing for America: Policy Struggles in the New Deal Era
by Gail Radford

Smoldering City: Chicagoans and the Great Fire, 1871–1874
by Karen Sawislak

Making the Second Ghetto: Race and Housing in Chicago, 1940–1960
by Arnold R. Hirsch

Faces along the Bar: Lore and Order in the Workingman's Saloon, 1870–1920
by Madelon Powers

Streets, Railroads, and the Great Strike of 1877
by David O. Stowell

The Creative Destruction of Manhattan, 1900–1940
by Max Page

Brownsville, Brooklyn: Blacks, Jews, and the Changing Face of the Ghetto
by Wendell Prichett

My Blue Heaven: Life and Politics in the Working-Class Suburbs of Los Angeles, 1920–1965
by Becky M. Nicolaides

In the Shadow of Slavery: African Americans in New York City, 1626–1863
by Leslie M. Harris

Downtown America: A History of the Place and the People Who Made It
by Alison Isenberg

Places of Their Own: African American Suburbanization in the Twentieth Century
by Andrew Wiese

BUILDING THE SOUTH SIDE

Urban Space and Civic Culture in Chicago
1890–1919

ROBIN F. BACHIN

UNIVERSITY OF CHICAGO PRESS
Chicago and London

ROBIN F. BACHIN

is the Charlton W. Tebeau associate professor of history
at the University of Miami.

The University of Chicago Press, Chicago 60637
The University of Chicago Press, Ltd., London

Printed in the United States of America

13 12 11 10 09 08 07 06 05 04   1 2 3 4 5

ISBN: 0-226-03393-7 (cloth)

Library of Congress Cataloging-in-Publication Data

Bachin, Robin Faith.

Building the South Side : urban space and civic culture in Chicago, 1890–1919 / Robin F. Bachin.

p. cm. — (Historical studies of urban America)

Includes bibliographical references (p.) and index.

ISBN 0-226-03393-7 (alk. paper)

1. Sociology, Urban—Illinois—Chicago. 2. Social values—Illinois—Chicago. 3. Chicago (Ill.)—Social conditions. 4. Working class—Illinois—Chicago. 5. Chicago (Ill.)—Race relations. I. Title. II. Series.

HN80.C5 B33 2004
307.76′09773′11—dc22

2003015711

♾ The paper used in this publication meets the minimum requirements of the American National Standard for Information Sciences—Permanence of Paper for Printed Library Materials, ANSI Z39.48-1992.

CONTENTS

ACKNOWLEDGMENTS

CHICAGO IS A CITY OF EXTREMES. Its image is shaped by gleaming modern skyscrapers and bleak public housing projects; the glistening waters of Lake Michigan and the barren landscape of the prairie; the wealth of the Gold Coast and the desolation of the slum; the celebration of diversity in this city of neighborhoods and the reality of ethnic and racial segregation, conflict, and violence. Yet one of the most striking features of this study in contrasts is Chicagoans' deep sense of civic pride and attachment to place. Perhaps it is the underdog appeal of being the "second city" or the celebration of grit and hard work that characterizes the "city of the big shoulders." Whatever the cause, Chicago, unlike many cities similar in size and scope, has been able to cultivate a clear sense of place and a commitment to civic ideals that often transcend the class, ethnic, racial, and religious backgrounds of its residents. This book explores the sources of these contrasts and the foundations of these civic ideals.

Many people and institutions aided in the preparation of this book. Several librarians and archivists proved invaluable in helping me identify sources and locate materials. I thank the special collections staffs at the Archdiocese of Chicago; the Burnham and Ryerson Libraries at the Art Institute of Chicago; the Chicago Park District; the Chicago Public Library; the Newberry Library; the Rockefeller Archive Center; and the University of Chicago. For help locating images for the book, I thank Julia

Bachrach at the Chicago Park District, Deborah Gillaspie at the Chicago Jazz Archive, Meredith Taussig at the Chicago Landmarks Commission, Debra Levine at the University of Chicago Library Special Collections Research Center, Bruce Raeburn at the Hogan Jazz Archive at Tulane University, and Piriya Vongkasemsiri at the Chicago Historical Society. For help in identifying sources on Comiskey Park, I thank Philip Bess, Robert Bluthardt, Douglas Bukowski, Charles Comiskey III, Richard Lindberg, and the Society for American Baseball Research. The Chicago Historical Society was my home for countless days as I made my way through their vast holdings of Chicago-related materials. That search was made much more efficient and enjoyable by the aid and support of archivist Archie Motley. It was with profound sadness that I learned of Archie's death as I was finishing this book. Archie was a model archivist; he knew the collections inside and out and constantly pointed researchers to materials they otherwise would not have found. His expert guidance, his passion for his work, and his love of all things Chicago will be sorely missed.

This book would not have been possible without the support of several grants and fellowships. An Andrew Mellon Foundation postdoctoral fellowship at the Newberry Library was crucial in helping me rework the manuscript and conduct new archival research. Participation in a National Endowment for the Humanities Summer Institute on the Built Environment of the American Metropolis helped me reframe some of my thinking about cities and civic culture, and I am indebted to the other seminar participants who shared their own work and ideas. The University of Miami provided support for research through Max Orovitz Summer Awards and General Research Support Awards. At the dissertation stage, I received support from the Rockefeller Archive Center in Pocantico Hills, New York, and from the Department of History and the Horace H. Rackham School of Graduate Study at the University of Michigan. The Richard H. Driehaus Foundation provided a subvention to offset publication costs of the book.

Several scholars read portions of the manuscript during various stages in the writing. For their time and thoughtful comments, I thank Henry Binford, Linda Borish, Robert Bruegmann, Michael Ebner, Elliott Gorn, Ann Keating, James Kloppenberg, Sherry Ortner, Dominic Pacyga, Steven Riess, Karen Sawislak, David Schuyler, Carl Smith, and Donald Spivey. I am deeply indebted to my dissertation committee—David Scobey, Earl Lewis, Terrence McDonald, and Rebecca Zurier—for their careful readings, continued encouragement, and perspicacious comments. For their friendship and support, and their constant willingness to share ideas from their own work,

I thank Georgina Hickey, Alison Isenberg, Erik Seeman, and Victoria Wolcott. For her unending hospitality during my numerous visits to Chicago, I am grateful to Carol Summerfield.

I also thank several colleagues in the history department at the University of Miami who have enhanced the intellectual environment here, including Edmund Abaka, Edward Baptist, Martha Few, and Hugh Thomas. Donald Spivey has been a wonderful colleague, mentor, and friend, and I value his guidance and support. Members of the University of Miami Humanities Colloquium pushed me to think more broadly about issues of urbanism, aesthetics, civic identity, and the public sphere. I especially thank Leslie Bow, Russ Castronovo, David Glimp, Michael Rothberg, and Maria Stampino. Finally, several students provided much-needed research assistance in the final stages of writing. They include Elizabeth Allard, Maria McCaughey-Rivas, James Otterson, and Aldo Regalado.

The series editors and the editors at the University of Chicago Press have been enthusiastic and encouraging from the start. Timothy Gilfoyle provided the most engaged and thoughtful reading of the manuscript I could have hoped for. James Grossman shared his insights on the South Side and also suggested stylistic changes that improved the quality of the book. Robert Devens expertly guided the book through every stage of revision and publication with unflagging patience and good humor. Alice Bennett's editing of the text was meticulous and masterly. I thank them all for lending assistance throughout the publication process.

My parents, Pearl and Zachary Bramnick, have provided constant support and encouragement throughout my academic career. From my earliest days in school, they stressed the value of education and encouraged me to pursue my academic goals. My husband, David Coppola, has been a source of continuous inspiration during the long days and nights of researching, writing, and revising. He provided the love, companionship, and reassurance that made completing the book much more enjoyable. After the birth of our daughter Marissa, he saw to it that the demands of parenting would not interfere with my need to finish this book on time. His unflagging support of my work has been a treasure; no words can convey how thankful I am for his presence in my life.

INTRODUCTION

IN THE FALL OF 1893, Universalist minister John Coleman Adams traveled to the South Side of Chicago to attend the World's Columbian Exposition, the celebration of the four hundredth anniversary of Columbus's landing in the New World. Adams was one of over 27 million people to visit the fair, which celebrated American technological, scientific, and social achievements (fig. 1). Gazing at the neoclassical buildings that dominated the fairgrounds, Adams reveled in the beauty of the glorious "White City." All the buildings, with a few notable exceptions, harked back to classical forms to showcase the ideal of democracy and its links to ancient Greek and Roman civilization. The buildings suggested the mastery of modern science and technology and at the same time drew connections to the past to show that America was the site of democratic progress (fig. 2). Adams envisioned the White City as a place that was "orderly and convenient. . . . Nothing in any of the exhibits within the walls of these great buildings was half so interesting, so suggestive, so full of hopeful intonations, as the Fair in its aspects as a city by itself. In the midst of a very real city, full of the faults which Chicago so preeminently displays, we saw a great many features of what an ideal city might be, a great many visions which perhaps one day will become solid facts."[1]

FIGURE 1. The classicism and symmetry of the City Beautiful ideal was embodied in the design of the 1893 World's Columbian Exposition. Courtesy of the Chicago Historical Society.

For Adams the fair symbolized the faith in the ability of the urban landscape to shape progress and foster civic order and harmony, the guiding principles of the emerging City Beautiful movement in urban planning. Fair promoters and many visitors alike saw head architect Daniel Burnham's White City as an embodiment of the ideal city. It represented the civic leaders' desire to control urban growth and create a planned environment in which beauty and harmony prevailed. The fair was an opportunity to create a model city in which the problems plaguing modern American cities—crowding, poor living conditions, class and ethnic tensions—would be eradicated.[2]

The fair was significant not only for reflecting the emergence of large-scale planning ideals but also for including sites of commercial leisure and mass amusement. The Midway offered a diversion from the White City and the grandiose ideas about planning, culture, and civic identity it embodied. Set up on a strip of land that connected Jackson Park, the location of the 633-acre fairgrounds, with Washington Park to the northwest, it functioned as a space quite distinct from the main fairgrounds. The Midway housed exotic and risqué exhibits, serving as a place of less controlled leisure and introducing elements of the emerging culture of amusement into the fairgrounds.

The Midway accomplished this carnivalesque atmosphere by linking "primitivism"

FIGURE 2. Frontispiece to 1893 World's Fair guidebook. Courtesy of the Chicago Historical Society.

FIGURE 3. Scene from the Streets of Cairo, World's Columbian Exposition. Courtesy of the Chicago Historical Society.

with the celebration of the burlesque (fig. 3). Initially under the direction of anthropologist F. W. Putnam, it showcased educational exhibits of "primitive" cultures in their "natural" habitats, showing the progress toward civilization. To demonstrate the supposed racial superiority of white Americans over other cultures, Putnam used the latest "scientific" evidence of the day, such as phrenology, which purported to assess brain functions by measuring head size and shape. Putnam traveled abroad and brought back examples of people and artifacts that he displayed on the Midway, including reconstructions of villages from China, Lapland, and Java and from American Indian reservations. Next there were Austrian, German, and Irish villages. As one traveled up the Midway, the visitor purportedly moved from least to most civilized, culminating in the figures of the perfect man and woman, created based on composite measurements of 25,000 white Americans. Yet fair organizers ultimately replaced Putnam with Sol Bloom, a protégé of P. T. Barnum, and the "anthropological" section of the fair took on the air of a carnival sideshow.[3]

In addition to housing the displays of "less civilized" races, the Midway was the site of exotic and risqué amusements. Here visitors witnessed a Cairo street fair, a Japanese bazaar, a Moorish palace, dancing animals, and hootchy-kootchy girls. So both elements—the progression of exotic foreign villages and the inclusion of risqué mass amusement, transformed the Midway into a place where one could glimpse the "exotic"—but at a safe distance. The Midway offered an opportunity for voyeurism into cultures that were deemed threatening or licentious, both the cultures of the "uncivilized" and the emerging mass culture of nickelodeons, vaudeville, and burlesque houses that challenged the values of middle- and upper-class America. One critic, writing in the *Dial* magazine, complained, "The commercial motive has forced its way to the surface, and has become the controlling influence in [fair promoters'] action." He continued, "Amusement, of cheap and even vulgar sorts, is being substituted for education, because most people prefer being amused to being instructed."[4]

Perhaps the most memorable symbol from the fair was the Ferris wheel (fig. 4). Designed by bridge builder George Ferris, the wheel was a steel testament to American

FIGURE 4. Ferris wheel, World's Columbian Exposition. Courtesy of the Chicago Historical Society.

ingenuity and scale, a symbol of progress, while serving a practical function of giving fairgoers a bird's-eye view of the entire panorama. And what they saw was the well-ordered city Adams discussed, as well as a clear separation between the classical design of the White City and the exoticism of the Midway.

The fair symbolized the emerging faith in the ability of the physical structure and design of cities to shape their civic and social cohesion. Its layout also inscribed in the landscape a sharp separation between places of cultural uplift (the White City) and areas of mass amusement (the Midway). This connection between the physical landscape of the city and broader civic ideals, and the circumscribed place of commercial leisure within urban spaces, constitute the subject of this book.

Building the South Side examines the relation between urban space and civic culture in Chicago during the Progressive Era. I discuss urban planning as a political and cultural process whereby various city leaders, both men and women, sought to create an urban public sphere that emphasized their (sometimes conflicting) visions of order, respectability, and civic identity. The University of Chicago, the South Park system, Comiskey Park, and the emerging Black Belt all were arenas in which community leaders looked to the physical design of the city to shape new public spheres of civic interaction (fig. 5). They represented what Nancy Fraser calls "arenas of discursive interaction" where citizens came together to address common experiences and concerns. These sites had within them the potential to create a shared sense of civic unity, but also the possibility of promoting diverse ethnic, racial, gender, and class interests.[5] Even in spaces outside the traditional political arena (of ward politics and ballot boxes), then, important conflicts were taking place that exposed the distribution of power and resources in the city and promoted new political coalitions. Thus the creation of a local terrain of civic culture was a contested process, with the battle for cultural authority transforming urban politics and blurring the lines between private and public, labor and leisure, and civic and commercial space.

The planning and use of urban space were integrally linked to a new civic culture emerging at the turn of the century. "Civic culture" was the desire to foster a shared sense of local identity and social engagement that had the potential to transcend boundaries of ethnicity, race, religion, and class. At the core of debates over civic cul-

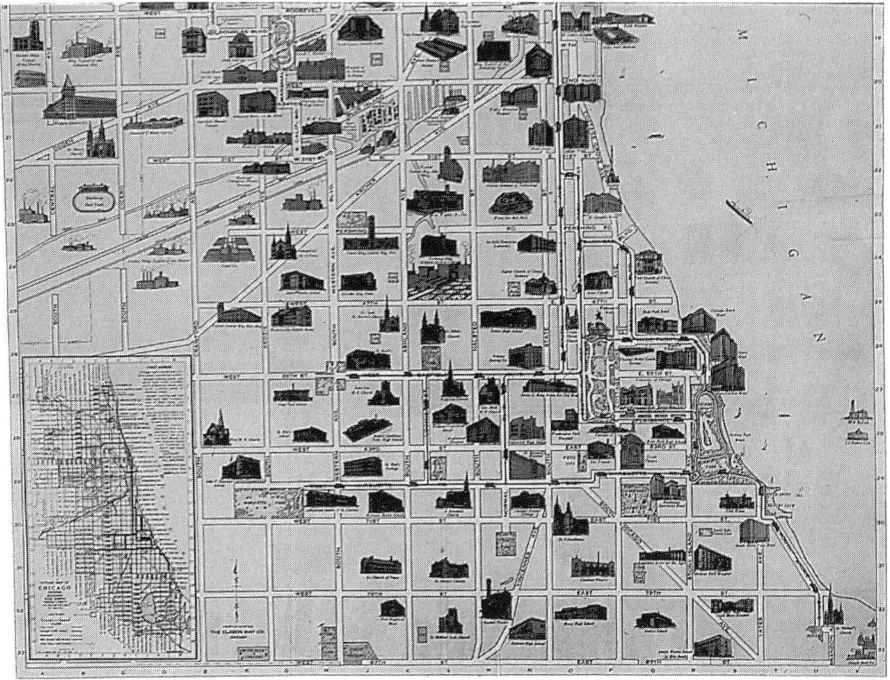

FIGURE 5. Location of cultural institutions in Chicago (South Side portion shown), *Chicago Motor Coach Map* (Chicago: Clason Map Company, 1926).

ture was the question of how social democracy could best be formulated within the city. These debates were shaped in part by a crisis of knowledge that challenged old certainties about social, cultural, and political authority. The emerging faith in the power of experts and social science to transform knowledge and shape urban growth forced a reexamination of the power of religious leaders, genteel elites, and ward bosses. In the process, a new language of politics and civic discourse emerged that emphasized the role of the expert in democratic culture but made the rhetoric of expertise available to a variety of groups in the city. Machine politicians, labor leaders, and female reformers appropriated this language of expertise in order to achieve public visibility and gain access to city spaces previously off-limits to them, thereby staking out spaces for themselves in the urban environment. At the same time, some of these groups challenged the notion that expertise should form the foundation of urban politics and posited alternative visions of how social democracy might be shaped.[6]

These efforts to shape civic culture were grounded in issues relating to the design, planning, and use of urban space. Civic leaders posited strong connections between the physical shape of the city and civic identity. This belief in the problem-solving and reforming capacity of the urban landscape—what I am calling "progressive urbanism" —assumed multiple forms between 1890 and 1920. Numerous leaders, including university administrators, park promoters, and mass culture entrepreneurs, looked to the physical design of the city to give form to their visions of urban culture. They linked city building with community building. The physical shape of the city was to reflect the values of order, harmony, and democracy that many believed were threatened in a rapidly changing urban environment. At the same time, though, various groups throughout the city often inscribed competing meanings on city spaces. Their alternative prescriptions for appropriate uses forced changes in the function and broader civic value of urban spaces.

Three different, and often competing, models of civic culture emerge from an examination of these diverse sites. One reflected the culture of centralization and consolidation that defined both the corporate world and the world of technocratic expertise. Civic leaders like University of Chicago president William Rainey Harper and architect and planner Daniel Burnham exemplified a belief in elite cultural uplift, in which reform came from above and was disseminated by trained experts who could be the best stewards of cultural refinement. Harper's plans for a centralized educational system and Burnham's model of city planning incorporated similar models of centralization, with all functions of a cohesive system emanating from one corporate center. This corporatist model of progressive urbanism was exemplified in part by the rise of a bureaucratic state that looked to trained experts to shape civic culture and public policy based on "scientific" principles of reform.

At the same time, an alternative vision of civic culture emerged, one that stressed citizen activism and cross-class alliances in promoting democratic culture and shaping civic institutions. This symbiotic model of urban reform saw dialogue between various groups in the city as the key to refashioning democratic culture by creating new spheres of social interaction. Reformers like Jane Addams and Mary McDowell, labor leaders like John Fitzpatrick and Margaret Haley, and black civic leaders like Ida B. Wells-Barnett saw in spaces like settlement houses and public parks the potential for forging new alliances that would overcome social distance among urban residents. Instead of consolidating political power in a bureaucratic government or expert elite, these reformers sought to diffuse power and reshape municipal government through coalition building and the multiplication of actors on the political stage.

Running through both of these reform ideologies was a strain of anticommercialism. Planners like Burnham and reformers like McDowell, Addams, and Wells-Barnett feared the effect of the rise of commercial culture on efforts to create a cohesive social order. In arenas of commercial culture like amusement parks and professional sports stadiums they saw the potential for behavior that distracted from, and even challenged, the promotion of a dynamic civic culture. Yet promoters of commercial culture, and many of the spectators who visited these sites, did not see these venues as antithetical to civic uplift, social cohesion, and respectability. Rather, promoters of commercial amusement like Chicago White Sox owner Charles Comiskey, black baseball entrepreneur Andrew "Rube" Foster, and black theater owner Robert Motts helped legitimize mass culture by infusing it with the rhetoric of Americanism, urban reform, and civic pride. They carved out alternative spaces of civic culture that stressed accessibility, entertainment, and working-class recreation as important features of public culture in the city. These spaces illustrated the multiple dimensions of urban citizenship, whereby city residents shaped their sense of civic identity based on participation in an emerging culture of leisure that ultimately helped forge broader access to the political arena.

THE POLITICS OF URBAN SPACE

Urban space and the power relations reflected in its arrangement are central elements in understanding the relationship between urban planning and politics. As geographer David Harvey explains, "The ability to influence the production of space is an important means to augment social power."[7] What architectural historian Dolores Hayden calls the "power of place" illustrates the variety of ways urban spaces are invested with meaning by multiple groups in the city. The processes that shape the physical landscape, including real estate development and speculation, architecture and design, state regulation and promotion, and residents' uses of city spaces, reflect the contested nature of urban development.[8]

This contestation in the process of planning and building the city points to the multiple ways urban residents imagined their place in the city and created public spheres of social interaction to foster civic engagement. According to political philosopher William M. Sullivan, "The social space of civic culture, embodied in institutions that enable public discussion and cooperation to take place, adds new norms to those that govern relations in civil society." He adds, "The social space of civic culture, then, structures a common point of view about what is rightfully 'public.' Participants in civic cultures in turn develop a sense of self for which common goods realized in the public sphere are critical aspects of individual identities."[9] He argues that one's sense of individual rights is shaped by the variety of interactions that take place within the public sphere. Yet he also exposes the importance of recognizing the existence of multiple public spheres in shaping civic engagement.

Feminist scholars have been at the forefront of highlighting how multiple public spheres structure the creation of political identities. They have pointed to the erosion of boundaries between the private and public, personal and political, and challenged the notion of a unified and cohesive public sphere.[10] Instead, feminist geographers like Linda McDowell suggest that by identifying multiple or alternative public spheres we might expand the meaning of political engagement while at the same time acknowledging the differences in power that allow some forms of civic discourse to eclipse others. She also argues that by locating multiple sites of civic culture, scholars might better understand the variety of groups that have a stake in the city-building process.[11] This model of urban politics locates spatial relations at the center of political debate and suggests how interactions in urban space expand and redefine the meanings and practices of citizenship.[12]

Recently, historians have explored the shifting meanings of citizenship in urban political history. In *The Public City,* Philip Ethington analyzes how people defined themselves as political actors in a democracy. Ethington views Progressivism as a process by which a variety of groups in the city "became mobilized and integrated into relations with the state." This model of "pluralist liberalism," whereby various groups claimed political rights based on need, transformed urban politics and created new relationships between individuals and the state.[13] Ethington, though, does not address the relation between public spheres and public space and the specific arenas in which civic discourse was shaped. In *Civic Wars,* Mary P. Ryan emphasizes the instability of national identity and citizenship in the nineteenth century and illustrates how numerous political actors represented these identities in a variety of public spaces. Ryan explores the shifting boundaries of private and public, with public spaces like parks becoming increasingly regulated and identified with markers of private largesse, and commercial sites like amusement parks becoming primary places of public interaction. Ryan stops short, however, of accepting these commercial leisure spaces as legitimate sites of civic culture.[14]

By contrast, in *The Park and the People* Roy Rosenzweig and Elizabeth Blackmar focus on the ways reform, leisure, recreation, and commercial culture increasingly structured civic debate and provided forums for various groups within the city to negotiate their changing roles as political actors and citizens.[15] Similarly, Jean-Christophe Agnew suggests that through access to spaces of commercial leisure immigrants acquired a sense of cultural citizenship "on terms far more generous and hospitable than those laid down by church and state."[16] Robin D. G. Kelley argues for the importance of examining the "hidden social spaces that tend to fall between the cracks of political history," especially in the case of African American history, so as to more fully understand the variety of meanings of citizenship.[17]

I build on the work of these scholars by illustrating the contested nature of forging civic identity and showing how a variety of sites could function as new arenas of public discourse.[18] The creation of new civic cultures in Chicago was not the sole property of cultural elites and middle-class reformers. Rather, leisure spaces such as parks, playgrounds, baseball stadiums, and dance halls embodied a new and distinct civic identity, transforming these sites into places of discursive political interaction. Instead of viewing commercial culture as an element of urban life that detracted from "authentic" working-class experience or as a site of alternative working-class subcultures, this book seeks a more nuanced interpretation. Commercial culture functioned in both of these ways, but it was also part of the larger project of the promotion of urban civic culture and changing definitions of citizenship.

Resituating debates over urban identity and civic culture allows scholars to rethink our understanding of Progressivism. In debates over the meaning of Progressivism, many scholars point to the difficulty of defining turn-of-the-century urban reform because its proponents pursued programs of both "structural" and "moral" reform.[19] Yet most of the discussion centers on the work of an elite group of reformers. Rather than emphasizing the desire of elites to recover an idyllic preindustrial social order, I examine Progressivism as a means through which various groups—industrialists, middle-class reformers, labor leaders, immigrant groups, and commercial entrepreneurs—sought to establish cultural legitimacy and authority within the terrain of class upheaval and cultural crisis that shaped the turn-of-the-century city. These groups used the language of reform to stake claims to city spaces to be designed and used according to their own prescriptions for creating a livable city. Progressivism, then, was not just a positivist, cause-and-effect response to perceived "problems" in the urban landscape, nor was it an example of elites' imposing social control on immigrant working-class populations in the city. Instead, Progressivism emerges as a process whereby numerous actors sought to reform the city based on their competing ideas of urban citizenship, city planning, and access to public space.[20]

This book also pushes the boundaries of historical definitions of urban planning and design. Recent historians of planning have illuminated the complex process of urban development. Yet much of planning history remains focused on the planner as the primary shaper of urban growth, often ignoring the roles played by urban communities in challenging both the design and the use of city spaces.[21] Other studies emphasize the promotional and regulatory nature of the state in shaping urban growth.[22] In addition, some recent scholars have demonstrated the strong connections between private interests and public policy in structuring city development.[23] This book offers a more expansive view of planning history, examining how various urban residents sought to imprint their identities and interests on city spaces through the ways they both designed and used them.[24]

Finally, I link the study of "high" and popular culture by examining arenas of recreation as important places for understanding American urban culture more broadly. Recent scholars have demonstrated how the public sphere of mass amusements and consumer pleasure helped break down some of the physical boundaries of class and gender that previously defined urban culture in America.[25] At the same time, though, the emergence of mass commercial culture had within it the potential for constructing new hierarchies that would define and circumscribe acceptable modes of public display. I show how leisure sites took on added significance as both reformers and promoters of mass amusement sought to make behavior in these spaces reflect their carefully delineated frameworks of acceptable social interaction—between classes, between men and women, and between races.

CHICAGO IN TRANSITION

The South Side of Chicago is a particularly salient site for studying these transformations in urban culture. The area encompassed a mix of people that crossed ethnic, racial, and class boundaries and comprised landscapes as diverse a prairie lands, industrial manufacturing districts, and elite suburbs. Many scholars have studied the growth of commercial culture and the rise of downtown to understand how the city grew at the turn of the century. Yet the central business district reflects only part of the urban vision that city boosters and other urban residents hoped to establish. Many promoters of civic pride looked to other spaces, those not associated with commerce, trade, and industry, to put forth an image of urban culture in Chicago.[26] The South Side was a microcosm of efforts to create a landscape that reflected civic pride and unity. At the same time, it pointed out the contradictions in these visions and exposed the tensions and conflicts that emerged as various groups came together to stake a claim to the urban landscape.

The South Side embodied many of the dramatic transformations Chicago experienced during the nineteenth century, transformations resulting from changes that allowed Chicago to become the metropolis of the Midwest. William Cronon's authoritative work on the growth of Chicago as an urban center points to the interaction between natural landscapes and built environments as a central feature of understanding urban development. As early as 1833, when white settlers signed a treaty with the Potawatomis and incorporated the town, Chicago boosters saw in this swampy prairie the potential for a great gateway between natural resources in the West and financial markets in the East. The Chicago River, while not a great waterway, provided a natural passage to the Mississippi River, the Great Lakes, and ultimately the Atlantic Ocean via the Erie Canal. This vast transportation system, with a little help from human alterations in the land through the construction of railroads, made Chicago into the gateway to the West (fig. 6). The city soon became a leader in the manufacturing and transportation of lumber, grain, meat, and related products throughout the nation. Moreover, the buying, selling, processing, and transporting of these products helped establish the Chicago Board of Trade as the center of commercial and financial growth in the city and the region. Land speculators, real estate developers, and manufacturers flooded into the region, platting out land, buying and selling parcels, and establishing industries. The population increased dramatically, and the city began annexing surrounding areas as early as 1850 (fig. 7).[27]

The rise of an industrial capitalist economy was reflected in the physical landscape of Chicago.[28] In place of prairie grasses and swamps, there now stood logging sheds, packing plants, grain elevators, steel yards, and railroad tracks. These physical artifacts were testimony to Chicago's phoenix-like rise from the ashes of the Great Fire of 1871 to become a leader in industrial growth. This image of the city was memorialized in literature and poetry about Chicago and often cast an unflattering shadow on the

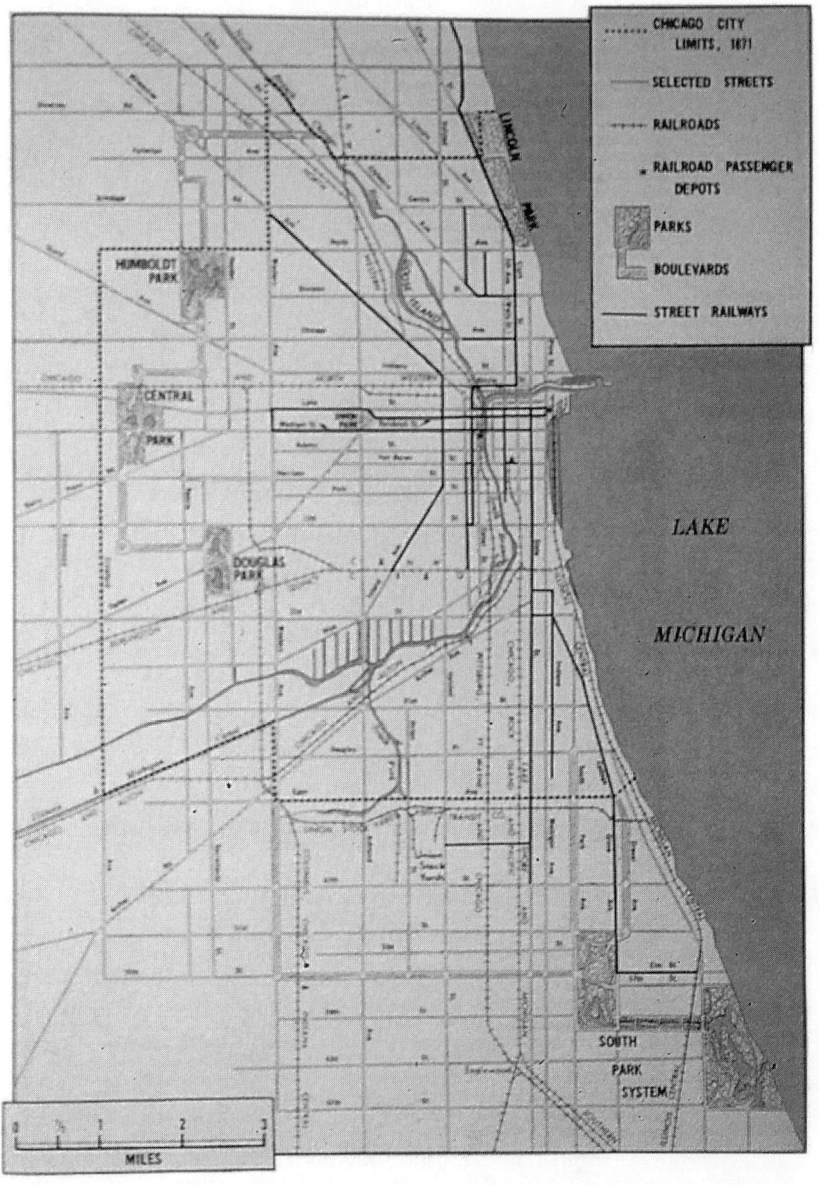

FIGURE 6. Parks and Railroads in 1871. Harold M. Mayer and Richard C. Wade, *Chicago: Growth of a Metropolis* (Chicago: University of Chicago Press, 1969), 69. Used with the permission of the University of Chicago Press.

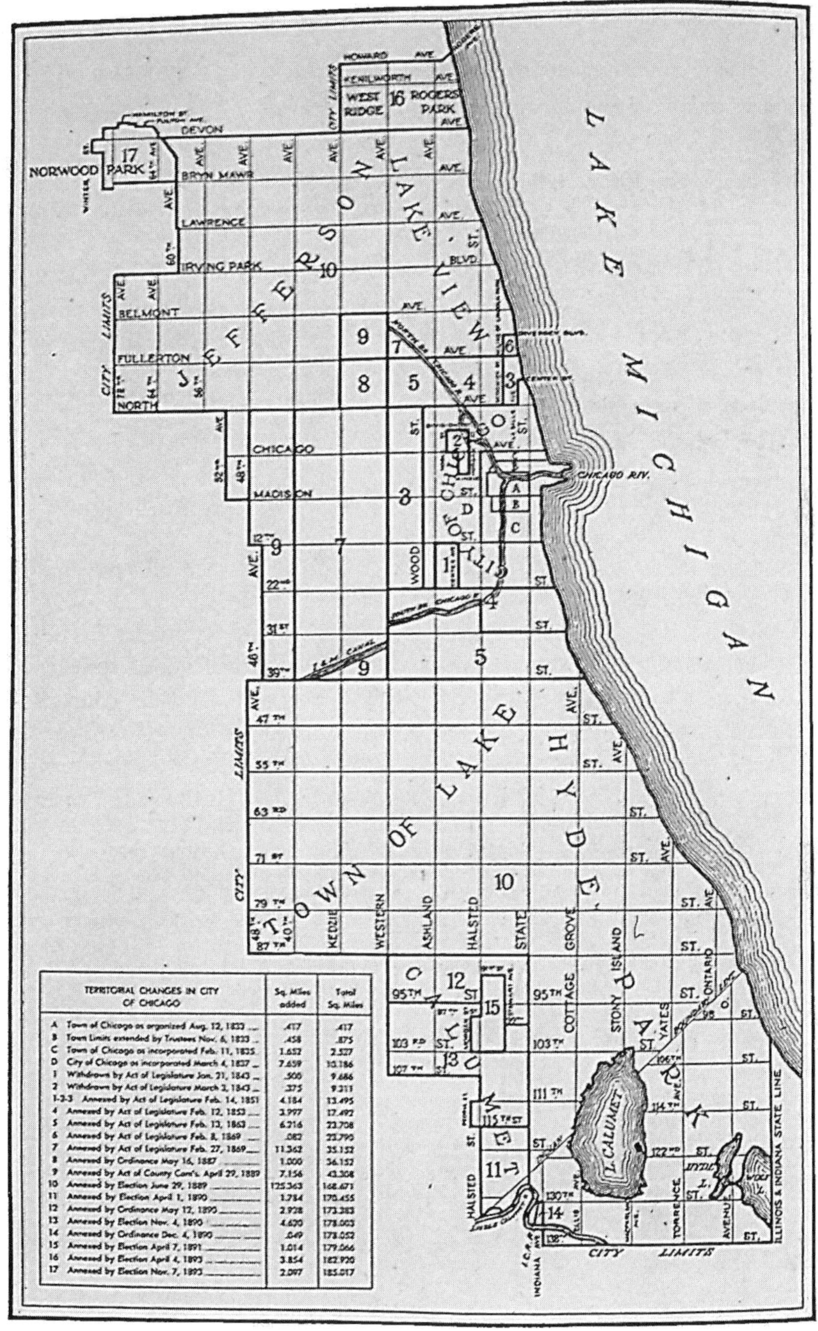

TERRITORIAL CHANGES IN CITY OF CHICAGO	Sq. Miles added	Total Sq. Miles
A Town of Chicago as organized Aug. 12, 1833	.417	.417
B Town Limits extended by Trustees Nov. 6, 1833	.458	.875
C Town of Chicago as incorporated Feb. 11, 1835	1.652	2.527
D City of Chicago as incorporated March 4, 1837	7.659	10.186
1 Withdrawn by Act of Legislature Jan. 21, 1843	.500	9.686
2 Withdrawn by Act of Legislature March 3, 1843	.375	9.311
1-2-3 Annexed by Act of Legislature Feb. 14, 1851	4.184	13.495
4 Annexed by Act of Legislature Feb. 12, 1853	3.997	17.492
5 Annexed by Act of Legislature Feb. 13, 1863	6.216	23.708
6 Annexed by Act of Legislature Feb. 8, 1869	.082	23.790
7 Annexed by Act of Legislature Feb. 27, 1869	11.362	35.152
8 Annexed by Ordinance May 16, 1887	1.000	36.152
9 Annexed by Act of County Com's. April 29, 1889	7.156	43.308
10 Annexed by Election June 29, 1889	125.363	168.671
11 Annexed by Election April 1, 1890	1.784	170.455
12 Annexed by Ordinance May 12, 1890	2.928	173.383
13 Annexed by Election Nov. 4, 1890	4.620	178.003
14 Annexed by Ordinance Dec. 4, 1890	.049	178.052
15 Annexed by Election April 7, 1891	1.014	179.066
16 Annexed by Election April 4, 1893	3.854	182.920
17 Annexed by Election Nov. 7, 1893	2.097	185.017

FIGURE 7. Growth of Chicago by annexations, to 1893. Bessie Louise Pierce, *A History of Chicago*, vol. 3, *The Rise of a Modern City, 1871–1893* (Chicago: University of Chicago Press, 1957), 334. Used with the permission of the University of Chicago Press.

progress that many Chicagoans wished to celebrate. Perhaps the most famous of these testimonies to Chicago's industrial and commercial growth is Carl Sandburg's *Chicago:*

> Hog Butcher for the World
> Tool Maker, Stacker of Wheat
> Player with Railroads and the Nation's Freight Handler;
> Stormy, husky, brawling,
> City of the Big Shoulders.[29]

Sandburg was not simply describing the conditions of economic growth in Chicago. Rather, he also was excoriating Chicago business leaders and industrialists for their apparent celebration of the greed, speculation, and cunning that created the great metropolis of the Midwest. Sandburg described Chicago as an immature city, one fueled solely by economic incentive, and lacking sophistication of culture and civilization. At the same time, he celebrated its brawny ethos:

> Laughing the stormy, husky, brawling laughter of Youth, half-naked, sweating, proud to be Hog Butcher, Tool Maker, Stacker of Wheat, Player with Railroads and Freight Handler to the Nation.[30]

Many civic leaders, including some of the industrialists responsible for Chicago's commercial growth, lamented this lack of "civilization" and "culture." They sought to create a sense of civic unity and urban order that would make Chicago one of the great cities in the world for cultural refinement and civic pride. Boosters turned to cultural philanthropy as a way to elevate its social character. They saw the opening of cultural institutions as a way to overcome the city's image as a bastion of crass commercialism, frenzied speculation, and unbridled industrial growth. The Art Institute of Chicago (1882), the Chicago Symphony Orchestra (1890), and the Field Columbian Museum (1893) served as emblems of an elite urban vision that linked real estate developers, bankers, and manufacturers in a shared culture of civic uplift.[31]

This model of urban culture resulted from the developing relationship between the city's industrial elite and the rising middle class. George Pullman, Gustavus Swift, Philip Armour, Martin Ryerson, Charles L. Hutchinson, and Marshall Field acquired their wealth through the vast opportunities for economic advancement available in Chicago in the 1880s and 1890s.[32] At the same time, the growth of the business, professional, and retail industries created opportunities for new nonmanual occupations.

Members of the new middle class developed skills and expertise in problem solving that helped them establish associations devoted to addressing problems in the urban environment.[33] Like the industrial elites of the city, many middle-class residents welcomed the opportunities made available by rapid economic growth but were apprehensive about what they saw as the resulting disorder and chaos.[34]

Indeed, Chicago in the nineteenth century experienced dramatic upheavals that challenged the very basis of a unified urban culture. Many of these upheavals resulted from the stark divisions of class and ethnicity that were exposed during and after the 1871 fire.[35] The fire changed the topography of the city in both physical and social ways. New fire codes meant that cheaper wood-frame construction could be used only outside the central business district (though these codes often were violated). As a result, many working-class groups were forced to rebuild shanties and frame homes close to industry, along the Chicago River, while wealthier residents constructed brick and stone homes near the lakefront, in the Gold Coast area, and farther north. Residential segregation created inequities in the distribution of city services, including sanitation, waste removal, water, transportation, and street paving, and resulted in outbreaks of typhoid and cholera.[36] These differences in access to city resources erupted during the 1877 railroad strike, the 1886 Haymarket affair, and the 1894 Pullman strike. At the heart of all these incidents were questions over the relations between capital and labor, politics and the economy, and American identity and ethnic culture.

All these elements of civic debate were symbolized by social and cultural life on the South Side. The annexation of 1889 expanded the South Side and made Chicago the second largest and fastest-growing city in the nation. The area within the city limits increased from 36 to 169 square miles, and the population swelled to over a million.[37] The annexed territory included the emerging Black Belt, the stockyards district and Packingtown, the steel mills, suburban Hyde Park, the South Side pleasure grounds, and the model town of Pullman (fig. 8). The demographic changes taking place in these diverse areas at the turn of the century meant that native-born elites, middle-class professionals, immigrant workers, and black migrants were brought into contact and often conflict with one another in a variety of urban spaces, from workplaces to leisure sites, public transit lines to city streets. How to negotiate the daily contours of these interactions and shape them into experiences of unity rather than division became a concern of many South Side residents.[38]

Indeed, many Chicago civic leaders were optimistic about the possibility of creating a more orderly and harmonious city. The 1893 World's Columbian Exposition embodied these hopes. Part of the reason Chicago was chosen as the host city was the

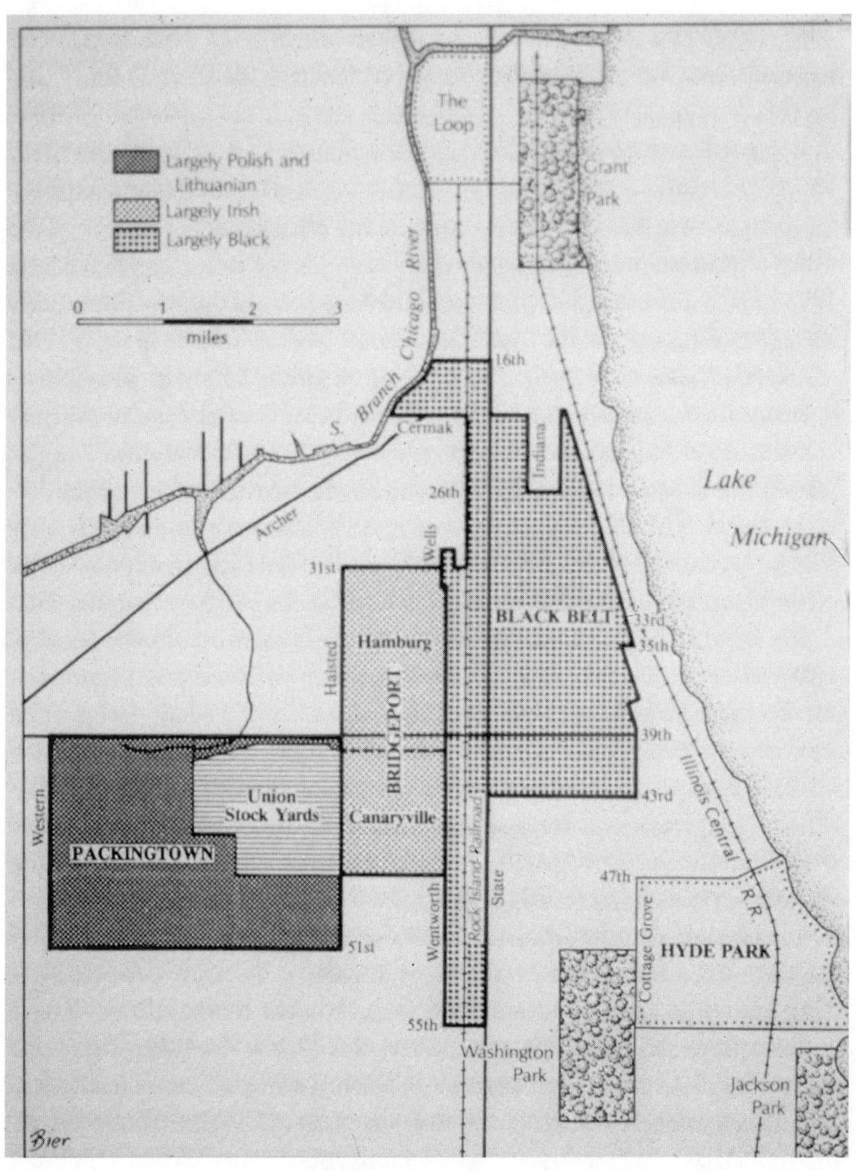

FIGURE 8. Three working-class communities on the South Side, 1920. James R. Barrett, *Work and Community in the Jungle* (Urbana: University of Illinois Press, 1987), 70. Copyright by the Board of Trustees of the University of Illinois, 1987. Used with permission of the University of Illinois Press.

belief that the midwestern metropolis best represented the future of American cities. By creating an ideal city in the midst of this representative American one, fair planners and city boosters could illustrate the promise of America's urban future. The fair dramatically symbolized a variety of groups' faith in the ability of technology and design to shape the physical landscape and lead to civic order and harmony. As a result, reforming the urban environment became a central feature of urban planning and politics in the Progressive Era, focusing on the crucial role urban design played in structuring people's sense of place and community in a rapidly changing American metropolis.

PART ONE

The University and the City

A NEW ORDER OF THINGS

Planning and Building the University of Chicago

IN AN 1895 ARTICLE, writer and University of Chicago English professor Robert Herrick spoke of the momentous development of the university in its few short years of existence. "The university has done more than grow," he wrote, "it has sprung into existence full-armed." He recounted its physical growth as well as the architectural design that gave the school its cohesive presence. Yet the most significant feature of the school's expansion, according to Herrick, was its emerging relationship with surrounding civic, educational, and cultural institutions in Chicago. The university was a "complex organism" that reached out to other institutions and brought them within its grasp.

For Herrick, the modern research university and its new system of affiliation with outside institutions represented the "democratic spirit" of the University of Chicago. The school forced exposure to a larger matrix of people and ideas, providing students with a wide range of associations and becoming a dominant presence in the civic life of the city. The new university was like the city of Chicago itself, according to Herrick, for it represented the hope that the West held for the nation.[1] In contrast to eastern institutions like Harvard, "We look to a new order of things in learning, as in national and social life. In that new life, one fancies, the dominating forces will be traditionless. . . . Our new student will be contemptuous of mere culture, of anything that derives its respect from the past alone; he will despise forms and ceremonies, but he will be powerful in life."[2]

Herrick's celebration of the vast possibilities for learning afforded students of this modern university highlights the University of Chicago's role in forging new ideas about student culture, "scientific" expertise, and the relation between knowledge and social action. Herrick captured the emerging faith in scientific investigation as a means of social action that was embodied in the ideas of those who would become leading University of Chicago scholars, especially pragmatist philosophers John Dewey and George Herbert Mead. The Chicago pragmatists offered theories of truth grounded in human interaction and lived experience, with the scientific study of social behavior shaping public life and political authority. The result of this new approach to learning, according to them, would be nothing less than the reformulation of American democracy, with a knowledgeable citizenry coming together to shape public policy and create a civic culture defined by active individual participation in community life.

Yet even before the official opening of the University of Chicago there were apparent tensions between its expressed ideals and their application. The goal of Chicago-area Baptists to create a college designed to offer a firm theological and classical education seemed at odds with the desire among some promoters to establish a university devoted to modern empirical investigation and scientific research. The founders, along with university president William Rainey Harper, attempted to mitigate this tension by suggesting that locating the university in a city like Chicago made it possible to jointly serve both goals: tending to the moral and theological needs of urban residents and using the city as a laboratory, with students applying the methods of scientific research to better understand the processes fostering social order and civic cohesion. At the same time that administrators supported this uneasy alliance between religion and science, they also created an institution that centralized all aspects of education. The university became what Robert Herrick called "a college trust," reaching out to local educational institutions and then swallowing them up. The university's relationship with the city developed as one based on control rather than collaboration, consolidation rather than cooperation.

The metaphor of the trust is significant because the university was indebted to several wealthy industrialists both within Chicago and outside. Its financing, and the real estate practices that grew out of it, made the university into a central player in shaping land-use decisions, real estate valuation, and spatial segregation in the city. These processes increasingly insulated the university from the city around it.

The planning, design, and building of the University of Chicago exemplified these practices and reflected the university's vision of its role in the city, for the school's prescribed function was reflected in the physical space it occupied. The built environment of the university suggested an institution that was insular, detached, and exclusive. The design of the campus exuded this aloof image not only through its spatial configuration but also through its vision of time. The University of Chicago represented a space where time stood still, shielded from the rapid change and expansion of a growing city by the walls of Gothic towers, a place where members were transported back to a place and time that symbolized stability and protection. The decision making regarding the design of the university hinted at some of the tensions that emerged over the nature of the institution's relationship with the city. As historian Neil Harris points out, the university was in the city but not of it.[3]

THE IDEA OF THE UNIVERSITY OF CHICAGO

On October 1, 1892, the new University of Chicago officially opened its doors. The first day of school exhibited a noticeable lack of fanfare. President William Rainey Harper, along with founder John D. Rockefeller, agreed to proceed as though the university had been operating for years and was simply continuing with its usual business. Harper wrote to Rockefeller, "After careful consideration I have proposed to our Board of Trustees that they hold no opening exercises; that the work of the University begin October 1 as if it were the continuation of work which had been conducted for a thousand years."[4] Harper here implied that he wanted to lend an air of authenticity and legitimacy to the new university by suggesting its timelessness. The university would stand as a symbol of new, modern methods of research and education but at the same time would insert itself into a historical tradition of the quest for knowledge and truth.

The uniqueness of opening day could not have been lost on students and faculty members, however, when they walked to classes amid construction crews and the lingering swampy areas that made up the "campus." The condition of the campus on opening day led Theodore M. Hammond, who was then in charge of buildings and grounds, to put his impressions into verse.

Mortar beds, and brick bats,
Lumber, lath, and lime,
Carpenters and plumbers
Pounding all the time.
"Of uninviting places
This is sure the worst!"
But we've kept the promise,
Moved in on the first.[5]

Despite this conscious downplaying of opening day, the rhetoric surrounding the birth of the university in the preceding months and years was far from mundane. Indeed, it reflected Harper's grandiose plans. The University of Chicago was to be worthy of the greatest institutions in the country, even in the world. Harper envisioned an institution designed on the German university's model of cultivating scholars at the graduate and professional level. Like Johns Hopkins University, the new University of Chicago embodied modern educational ideals, as a research institution at the forefront of scientific advances. Harper exhibited his faith in positivist science and its social function, advocating educational programs to produce "objective" research that could be used for practical social and civic betterment. Moreover, Harper believed that such a focus could attract the best students and the best faculty, even inducing prominent scholars and presidents from other top colleges to join him at Chicago.[6]

The University of Chicago opened just at a time when higher education itself was being transformed. More and more institutions reformed their courses of study at the turn of the century, moving away from purely classical education and incorporating new models of professionalization and specialization. Northwestern University, just north of Chicago, began as a Methodist institution offering a classical education to undergraduate students. By the time the University of Chicago opened, though, Northwestern was establishing more highly specialized disciplines and was also incorporating graduate programs. By contrast, the Roman Catholic universities in the city, St. Vincent's College (renamed DePaul University in 1907) and St. Ignatius College (renamed Loyola University in 1909) had a primary devotion to the ideals of the church rather than to the increasing emphasis on highly specialized and increasingly scientific knowledge. Still, changes in higher education nationwide forced both schools to expand their offerings and create professional schools in law, medicine, and business. Administrators argued that they made these changes to meet the needs of their Catholic constituents within the city.[7]

The University of Chicago sought a unique role in the city. It would be a world-class institution devoted to both undergraduate study and graduate research. It combined Baptist missionary ideals with a catholic atmosphere to foster the free exchange of ideas. And it was a self-consciously urban institution, dedicated to addressing the issues confronting the city of Chicago even as it cultivated a national and international community of students and scholars. The initial charter for the university said that it must be located within a city, not in a suburb or rural area. According to Harper, the city would serve as a vast laboratory in which students and professors could explore contemporary problems and find solutions through the scientific method. Harper hoped that the university would be a central fixture in the city. Speaking at Columbia University in 1902, Harper expressed his view of the role of urban universities: "A university which will adapt itself to urban influence, which will undertake to serve as an expression of urban civilization, and which is compelled to meet the demands of an urban environment will in the end become something essentially different from a university located in a village or small city. . . . It will gradually take on new characteristics both outward and inward, and it will ultimately form a new type of university."[8]

According to the rhetoric, then, the new University of Chicago was not a remote ivory tower, but rather an integral part of a rapidly developing urban center. For Harper, the production of knowledge went hand in hand with public service and civic engagement, at least initially.

The new University of Chicago opened two weeks before the dedication of the World's Columbian Exposition. Since the site for the exposition was to be just south of the new university in Jackson Park, all attending would have an opportunity to see the future of Chicago and the nation as they glimpsed the progress made possible by grand design working in tandem with modern research facilities. From the Ferris wheel, the symbol of technological innovation and commerce, they could see the Gothic buildings reminiscent of earlier days. This image of the Ferris wheel rising up from the Midway, with riders peering in from the outside, also illustrated the tensions between proximity and distance that came to characterize the university's relationship with the city around it.[9]

PLANNING THE UNIVERSITY OF CHICAGO

The idea of creating a new Baptist university in Chicago dedicated to promoting modern research methods stemmed from both local and national concerns. The initial impetus came after the failure of the first University of Chicago in the 1870s. Established in 1857 by Stephen Douglas as a Baptist mission school, the university soon encountered financial setbacks and was forced to close in 1879. Several scholars and administrators affiliated with the old University of Chicago, most notably Thomas Wakefield Goodspeed, appealed to the Baptist community in Chicago to help establish a new Baptist university in the city. When Goodspeed heard that industrialist and philanthropist John D. Rockefeller was interested in donating money to found a Baptist school, he quickly appealed to him for help. Goodspeed pointed out that the Baptists had no first-rate institution of higher learning in the West. He argued they must educate the intelligent members of their religion or lose them: "Our Baptist youth must be educated somewhere and they will be mightily influenced by their religious surroundings in college. If we neglect to provide for their education we shall lose them and the generations after them."[10]

Goodspeed organized the American Baptist Education Society in 1888 to rally more Baptist leaders to the cause. Frederick T. Gates, the minister of Central Baptist Church in Minneapolis, became corresponding secretary, and several months later he issued a plea for the establishment of a new Baptist college in Chicago. Like Goodspeed, Gates pointed to the incredible population growth in the West. He also made his request on moral grounds. "If some Christian denomination does not go in and capture the city," he argued, "infidelity will." Gates envisioned

> an institution with an endowment of several millions, with buildings, library and other appliances equal to any on the continent; an institution commanding the services of the ablest specialists in every department, giving the highest classical as well as scientific culture, and aiming to counteract the Western tendency to a merely superficial and utilitarian education; an institution wholly under Baptist control as a chartered right, loyal to Christ and his church, employing none but Christians in any department of instruction; a school not only evangelical but evangelistic, seeking to bring every student into surrender to Jesus Christ as Lord.[11]

Gates's report is striking in its emphasis both on Christian duty and evangelism and on scientific research and the cultivation of expertise. For Gates, and eventually for Harper, the Baptist missionary ideal and the goal of promoting scientific inquiry were not mutually exclusive. Yet how to strike an appropriate balance between the two, or to demonstrate how these ideals were integrally related, was the central question they faced as planning went forward. Initial debates about the location of the new institution and the nature of the curriculum reflected this tension.[12]

Gates helped convince Rockefeller of the need for a Baptist institution of higher learning in Chicago. Yet the decision to locate the new college there was not immediate. Augustus H. Strong, president of Rochester Seminary, argued in favor of endowing a Baptist institution in New York. His argument centered on the additional question of whether the institution should be a college or a university. Rockefeller was in favor of endowing a college; Strong favored a university. Strong felt New York would be an appropriate site, since the city offered "conditions of highest mental activity and growth" necessary for advanced scholarship and the study of professions.[13] He argued that Chicago was not the appropriate site for a graduate institution. "That is what Baptists hitherto have always been doing—building their churches on the back streets, and their colleges in the country towns," claimed Strong. A university established in Chicago would be "a mongrel institution," provincial rather than cosmopolitan.[14]

Goodspeed envisioned a Baptist institution in Chicago that would be regional but not necessarily provincial. Chicago was the natural location for the new college precisely because it was such a new and dynamic city: "A first class institution here is certain to become the greatest in our denomination. Chicago is the commercial, political, social, religious, educational center of a wide empire. It is the natural place for everyone in the West to come to. . . . Of all places in the world, this is the location plainly designated by nature for a great University for our people."[15]

Goodspeed sought to aid his cause by securing the support of prominent Yale Semitics professor William Rainey Harper, considered as a possible president of the new university. Harper was arguably the nation's leading Baptist scholar of the Old Testament, and he favored the Chicago site. A prodigy who received his doctorate in philosophy from Yale at age eighteen, he later joined the faculty of the Theological Seminary in Morgan Park, just outside Chicago. His dedication to improving Baptist education in the West made him the perfect leader for this new institution.[16]

Harper was perhaps best known for his role in shaping the Chautauqua movement, an educational experiment started in upstate New York in 1874 that was devoted to providing summer educational programs for Sunday school teachers. Chautauqua's popularity led scholars like Harper to expand the program and offer more secular programming for anyone interested in pursuing adult education outside traditional university settings.[17] Harper also instituted an extension program in which university professors traveled to towns across the East, presented lectures, and helped their students earn credit toward a college degree. Perhaps most important, however, Harper challenged orthodox theology and brought to his study of biblical texts what he referred to as a "rationalist" perspective. He embraced a critical approach to biblical language and literature, though he argued that his thinking represented views that "accord well with those of the average intelligent Baptist minister of today."[18] This blend of intellectual rigor and commitment to Baptist teachings made Harper the ideal choice to lead a modern Baptist university.[19]

In May 1889, after several months of negotiation, Rockefeller agreed to establish a Baptist institution in Chicago instead of in New York. That a large-scale university ultimately was established in Chicago illustrated both the underlying goal of many Baptist educators to create a university to serve both the regional and national needs of the Baptists and the desire to create a world-class research institution in the city of Chicago. Promoters reconciled the two by equating local Christian duty with national civic culture and patriotism. In a speech celebrating the selection of Chicago as the site of the new school, Dr. P. S. Henson, pastor of the First Baptist Church of Chicago, expressed this religious and nationalistic mission of the university: "We have come to a new era in the history of Chicago. We stand tonight in an august presence. . . . Brethren of Chicago and the great Northwest, for us this is a day of days, a day of Appomattox triumph after a Bull Run defeat, a day to rejoice in with humble, hearty gratitude to God, a day to tell our children's children, and for remotest posterity to celebrate. . . . May God crown with blessing the embodiment of so many hopes and the answer to so many prayers—the new University of Chicago."[20]

By infusing the founding of the university with both religious and patriotic rhetoric, Henson suggested the symbiotic relationship between the two that would characterize the early mission of the University of Chicago.

The founders saw scientific inquiry as a means of unlocking the mysteries of the universe and coming closer to God and "truth." Harper illustrated this connection between science and religion. "The circle of scientific investigation has gradually extended itself, until it includes everything from God himself to the most insignificant atom of his creation," he argued.[21] Science would therefore be used in the service of religion in the quest for truth. This blend of religious ideals and scientific models of investigation could help address pressing needs and concerns in modern society. Martin Ryerson, director of the Corn Exchange Bank and president of the university's Board of Trustees, expressed his belief in the social role of the university. According to Ryerson, "We know that in the presence of the great social and industrial problems of the day we cannot afford to leave concealed any part of the truth which the human is capable of grasping, and that this truth must be sought in the domain of natural science as well as in the domain of religion, ethics, and political science."[22]

This emphasis on the role of scientific investigation in the welfare of the community brought together the Baptist missionary ideal with the desire to promote scholarly research. Science and technology, when put to proper use, would lead to progress and ultimately to a more harmonious social order. The University could provide a new model of civic culture in Chicago, then, one defined by the scientific pursuit of truth rather than by cultural uplift through the stewardship of commercial elites.

FINANCING THE UNIVERSITY

The financing of the university illustrated the tensions and contradictions in some of its founding ideals and their implementation. Indeed, rather than challenging the rise of commercialism in Chicago, the financing reflected the central role of corporate capital in promoting and defining culture in the city. The bulk of the funds came from the John D. Rockefeller endowment. On May 15, 1889, Rockefeller wrote to Gates agreeing to contribute $600,000 toward the new university as long as an additional $400,000 could be raised by June 1, 1890. Rockefeller agreed to fund a college, with the question of whether to expand into a university put off for the present. His endowment would pay for operating expenses for the college but not for land, buildings, or graduate programs. The funds for these needs would come from the $400,000 raised by the Baptist Education Society as well as future fund-raising.[23]

Goodspeed and the American Baptist Education Society first appealed to Chicago-area Baptists to raise the money stipulated by the Rockefeller gift. After two months the Society had raised close to $200,000. Members realized, though, that they could not expect much more from the Chicago Baptist community.[24] They then appealed to Baptist communities throughout the West for subscriptions. When pledges came in slowly, Gates issued an appeal in the *Standard,* the American Baptist journal. "The issue of the whole enterprise [of the founding of a university] now depends on whether the brethren outside this city will pledge one hundred thousand dollars rather than see the great undertaking fall to the ground in failure. We ask, therefore, every pastor living between Ohio and the Rocky Mountains to preach one sermon on Christian education during the month of January."[25] By February 1890 they had raised an additional $30,000 but were still far short of the $400,000 goal.

Gates and Goodspeed also solicited financial support from the business community of Chicago. They recognized the abundant wealth of many of Chicago's leading industrialists and sensed that since many were already actively involved in philanthropy they would be willing donors to the university. They first approached Charles L. Hutchinson, the banker who was also director of the World's Columbian Exposition and president of the Art Institute. Once he agreed to make a subscription and serve as a trustee, it became easier to obtain the support of other Chicago elites. Hutchinson presented the case of the university to the Commercial Club and promised to help secure funds from its members. Gates also approached the sleeping car magnate George Pullman. Evidently Pullman had plans to open either a university or a scientific academy on the South Side of Chicago and wondered if his project and Rockefeller's might be merged. Gates explained to Rockefeller that though he did not take this offer seriously, they did want to appeal to Pullman for funding. Gates also said that Pullman thought the new university would be a theological seminary and had reservations about supporting it since he was a Universalist. Gates explained to Rockefeller, "We thought that if you were to assure him that this is a College, not designed in itself to teach theology, that he might give us $5,000 or $10,000."[26]

Goodspeed and Gates also appealed to prominent men of means from other faiths. Yet this appeal to non-Baptists was not as easy as Goodspeed and Gates had hoped. At one point Gates conceded to Harper, who had not yet affirmed his acceptance of the presidency, that men of means from other faiths were undermining the Baptists. Gates wrote:

> The fact is that the other denominations have waked up and passed the word around that we must not be encouraged. At least it seems to appear that way. Sectarian! Sectarian! Baptist! Baptist! That is the eternal cry in nearly every office and our utmost endeavors on the street and in the papers are powerless to arrest the note of alarm. I do privately believe that Lake Forest and Evanston are quak-

> ing, and that the whole [Presbyterian] and [Methodist] denominations . . . have come to fear Baptist supremacy in this city and the West educationally, and have rallied their friends against us.[27]

With these concerns in mind, Goodspeed and others targeted non-Protestant groups who might be persuaded to support the university. In a letter to his sons, Goodspeed said that he approached John R. Walsh, president of the Chicago National Bank, "a Catholic, sometimes a rough man, and I went with fear and trembling."[28] Goodspeed noted that he was well received and hoped that Walsh might help with an appeal to local Catholics. The American Baptist Education Society also appealed to Jewish Chicagoans, and on April 8, 1890, the Standard Club, composed of the city's wealthiest Jews, voted to raise $25,000 to support the new university. By June 1890, Rockefeller's deadline for subscriptions, the Society had raised the necessary money.[29] Even with regard to fund-raising, the university was juggling the goal of being an explicitly Baptist institution with the desire to be cosmopolitan. By appealing to Chicagoans of all faiths, the University of Chicago became an institution that diverse Chicagoans could claim as their own. Yet some founders, including Rockefeller, worried that this broad-based financing might affect the university's goals and mission.

The new University of Chicago was chartered on September 10, 1890, as a coeducational college founded under the auspices of the American Baptist Education Society. The articles of incorporation, signed by Rockefeller, Harper, Gates, Goodspeed, Marshall Field (a department store magnate), E. Nelson Blake (a leader among the Baptist laity), and Francis E. Hinckley (who contributed the first $50,000 after Rockefeller's gift), stipulated that at all times two-thirds of the twenty-one members of the Board of Trustees, and the university president, should be members of Baptist churches.[30] This condition reflected Rockefeller's concern that control of the university might be wrested from the American Baptist Education Society and fall into the hands of Chicago's merchant elite. During the final stages of the fund-raising campaign Gates reported to Rockefeller that one potential donor expressed interest in giving as long as the university exhibited a "catholicity of spirit." Rockefeller responded that he believed in this spirit but was not sure what the donor meant by it. "The question of money may not be so important a factor later on," he argued, "as that freedom which we always want to have in the administration of the proposed university."[31] Once the university was incorporated, additional gifts from leading Chicago businesspeople came in. Rockefeller made an additional donation of $1 million in late 1890.

The original trustees of the university were a virtual who's who of Chicago's elite. E. Nelson Blake, Martin Ryerson, Charles Hutchinson, Thomas Goodspeed, and William Rainey Harper served on the original executive committee. Other board members included Eli B. Felsenthal (lawyer), Andrew MacLeish (founder of Carson, Pirie, Scott department store), Henry A. Rust (railroad merchant), and Daniel L. Shorey (judge). Most trustees worked in business or the professions. All the non-Baptist board members who listed their religion in *Who's Who of Chicagoans* were either Protestants or Western European Jews. That many of these individuals were active in other cultural institutions suggests the close link between wealth, status, and cultural promotion in Chicago. Through both money and power, these elites hoped to exert pressure on the shape and scope of culture in the city.[32]

THE UNIVERSITY AND THE CHANGING DEMOGRAPHICS OF HYDE PARK

The connection between the development of the university and business interests did not end with its funding. The Board of Trustees needed to acquire real estate holdings, and the university's policies of expansion profoundly affected the landscape of the surrounding community of Hyde Park. The building of the university influenced not only land-use patterns but also property values. Moreover, many of Chicago's leading land speculators made substantial profits on the land they sold to the university. The University of Chicago's policies of land acquisition demonstrated that its relationship with the surrounding neighborhood would be hegemonic rather than symbiotic.

The most significant gift after the Rockefeller endowment was Marshall Field's donation of ten acres of land along the Midway. Field pledged this land in January 1890, stipulating that the $400,000 Rockefeller required the university to raise be independent of the value of his land. On May 26, 1890, Field wrote to Gates stating that as soon as Rockefeller's conditions for endowment were met, he would donate the land. After the announcement of the fund-raising success, Field stated, "I congratulate the people of this city and the entire West on the success achieved, and with all friends of [the word "higher" was crossed out] culture I rejoice that another noble institution of higher learning is to be founded, and founded in the heart of the continent."[33]

The original proposal called for Field to donate land between Fifty-fifth and Fifty-eighth Streets, Ellis and Greenwood Avenues. A modification in the plan provided a ten-acre site between Fifty-sixth and Fifty-ninth (Midway Plaisance) and Ellis and

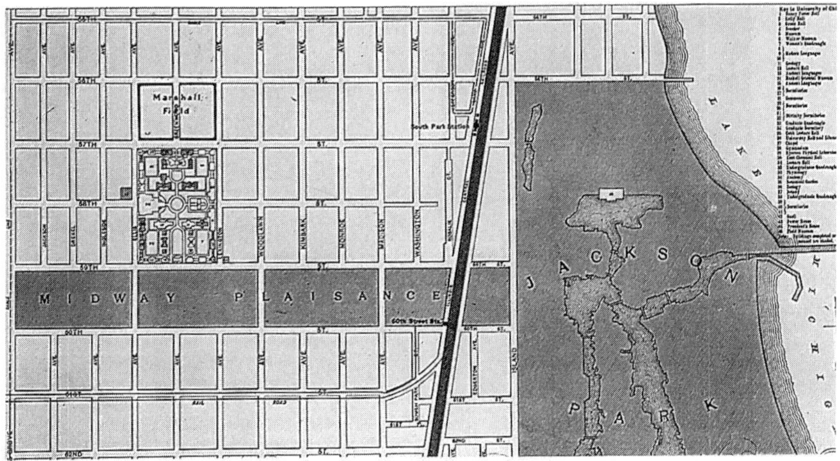

FIGURE 9. Map of the Campus, 1901. *University Register,* 1901–2.

Greenwood. Field then offered the university an option to purchase the ten acres immediately south of the site. The final agreement had Field donating one and a half blocks and selling the university another one and a half blocks for $132,500. Thus the total site consisted of three blocks beginning at the Midway and running north along the east side of Ellis Avenue two blocks to Fifty-seventh and east along the south side of Fifty-seventh two blocks to University (then Lexington) Avenue (fig. 9).[34]

By the later months of 1890 some trustees already feared that the site was not large enough. Field then offered to sell the university a fourth block for $150,000 and exchange a block so that the site would be contiguous. Some trustees were apprehensive about such a large expenditure to expand the site of the university. Goodspeed was concerned that building could not begin until the site was secured and also feared spending more money on the site when funds were needed for buildings, libraries, and equipment. The trustees also found it hard to negotiate with Field. Goodspeed expressed his frustration in a letter to Harper: "The difficulty in the case is that Mr. Field is not willing to sell for a price we are willing to pay."[35]

In the meantime, Harper accepted the presidency of the school. Since board members knew that Harper wanted to create a great research institution, they deemed it wise to make provisions for expansion. On April 23, 1891, the committee agreed to Field's terms for the purchase of the additional land. Hutchinson argued that they should buy the fourth block because many other Chicago institutions had made the mistake of planning on too small a scale and thereby hindering future growth. The University of Chicago was assured of rapid growth and needed to be adequately prepared for it.[36]

Gates found the site ideal, since it was close to several railroads (including the Illinois Central Railroad) and to streetcar lines. He also spoke highly about the general character of the neighborhood, for "in every direction from the site is residence property and forms the location of the higher middle and aristocratic classes." He also pointed to Washington and Jackson Parks bordering the campus and noted that no manufacturing ever would take place in the vicinity—valuable features of this location.[37] For Gates this meant that the university's future expansion was likely, and without worry about the devaluation of its real estate holdings. Yet changes in the city of Chicago eventually challenged this belief.

Even before plans for the university began, Hyde Park was in the midst of rapid growth and change. Paul Cornell, the founder of Hyde Park, bought his first parcel of land in 1853 between Fifty-first and Fifty-fifth Streets and Lake Michigan and Cottage Grove Avenue, hoping to establish a suburban resort town directly south of Chicago. He then deeded sixty acres to the Illinois Central Railroad on condition that it build a station at Fifty-third Street. In 1856 the railroad opened Chicago's first suburban station at Fifty-third Street and Lake Park Avenue. This transportation line made Hyde Park accessible to people in the city and therefore increased the value of the land.[38]

The Hyde Park economy continued to center on real estate development and residential building. Cornell specifically wanted to keep Hyde Park suburban and industry-free. Friends and relatives of Cornell purchased land in and around Hyde Park over the next few decades. Soon other developers and businesspeople, including Marshall Field, bought land there for speculation, and the section of town just north of Cornell's land became another fashionable residential district.[39]

The township of Hyde Park, a forty-eight-square-mile village that included what would later be called Hyde Park–Kenwood on the north, was incorporated in 1861. It was bounded by Thirty-ninth and 138th Streets, State Street and Michigan Avenue (fig. 10). In order to control the town's development, Cornell and other property owners initiated plans for the South Park system. They felt that with a large-scale park plan the town would remain a residential retreat and ward off the encroachment of negative features of the city. Already they had seen the southern portion of Hyde Park Township become rapidly industrialized as steel plants proliferated with the opening of Calumet Harbor and the growth of the railroads. Real estate agents billed Hyde Park–Kenwood as "exclusive" and "elegant." A system of parks would further enhance

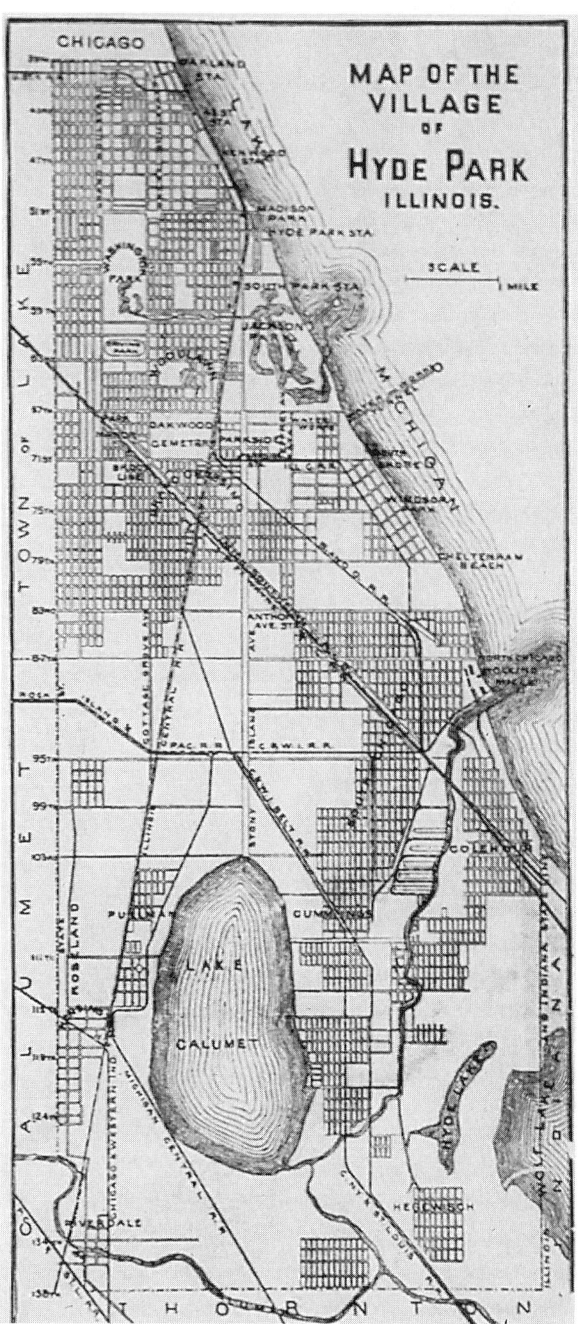

FIGURE 10

"Map of the Village of Hyde Park, Illinois," 1888. Courtesy of the Special Collections Research Center, University of Chicago Library.

their claim while maintaining and even raising the value of property fronting the parks.[40]

In 1867 Cornell successfully lobbied the state legislature for a bill establishing the park system, but the proposal was voted down in Hyde Park. The issue was resolved in April 1869 when plans for specific sites were spelled out. The town of Hyde Park passed the bill, and work began on the South Park system, including Washington and Jackson Parks, with the Midway Plaisance connecting them.[41] The state legislature authorized a bond issue of $2 million to purchase land for the South Parks. Between 1869 and 1870 the South Park Commission bought 1,100 acres of land, with local property owners making a hefty profit. The park purchases also initiated a flurry of speculation around property fronting the chosen park sites.[42]

Although the Great Chicago Fire of 1871 destroyed the building that housed landscape architects Frederick Law Olmsted and Calvert Vaux's blueprints for the parks, all was not lost for property owners. Indeed, the fire brought on another swell of speculation in areas outside the burned-out district, and on the South Side in particular. Between 1866 and 1873 property values rose from $1,000 to $20,000 an acre at Fifty-first Street and Drexel Boulevard, from $500 to $10,000 per acre at Forty-seventh and State, and from $100 to $15,000 an acre around Fifty-third and Fifty-fifth Streets. At the height of the land boom in 1873, values of property south of Thirty-ninth Street reached $123,000,000, from about $3,000,000 in 1862.[43] The opening of new suburban railway and horse-car lines, along with progress toward the completion of Olmsted and Vaux's South Parks and Boulevards, accounted for much of the growth. Although the depression of 1873 thwarted this rapid rise in values and speculation, landowners in Hyde Park soon recouped most of their losses as a large migration of Chicagoans moved outside the city limits and to the South Side.[44]

The fire significantly affected the growth of Hyde Park in the 1870s and 1880s. As the Chicago City Council established new fire codes banning frame construction within the center of the city, many developers began purchasing land and building in suburban Hyde Park. As the town grew and developed, subtle shifts in demographics began to occur. While the bulk of newcomers to Hyde Park–Kenwood remained wealthy Chicagoans looking for suburban residences, many middle- and lower-income people moved to the area as well. This change resulted as more frame workers' cottages were built on the outskirts of the city, outside the fire code boundaries, and as the increased wages for workers in the building trades made homeownership possible for some of them.[45]

Historian Jean Block's analysis of the 1870 census shows that in addition to seventy-five businessmen and forty-seven professionals in the town, there also were seventy-nine skilled workers, thirty-three common laborers, and more than a hundred domestic servants, both male and female. There were eight African Americans, five of them domestic servants, and three children. The foreign-born made up less than one-third of Hyde Park-Kenwood residents in 1870, but by 1880 this number had increased to nearly half. Already this shift in population began to show itself in a differentiated spatial structure of the town. Within the north end of Hyde Park Township were the three smaller communities of Kenwood, Hyde Park Center, and South Park. Each developed distinct features as the town expanded.[46]

Hyde Park Center developed as the main commercial section of town, between Fifty-first and Fifty-fifth Streets. The first cluster of retail establishments opened at Fifty-third Street and Lake Park Avenue in the 1870s and expanded in the 1880s. Soon liquor stores, coal yards, and livery stables opened there as well. While Hyde Park Center initially contained large single-family homes, during the 1880s it developed into a largely middle- and working-class neighborhood between Fifty-third and Fifty-fifth. The large homes of the earliest residents were converted into hotels and boardinghouses for railroad workers. Around Lake Park Avenue near the Fifty-third Street station, urban rowhouses, three-flats, and workingmen's cottages proliferated. Most of the common laborers, many of them Irish, lived in cottages near St. Thomas the Apostle Church at Fifty-fifth and Kimbark. Saloons and billiard halls also opened on Lake Park, evidence of the development of a working-class neighborhood.[47]

As Hyde Park Center became more commercial and as more workers moved in, many of them immigrants from Germany, Sweden, and Ireland, the earlier settlers moved to the exclusive suburb of Kenwood, north of Fifty-first Street. Residents were white native-born Protestants, along with a few German Jews, who were middle and upper class.[48] Martin Ryerson, Julius Rosenwald of Sears, Roebuck and Company, and Joseph Schaffner of Hart, Schaffner and Marx lived in the neighborhood. Their homes were large, set far back from the street, with ample room for coach houses and barns. Most were constructed of stone, stucco, and brick, with few wood-frame homes. They contained intricate ornamentation, with stained glass windows, gables, and turrets. Kenwood also remained entirely residential with no retail development until 1894, when the first stores selling food and household supplies opened at Forty-seventh and Lake Park.[49]

South Park, between Fifty-fifth and Fifty-ninth Streets, comprising mostly middle-class and upper-middle-class homes, would later become the site of the University of Chicago. Its homes were more modest than those in Kenwood, and the area was less densely populated than Hyde Park Center. The exception was the home of Jonathan Y. Scammon, a banker and lawyer whose Fernwood estate on Fifty-ninth between Dorchester and Woodlawn later would be partially sold and donated to the university. The most significant feature of South Park was Rosalie Court, on Harper Avenue between Fifty-seventh and Fifty-ninth Streets. In 1883 Rosalie Buckingham bought these two blocks and subdivided them into sites for forty-two villas and cottages.[50] Many of the residents in Rosalie Villas were recent immigrants earning enough as skilled or semi-skilled laborers to afford to buy them.[51] Almost as soon as Rosalie Villas was completed, the first apartment house in South Park was built in the same area. Thus the future density of this section of Hyde Park could already be predicted.

The class and ethnic division that existed not only in Hyde Park–Kenwood but between the northern and southern sections of Hyde Park Township came to a head in 1887. Already in the early 1880s there were residents calling for Hyde Park to be divided into three separate villages: Hyde Park, South Chicago, and Pullman. Others argued that Hyde Park should create a city government with the district divided into seven wards. Both of these petitions failed, but they reflected the dissatisfaction many residents felt with the current village government.[52] The main reasons for this dissatisfaction were the rapid increase in population, the need for additional services, and the increased class and ethnic tensions in the area. The president of the Board of Trustees of Hyde Park Village, a resident of South Park, captured this tension in a speech in 1884: "The foreign population of our large cities is already either in the majority or possess the political power of controlling the election. So long as this is so, American ideas are in danger of being subordinated."[53] When the Chicago consolidation and annexation bill allowing Chicago to annex adjacent territories passed the state legislature in 1887, some Hyde Parkers saw this as a solution to their problems, while others feared the loss of autonomy. But when it became clear that the rules for governance after annexation were insufficiently established, the Illinois Supreme Court found the annexation law invalid and nullified the bill.[54]

After amending the bill to address the problems raised by the court, Chicago and the annexation districts of Hyde Park, Lake, and Lake View voted again on annexation on June 28, 1889, with the legislation passing. In general in Hyde Park village, the more heavily industrialized and immigrant working-class precincts to the south favored annexation, allegedly for the benefits of services for water, roads, and general improvements. By contrast, the wealthier and more residential northern section of Hyde Park opposed annexation, fearing the infringement of city government on their autonomy and the possible rise in taxes and urbanization of the neighborhood.[55] Many early residents of Hyde Park lamented annexation and the loss of "suburban identity" and natural serenity. John D. Sherman, a member of the second family to settle in Kenwood, wrote:

> Maybe it was because there were so many ponies hitched to that barnyard fence that the quail nesting in the old place and the rabbits didn't seem to like our hazel bushes any more, and the wild pigeons didn't stop to rest in our big oaks, and the spring beauties, and pinks, and prairie flowers. . . . Or maybe lake water, and gas, and paved streets, and electric lights, and taxes had something to do with it. At any rate, the birds,—sparrows don't count—and the rabbits, and the flowers are all gone—and the boys too. And so is Hyde Park.[56]

Clearly villagers like Sherman saw the city overtaking their serene, pastoral landscape as a result of this political change.[57]

Yet such descriptions ignored they way wealthier residential sections of Hyde Park, and especially Kenwood, remained relatively unchanged immediately following annexation. In addition, land values rose in Hyde Park as new transportation systems, including the South Side elevated line, and new services, including better streets, water, police, and fire prevention systems, were implemented.[58]

The awarding of the World's Fair was the single most significant factor affecting land use and development in Hyde Park. When Jackson Park was chosen as the site, nearby land values rose to "crack-brained altitudes," increasing by as much as 1,000 percent in one year.[59] Tracts of land south of the park, still partially covered by water, were bid up from $600 to $6,000 and even as high as $15,000 an acre.[60] More important was the type of development occurring on these tracts of land. Property owners unable to sell land for single-family homes at a profit instead built hotels and apartment houses along Fifty-fifth Street and near Jackson Park in preparation for the fair. Building was at a peak, and the South Park section of Hyde Park that had been mostly residential took on a more commercial feel.[61] Again many residents lamented the impact of this building on the residential character of Hyde Park. One stated, "These sections, under ordinary conditions, would have developed as high class residence districts exclusively. The location of the fair, however, has stimulated the construction of apartment houses in neighborhoods where they are not appreciated by the surrounding owners."[62]

The district of South Park also became more commercial as this large-scale building took place. Along Cottage Grove Avenue, on the western edge of South Park, low-rent cottages and boardinghouses went up. Shopping areas were built along Fifty-seventh Street that included a grocery store, a Chinese laundry, a pharmacy, a soda fountain, and a home furnishings store.[63] This commercial growth transformed the demographics of South Park, for when the influx of fair visitors proved smaller than expected, the low rents and vacant apartments attracted laborers from across the city, many of whom had constructed buildings at the fair. Throughout the 1890s South Park became home to Irish, Germans, Swedes, Greeks, Chinese, and African Americans. Laborers, carpenters, tailors, and railway workers moved into the area, along with clerks, artists, and actors. Thus, during and after the fair the demographics of South Park were more similar to those of the rest of Chicago than they were to Kenwood.[64]

These changing residential patterns and increased land values affected the planning and development of the University of Chicago. Building the fair commenced nearly simultaneously with building the university, and as hotels and apartment complexes went up, so did property values.[65]

When Marshall Field purchased his land in Hyde Park in 1879, he paid $79,166 for sixty-three and one-third acres, or $1,253 an acre. The *Chicago Tribune* described the site as an area of "sand and swamp."[66] After the Board of Trustees recognized the need to expand the campus, Field was able to sell them the additional land for $10,000 an acre. Field therefore made a substantial profit from his "gift" to the university. He also sold university faculty plots on Woodlawn and University Avenues. Over the next eleven years the university added over $1 million worth of property to the initial site on both sides of the Midway from Cottage Grove to Dorchester.[67] By 1903 the university's landholdings around the campus totaled over $3.5 million exclusive of buildings.[68]

The rise in property values was partly precipitated by the expectation that the district would remain residential as professors moved into the surrounding neighborhood. Many residents saw this as a way to stem the flow of immigrants and laborers into South Park that occurred during the construction of the fair.[69] Indeed the university's first act on acquiring the Field property was to vacate the land, closing off and clearing all streets and alleys that ran through the site.[70]

Vacating the Field property created a self-contained campus separated from the surrounding neighborhood. The enclosed quadrangle design shut the campus off from the larger Hyde Park community. In addition, the university's land acquisition and building patterns curtailed the demographic changes occurring in South Park.

DESIGNING THE UNIVERSITY

Once the Board of Trustees had secured the site, members made plans for building the campus. The committee on buildings and grounds was the first subcommittee established after the university was chartered. In April 1891 it initiated a campaign to raise funds for campus buildings. Once again the university appealed to Chicago's elite. Already in 1891 the university had received an endowment from the estate of William B. Ogden, former mayor of Chicago, to establish the Ogden Scientific School of the University of Chicago, a graduate school devoted to scientific research. Members of the board went to other businessmen as well as the expanding network of women's clubs in Chicago to obtain the necessary subscriptions. The response was overwhelming. The board raised over $1 million in ninety days. Many donors continued to provide financial support to the university throughout their lifetimes.[71]

Members of the committee on buildings and grounds took an active role in the planning and design of the campus right from the start. At their first meeting, on July 10, 1890, Martin Ryerson, the committee chair, sketched out the immediate needs of the new university. The committee focused on planning three buildings: a general recitation hall, a Divinity School dormitory, and a university dormitory.[72] Committee members then solicited plans from six of the leading architectural firms in Chicago. Those that responded with plans were the firms of Patton and Fisher, Flanders and Zimmerman, and Henry Ives Cobb. Trustees shared a sentiment that the award should go to an individual architect rather than a firm so that the members of the board could work more directly with the architect and have significant input in the planning.[73]

On June 4, 1891, the committee selected Cobb as the architect. He submitted his sketches on June 25 for a campus laid out on a quadrangle with a Romanesque building design like that of the Newberry Library, a project he oversaw simultaneously with the university commission. Ryerson favored a Gothic design and urged Harper to visit Trinity College in Hartford, Connecticut, and also to obtain Yale's plans for Gothic buildings. Committee members made their preference for Gothic known to Cobb and

FIGURE 11. Henry Ives Cobb final campus plan, 1893. Courtesy of the Special Collections Research Center, University of Chicago Library.

then stayed in constant contact with him throughout the summer, meeting every four or five days to refine the design accordingly. They selected Gothic to evoke the history of Oxford and Cambridge, believing this style would give the new university in the West a sense of tradition amid its gabled walls and towers (fig. 11).[74]

The choice of Gothic reflected the university's broader cultural and educational goals. Committee members pointed out that Gothic design allowed for unity and fixity of form while providing for variation and future expansion. As trustee Charles Hutchinson explained, the buildings were to "stand as the expression of a great University."[75] The design also evoked the religious values the university was founded on. It harked back to a monastic ideal, suggesting images of piety, age, and order. President Harper captured this priestly function of the university in *The Trend in Higher Education:* "The University is the keeper, for the church of democracy, of holy mysteries, of sacred and significant traditions.[76]

The religious symbolism reflected in Gothic design, though, raised concern about how effectively this style also could convey the modern scientific focus of the university's mission. This tension between the religious and scientific foundations of the institution played itself out in discussions over building and design, epitomized by the debate over which building to erect first. Goodspeed expressed this concern in a letter to Harper: "If we begin with the Theological Seminary, erect its building first and open it first on our campus we cannot but convey to the public the idea that we are sectarianizing the entire enterprise. They will say, this is Baptist and nothing but Baptist, sectarian all the way thro', and if we let this impression go abroad we destroy ourselves."[77] The trustees thus decided to erect the recitation hall, the dormitory for incoming undergraduates, and the Divinity dorm simultaneously.

After several revisions of Cobb's plans, the committee on buildings and grounds chose the sites for the first three buildings. The undergraduate dormitory would be on Ellis Avenue at Fifty-seventh Street, the recitation hall south of this on Ellis, and the Divinity dorm on Ellis near Fifty-ninth, all fronting east and west on Ellis. The committee members' high level of involvement in the design was shown by their role in the minute details of planning. They voted that buildings be set back ten feet from the street, that stairways be placed on the east side of dorms, plumbing on the street side, and bay windows on the street side.[78] Members selected granite as the building material, along with Blue Bedford limestone and brick, maple for the floors in the dorms, bronze hardware for the interior of the buildings and iron for the exterior. The selection of Bedford limestone proved significant, for it became the predominant building material for the university and helped achieve a unity of design even after several expansions. The stone had the added bonus, according to a report to the trustees, of quickly taking on a weathered look, thereby giving the university an appearance of age and tradition despite its youth.[79]

Henry Ives Cobb's building designs combined elaborate Gothic ornamentation with the simplicity of a quadrangle plan. Both the lecture hall and the dorms featured steep-roofed gables, turrets, and dormers, along with pointed archways and deep-set rectangular windows. Additional Gothic elements like gargoyles and griffins graced the buildings.[80] These symbols suggested the sculptural ornamentation of the Middle Ages. Just as many Protestant churches in the city chose Gothic to symbolize the rootedness of religious tradition, so too did the university select this style as a means of communicating the medieval connection between piety and community.[81]

On November 26 building began with the breaking of ground for Cobb Hall, the recitation hall financed by Chicago industrialist Silas Cobb (no relation to the architect). Henry Ives Cobb created a building that was a model for all future ones. He made the entrance the most elaborate feature of the building, a practice he continued in other buildings, especially the more austere scientific ones. He designed an elaborate

FIGURE 12. Cobb Hall from the east, 1892. Courtesy of the Special Collections Research Center, University of Chicago Library.

archway with rising tiers of windows reminiscent of Notre Dame cathedral in Paris. He also recessed the portions of the building that flanked the entrance to create a more dramatic entry (fig. 12).[82]

Cobb Hall served a variety of functions that reflected Harper's goal of providing multiple fronts for the dissemination of knowledge in the new institution (fig. 13). The first floor contained a chapel, a large lecture hall, offices for deans to consult with students, and administrative offices. It also housed the University Press and the offices of University Extension, both of which reflected Harper's desire to make educational outreach and the dissemination of knowledge central features of the modern university. The rest of the building housed individual departments, classrooms, and a library, uses designed to change as new buildings were built.

The plans for the dormitory buildings were carried out in a similar manner. Cobb extended the Gothic ornamentation developed in Cobb Hall to the Divinity dorms, later named Gates Hall and Goodspeed Hall, the graduate dorm, later named Blake Hall, the undergraduate dorm (Snell Hall), and the women's dorms (Foster, Beecher, Kelly, and Green Halls). There was some difference, however, in the interior designs

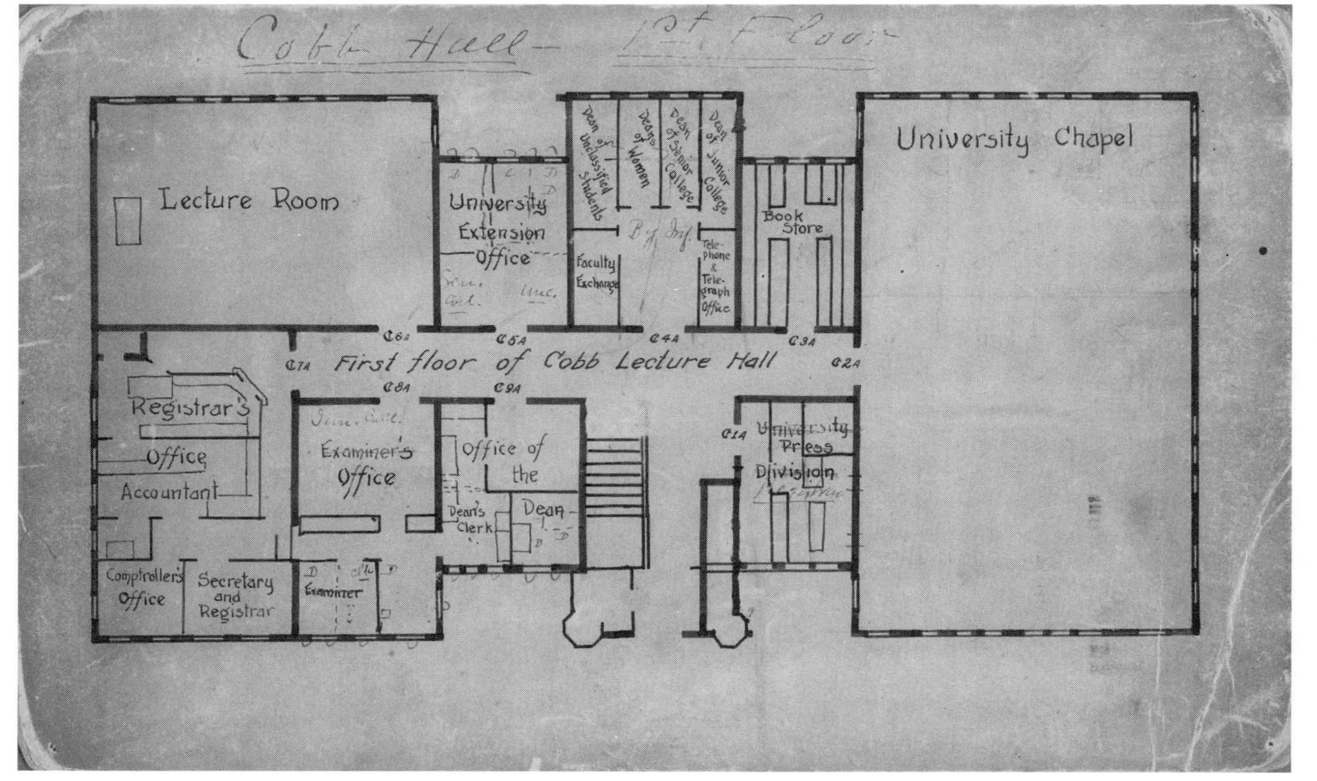

FIGURE 13. First floor plan of Cobb Hall. Courtesy of the Special Collections Research Center, University of Chicago Library.

FIGURE 14. Foster Hall, 1893. Courtesy of the Special Collections Research Center, University of Chicago Library.

of the dormitories. The men's dorms initially featured no area for the social gathering that Harper felt so essential to the collegiate experience. Soon a room in the basement and one on the first floor were set aside for group assembly.[83]

By contrast, the women's dorms provided ample room for social gathering and communal assembly. This was primarily because the women's deans, Marion Talbot, Alice Freeman Palmer, and Julia Buckley, were involved in the design. Parlors and dining rooms provided suitable sites for sociability while single rooms with connecting doors allowed for privacy. Thus the women's dorms became centers for campus receptions and gatherings (fig. 14).[84]

Planning for university museums and science buildings illustrated the flexibility of the Gothic design. The George C. Walker Museum of Natural History, dedicated in December 1893, and the Frederick Haskell Oriental Institute, dedicated in 1895 and devoted to the study of the Oriental roots of the Judeo-Christian tradition, followed the Gothic design established in the original buildings. In reference to the Oriental Institute, Cobb thought it was "unnecessary to make the building at all ornate in its outline."[85] Instead the buildings were more simply designed to reflect the serious function of study that would be carried out inside (fig. 15). This design scheme also reflected the fact that Harper and the trustees viewed the museums as teaching and research facilities for university students and faculty, not as cultural institutions for the public.

The science buildings—Kent Chemical Laboratory, Ryerson Physical Laboratory (both opened January 1, 1894), and Hull Biological Laboratories (completed in 1897)—demonstrated a similar simplicity in building style (fig. 16). Cobb paid particular attention to the functional needs of the buildings, providing temperature-regulated rooms, darkrooms, and areas with ample sunlight. He consulted with prominent scientists before designing the laboratory buildings to be sure he included the latest tech-

FIGURE 15. Haskell Oriental Museum, 1896. Courtesy of the Special Collections Research Center, University of Chicago Library.

FIGURE 16. Ryerson Physical Laboratory, 1894. Courtesy of the Special Collections Research Center, University of Chicago Library.

nology in the field. Ryerson, for example, featured "constant temperature" labs, a mercury room, iron-free labs, and calorimetry labs to produce chemical reactions through heat flow. The building also housed classrooms, large lecture halls, and a library. The technical requirements of the science buildings made them extremely costly, but Harper convinced Rockefeller that no cost could be spared in making these buildings state of the art. Cobb's wrought-iron gate that served as an entrance to Hull Biological Laboratories provided the ornamentation that was lacking in the exteriors of the science buildings (fig. 17).[86]

The versatility of the Gothic style allowed Cobb to maintain a comprehensive design scheme while making individual variations among buildings. He used slight modifications in ornamentation to communicate the variety of functions, from residence halls with ominous griffins to science laboratories with larger windows to admit more light. By incorporating spaces that served religion and those that housed scientific

FIGURE 17. Anatomy building with Cobb Gate, 1897. Courtesy of the Special Collections Research Center, University of Chicago Library.

investigation into a cohesive Gothic design motif, Cobb and the trustees inscribed their vision of the modern quest for truth on the physical fabric of the campus.

Yet some critics believed that the symbolism of the Gothic design of the campus undermined the values of research and quest for knowledge that the university sought to promote. Thomas Chrowder Chamberlin, president of the University of Wisconsin, criticized the monastic medievalism that infused the design of the university, as well as its ceremonial rituals. He disapproved of the revival of "the ceremonials of medieval institutions which . . . are associated with an undeveloped stage of scholarship." He argued that "real scholarship . . . associates itself more and more with simplicity."[87] Architect Frank Lloyd Wright was critical of the university's design on similar grounds: "Our Chicago University, 'a seat of learning,' is just as far removed from truth. If environment is significant and indicative, what does this highly reactionary, extensive and expensive scene-painting by means of hybrid Collegiate Gothic signify?"[88]

The choice of Gothic architecture was even more significant because of the changing styles of architecture in late nineteenth-century America, some of which were pioneered in Chicago. For example, Chicago was the home of the skyscraper, a marvel of modern technology and design that revolutionized building construction and connected street to sky. The invention of the passenger elevator, combined with the development of steel-frame construction, made the skyscraper possible. No longer was it necessary to build only as high as masonry weight-bearing walls allowed. Now the exterior walls of buildings were mere "curtains" supported by internal framing. Although skeletal framing existed in several buildings in Chicago in the 1880s, the completion of William Le Baron Jenney's Home Insurance Building in 1885 forever transformed the skyline of Chicago and prompted the rise of Chicago as the first skyscraper city.[89]

Chicago architect Louis Sullivan also was at the forefront of modern building design. He saw the development of the skyscraper as a unique American contribution to the history of architecture, arguing that a distinctive American style should follow suit. For Sullivan, the skyscraper represented "the formative beginnings of [a] national style" in America, and he urged architects to be innovative in technology as well as in design, rather than copying the artistic styles of the European past.[90] He also posited a direct relation between the function of a building and the form it should take: "It is the pervading law of all things organic, and inorganic, of all things physical and metaphysical, of all things human and all things superhuman . . . that form ever follows function. This is the law."[91] Rather than layer buildings with superfluous ornamentation, architects should focus on how the form of the building itself becomes its artistic expression. Moreover, they should look to nature, and specifically to the American landscape, for ideas about form and function. Sullivan believed this sensibility not only would create an "organic" American architecture but also would represent "an art that will live because it will be of the people, for the people, and by the people."[92] For Sullivan, modern technology, architectural form, and democracy were all integrally related. By directly linking form and function, the built and the natural landscapes, Americans could achieve a distinctive artistic style that reflected the ideals of the nation.[93]

The notion that artistic expression was best realized through an ideal of "domestic vernacular"—with an organic style emerging from the natural landscape of different regions and locales, grew out of the Arts and Crafts movement in Britain. This movement stressed the integrity of materials and the beauty inherent in natural finish and simple design. Both John Ruskin and William Morris, leaders of the movement in England, stressed the connections between beauty, simplicity, and hand craftsmanship. They argued that working with one's hands restored the dignity of labor in an age when it was becoming degraded because of industrial production and technology. Ruskin and Morris found in Gothic architecture a vehicle for achieving the integration of beauty, craftsmanship, and close-knit community. These monastic qualities, they argued, helped overcome the alienation of the worker from the work process and also revived the ideal of simplicity in design.[94]

When the Arts and Crafts movement was translated into American design, however, its focus shifted. Like Ruskin and Morris, American architects stressed the importance of opening built structures to the natural environment. Yet for them this meant rejecting what they considered anachronistic design ideals from the European past and embracing a new "domestic vernacular" of their own. Architects who were part of the nascent prairie school created designs that integrated buildings with their surroundings and broke down barriers dividing the interior and exterior of the home. Thus nature motifs in stained glass windows reflected the belief in domestic architectural design as both an art form and a source of communion with nature. These designs also grew out of Sullivan's desire to create an organic American architecture inspired by the American landscape. In addition, American architects like Sullivan and his protégé Frank Lloyd Wright urged architects not to turn their backs on modernity and technological change but instead to embrace them to foster progressive design. Proponents of the Arts and Crafts movement in America, then, rejected Gothic or Beaux-Arts design (like that of the World's Columbian Exposition) as remnants of historical memory. Hence Wright criticized the use of Gothic at the University of Chicago, a place that supposedly symbolized the progressive spirit of the modern American heartland.[95]

Wright, Dwight Heald Perkins, George Maher, and Howard Van Doren Shaw became some of the premier architects of prairie school design, and they received many of their first commissions for private homes right in the Hyde Park neighborhood of the University of Chicago. Indeed, several university professors chose these architects precisely because they represented a new school of design. Faculty members soon began buying lots from Marshall Field on Woodlawn and University Avenues, and the simplicity of design of their prairie school homes and apartments contrasted sharply with the ornamentation of the Gothic University across the street.[96]

The university campus stood apart from the surrounding neighborhood because of the unified Gothic design and the barriers created by the quadrangle plan (fig. 18).

FIGURE 18. Aerial view of the university looking north from the Midway. Courtesy of the Special Collections Research Center, University of Chicago Library.

Rather than opening out into the community and standing as an integral part of the city, the university closed itself off from the outside world with imposing stone walls, gabled roofs, and gargoyles. Building names were engraved on the facades that faced the quadrangles; therefore only people inside the quadrangles could distinguish between buildings.[97]

Many observers admired this image of enclosure and seclusion in the campus design. One critic writing in the *Architectural Record* explained, "The reason for this arrangement was to, as far as possible, exclude all outside conditions from the student when he had once entered the University grounds . . . and to remove the mind of the student from the busy mercantile conditions of Chicago and surround him with a peculiar air of quiet dignity which is so noticeable in old university buildings." The author added, "When the quadrangles are completed this will be very marked and, as this style of English Gothic architecture easily takes on an air of age by the help of a few vines and weather stains, the effect will certainly be most restful and suggestive of university conditions."[98]

Moreover, some faculty members argued that more could be done to create this sense of enclosure. According to Ernest D. Burton, who later became the third president of the university, the full benefits of the quadrangle idea were unrealized even as late as 1910 because there still were gaps in the enclosure. He argued that the university could contribute to the "quadrangle sense" by placing a "high, closely trimmed hedge along the side of the main quadrangle, wherever buildings have not yet been erected."[99]

Two styles of architecture, one identified as modern and American and the other as traditional and European, competed to define the community around the University of Chicago. This contrast created a visual disconnect between the university and its immediate surroundings.[100]

LAND USE AND REAL ESTATE SPECULATION AT THE UNIVERSITY OF CHICAGO

This process of creating borders did not end with the design and building of the campus. Tied to this project was the university's expanding role as a property owner and landlord. By acquiring property not intended for campus grounds, the university linked raising money by acquiring real estate with the desire to create a buffer zone between the campus and the surrounding city. While this practice would begin with the goal of guaranteeing the potential for campus expansion, it ultimately ended with restrictive covenants that ensured, at least for a time, the racial segregation of the campus neighborhood.

As early as 1888 the promoters of the university raised some of its initial funding through real estate sales. Gates and Goodspeed sought to acquire property from the Blue Island Land and Building Company, which owned land in Morgan Park (the location of the Baptist Theological Seminary) and was improving it for residential development. Potential earnings from this acquisition were valued at close to $100,000 and became an important early source of income for the university.[101] In 1892 Board of Trustees member Charles Hutchinson sent a letter to Gates, now Rockefeller's corresponding secretary, asking him about the propriety of the university's dealing in real estate. "We have an opportunity of purchasing for the University a choice piece of downtown property . . . and I think we ought to avail ourselves of it," said Hutchinson. He went on to claim that the board believed "it would be wise to put a portion of our money into good, improved Real Estate in Chicago."[102] Rockefeller responded with a telegram to Gates saying that he did not object to the sale of bonds to secure good real estate in Chicago, but he thought the board should "take great caution" in working off bonds in the current market "so as not to depress them."[103]

Indeed, part of the reason the board turned to real estate as a source of fund-raising was the recession that ultimately made it difficult to collect many of the pledged gifts. By 1893 the failure of several banks in Chicago, combined with the delays in opening the World's Fair and the outbreak of cholera, meant that less and less money was coming in to the university. Real estate was an attractive alternative to secure the school's future, both because some properties off site could be purchased less expensively and because some investors had an easier time donating property than giving money.[104]

The legality of the arrangement, though, was not immediately clear. The board consulted one of the university's attorneys, who said he believed the institution could hold only the real estate "necessary for its use." Board member Eli Felsenthal reviewed the statutes of the State of Illinois and opined that the university could use gifts only as intended by the donor.[105] The board interpreted this statute to mean that the university could purchase real estate and accept gifts of land as long as Board members made clear arrangements with donors about the specific use to which the property would be put. This mandate would become increasingly important as the university accepted more and more subscriptions in the form of donated land and buildings. The university soon found itself a partner with leading developers in Chicago trying to protect and even inflate land values, particularly on the South Side.

The university committed itself not only to accepting real estate as a source of financing, and to purchasing real estate to enhance the financial standing of the institution, but also to using funds from the Rockefeller endowment to erect income-producing buildings. This policy emerged after the board negotiated the terms of the gift of Helen Culver in 1895. Culver was the cousin of Charles T. Hull, the benefactor of the Hull House settlement on the West Side of Chicago and also a member of the board of the old University of Chicago. Indeed, much of the estate that she proposed to donate to the university came from Hull. This property would be worth over $1 million; Harper called the gift "the single greatest thing that has yet been done for the University outside of Mr. Rockefeller's gifts."[106] Culver wanted to use the money generated from the gift to create an art institute on the West Side, along with a school of music. She also proposed to endow the Department of Biology. Harper persuaded her to put half of the money toward establishing and equipping biological laboratories for the university (the Hull Biological Laboratories) and the other half toward the endowment. Harper also pointed out that the property consisted of some scattered tenements, and he believed the university should "take hold of it at once, concentrate it, dispose of it, and get it into better shape."[107]

The process by which the university "disposed of" this property established the pattern for the future. It quickly razed many of the tenements and then erected new buildings. On one site, at the corner of Park Avenue and Ashland, the university demolished a four-story brick flat and erected a "high class modern apartment building." According to the board, this building represented "an entirely safe investment of endowment funds realizing a satisfactory income and incidentally enhancing the value of adjacent properties belonging to the University."[108]

The university soon purchased or acquired through gifts numerous properties both on the South Side and scattered throughout the city. And it now found itself a landlord forced to handle tenant disputes. In one case the university attempted to lease a property at 249–51 Jefferson Street, but the lease fell through because some tenants refused to vacate. According to the comptroller's report, "they are undesirable tenants and must be dispossessed whether the lease is or is not executed."[109] The university aroused the ire of residents of the western suburb of Berwyn when the board proposed erecting a fence along the university's property line. After several protests by residents, the university agreed to put up a post instead of a fence so as not to cut off access for residents.[110] By 1912 the university rented 328 flats, and at that time only 5 were vacant. The business manager, Wallace Heckman, reported that rents were steadily rising.[111]

The university also continued to purchase properties close to campus. Many were rented to those affiliated with the school, including faculty and students. Others were rented to workers and professionals in the neighborhood. By 1918, for example, the university had a total of 294 tenants in properties surrounding the campus, and those properties generated $116,769 in rent.[112] The finance committee of the Board of Trustees suggested that rents in these properties should be increased, though, since it appeared that they were below market rate. The solution the board proposed included raising the rents on these properties so that they would generate an additional return of $16,638 a year, even after providing a 10 percent discount to university occupants. The board's minutes regarding this discount explain that raising the rent and then giving faculty a discount would ensure that most of the property south of the Midway would chiefly house university tenants, thereby keeping out other groups and consolidating it for the university.[113]

The university grew increasingly concerned over the lack of housing available to faculty during World War I. Its addressing this issue dovetailed with the growing fear of declining property values around the campus. These dual concerns were fueled in part by the expansion of the Black Belt in the neighborhood west of the university during and after World War I. Between 1890 and 1915 the African American population of Chicago grew from fewer than 15,000, or a little over 1 percent of the city's population, to approximately 50,000, or over 2 percent. After the Great Migration of black southerners to Chicago during World War I, the number increased to over 100,000, with the black population rising 148.5 percent between 1910 and 1920 while the white population increased 21 percent.[114] Before 1900, African Americans lived primarily on the South Side but were scattered in various neighborhoods. After 1900, and clearly by 1915, the narrow Black Belt south of the central business district, bounded by Twelfth and Thirty-ninth Streets, State Street and Lake Michigan, solidified. White residents from these areas, fearing the "Negro invasion," moved southward, into neighborhoods around the University of Chicago (fig. 19).[115]

The university increasingly supported neighborhood organizations pushing for racial restrictions in their homeowners' associations. These associations often started as local neighborhood improvement groups. As early as 1894 the Hyde Park Protective Association (HPPA), a group devoted to keeping Hyde Park a dry district after the 1889 annexation to the city, appealed to the university for subscriptions to support its work. Although the university initially declined to give money, it soon made regular contributions of over $200 a year. The university worked closely with the HPPA to be sure that the area around the university remained clear of "vicious resorts."[116] In 1916, for example, newspaper reports claimed that the amusement park Midway Gardens, at Cottage Grove Avenue and Sixtieth Street, was going to reopen as a beer garden. The Board of Trustees minutes noted that the HPPA had played a crucial role in "protecting the neighborhood of the University from 'blind pigs,' gambling, and immorality."[117] For the university, this connection both enhanced the value of real estate around campus and helped protect its borders from undesirable elements.

The university contributed to property owners' associations for largely the same reasons. The neighborhoods of Hyde Park, Woodlawn, and Kenwood had improvement societies designed to keep the neighborhoods clean. Many of the associations, however, soon turned to racial restriction. As early as 1909, attorney Francis Harper formed the Hyde Park Improvement Protective Club to hold "the color line" in Hyde Park.[118] Homeowners' associations increasingly worked with the Chicago Real Estate Board to ensure that blacks could not "invade" white areas of the city. In 1917 the board proposed a formal scheme of racial segregation. The Hyde Park and Kenwood Property Owners' Association was at the forefront of this movement. On January 10, 1920, the Chicago Real Estate Board congratulated the Association after it "proclaimed that in sixty days it had forestalled Negro occupancy of fifty-seven houses south of Thirty-ninth Street."[119] The following year the Real Estate Board voted to expel "any member who sells a Negro property in a block where there are only white members."[120]

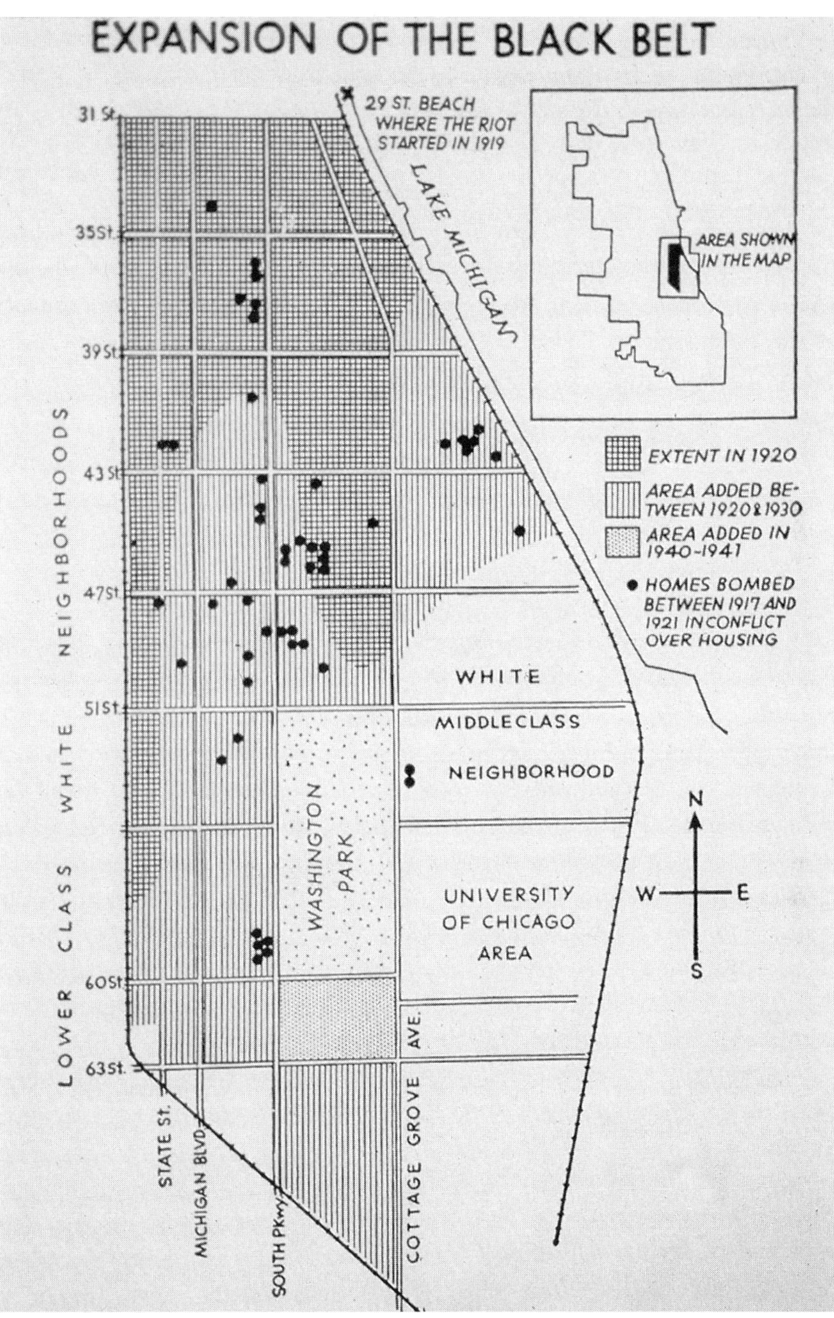

FIGURE 19. Map of the expansion of the Black Belt. From St. Clair Drake and Horace R. Cayton, *Black Metropolis: A Study of Negro Life in a Northern Ghetto*, 2 vols. (New York: Harcourt, Brace and World, 1945).

The Woodlawn Property Owners' League was even more directly responsible for keeping blacks out of the immediate vicinity of the University of Chicago. The League covered property in the Washington Park subdivision, to the west of the university. By the 1920s many residents referred to this district as "the white island" because it was surrounded by the expanding Black Belt. Over 95 percent of the property frontage in this subdivision was covered by restrictive covenants.[121] The University of Chicago owned much of this property. The *Chicago Defender,* the leading black newspaper in the city, reported, "It is well known in Woodlawn that this university is the motive power behind the Restrictive Covenants. In fact, many of the real estate owners in that area refer to the Restrictive Covenants as 'the University of Chicago Agreement to get rid of Negroes.'"[122]

The university often hid its ownership of land around the campus by keeping its title in the name of an individual who served as a leasing agent. A newspaper article in 1903 explained that the university often made real estate purchases secretively, thereby obscuring its role as landowner.[123] This arrangement grew increasingly common in the 1920s as the university bought more properties close to the Midway. A 1924 Board of Trustees meeting reviewed many of the school's recent real estate purchases and noted that most of them were apartment buildings between Fifty-sixth and Fifty-ninth Streets on Drexel, Ellis, and University. In the case of the University Avenue property, the minutes specify that the title was placed in the name of Allen B. Pond, one of the architects for the university, who gave "a declaration of trust and a special warranty deed conveying the property to the University both of which are held unrecorded." The minutes further note that the university's ownership was not disclosed.[124] The university kept its landholdings secret, in part, to divert attention from its role in shaping land use in Hyde Park. At the same time, though, this practice disguised its role in the increasingly pervasive use of restrictive covenants promoting racial segregation.[125]

For the University of Chicago, then, real estate acquisition was a significant part of its fund-raising strategy, but it also became an important tool in creating protective borders around the campus. The minutes of the Board of Trustees make it clear that a variety of factors shaped real estate decisions. First, real estate was an effective way for wealthy Chicagoans to donate to the university. Through careful estate planning, they could contribute and at the same time (in some instances) receive a per annum payment from the university for the rest of the donor's lifetime of a percentage of the amount generated by the sale of the property. In addition, the university could invest in real estate outside Hyde Park that provided substantial returns, in many instances higher than the returns on its bonds and other investments. Finally, land purchases helped secure additional space for expansion. Yet the minutes also indicate that land acquisitions in Hyde Park often had less to do with the need for added space than with the desire to create carefully delimited boundaries around the campus. Just as the Gothic quadrangle design suggested an enclosed space separate from the surrounding city, so too did real estate practices.

UNIVERSITY AFFILIATION AND THE CONSOLIDATION OF EDUCATION IN CHICAGO

Harper's program of affiliation further exposed the tensions between the university and the city, not just in terms of physical layout but also with regard to the increasing centralization of urban education within its borders. Harper revolutionized higher education by making the University of Chicago an umbrella organization under which nearly all other facets of education within the city were controlled. This model of affiliation allowed the campus proper to serve the intellectual and scholarly interests of matriculating students and faculty—thereby creating a cohesive and insular academic culture—yet bring the work of the university to the wider public by extending its grasp to the communities outside its doors. Through its affiliation programs, the university carved out a niche for itself by contributing to the rising emphasis on expertise. In the process, it also contributed to the differentiation of city space in which areas of the city took on specific functions and purposes and were distinguished by the groups of people they served.

For Harper, affiliation was an example of how higher education played a central role in the moral and civic uplift of the urban community. This sense of moral uplift came in part from Harper's, and the university's, strong connection to religious ideals and a social mission. Since the university was founded on the notion that Christian ideals would supplement modern scientific inquiry and that the two were compatible and defining elements of the modern research university, the first plan for affiliation involved the union between the new University of Chicago and the Baptist Theological Seminary that was part of the old university in Morgan Park.

In March 1889 Goodspeed wrote in favor of this union between the theological seminary and the new university, stating, "One institution, one interest, one great and united constituency would seem to be the wise and successful policy."[126] When the university opened in 1892, the seminary relocated there and became the university's Divinity School, devoted to providing Baptist ministers the advantages of training at a modern research institution. In its first year the seminary brought the university 191 students, over 600 alumni, and assets of nearly half a million dollars.[127] Affiliating with other institutions, then, had both pedagogical benefits and fiscal ones.

In addition to making the Divinity School an organic part of the university, Harper sought further affiliations to strengthen the institution's religious character without compromising either its scholarly and scientific nature or its commitment to catholicity of spirit. The issue of what form the school's religious mission would take came to the fore when the Young Men's Christian Association sought affiliation with the university. While Harper supported the work of the organization, he objected to what he considered the narrowness of its program and felt it might not be appropriate for an outside organization to direct the religious work of the university.[128] As a result, Harper organized the university's Christian Union. The Union was open to students and faculty and by 1901 was controlled by a board similar to those that directed other university departments. The Union could affiliate with a variety of Christian organizations, thereby enabling the university to avoid being identified with any one branch of religious activity.[129] Charles R. Henderson, professor of sociology who was appointed university chaplain, expressed this about the religious life of the university: "Those who lead in the conduct of worship are Christians, and their expression of religion is in the language of the Christian world, sacred to most of us from the dawn of consciousness. But this does not exclude other dialects of the common faith of the world, and the freedom to voice the deeper feelings of the soul in any form hallowed by reverence and family associations is permitted and encouraged."[130]

While affiliation enabled the university to stress the missionary nature of its work, it also reflected Harper's plan of consolidation in creating a model research university. The university sought to form alliances with other educational institutions within the city in order to streamline the delivery of education and bring it under the control of a rationally organized structure. According to Harper, "In seeking to co-operate with colleges, high schools, and academies, the University confesses frankly its desire so to affect the work of these institutions as to secure more thoroughly prepared students for college and university work."[131] Harper proposed affiliation with both colleges and secondary schools so that "the slovenliness which characterize[d] the earlier educational work" could be organized and brought into a coordinated system of management.[132]

According to the plans for college affiliation, the university offered a number of benefits, including college examinations at no cost, joint diplomas and degrees with the college and the university, fellowships for one year of graduate school at Chicago to the top three students, and free use of laboratories and libraries. In turn, the university's Board of Trustees had a role in hiring, promoting, and firing college faculty. By 1902, six institutions of higher learning were affiliated with the University of Chicago: Des Moines College, Kalamazoo College, John B. Stetson College (the previous three with Baptist affiliations), Butler College, Bradley (a polytechnical institute), and Rush Medical College.[133]

The merger with Rush Medical College demonstrates how the goals of educational efficiency, university expansion and consolidation, and financing all came together. From the start Harper envisioned his university incorporating not only graduate schools for advanced training in the arts and sciences but also professional schools, including law and medicine. Harper began corresponding with the registrar at Rush Medical College, Dr. E. Fletcher Ingals, as early as 1894. Rush was founded in 1837 and initially was affiliated with the old University of Chicago. After the university closed, Rush developed a loose affiliation with Lake Forest University, a Presbyterian school north of Chicago. Harper believed the faculty at Rush represented some of the most advanced training in medicine, and he sought guidance on whether to seek affiliation with them. Frederick Gates, for example, opposed the union with Rush, arguing that it would be better for the university to wait and develop its own medical program from scratch so that it had complete control over all phases of its governance.[134] Yet Harper felt that the terms of affiliation, whereby Rush was forced to pay off its existing debt, raise admissions requirements, and dissolve its doctor-headed board in favor of a board approved by the University of Chicago trustees, made this an extremely attractive possibility for bringing medical education to the campus. The Board of Trustees approved the affiliation in 1898.[135]

In part, Gates opposed the affiliation because he and Rockefeller both argued that the exact terms of the relationship were not fully detailed. They were concerned that Rush would eventually merge with the university and become its medical school. According to Gates, this possibility violated one of the understandings Rockefeller believed he had with Harper: that he would not form an alliance with another medical college in Chicago. In addition, Gates argued that Rockefeller felt pressured to make contributions to the university based on decisions Harper made without consulting him. According to Gates, "Mr. Rockefeller came instinctively to feel that the methods of securing his assistance are too often methods of compulsion."[136] A cartoon of Harper holding a sack of money in one hand and a model of Rush in the other illustrated the sense that affiliation, especially in this case, was a program for gouging funds from Rockefeller, with dubious merit on intellectual or pedagogical grounds (fig. 20).

In addition to using affiliation as a vehicle for incorporating professional schools into the university, Harper also sought affiliation with secondary schools that would serve as feeders for the university. An affiliated high school was established coincident with the opening of the university. Morgan Park, the site of the old university and Baptist Seminary, became home to Morgan Park Academy. The academy was to have a close relationship with the university, functioning as a preparatory school for students before they began college work. According to Harper, it was intended to prepare students to enter the university, serve as a site for experiments in secondary education, and bring secondary and higher education close together.[137]

The academy was riddled with financial problems from the start. Gifts from other donors, not Rockefeller, were supposed to be the source of funding. When the trustees of the university could not raise the money, Rockefeller made a contribution to help the academy get started. But unable to raise enough money and maintain enrollments, the school closed at the end of 1907.[138]

The closing of Morgan Park did not greatly affect the university's role in linking secondary education with college work, for it had already established affiliations with other secondary institutions as well as the regional colleges.[139] Harper's affiliation program reflected his belief in the benefits of efficiency and rationalization in education. He argued in 1893, "With our thousands of educational institutions, there is at present no trace of system and order."[140]

Harper's attempts to create an all-encompassing department of pedagogy and educational training at the university illustrate his vision of centralization and consolidation. Harper hoped this department would become part of a larger pedagogical program that would serve as the basis of a professional school. Accordingly, he sought to bring two secondary schools into affiliation with the department, the South Side Academy and the Chicago Manual Training School. The former was a preparatory school established by a Chicago graduate student in the early 1890s. In June 1897 the head of the South Side Academy, E. O. Sisson, offered to make the school an affiliate of the university's Department of Pedagogy for observation and experimentation.[141]

Harper also recognized the importance of training in the practical arts, and he wanted the university involved in promoting manual training. He hoped it could

FIGURE 20. Caricature of William Rainey Harper holding Rush Medical College. Courtesy of the Rockefeller Archives Center.

establish a department or school that linked vocational training with academic coursework, and he looked toward a variety of models to shape the program. In 1896 Harper approached the Chicago Manual Training School (CMTS), an independent school of vocational arts and academic instruction founded in 1884 by the Commercial Club of Chicago. Again Rockefeller feared the problems that could arise as a result of bringing in a separate body to do the work of the university. In response, Harper proposed that the name be changed to include "technology," and that university board members be appointed as new trustees, so that the school might become the nucleus of a university school of technology.[142] The final agreement involved keeping the original name, as well as maintaining the institution as a separate but affiliated secondary school. All property belonging to the CMTS (one four-story brick building on the corner of Michigan Avenue and Twelfth Street) became the property of the university, and some of the trustees of the CMTS were replaced by university trustees.[143]

Harper's plans for a comprehensive program in pedagogy received an additional boost in 1898 when Chicago philanthropist Anita McCormick Blaine initiated a program to fund an experimental school, the Chicago Institute, under the direction of Colonel Francis Wayland Parker, the progressive principal of the Cook County Normal School. Blaine was the daughter of McCormick Reaper Works president Cyrus McCormick, and she was drawn into the Rockefeller family web after her brother Harold married Rockefeller's daughter Edith. Blaine offered to provide a $1 million endowment for the creation of a teacher training institute and an attached elementary school under Parker's direction. Already she had organized a board of trustees and created the endowment. She then consulted several leading reformers and educators, including Harper, about the best location for the new school. Harper saw the new Chicago Institute as a model for the type of teacher training school he wanted for the university, and he persuaded Blaine to incorporate the Institute into the educational program at the University of Chicago.[144]

The agreement between Harper and Blaine set the foundation for the establishment of the University of Chicago School of Education. On March 4, 1901, Blaine transferred $1 million worth of Institute assets to the university. In return, Harper guaranteed Blaine, Parker, and Institute trustees that the educational programs Parker initiated at the Normal School would not be hampered by allegiance with a large educational system and that the university would provide a suitable site and buildings for the School of Education.[145] This merger with the Institute prompted the South Side Academy to make its agreement with the university final, and by May 1901 the school and its endowment were placed in the hands of the university. The university's School of Education now was complete, with the CMTS, the Chicago Institute, and the South Side Academy forming a comprehensive program of pedagogy and educational training.

PRAGMATISM AND PEDAGOGY AT THE UNIVERSITY OF CHICAGO

The programs of the School of Education were structured by the Department of Pedagogy, which was organized in 1894 with recently appointed philosophy professor John Dewey as its head. Dewey taught philosophy at the University of Michigan at the time Harper hired him, and he already was regarded by many intellectuals as one of the leading philosophers of education in the nation.[146] Harper looked to Dewey to create an innovative program of educational research and training to bring together new studies in psychology and philosophy, pioneered by Dewey, fellow philosophy professor George Herbert Mead, and Harvard professor William James. The goal of the new pedagogy department was to "train competent specialists for the broad and scientific treatment of educational problems."[147]

In 1896 the university established an elementary school that would serve as the educational "laboratory" of the Department of Pedagogy. The University Elementary School, which came to be known as the Laboratory (Lab) School, provided an arena for Dewey, Mead, and other educational theorists to experiment with a variety of methods and ideas. Under Dewey, the Lab School gained international prominence as a model for progressive education and scientific pedagogical investigation.[148]

Dewey believed that the training of teachers and the development of educational theories through research and experiment went together. This connection between theory and practice grew out of his philosophy of pragmatism. Dewey was the leading proponent of pragmatism at Chicago, and he linked this developing philosophy directly to ideas about pedagogy and social activism. He pointed out the connections between the search for knowledge, the process of social engagement, religious commitment, and democracy. "If God is, at the root of life, incarnate in man, then democracy has a spiritual meaning which it behooves us not to pass by," he argued. "Democracy is freedom. If truth is at the bottom of things, freedom means giving truth a chance to show itself, a chance to well up from the depths."[149] Dewey's belief in human rationality and social interaction as the bases of truth and knowledge would lead him to move from formal religion toward a civic humanism that saw freedom and radical empiricism as the foundation for a spiritual democracy.

Dewey modeled his concept of truth on the work of philosophers Charles Sanders Peirce and William James. Both Peirce and James challenged the religious belief in truth as fixed and absolute, instead positing truth as a process that could be understood only through scientific inquiry and collective conversation and action. Dewey followed both Peirce and James in arguing that the process of knowing itself constituted knowledge. Knowledge was linked directly to experience and tied to the unfolding of history. Dewey's understanding of the structure of knowledge led him away from a Kantian distinction between experiential knowledge and intuitive knowledge and toward a Hegelian understanding of the role of history and lived experience in shaping knowledge.[150]

This belief in active social engagement served as the foundation for theories of progressive education that Dewey elaborated at the University of Chicago Elementary School. Dewey, along with other educational reformers such as George Herbert Mead and Colonel Francis Parker, believed that communities sustain themselves through continuous self-renewal. "This renewal takes place," argued Dewey, "by means of the educational growth of the immature members of the group."[151] In order to foster democratic institutions and an active civic culture, progressive educators demonstrated how learning was an ongoing process that united individual knowledge with social interaction. In this way, education helped forge a dynamic and continuously evolving public sphere. The promotion of democracy, then, was integrally linked to education:

> A society which makes provision for participation in its good of all its members on equal terms and which secures flexible readjustment of its institutions through interaction of the different forms of associated life is in so far democratic. Such a society must have a type of education which gives individuals a personal interest in social relationships and control, and the habits of mind which secure social changes without introducing disorder.[152]

Dewey argued that the learning environment for children should be modeled on practical experiences from everyday life and should encourage cooperative forms of social engagement. At the University Elementary School, problem solving was the basis of learning, with concrete experience replacing abstract theory as the source of knowledge. For example, students learned mathematics by making measurements for carpentry projects, botany by creating their own gardens, and chemistry through kitchen experiments. By engaging in these experiments cooperatively, they could place their acquired knowledge within the context of their environment and peer group. According to Dewey, "A fully integrated personality . . . exists only when successive experiences are integrated with one another. It can be built up only as a world of related objects is constructed."[153]

Both Dewey and Mead believed that experiential learning offered a way to reintegrate mind and hand, art and experience, labor and leisure. They shared with other progressives like settlement house founder Jane Addams and architectural critic Lewis Mumford a belief in the restorative qualities of manual education. Following John Ruskin and William Morris in England, they argued that "industrial education," which linked the creative process of artistic production and manual labor with social education, could lead to the creation of a unified and organic community. Self-fulfillment would come from the individual's becoming part of a cohesive community in which art was part of everyday experience. These educators shared with architects Louis Sullivan and Frank Lloyd Wright an understanding of how linking form and function, culture and community could help overcome the alienation created by the modern industrial factory system and the growth of a bureaucratic state. They argued that art and symbolic form could contribute to both individual and civic regeneration.[154]

Progressive educators also believed that reintroducing manual education and crafts into the school curriculum would help overcome the rising tensions and divisions between labor and capital. Hull House settlement founders Jane Addams and Ellen Gates Starr created a labor museum at the settlement in 1900, following William Morris's prescriptions for connecting art, work, and community. The Labor Museum, along with the Manual Training School at the University of Chicago, pioneered the movement for linking industrial education programs with a liberal arts curriculum. This connection in education could benefit all children, according to Addams and Dewey, since it would make them aware of the connections between work processes, labor relations, and industrial America. Addams also believed that industrial education would provide a foundation for appreciating and understanding diverse ethnic cultures. "It seemed to me that Hull-House ought to be able to devise some educational enterprise which should build a bridge between European and American experiences in such ways [*sic*] as to give them both more meaning and sense of relation."[155] Through progressive education, Dewey and Addams saw the potential for linking a fluid and diverse urban culture with a renewed public sphere to refashion social relations.

Tensions emerged between Dewey's conception of progressive education and Harper's. In particular, Harper's promotion of academic centralization contrasted sharply with Dewey's ideas about the links between pragmatism, pedagogy, and democracy. The increased consolidation of education under the auspices of the university illustrated how centralization could undermine the very ideas of democratic social engagement that progressive education was based on. The university, argued some critics, was becoming more and more like a corporation, not only in its structure but also in its values. The absorption of so many educational facilities "would enable the University to achieve on its own campus the equivalent of vertical integration in industry: a child could enter the orbit of the University from the nursery and remain until leaving with a Ph.D. degree."[156]

This tension between Harper and Dewey about the university's role in promoting urban education was exposed in debates over the future of the Chicago public school system. With the success of the university affiliations laying the groundwork, Harper sought a more active role for himself and the university in coordinating all phases of education in Chicago. As early as 1895 Harper wrote to Gates, "We have just succeeded in carrying through a plan which gives us very close control of the High Schools of the City of Chicago."[157] Here he referred both to his affiliations with local schools and also to plans to work with the mayor's office to reorganize the public school system. In 1899 Harper wrote a report, commissioned by Mayor Carter Harrison Jr., that recommended using business principles of efficiency and centralization in reformulating the Chicago Board of Education.[158] The report called for the concentration of authority in the office of the superintendent, with the mayor continuing to appoint members of the board. More important, Harper argued for professionalizing teaching by requiring a college degree for all who wanted to be teachers.[159] By coordinating all aspects of teaching and education, from the structure of the public schools to the curriculum for teachers' education, Harper hoped to make the university the leader and beacon of educational reform.

Harper's plan for bureaucratizing secondary education reflected both class and gender tensions. The "Harper Plan," as it came to be known, effectively removed control over the selection of teachers from local school boards and placed it in the hands of appointees in the superintendent's office. The plan also sought to create a system of meritocracy and professionalism through testing and the college degree requirement. In addition, Harper argued that male teachers (who usually were the ones with college degrees) should receive higher salaries than female teachers, since the men were career professionals.[160]

The Harper Plan diametrically opposed the reform efforts of the Chicago Teachers' Federation (CTF), a union organized in 1897 and headed by Margaret Haley and Catherine Goggin. The CTF sought to protect teachers' control over the classroom and the curriculum and to preserve the local attachments between teachers and the communities they served. Haley and Goggin allied themselves with the Chicago Federation of Labor (CFL) and linked union efforts to thwart the Harper Plan with broader class-conscious arguments over access to democratic institutions. According to Haley, the CTF represented a "struggle to prevent the last institution of democracy, the public school, from becoming a prey to the dominant spirit of greed, commercialism, autocracy & all attendant evils."[161] The CTF, with support from the CFL and University of Chicago faculty John Dewey and George Herbert Mead, repeatedly challenged efforts to institute the Harper Plan. Their efforts were thwarted in 1917, however, when the Illinois legislature upheld the Loeb rule, which outlawed union membership for teachers.[162]

The battle over school reform demonstrates the competing visions that were emerging at Chicago over what form modern American education would take in the wake of the rise of modern research institutions like the University of Chicago. Harper emphasized business models of consolidation and efficiency for his vision of modern education. His school reform bill reflected the rising belief in the power of centralized coalitions of trained experts to direct all phases of education. Because the university offered the most efficient and professional model for shaping education, Harper sought to bring other educational institutions under its control.

By contrast, Haley, Dewey, and Mead saw the potential for engaged public participation, with decentralized teacher control, as the best course for providing democratic education in modern America. Union advocates used the same language of expert guidance that Harper employed, but they did so to legitimize the authority and expertise of union teachers whose experience in their own communities enabled them, they argued, to best meet the educational needs of Chicago's youth. Moreover, John Dewey's alliance with Haley instead of Harper in the school reform debate reflected the fundamental differences between his goals for education and Harper's.[163]

This pedagogical debate further underscored the tensions over civic culture emanating from the University of Chicago. The processes of centralizing education in Chicago, designing the university, and regulating land use all suggested a model of civic engagement different from the one initially invoked by Harper. Rather than seeing the university as a neighbor and partner in shaping knowledge in the city, the administration envisioned a more paternalistic role. Just as the university centralized and consolidated the production and dissemination of knowledge, so too did it try to exert direct control over the process of shaping its physical borders and isolating itself from the rest of the city. These practices went hand in hand, for they illustrated both the physical and the intellectual barriers the university erected as it developed into a leader of higher education both in Chicago and across the nation.

Some critics even compared the tactics of the University of Chicago to those of Standard Oil, arguing that taking over smaller competitors in the realm of education was the equivalent of John D. Rockefeller's trust-building project. By swallowing smaller competitors and supplanting competition with a system of corporate consolidation, the university—like Rockefeller—undermined the democratic ideal. Affiliation, for example, enhanced the university's control over education instead of brokering a new agreement between institutions to reshape education in the city. Rather than mediating between different constituencies, the affiliated institutions became sites that augmented the university's power in controlling the educational enterprise in Chicago.

This consolidation manifested itself in the physical shape of the university. The Gothic towers, emblems of insularity, gave visible expression to the deepening rift between academic scholarship and civic engagement at the University of Chicago. While Dewey and others offered a model of civic culture defined by social activism, the university administration increasingly looked to the construction of expertise within the quadrangles of the campus as the best model of creating knowledge and fostering civic leadership.

The Gothic design of the campus united two ideas of civic culture that increasingly were linked. On one hand, it helped give cultural legitimacy to the Chicago elites who funded the university. The link between Gothic architecture and moral values allowed Chicago's industrialists to divert attention from their mercenary practices and emphasize their contribution to the culture of the city.[164] The campus design also illustrated the segmentation and specialization of knowledge created by the modern research university. Both models of civic culture, though, drew sharp distinctions between the purveyors of civic leadership and its recipients. The more activist and democratic model of civic engagement promoted by Dewey became an auxiliary function of the university rather than a defining component of it.

2

THE CITY SEEKING AID FROM ALMA MATER

Collegiate Culture, Coeducation, and the Boundaries of College and Community

IN 1912, FEMALE FACULTY AND STUDENTS at the University of Chicago launched a campaign to raise funds for a building devoted to "the social activities and physical training of the women."[1] This call was prompted both by the lack of adequate social and athletic facilities for women at the university, and by the fact that such buildings for the men had been dedicated several years earlier. Once the women secured a major donor, they set about designing the building to reflect their ideas about the relation between their roles as women, their university education, and their broader contributions to society. The building design, decor, and dedication ceremonies for Ida Noyes Hall exhibited the ideal to which many university women, both students and faculty, ascribed. The dedication featured the performance of a masque intended to dramatize the larger civic purpose that would be fostered in Ida Noyes Hall. The allegory of "The Masque of Youth" read:

> In comes Youth, joyous in unawakened power. . . . Guided by her angels she has come to Alma Mater seated on her Gothic throne. . . . Youth throws herself at Alma Mater's feet, eager for a test of her young strength. . . . In answer come, in their turn, the Olympic games, for the perfection of her body's growth; . . . the Romance of Literature; . . . the Spirit of Worship. . . . Then comes the City

> seeking aid from Alma Mater, and the wise mother, knowing that her child must spend her strength for others before it shall be truly hers, bestows on Youth the gift of Service.[2]

The masque clearly reflected the links between the university as the seat of maternal protection and source of knowledge and as the home of larger civic ideals. Not only would women's bodies, minds, and spirits be nurtured by Alma Mater, so too would the female dedication to service transcend the boundaries of the campus and exert a presence within the city itself.

The masque also invoked larger debates structuring higher education at the turn of the century. In his December 1901 convocation address, President William Rainey Harper discussed a growing concern among administrators at colleges and universities throughout the country. He pointed to the nationwide trend of increased female enrollment and the possibility of the "feminization" of the university. Chicago was at the forefront of this trend, since it had been a coeducational institution from the time of its founding in 1890. During its first year, there were 750 students enrolled at the university, and more than a quarter were women. The largest group of students entering the Graduate School came from Wellesley, a women's college.[3] The percentage of female students rose steadily, from 24 percent in 1892 to 52 percent in 1902. Moreover, between 1892 and 1902 women received 56 percent of the Phi Beta Kappa awards at Chicago.[4] Harper's solution was what he called a system of "sex segregation" among undergraduates in the first two years of college. Harper believed this policy would attract more male students, help preserve the masculine character of the learning environment, and benefit both males and females intellectually.[5] Indeed, Chicago sociologist Albion Small spoke for Harper and many other faculty members when he argued in favor of sex segregation on supposedly intellectual grounds: "In a word, the massing of large numbers of young men and women in a mixed company for educational purposes is, in my judgment, the most certain device that could be imagined for reducing the educational influence upon both sexes below a respectable level of seriousness and dignity. . . . This spontaneous matching or attractions by people of that age . . . lowers the dignity of the University to the level of a pre-matrimonial experiment station."[6]

The concern about coeducation and how best to shape it reflected broader tensions over how student culture would be shaped, knowledge would be structured, and the university would fulfill its mission to engage with the city. By the first years of the twentieth century, the university increasingly moved away from a model of direct civic engagement and more toward notions of scientific research and expertise that stressed neutrality, objectivity, and distance from larger political concerns of the day. Faculty found their roles more circumscribed as the university's commitment to the larger civic culture of Chicago was redefined. Just as the university imposed physical boundaries that demarcated the campus from the surrounding city, so too were expertise, professionalism, and scientific investigation defined as projects to be contained within the boundaries of the campus rather than outside them.

These battles over the meanings and sites of knowledge production exposed many of the ambiguities over women's place, both within the university and outside in the city. Moreover, the spatial dimension of these debates about gender illustrated how the presence of women in an institution often perceived as male (the university campus) led to the creation of plans intended to contain women's place so as not to "overfeminize" and thereby devalue university education.[7]

At the same time, the training that women received at the university gave them the expertise that helped legitimize their expanded roles beyond the Gothic quadrangles. Indeed, it was largely through women's efforts that the presence of the university within the city was felt. Through civic activism, social work, and settlement house leadership, university women created arenas where the meanings of social science and expertise could be destabilized. Their training allowed them to reshape the boundaries between university and city, mind and body, knowledge and action and to construct a new model of the public sphere that recognized the importance of multiple definitions of expertise and political engagement.[8]

STUDENT CULTURE AT THE UNIVERSITY OF CHICAGO

Student demographics nationwide changed radically at the end of the nineteenth century, as the percentage of youth aged eighteen to twenty-one attending college skyrocketed. In 1840, 16,233 students attended college at 173 institutions. By 1880, 85,378 students were enrolled in 591 institutions of higher learning. In 1880, roughly 2 percent of college-age Americans went to college, while by 1900 that percentage jumped to 4 percent.[9] The rapid rise in the number of students attending college reflected new opportunities available to people for whom in the past college was not a possibility. Traditionally, those who attended were sons of the elite. For them college was a way to shape character, forge economic and political connections, and become part of the social and cultural networks promised by clubs and societies at places like Harvard, Yale, and Princeton. Before the nineteenth century, the other large group of college graduates entered the ministry, attending seminaries in order to be ordained. The Morrill Land Grant Act of 1862 did much to democratize higher education by providing federal lands for the creation of colleges to promote the study of agriculture. Higher education now was available to children of farming families, and colleges and universities proliferated through the Midwest and West in the late nineteenth century.[10]

Students from both rural and urban settings looked to college as a way to gain entry into the world of expertise that was becoming so central to the rising corporate marketplace. Many schools, including Harvard and Yale, modified the college curriculum, focusing less on the classics and more on science and the liberal arts. Students saw attending college, with its increasing emphasis on science, efficiency, and professionalism, as a way to achieve economic and social mobility. Although the student population was extremely diverse by the turn of the century, and the types of institutions they attended varied greatly, a noticeable shift in both the backgrounds and educational goals of the nation's college students was evident.[11]

One of the most important changes to occur in higher education in the late nineteenth century was the rise of coeducation. Between 1900 and 1916, the number of men attending college tripled, while the number of women quadrupled. By 1915, 75 percent of these college women were attending coeducational institutions. This interest in coeducation among female students reflected a dramatic change in the place of higher education in women's lives. Like the men's colleges of the eighteenth and nineteenth centuries, most of the women's colleges catered to an elite clientele. Women's colleges served much the same purpose as men's colleges—fostering an atmosphere conducive to the development of character through a general classical education.

The setting of early women's colleges was designed to consolidate women's roles by creating a feeling of shared domesticity. Their founders stressed the need for a protective environment for the young women leaving home to pursue higher education, and they adopted the model of the seminary for campus design. At Mount Holyoke (1837) in Massachusetts and Vassar (1861) in New York, all activities took place in one building erected on a picturesque hillside. This seclusion allowed teachers and supervisors to monitor the female students, thereby creating an insular college experience. Later women's colleges, including Smith (1875) in Massachusetts and Bryn Mawr (1885) in Pennsylvania, sought to distance themselves from the bonds of domesticity symbolized by the earlier seminary-like campuses. The Gothic quadrangle, symbolic of the best tradition of (male) collegiate culture in England, became the favored style for the new women's colleges, reflecting the desire to create institutions of higher learning equal in stature to those of men.[12]

By the late nineteenth century, justifications for women's education changed. More women attended college to further careers as teachers, nurses, doctors, or librarians, mirroring the professional concerns of male students. New research universities like Johns Hopkins, Clark, and Chicago offered specialized departments and graduate training that fostered the rise of professionalism. As a result, many women looked to coeducational institutions like the University of Chicago to pursue professional degrees and graduate training.[13] The university attempted to strike a balance between its goals of promoting scientific investigation, rigorous research, and professional training and opening up higher education to a broader spectrum of Americans, one of Harper's interests.

A university survey illustrates some demographic features of the early student body. During the inaugural year, 750 students enrolled at the university, one-third undergraduates, one-quarter graduates, and the rest in the Divinity School. These figures were significant, for they illustrated the central place of the Divinity School in the early growth of the university. More than a third of the undergraduates were transfers from other institutions, while the Graduate School received students from ninety-five institutions.[14]

The graduate schools clearly were attracting students from other regions, but the university as a whole mainly served a regional student population during its first years. In the first class, three-quarters of the students came from Chicago and the Midwest. One in seven came from New England and the mid-Atlantic states, and less than 3 percent came from the South or the West. Twenty students came from Canada, and a total of a dozen came from other countries.[15] Interestingly, a large portion of female students came from the East and the South, while most men came from the Midwest. Yet the numbers of students, both male and female, from outside the Midwest rose quickly as the university established its reputation as one of the premier research universities in the nation.

Other demographic factors illustrated how the University of Chicago reflected changes occurring in higher education at the turn of the century. Although the university was founded under Baptist auspices, students came from a range of religious backgrounds. A survey of 199 students in the 1903 graduating class revealed that Baptists were the most numerous group in the class but not a majority. There were twenty-four Baptists, nineteen Presbyterians, fifteen Episcopalians, thirteen Congregationalists, thirteen Methodists, ten Jews, and eight Roman Catholics.[16]

Despite this religious diversity, the university had a reputation as being unfriendly toward non-Protestants. Irish Catholics were one group that experienced this hostility. In 1890, first- and second-generation Irish made up over 16 percent of the population of Chicago. Large numbers of Irish had started coming to Chicago in 1836 with the promise of employment generated by the massive Illinois and Michigan Canal project, which linked Lake Michigan to the Illinois River. By the 1890s, many second-generation Irish families had achieved middle-class status and moved from Bridgeport, near the canal, to areas like Washington Park, just west of the university.[17] Irish Catholics migrated there just at the time the university was seeking to acquire more property around the campus, sparking some tensions with the residents.[18]

Chicago writer James T. Farrell recounted these antagonisms in both ethnic and class terms. In his autobiographical novel *My Days of Anger,* Farrell described how his protagonist, Danny O'Neill, faced the difficult decision of whether to attend the university. His Irish Catholic neighbors were hostile toward the school and believed that anyone from their parish who attended had betrayed the group. They described it as atheistic and anti-Catholic, and undergirding their hostility was a feeling of exclusion and separateness tied to class. Danny felt divided loyalties after he decided to attend the University of Chicago, as if his identity had been torn apart and reshaped by his decision to enter the Gothic gates. Farrell wrote about Danny, "Yesterday at mass he had realized he was growing away from the life of the neighborhood. With the family, he had seen himself more or less a stranger looking on at them. New attitudes had been quietly developing in him and now they were making themselves felt." Here the physical boundary between the university and the parish was symbolic of deeper social and psychological divisions that characterized the way residents of this community understood their place in it.[19]

One of the earliest Catholic churches in Chicago was founded in 1869 just steps from what would become the campus of the University of Chicago. St. Thomas the Apostle Church started in a small frame structure at Fifty-fifth Street and Kimbark Avenue, but the congregation soon outgrew the building and it was replaced with a substantial Gothic brick church in 1890, just as the university was planning its Gothic campus. So even as these neighbors—the church and the university—appealed to different local populations, they selected the same design style evoking the symbols of religious piety, fixity, and order.[20]

The university did establish an informal relationship with St. Thomas Church after Father Thomas Vincent Shannon was appointed rector in 1916.[21] Shannon was a graduate of the old University of Chicago, and this connection prompted George W. Mundelein, archbishop of Chicago, to appoint him to St. Thomas. Mundelein hoped Shannon "might establish friendly relations and be a source of information to the Faculty connected with the University."[22] On the surface, Mundelein maintained a cordial relationship with the university, but his private correspondence suggests his ambivalence and even hostility toward the institution. "Those of you who have had any experience, will agree with me that its tendencies are in many of its courses aetheistic, are materialistic, and are socialistic," he argued. He further claimed, "Nine out of ten Catholic girl students who enter there come out decidedly the worse for wear as far as their spiritual side is concerned."[23] Mundelein, then, affirmed the religious tensions that many Catholic students claimed to experience.[24]

Jews experienced different kinds of tensions with the university. Wealthy German Jews were active in its founding and instrumental in helping the institution raise local funds to ensure additional support from John D. Rockefeller. Board of Trustees member Eli B. Felsenthal, a Jewish graduate of the old University of Chicago, proved crucial in forging ties with other prominent Chicago Jews, including Reform Rabbi Emil G. Hirsch, who would become a faculty member.[25] As the Chicago Jewish community expanded in the 1880s and 1890s, with poor Eastern European Jews arriving and congregating in neighborhoods like Maxwell Street and the West Side, wealthier and more established German Jews moved south of the central business district, into the Grand Boulevard neighborhood and eventually to Washington Park, Hyde Park, and Kenwood. As they moved, they built new synagogues in these neighborhoods, creating a visible presence of Jewish culture within the urban landscape of the South Side. The most spectacular testament to this presence was the Kehilath Anshe Ma'ariv (KAM) Temple, built in 1891 by renowned architect and engineer Dankmar Adler (partner of architect Louis Sullivan), whose father was a rabbi at KAM.[26] German Jews became a vital part of the cultural life of Hyde Park, but they were more alienated as students within the university.

Jewish students at the University of Chicago were subject to patterns of discrimination that shaped their collegiate experience nationwide.[27] At most universities, they were excluded from fraternities, athletic clubs, literary magazines, debating clubs, and newspapers. At Chicago, Jews could not be elected to class office, hold office in any club, or join a fraternity that was not one of their own. Vincent Sheean, a writer and University of Chicago alumnus, recounted a story from his college days, during which time he accidentally pledged a Jewish fraternity (he was not Jewish). He said he was unaware that the fraternity was Jewish until a female friend enlightened him. "'It's that damned fraternity,'" she explained. "'You can't possibly belong to it and make anything out of your college life. . . . No girl will go out with you—no nice girl that is. And you're barred from everything that makes college life what it is.'" When Sheean told her he did not realize the fraternity was Jewish, she replied, "'You're sixteen years old. You've got a fair amount of brains. My God, do you mean to tell me you don't know a Jew when you see one? Look at them, idiot, look at them. They have noses, hair, eyes, features, mouth, all different from everybody else."[28] While the University of Chicago was more open and democratic in its admission policies than older universities, the cultural life of the institution helped reproduce class, religious, and ethnic cultural hierarchies. Jewish students were set apart from the mainstream student body based on a combination of religious, ethnic, and often class differences that were difficult to overcome despite the increasing public role of Jews in the cultural life of Hyde Park.[29]

African Americans had even fewer opportunities at the University of Chicago. While the university did not have an official color line, it discouraged black students' presence. In 1899, Harper advised a recruiting agent in Texas that he should "get rid of anyone who may be obnoxious to you" and explained that the university was reluctant to admit "Negroes." Some African Americans did matriculate at the university, and they tended to come from either highly privileged or extremely deprived circumstances. Still, in 1901, only 5 out of 3,500 enrolled students were black. This number did not increase significantly until after World War II, despite the growing presence of black residents in neighborhoods close to the university.[30]

While the university had a somewhat antagonistic relationship with neighborhood residents based on racial and ethnic barriers, it was a bit more sensitive to issues of class. Harper observed in 1902 that many of the students, especially those from Chicago, were from working-class families. Harper explained that the need to work provided them with the characteristics of "steadiness, sturdiness, strength, strong individuality, high ideals, and clear purpose." Robert Herrick agreed. In his *Scribner's* article, he celebrated the admirable characteristics of University of Chicago students with as much enthusiasm as Harper. He also explained that students "who are earning the means to study are the rule, not the exception." Herrick argued that this condition of "strenuous poverty" created "a very different atmosphere in the college world from the opulent spirit of our older institutions."[31]

The structure of the university, according to Harper, made it more feasible for higher education to be opened up to a broader class of students. Instead of adopting a semester system, where students had long vacations in the winter and summer, Harper instituted the quarter system. Students who so desired could attend school throughout the year, with one-week breaks between quarters, thereby completing their education in less time. Other students could work for part of the year if necessary and not feel they had lost time in a tightly structured course of study. Harper articulated his belief in the intellectual benefits of the quarter system during a discussion of the lack of annual graduation ceremonies under this system. "It is only a rigid arrangement, which treats alike all students of whatever capacity, which can secure an annual graduation day," he explained. He added, "The fact is that each individual student should be treated separately, and when his course of study is completed he should be given his diploma."[32] The quarter system stressed academic achievement rather than a student's ability simply to remain in the confines of the quadrangles for a specified period. The creation of this type of meritocracy, according to Harper, did away with class distinctions and made a college education a reasonable prospect for a wider range of students.[33]

PROMOTING COLLEGIATE SPIRIT AT CHICAGO

This emphasis on the efficiency and intellectual rigor of the university generated criticism regarding the lack of cohesiveness and collegial spirit that the traditional college calendar created. Indeed, a letter to Harper from Frederick T. Gates, founder John D. Rockefeller's secretary, addressed this concern. Gates's son Fred attended the university, and Gates shared some of Fred's thoughts from a recent visit home. "He complains a little of the lack of what he calls 'college spirit' and what I should prefer to call 'cohesion and communal social and intellectual life among the students.'" Gates believed this feeling was most likely a result of the quarter system, combined with the fact that many of those who lived on campus were graduate students, and many undergraduates were from Chicago and lived at home.[34] Harper responded to these criticism about the quarter system destroying "class spirit" by arguing, "There is a certain kind of class spirit which ought to be destroyed. A class spirit which rises superior to the college spirit and to the spirit of scholarship deserves no existence." The university plan emphasized this "spirit of scholarship," for Harper the most important element of collegiate life.[35]

Still, Harper hoped that the creation of a house system of college residence would alleviate these feelings of alienation among students. Under this plan, faculty lived with groups of students who were entitled to continuous residence in one hall. Each house had a head appointed by the president, a counselor chosen from the faculty of the house, a house committee, and a secretary and treasurer. This system was stalled, though, because there was inadequate dormitory space for a few years after the founding of the university. Foster Hall was completed as part of the original quadrangle, but Kelly, Beecher, and Snell Halls still were under construction after the university opened its doors. Until 1898, most students were forced to live off campus. As a result, the university rented the Beatrice Apartments, a new building erected to house visitors during the fair.[36]

While many male students lived in the apartments during their early years at the university, their housing situation improved with the introduction of fraternity houses. Harper's initial plan for the university did not include fraternities. In an article titled "The Antagonism of Fraternities to the Democratic Spirit of Scholarship," Harper argued that traditional clubs and literary societies were more advantageous for promoting social life than were fraternities.[37] Yet when the issue was raised at the first meeting of the Faculty of Arts, Literature, and Science, he appointed a committee to review it. The committee advised that it would be unwise to forbid students to establish fraternities but that the university should discourage them, since "the end sought by these societies so far as they are laudable, may be secured by other means which shall be free from the objections of secrecy, of rigid exclusiveness, and of antagonism to the democratic spirit which is inherent in the highest scholarship and manhood, and the most exalted citizenship."[38]

The Board of Trustees responded to these recommendations by stating that fraternities should be allowed on campus, but that each chapter must submit its house rules for approval, appoint a representative the faculty might consult with, and restrict membership to students in their second year in the Academic (Junior) College (freshmen and sophomores) and the University (Senior) College (juniors and seniors).[39] This plan fit neatly within the framework of the house system Harper outlined for dormitories, so fraternities were subject to the same university regulation as other clubs and resident houses.[40]

The advent of fraternities opened up the possibility of introducing sororities on campus, but the misgivings of the assistant dean of women, Marion Talbot, led to their exclusion.[41] Talbot had accepted the position in 1892 so she could "cast her lot with the new University and the growing city." Here she saw a chance to be an active contributor to women's higher education on an egalitarian basis with men.[42] She argued that the formation of women's secret societies was not the best "form of social organization" for university women given "the special conditions which prevail at the University of Chicago."[43] By this she meant that the place of women at the university was in a formative stage and that all should work together for the benefit of other female faculty and students.

Talbot was a perfect choice to serve as an assistant dean of women. She had collaborated with her MIT professor Ellen Swallow Richards, a chemist who developed the field of sanitary science and the concept of human ecology, the study of the environment that humans interact with daily, including the city and the home.[44] Talbot and Richards together edited *Home Sanitation: A Manual for Housekeepers* (1887), one of the foundation texts for home economics. She joined the faculty at Wellesley College in 1890 to establish a course in domestic science, one of the first in the nation. This work formed the basis of Talbot's intellectual pursuits at the University of Chicago, and also her approach to shaping women's roles in the city.[45]

Once Talbot arrived at Chicago, she quickly sought to establish a residence model similar to the house system while still boarding at the Beatrice Apartments. Talbot, along with Alice Freeman Palmer, dean of women and professor of history (and former president of Wellesley College), wanted to create a "family" atmosphere for the female students, particularly since most were coming from farther away than the male students. Talbot recognized that much of the student culture on campus was dominated by men, including clubs, athletics, and student government. She wanted to strike a balance between the cohesion that female students at women's colleges experienced and the independence a coeducational university afforded them. Throughout her tenure, Talbot attempted both to promote equal access for women in all university programs and to ensure that the needs of female students—social, educational, and professional—were adequately addressed by the university.[46] She argued that the best principle for establishing a cohesive community of female faculty and students in the makeshift living conditions of the Beatrice Apartments was "the co-ordination of individual liberty and organic union."[47] Rather than the atmosphere of exclusivity embodied in the fraternity, Talbot emphasized the importance of cooperation and conviviality. The model of sociability Talbot established while at the Beatrice became the example for the house system at the university while inspiring the plans for the women's dormitory buildings.

COEDUCATION, SEX SEGREGATION, AND THE RISE OF COLLEGIATE CULTURE

Different notions of male and female patterns of sociability on campus extended to other realms of college life, including scholastics. Administrators at several universities, including Chicago, made it clear that they feared the effect that "feminization" of higher education would have on the prestige of the university and on collegiate culture in general. At Chicago and elsewhere, some administrators worried that continuing to admit more women would "divert . . . a large number of the best class of college men" to all-male schools like Yale, thereby dooming other schools' ability to compete with the most prestigious institutions across the nation.[48] At the University of Wisconsin, President Charles Richard Van Hise articulated a similar "sex repulsion theory," asserting that the growing number of women was driving men out of the classroom.[49]

Some faculty and administrators revived older arguments against women's higher education in general. As early as 1873, Dr. Edward Clarke published *Sex in Education,* in which he applied Darwinian principles of evolution to the study of female education. He argued that if women used up their "limited energy" through study and intellectual exertion, they would harm their "female apparatus" and thereby threaten the future of the race. Clark University president G. Stanley Hall outlined how higher education threatened the race on social and psychological grounds. In his study of sexual attraction during adolescence, he argued that if women received higher education, they would "become functionally castrated, unwilling to accept the limitations of married life," and resentful when it came time to perform "the functions particular to their sex." He believed that if women were to be educated at all, it should be in colleges and facilities separate from those of men, since the sexual attraction would disturb males during their studies.[50] Chicago sociology professor Albion W. Small concurred, arguing, "Speaking now of the boys, if we want to emasculate them mentally I know of no surer means of doing it than by putting them, at the Junior College age, into the same classes with girls."[51]

At the University of Chicago, President Harper proposed his solution of "sex segregation" among undergraduate students in the Junior College. Men and women would receive instruction separate from one another, thereby maintaining the university's commitment to coeducation. Harper claimed this plan offered a way to address the perceived difference in needs of male and female students and to provide a strong intellectual and social atmosphere for each.[52]

Many alumnae felt differently, arguing that segregation of education was the first step toward doing away with coeducation altogether. Chicago graduate Madeleine Wallin, who became a leader in the campaign for municipal suffrage, opposed the plan, arguing that it was a "halfway method" that would lead to "self-consciousness and exaggeration of sex differences." Marion Talbot led the protest among the faculty. In addition to speaking out against the policy within the university, she also wrote directly to Mrs. John D. Rockefeller to express her concern that the position of female faculty was not taken into consideration. She argued that the plan was designed "chiefly in the interests of men," as evinced "by the fact that the protests of every woman connected with the administration and instruction and of nearly every woman graduate received no official recognition."[53] Over fifty faculty members supported Talbot's efforts, including John Dewey, who argued that the policy of sex segregation was an "un-American, anti-democratic, and reactionary policy."[54]

Despite these protests, which according to Frederick T. Gates came from those commonly regarded as some of the "ablest men of the Faculty," and which illustrated "how acute the spirit of irritation is in the institution," on October 22, 1902, the Board of Trustees voted in favor of segregation.[55] Initially Harper hoped to build a separate quadrangle for women that included a clubhouse, gymnasium, classroom, and laboratory facilities for female freshmen and sophomores. Rockefeller made it clear, however, that while he approved of the separation of men and women in the Junior College if the Board of Trustees and president recommended it, he would not contribute financially to allow for the "practical execution of the policy."[56] Yet lack of funds meant that the dramatic physical separation between men and women would be scaled back, and the policy of sex segregation implemented on a more limited basis.

Rather than build the separate women's quadrangle, the university devoted Ellis Hall, already built, to the Junior College men and built Lexington Hall to accommodate the women. Junior College students were divided, for purposes of "administration, instruction, and personal association," into eight colleges, based on Oxford's program of residential colleges. There were separate colleges for men and women in Arts, Literature, Philosophy, and Science, each with its own dean and faculty. Harper's plan stipulated that at least one-third of every student's work each quarter had to be taken from instructors assigned to the student's own college.[57]

By implementing the plan of sex segregation, Harper and the Board of Trustees believed they were fostering the kind of collegiality previously missing from the campus. The plan would create a residential community of scholars who shared not only intellectual pursuits but also camaraderie, thereby linking the academic and social aspects of collegiate life. Indeed, future university president Harry Pratt Judson said as much in his letter of support for sex segregation. "In the old-fashioned men's colleges there is a sense of unity," he argued, "a feeling of social solidarity, which is notably lacking in coëducational institutions, and which in itself is a powerful educational agency."[58] Fostering male patterns of sociability similar to those at single-sex colleges, according to Judson and others, would provide the most effective learning environment for men and women. That this gendered division of learning was reflected in the physical form of the campus further reinforced rather than challenged traditional assumptions about the intellectual differences between men and women. These divisions between male and female sociability, linked to ideas about gender difference in intellectual proclivities, were underscored by debates over another feature of collegiate culture—athletics.

THE "COLLEGE SPIRIT": GENDER, ATHLETICS, AND SOCIABILITY AT CHICAGO

Debates over athletics at the university illustrate the gendered underpinnings of efforts to foster a stronger sense of collegiate spirit across campus. Administrators' understanding of men's and women's physical capacities, as well as their patterns of sociability, were shaped by the assumption of gender difference. This mark of difference forced female students and educators to walk a fine line between providing for the "special needs" of women and fighting for equal status within all university programs, including athletics.[59]

Harper demonstrated his support for university athletics when he hired Alonzo Stagg, a former Yale Divinity School student who had played football under legendary Walter Camp, as football coach and director of physical culture. Harper argued that a strong athletic program was every bit as essential to the modern university as was the scientific laboratory. He wrote, "The athletic work of the students is a vital part of the student life. Under the proper restrictions it is a real and essential part of college education. The athletic field, like the gymnasium, is one of the University's laboratories and by no means the least important one."[60]

Harper linked athletics directly to manhood and morality. In a speech praising Stagg he affirmed, "In the director of the work [of college athletics], . . . we have an example of earnest and conscientious manhood which exerts a powerful influence among the men themselves toward right conduct and right living."[61] Albion Small agreed, identifying college sports as one of "the most important moralizing influences at our disposal."[62]

Both Stagg and Harper invoked the rhetoric of "muscular Christianity" to articulate the central role competitive sports played in promoting the best attributes in college students. Muscular Christianity emerged in the mid-nineteenth century as a concept that linked exercise, health, and hygiene with moral purity and national strength, combining millennial ideas about human perfectibility with health reform programs designed to purify "the race." Social reformer Thomas Wentworth Higginson, among others, found that the physical degeneracy he witnessed in mid-nineteenth-century America mirrored the moral degeneracy he wanted to overcome. He linked self-betterment through physical exercise directly to moral improvement and national power.[63]

By the turn of the century, this rhetoric of muscular Christianity shifted slightly, with athletics serving the interests of morality and nationalism, but also of the modern corporate workplace. University of Chicago faculty, for example, pointed out that the values and discipline learned on the athletic field would have important applications within society at large. For Alonzo Stagg, the drive to win promoted principles of conduct that transcended the football field: "It will be a pleasure to create a strong college spirit which means so much to a boy's life. And last and best of all, it will give me such a fine chance to do the Christian work among the boys who are sure to have the most influence. Win the athletes of any college for Christ, and you will have the strongest working element attainable in college life."[64]

Harper believed that athletics played a central role in fostering the "college spirit" critics claimed was missing at Chicago. Rooting for the college team, according to Harper and other promoters of intercollegiate athletics, would unite students in a common cause and create the bonds that were so integral a part of college life historically.[65] Chicago English professor Robert Herrick noted the role of athletics in creating loyalty both to the university and to the nation. Team sports helped male students "feel the exhilaration and loyalty to the scope of the institution as men working shoulder to shoulder in a new country, planning for a brilliant future."[66] According to many promoters of athletics, competition and loyalty, the two fundamental elements of collegiate sports and male culture, would become the basis of corporate culture in America. By making sports a prominent feature of university life, college presidents and athletic directors helped refocus higher education, joining academic development with physical prowess in the creation of a masculine collegiate culture.

Harper and Stagg were not the only Americans championing the virtues of athletics at the turn of the century. Many American civic, political, and business leaders argued that athletics and teamwork could serve as antidotes to the growing discomfort with the rise of the modern bureaucratic culture. A *New York Times* editorial captured this faith in the potential of physical exercise to overcome what many regarded as the effeminacy of modern urban commercial culture. "A weakly, sickly, flabby race may be a pleasing spectacle to theorists who live chiefly in the clouds, but for the destiny yet lying before us we cannot have too much of the attributes which are popularly included in the word 'manliness.'"[67] Leaders like Theodore Roosevelt saw in "the cult of strenuosity" and "muscular Christianity" a means to find intense experience and reassert masculine prowess through physical activity.[68]

Women, however, were not excluded from these prescriptions to exercise. Some scientists stressed the need for exercise, especially among college-educated women, so they could effectively carry out the demands of motherhood. University of Chicago sociologist William I. Thomas, in *Sex and Society: Studies in the Social Psychology of Sex*, argued that women's participation in athletics was essential as an antidote to neurasthenia and other aliments that elite and middle-class women suffered as a result of their "passive" social role.[69] Dr. Dudley Allen Sargent, director of the Hemenway Gymnasium at Harvard University and founder of the Sargent School for Physical Education, pointed to the enormous benefits of sports for women, including "concentration, accuracy, alertness, . . . perseverance, reason, judgment, . . . grace, poise, suppleness, courage, strength, and endurance."[70]

These advocates of women's exercise echoed the ideas of earlier women's health reformers, including Catharine Beecher and Frances Willard, by linking women's physical health with their ability to carry out their duties as wives and mothers. The "cult of true womanhood," which maintained that women's proper sphere was in the home providing nurture and maintaining piety among all members of the household, required women to be both morally and physically robust. This idea was the women's equivalent of muscular Christianity, and its proponents stressed that a woman's physical well-being was tied directly to her roles as wife and mother. According to Catharine Beecher and her sister Harriet Beecher Stowe, exercise offered women a chance to enhance their daily lives while at the same time taking more control over their domestic duties: "Young girls can seldom be made to realize the value of health, and the need of exercise to secure it, so as to feel much interest in walking abroad, when they have no other object. But, if they are brought up to minister to the comfort and enjoyment of themselves and of others, by performing domestic duties, they will constantly be interested and cheered in their exercise by the feeling of usefulness and the consciousness of having performed their duty."[71] While Beecher and Stowe's advocacy of exercise was framed within the narrow limits of the cult of true womanhood, they nonetheless challenged the idea that physical weakness was an essential element of the female constitution.

By the turn of the century, several female physicians and scientists broadened this interpretation of the role of exercise for women, showing how control over one's body could be liberating in other realms of life as well. Female scientists like Helen Bradford Thompson (who studied with James Angell at Chicago) linked their pioneering studies in physiology and social psychology to the New Woman. Challenging ingrained beliefs about the inherent inferiority of women, these scientists demonstrated how slight sex differences were in terms of both physical and mental abilities. Physical exercise (as well as intellectual stimulation), according to these studies, was beneficial for both men and women.[72]

In a *Ladies' Home Journal* series titled "What Has College Done for Girls?" writer Edith Rickert assessed the benefits and drawbacks of higher education for women and included a discussion of athletics among college women. Rickert's series was based on interviews with hundreds of women who had attended college between 1849 and 1909. Respondents to her survey stressed the importance of physical education in allowing college women to preserve "the balance of a sound mind in a healthful body." Many respondents also believed that women's specific needs should be more directly addressed in college. "That is," according to Rickert, "the special handicaps of women should be more carefully weighed in the scheme of physical training, particularly athletics, and this training should be directed more definitely toward the strength that is needed for motherhood rather than the muscularity that shows up well in contests."[73]

Many women, along with men, believed that physical exercise ought to be used to improve women's health, fitness, and by extension, beauty, but that athletic competition was an altogether separate matter, one that could introduce masculine characteristics such as competitiveness, aggression, and even violence. In his *Ladies' Home Journal* article "Are Athletics Making Girls Masculine? A Practical Answer to a Question Every Girl Asks," Dudley Sargent discussed the fear that competitive sports could undermine women's femininity and pose a threat to the race. "Many persons honestly believe," he stated, "that athletics are making girls bold, masculine and overassertive; that they are destroying the beautiful lines and curves of her figure."[74] Indeed, Sargent argued, women who excelled in competitive sports may have inherited male physiological features. This was necessarily so, he pointed out, because only by taking on "masculine attributes" could they succeed in certain forms of competition. While Sargent believed that some degree of competition was beneficial, he did not wish to see women engaged in rough contact sports that threatened their health. Instead, he argued for rules changes that took into account the different physical and emotional capacities of men and women.[75]

This tension between athletics as a means of exercise and as form of competition structured early debates about women's athletics at the University of Chicago. When the Department of Physical Culture and Athletics was organized on October 1, 1892, members emphasized the importance of tending to the physical fitness of all students. Part of the General Regulations of the University stated, "All students will be examined as to their physical condition on entering the University, and at intervals during the course." The university physician would make the examination and provide each student with a detailed written report "indicating constitutional weaknesses, and forms of exercise desirable and undesirable for the individual in question." The regulation stipulated that Alonzo Stagg, as the director of the Department of Physical Education, "give his personal attention, not only to the organization and training of athletics teams . . . but especially to the physical training of each student, in so far as it is practicable."[76]

The Women's Division of the Department of Physical Education, under the leadership of Gertrude Dudley, emphasized how exercise improved physical fitness and dealt cautiously with the issue of competitive sports for women. The purpose of the Women's Division was to promote good health, provide wholesome forms of recreation, and teach skills in an individual sport that graduates might pursue in their leisure time.[77] Professor Dudley met with each student to discuss recommended programs and made suggestions for personal health habits, as well as sleep, food, and exercise regimen. Dudley worked in conjunction with Marion Talbot, furnishing her with a list of all female students who "in her opinion, were not in average physical condition."[78]

The Women's Division set as its goals not only health and fitness for women, but also the creation of a new sphere of female sociability at college. Women were instructed in a variety of activities that they selected themselves and that allowed for "differing degrees of physical fitness." "In all of the teaching, emphasis is placed on the Joy of activity. If a student seems unable to get that result, change of activity is not only suggested but urged."[79]

Regarding the possibility of competition, Marion Talbot advised the Board of Physical Culture in 1894 that "contests in women's training" should be "very carefully watched and guarded."[80] Women engaged in rowing, tennis, golf, swimming, ring hockey, and calisthenics to stress the "corrective" aspects of individual exercise over team competition.[81] By 1904, though, team sports had become an important feature of the physical culture program for women and included basketball, baseball, captain ball, and field hockey. This change was largely a result of the growing belief that competition in moderate form (though not intercollegiate competition) had social benefits for women athletes. Dudley stressed that team sports, when the element of competition was properly regulated, provided college women with a sense of belonging. By becoming members of a team, she argued, they became an integral part of a group. "The early realization of a definite place in the life of a large University is important, especially in a non-residential campus like Chicago with so large a proportion of women living at home."[82] Team sports offered this element of camaraderie.

The rules for intramural basketball reflected this emphasis on democracy, sociability, and belief in the need to protect women's health. Women's basketball was played in colleges and universities throughout the nation by the turn of the century, structured by a variety of rules modifications first introduced in 1901 by Senda Berenson, director of women's physical culture at Smith College.[83] When Alonzo Stagg asked which rules for basketball the Chicago women employed, intramural coach Marie C. Ortmayer responded that they used the American Amateur Athletic Union rules with two modifications. No one could "tackle" the ball after a fair catch by the opposing team, and only forwards could shoot the ball. She explained that these rules had educational as well as physical benefits for women.[84]

In 1903 the National Conference of Deans of Women made clear these connections between promoting female sociability and teamwork and limiting athletic competition. The conference adopted resolutions that furthered these goals. "Resolved, that the social life shall be regulated and that the tests of good health and high scholarship should be applied" to be sure female students are not engaged in "social dissipation." Furthermore, intercollegiate athletic contests for women were not approved.[85] Moderated competition would protect the health of women, and it also offered an alternative to the spirit of aggressive competition that structured male sports, as well as male collegiate culture more broadly.

Part of the admonition against intercollegiate competition for women resulted from the increased evidence of scandal and corruption plaguing men's athletic competition, especially intercollegiate football. Female physical educators argued that women's athletics represented the true spirit of the amateur ideal, as opposed to male competition, increasingly entwined in a web of commercialism and professionalism. Scandal regarding the amateur status of football players, at the University of Chicago and at other leading institutions, illustrated how much big-time athletics potentially undermined the educational values and ideals of the university experience.[86] According to many female educators, women's model of athletic engagement, emphasizing participation, served as an antidote to the more brutal and commercial tendencies within male competition, which emphasized winning. These discussions also prompted many educators to question how the values associated with sports were being promoted or corrupted on college campuses.

Yet despite the efforts of educators like Gertrude Dudley, competition continued to flourish on college campuses. Immediately after his arrival, Stagg wanted to see competitive sports integrated into the built environment of the university as well as into collegiate culture. Football took precedence. In 1893 Marshall Field, who had donated the original block of land the campus was built on, provided another tract adjoining the campus for an athletic field. Stagg, working with many of the athletes on his football team, built a fence around the field with boards and posts, graded the field, and eventually built seats.[87] Marshall Field (named for its donor but later called Stagg Field in honor of the athletic director) became the home of the University of Chicago Maroons football team as well as other organized sports teams. Crowds of over ten thousand filled the stands to support their team, and members of Chicago's elite were among the loyal rooters. By 1914 the University of Chicago had the funds to erect massive medieval stone towers that marked the entrance to Stagg Field.[88]

As football became one of the leading sources of campus pride—at the University of Chicago and throughout the nation—and as victory promoted greater alumni loyalty and fund-raising, women's athletics were further marginalized. Collegiate athletics increasingly placed women on the sidelines, supporting their male counterparts on the field. Demia Butler, a member of the first class at the University of Chicago, recalled a visit to the Beatrice, the apartment house rented for students, by Stagg and Joseph Raycroft, a quarterback for the team who later became assistant professor of physical culture (and who married Demia's sister Elizabeth). Stagg and Raycroft sang, entertained the women, and invited them to attend a football game the next day in Washington Park. A week later, the Beatrice hosted a reception where Stagg spoke about the demands of football. Butler recalls, "After he told us of the great physical, mental, and moral strength the game demanded, and what a fine discipline it is in all the times, we were prepared to enjoy it with greater zest than ever."[89]

Ironically, Marion Talbot led one of the initial efforts to create university cheers in support of the football team. She held a competition among the female students for "the best gridiron lyric."[90] In addition, Agnes Wayman, captain of the women's basketball team and assistant instructor in the women's gymnasium at the University of Chicago Settlement, spoke at a rally for the defeated Chicago football team in which her words helped console the players after their loss. These episodes demonstrate that cheerleading and rallying around the football team became increasingly important ways for women to take part in the culture of collegiate athletics. Yet they should not mask the constant struggles by women like Talbot and Dudley to challenge and redefine the place of women in athletics, and in collegiate culture more broadly.[91]

The idea that women best served the athletic program as sidelines fans, instead of as competitors, was apparent in discussions over women's part in the Athletic Department's portion of the annual Spring Festival program in 1913. Stagg asked Dudley and the female students to put on a series of maypole dances. He reminded her that "the women's work for several years has been receiving approximately $2,000 from the athletic fund. . . . The athletic fund, as you know, is created entirely by the receipts from the men's athletic contests. The women have shared in its beneficence without really giving a single income-producing event."[92] What he did not tell Dudley, but shared with Athletic Department physician Dudley Reed, was that he believed the maypole dance could raise a great deal of money for the athletic fund. He told Reed that "last year four thousand people paid twenty-five cents at Illinois to see the dances put on by the women in their May Day Festival. You can readily see from the success of the affair at Illinois what the prospects are for Chicago."[93]

The discussion about the Spring Festival reflected the notion that women best served the sports program by being ornamental. Dudley and Talbot, however, wanted to showcase the achievements of women in all aspects of university life. If women took part in the athletic program, they would do so as athletes, not as dancers.[94] Stagg recalled, though, that at the first festival, held three years earlier, several faculty members objected to the hockey game put on by the women. Apparently they "objected to having the women exhibit publicly." Stagg added that for the current year's events there likely would be no objection to a maypole dance.[95] The female body, then, became an object of display, showcasing femininity and beauty rather than athleticism, skill, and strength.

FIGURE 21. Bartlett Gymnasium. Courtesy of the Special Collections Research Center, University of Chicago Library.

The secondary status of women's athletics became a central issue in efforts to improve the facilities available to women. Dudley, and alumnae, regularly lamented their lack of adequate facilities.[96] A campaign launched by the Alumnae Club to raise funds for a women's gymnasium displayed women's loyalty to the university and their desire to have the university repay this loyalty with a women's building. A pitch in the *University of Chicago Magazine* exclaimed, "Oh, Chicago! It is time to wake up, time to take advantage of this love and loyalty while it is yours. Give us a woman's building worthy of this great institution, worthy of the women who crowd your halls, a place where every girl might have a fair chance."[97] The article pointed to the lack of space and dearth of equipment for women's athletics. It mentioned how a corner of the library was used for a gymnasium for women in the early days, as were lecture rooms in Ellis and Cobb Halls. Alumnae also recounted the lack of field space for women's outdoor athletics.[98]

These battles over facilities heated up after the new state-of-the-art men's building, Bartlett Gymnasium, opened with great fanfare in 1904 (fig. 21). Even before the gym was built, the committee on buildings and grounds voted that "the women should not occupy a portion of the new gymnasium, even temporarily."[99] Indeed, it was clear from the start that Bartlett was designed to be a monument to manly sports. During his convocation address in 1900, Harper announced plans for the new building. "A father will erect this building, which shall be dedicated to the work of the physical upbuilding of young men, in memory of his son taken suddenly from life in the midst of a splendid and vigorous young manhood." Trustee A. C. Bartlett eventually donated $150,000 for the gymnasium that was dedicated to "the Advancement of Physical Education and the Glory of Manly Arts."[100]

The design of the building reinforced this celebration of virility. The entrance contained a stained glass window above the main door depicting triumphal tournament scenes from Sir Walter Scott's *Ivanhoe.* The entry also featured an Arthurian mural picturing medieval quarterstaff and sword fights, suggesting the links between male athletic competition and medieval honor (fig. 22). In addition, a stone relief on the north

FIGURE 22. Medieval imagery in Bartlett Gymnasium. Courtesy of the Special Collections Research Center, University of Chicago Library.

side of the building showed two rams butting heads and recalled one of the speeches given on opening day in 1904, describing men as "the noblest of animals," celebrated for their "tough muscles and steady nerves, vital force and elastic vigor."[101]

All of this celebration of manliness, and its embodiment in the gymnasium's design, clearly marked it as off limits to women. The lack of adequate facilities for women, though, led Stagg and Harper to agree to open the swimming pool to women on Monday afternoons.[102] But the rest of women's athletics labored under the same constrained conditions until women could raise enough funds for a building of their own. The Women's Athletic Association offered subscriptions and staged a variety of plays to purchase equipment, and it worked at forging relationships with donors that might lead to the construction of a gymnasium for women. Along these lines, the Gymnasium Committee of the Alumnae Club asked Chicagoans, "Isn't there among us some large-hearted, public spirited Chicago man or woman who, recognizing our needs, will feel honored to have his or her name carved above the entrance to a women's building?"[103]

They found a supporter in La Verne Noyes, a prominent Chicago businessman who wanted to erect a building in honor of his dead wife, Ida. Noyes told Stagg, and later university president Harry Judson, that he would give $300,000 to be used, in part, for a women's gymnasium. Julius Rosenwald of Sears, who would become one of the largest contributors to the university, also made a gift toward the building.[104] On hearing of the gifts, members of the Women's Athletic Association exclaimed, "The millennium for University women seems at last to be at hand. We are to have a gymnasium and a club house!"[105]

Indeed, unlike Bartlett Gymnasium's focus on virility and competition, the new women's gym was structured around patterns of appropriate female physical activity and sociability. Ida Noyes Hall was built to resemble a Tudor manor house, with elegant interior details that symbolized women's domestic arts (see figs. 23 and 24). The hall contained a large common room as well as a library, social rooms for serving refreshments, offices for women's clubs, and a sun parlor. It also housed a personal service department, with provisions for shining shoes and giving manicures. The hall included a swimming pool, a game room, two bowling alleys, and a large room for "corrective gymnasium work."[106] This last room featured a large mural depicting the Masque of Youth and the Spirit of Gothic Architecture (quoted at the start of the chapter), illustrating, according to university president Harry Pratt Judson, that "beauty" is "educative" (fig. 25).[107]

The gendered differences between Ida Noyes Hall and Bartlett Gymnasium also were made clear in the dedication remarks. At the cornerstone ceremony on April 18, 1915, Marion Talbot spoke about the joy and importance of seeing this building come to fruition, and highlighted the role it would play in the lives of university women. "Here self-discovery and self-control will lead to social co-operation and mutual understanding. . . . Tolerance, sympathy, kindness, the generous word and the helpful act . . . will be the contribution of the women who go forth from Ida Noyes Hall to take part in the upbuilding of the new civilization which is to come."[108] The gymnasium would enhance feminine characteristics, not detract from them, and would reinforce women's role as the keepers of cooperation instead of competition.

Promoters of women's athletics walked a fine line between seeking equal access for women and safeguarding the femininity of female athletes. At the same time, they attempted to ensure that women's bodies did not become commodified and placed in the service of male commercial athletics. Dudley's efforts to secure funds and facilities for women illustrates her commitment to the goal of equal participation that was supposed to be the foundation of the new coeducational institution. Yet in athletics and other curricular programs, the university's commitment to coeducation did not equate to support of integrating men and women, or even developing similar courses of study for them. Indeed, the construction of separate facilities for men's and women's athletics gave physical expression to the stark differences in the ideals and goals for men and women, not only in their involvement with sports, but in their lives more generally. That women like Gertrude Dudley and Marion Talbot fought at once for greater access to previously male domains and for recognizing women's "special needs" within the university illustrates the multiple ways women needed to position themselves to gain a place in the modern research university. Their efforts went not only toward securing facilities and funds for women's programs, but also toward reshaping perceptions about the proper relation between gender and athletics, women and higher education.

The athletic program at Chicago embodied many of the trends shaping higher education in the Progressive Era. Athletics underscored the scientific element of exercise in the promotion of health, fitness, and "good living" and at the same time reflected the growing influence of commercialism in the spectacle of college sport, especially football. By structuring rituals and ceremonies around collegiate football, universities linked sport with fund-raising and public visibility, thereby tying promotion of the university directly to sports. In doing so, they contributed to the commodification of

FIGURE 23. Ida Noyes Hall, exterior. Courtesy of the Special Collections Research Center, University of Chicago Library.

athletics that made organized sport increasingly at odds with the professed educational and moral mission of higher education. Both the scientific and the commercial aspects of athletics reified gender difference on college campuses by circumscribing appropriate forms of physical and social activity for women, especially on coeducational campuses. Yet athletics also opened up new possibilities for women—to use scientific notions of fitness and health to take greater control over their own bodies, and to shape new models of collegiate sociability based more on (female) ideals of cooperation than on (male) competition. These ideals transcended the playing field and found their way into curricular programs within the university and into women's public roles within the city.[109]

FIGURE 24. Ida Noyes Hall. Courtesy of the Special Collections Research Center, University of Chicago Library.

FIGURE 25. "Masque of Youth" mural. Ida Noyes Hall. Courtesy of the Special Collections Research Center, University of Chicago Library.

GENDERING THE CURRICULUM: SANITARY SCIENCE VERSUS HOUSEHOLD ADMINISTRATION

This balance between providing for women's practical needs and at the same time making campus life fully accessible to both men and women also shaped debates over the university curriculum. Harper's sex segregation plan was linked to a subdivided curriculum that broke fields into subdisciplines and categorized intellectual investigation by more narrow definitions of field. This elaborate model of university management and the division of the curriculum into discrete units, seemingly based more on disciplinary specialization and corporate strategies of efficiency than on the promotion of broad-based intellectual inquiry, led many faculty members to question the intent of Harper and the administration. It appeared to many that the administration was taking too much control over academic aspects of the university that were better left to faculty.

Robert Herrick, more often than not a supporter of Harper, called Harper's administrative plan a "ward-politician method of bottling up his faculty in three small bottles to be carried about in his pocket."[110] John Dewey argued, "A ponderous machinery has come into existence to carry on the multiplicity of business and quasi-business matters without which the modern university would come to a standstill."[111] Other faculty members recommended eliminating the Junior and Senior Colleges, arguing that they unnecessarily increased the powers of a central administration.[112]

Dewey tied this administrative centralization directly to the rise of specialization within the curriculum. Virtually from the time of the establishment of the university, Harper started dividing the academic units into smaller and smaller components to reflect new disciplinary specialties, particularly within the sciences. The Biology Department, for example, was divided into separate departments for botany, zoology, paleontology, anatomy and histology, physiology, and neurology.[113] While these divisions reflected larger trends in higher education, particularly at research universities, Chicago was at the forefront in implementing these proposals. Dewey argued that this specialization detracted from the ability of teachers and students to address the larger questions of life in a holistic and cohesive way: "Specialization . . . leads the individual, if he follows it unreservedly, into bypaths still further off from the highway where men, struggling together, develop strength."[114] For Dewey, specialization challenged the mission of the modern research university to tackle the issues and problems confronting society in an integrated way. For Harper, specialization meant greater precision and more exact knowledge. These diverging ideas about curriculum structure and the production of knowledge affected the university's level of civic engagement and exposed some of the ways ideas about gender entered into the intellectual work of the university.

Marion Talbot was one of the strongest critics of these plans for simultaneous differentiation of curriculum and consolidation of administrative power. She feared that the subdivision of academic life led to the narrowing of the course of academic pursuits open to women, and that a centralized administrative body only silenced the concerns of women, both students and faculty. Rosalind Rosenberg's work has shown how the trend toward specialization in higher education merged with traditional assumptions about women's proper roles, thereby limiting women's influence within the university.[115] Talbot pointed to the potential effects of this trend when she claimed that, based on her experiences at a modern research university like Chicago, the "current discussion of educational aims and methods does not adequately take into account the needs of women and girls."[116]

Talbot tried to strike a balance between promoting departments and courses that helped prepare women for their most likely future occupations as teachers, librarians, and nurses and advocating equal access for women to all fields and disciplines. For example, she addressed charges that women had fewer proclivities for math and science than men and should perhaps pursue a curriculum geared more toward literature and vocational training (like courses in domestic science) rather than a classic liberal arts curriculum. In her 1902 study of female students at Chicago, she showed that perceived gender differences in course selections were exaggerated. More women than men took physiology, for example, and 16 percent of female students took mathematics beyond the required course.[117] Above all, she advocated equal support for female scholars, through fellowships, teaching positions, and intellectual guidance.[118]

At the same time, Talbot pushed for the development of domestic science courses, as well as courses in hygiene and social service, so that scientific models of scholarship would be presented in all aspects of the university curriculum. Talbot and other female educators across the country fought to have universities seriously consider the practical needs of both men and women on graduation from college. They recognized that most women had few options after graduation. Wanting to prepare women for their most likely postcollege pursuits, they sought to open up other fields.

These educators were responding to concerns expressed by female college graduates, especially those from women's colleges. In one segment of her *Ladies' Home Journal* series, Edith Rickert asked female college graduates to assess their overall college experience and its current roles in their lives. In general, she found that most believed college education made them better prepared not only for potential careers but also for household duties and motherhood.[119] Other women were less enthusiastic, lamenting their lack of viable career options on graduation and feeling that the liberal arts curriculum failed to prepare them for their lives as wives and mothers. As one respondent noted, college women "have studied chemistry . . . but they could not make their own baking powder."[120] Many women pointed to the need for training in domestic science, sanitation, and women's health, the very programs Marion Talbot was a leader in developing.

In addition to addressing the practical needs of women, Talbot also realized that one of the justifications for giving women access to higher education was to allow them to use their perceived attributes of cooperation and nurturance to foster community involvement. Courses in social science seemed particularly well suited to women in that they could apply the rigor of scientific research to expand their roles in community service. Building on both middle-class women's domestic roles and their history of club activity, university-educated women could link these traditional roles to public social service.[121]

Talbot's attempts to establish a department of sanitary science at the University of Chicago illustrated the difficulties in bridging this gender gap within the context of the modern research university. She approached Harper about creating this department in order to train both men and women to deal with issues of urban planning, sanitation, and consumer protection. Talbot's plan included courses in chemistry, physics, physiology, political economy, and modern languages. She stressed the importance of an interdisciplinary and gender-neutral structure, for she argued that the issues confronting modern cities entailed the integration of (male) scholarly scientific research with (female) social reform activity and required that the two come together in the curriculum.[122] Her plans for this program reflected the attempt to use scientific method to make the traditional roles of women legitimate elements of the university curriculum. One supporter of the new department wrote to Talbot, "When housekeeping becomes the applied science you would make of it, it will no longer be regarded as drudgery."[123] By making these courses available to both men and women, the sanitary science program might help reshape the academic curriculum. Instead of addressing the career options of men only, Talbot's department of sanitary science would insert areas of expertise traditionally associated with women into the broader structure of higher education.

Harper denied Talbot's request for funding for the department, citing the university's limited resources. Instead, he suggested that she carry out her work under the auspices of the Department of Sociology. Talbot believed that sanitation and sociology were intimately connected, for she argued that improved sanitary conditions would foster broader social progress.[124] Yet, like Dudley in athletics, she frequently had to plead with colleagues and her department head, Albion Small, to allocate funds for materials to support her work, including books, laboratories, and equipment.[125]

In 1902 Harper agreed to establish a separate department of "household administration" under Talbot's direction.[126] Talbot attempted to make this department fit within the structure she had envisioned for sanitary science, though the focus of the new department obviously shifted toward the household rather than society at large. The object of the department, according to Talbot, was to train men and women for the "rational and scientific administration of the home as a social unit"; to teach the basics of household administration to teachers, health engineers, and social servants who would serve in public institutions; and to educate students in the role of the household in society.[127] One member of Talbot's staff argued that gender should play no role in structuring the curriculum or determining who took the courses. "Domestic Science," she explained, "should form part of the education of every woman and every man." Still, most of the students in the program were female, as were the instructors.[128]

The creation of a distinct department of household administration symbolized the central role of specialization within modern academic culture and illustrated how the debate over the physical separation of college men and women translated into larger patterns of gender differentiation in intellectual work. Indeed, many faculty members, including Chicago economist J. Laurence Laughlin, saw professionalization in the academy, and greater subdivision of the curriculum, as a way to counter the "feminization" of the college campus. Creating distinct programs in fields like household science meant women would no longer dominate courses in the liberal arts curriculum, and the university could successfully attract the best male students without fear of a significant female presence.

This trend toward gender differentiation in the curriculum also led to an increasing division between scientific research and social activism. Academic women like Talbot would then have to fight on a variety of fronts to maintain the connection between academic training and civic engagement as this connection was threatened by the rise of the culture of expertise within the university.[129]

PRAGMATIST PHILOSOPHY, THE UNIVERSITY OF CHICAGO SETTLEMENT, AND CIVIC CULTURE

Many college-educated women found a vehicle for using their skills and training in social settlement work. Women combined the scientific models of investigation they learned at universities like Chicago with the female tradition of benevolent work. The founding of social settlements in Chicago provided an arena in which social science and reform could be joined. Settlements also offered an environment where a variety of groups in the city came together to interact on a personal level and share common interests. They brought together university professors, labor leaders, middle-class reformers, and ethnic community residents in a setting that fostered the dynamic civic engagement that Progressives hoped would lead to the social reconstruction of American democracy. Settlements combined Christian ethics with scientific methods of investigation developed at universities like Chicago to create a new brand of social reform.[130]

Settlement houses also offered college-educated women an arena in which they could break down barriers between private and public and become a visible presence in urban culture and politics. In addition, women without college degrees who were active in reform politics found settlements places where they could cultivate a women's sphere that transcended the private world of the home and club life to create a "social center for civic cooperation."[131] Female reformers often drew on the rhetoric of domesticity to justify their increased public presence. For example, reformer Louise de Koven Bowen argued, "If a woman is a good housekeeper in her own house, she will be able to do well that larger housekeeping."[132] Clearly social reform and the emerging discipline of social work fit popular conceptions of women's nurturing role in society. These fields also offered professional opportunities for women when university positions and research jobs were extremely limited. Yet this language of "municipal housekeeping" masked the important role these women played in shaping scholarly investigation in the social sciences, labor organizing, and urban politics.

Settlements reflected pragmatist notions of knowledge, experience, and social action. Educators like John Dewey linked Christian idealism, scientific method, and the promotion of democratic community not just to education but to society more broadly. Dewey was joined by educators in other fields in structuring these ideas of knowledge and experience. George Herbert Mead, who was brought to Chicago to help establish the burgeoning field of psychology there, became a central player in settlement activities. In addition, Albion Small left his presidency at Colby College to head the Department of Sociology. These scholars, along with Marion Talbot and Alice Freeman Palmer, the first dean of women, played prominent roles in shaping the social sciences, both at Chicago and throughout the nation. With the help of several of their graduate students, including Sophonisba Breckinridge and Edith and Grace Abbott, these scholars became leading figures in linking the intellectual foundation of social science with civic activism, social reform, and public policy.[133]

These educators' belief in the social foundation of knowledge and selfhood led directly to a view of democratic renewal whereby citizens became active participants in civic culture in order to reshape it and continually contribute to a revitalized public sphere. Pragmatist philosophers constructed what historian James T. Kloppenberg calls a *via media,* whereby thinkers like Dewey and Mead tacked between constructing philosophical ideas of knowledge and political theories of social democracy.[134] The artificial divisions between thought and action, individual morality and social structure, were broken down. The pragmatists sought an organic understanding of the self and its relation to society, positing a view of social relations that stressed active participation in the public sphere as the path to individual self-fulfillment.[135]

Dewey's emphasis on the social role of knowledge and the dialectical relation between thought and action contributed to the rise of sociology as a distinct scientific discipline. The pragmatist connection between knowledge and experience converged with a new understanding of the role that environmental factors played in shaping the individual and society. These ideas shaped the emergence of psychology, sociology, and anthropology, and contributed to Chicago's prominence in shaping these fields. Sociologists applied their belief in scientific theory to the study of human behavior and social conditions, grounding sociological theory in empirical research and firsthand experience.

Like Dewey and Mead, the early Chicago sociologists had backgrounds in religion and theology that contributed to their approach to scholarship and scientific investigation. Albion Small was a Baptist with training as a minister who, along with Harper, was active in the Chautauqua movement (he also coauthored his first book, *An Introduction to the Study of Sociology* [1894], with George E. Vincent, son of the founder of

Chautauqua). Small sought to establish a scientific basis for the discipline of sociology (he founded the *American Journal of Sociology* in 1895), but at the same time he believed that sociology had a larger social purpose. He linked his Christian idealism with a faith in scientific progress based on the research ideal of the modern university. Like Dewey, then, Small sought to transcend the dichotomies of religion and science, scholarship and civic engagement. Other early Chicago sociologists, including Vincent, Charles R. Henderson, and William I. Thomas, embodied this transition. To varying degrees, they all sought to develop a new type of civic discourse in which there was a symbiosis among knowledge, social cooperation, and an activist reform community.[136]

According to the Chicago sociologists, science should have a crucial part in shaping our understanding of social behavior. By linking natural history to the study of human society, Small, Henderson, and Thomas argued that scholars could gain a greater appreciation of the "organic" nature of social relations and understand the role each individual played within the wider community. In *The Meaning of Sociology* (1910), Small explained that the relationships among people, and between people and the natural environment, were integrally connected.[137] Like Dewey and Mead, the Chicago sociologists argued that individuals were not simply instinctual beings directed by predictable patterns of behavior, but instead were conscious actors constantly adjusting to the environments around them. Small, Henderson, and Thomas applied their ideas about social relations and human conditions to studies of the surrounding city, launching the community study as the foundation of the discipline of sociology.[138]

The Chicago sociologists reiterated Harper's contention that the city of Chicago offered wonderful opportunities to formulate a science of society. A discussion of the Sociology Department's relationship with the city identified Chicago as "one of the most complete social laboratories in the world." Cities, the author argued, present the "most serious problems of modern society," and he added, "No city in the world presents a wider variety of social problems than Chicago.[139] Sociologists sought to overcome its problems by better understanding the geography of the city. They posited a spatial view of social pathology and its links to urban growth and used a variety of first-hand accounts to study these conditions. Sociologists, along with urban reformers, believed that by observing urban life through scientific investigation, they could understand the social, economic, and cultural factors shaping society and formulate methods for social improvement.

Most often these ideas for improvement involved reshaping the spatial geography of the city. By linking physical space to social conditions, Small, and especially

Thomas, created a model of investigation that built on the "human ecology" of the city. Using mapmaking as the basis of social investigation, the sociologists collected data on poverty, vice, delinquency, and ethnicity to formulate a comprehensive picture of city life. Social investigation and public policy drew their reasoning from community studies, with early investigations including *The Slums of Chicago* (1894), *The Housing of Working People* (1895), and *The Italians in Chicago* (1897). The publication of Florian Znaniecki and W. I. Thomas's *Polish Peasant in Europe and America* (1918–19) represented the culmination of these community investigations and the movement toward empirical investigation that would characterize the "Chicago school" under Ernest Burgess, Robert Park, and Louis Wirth throughout the 1920s and 1930s.[140]

The Chicago school's theories of urban community formation grew directly out of the pioneering community studies prepared under the auspices of Chicago's social settlements, especially Hull House and the University of Chicago Settlement. Settlements allowed sociologists to observe firsthand how a variety of cultures came together in physical proximity and created community institutions that helped them adapt to changing social conditions. Small, Park, and Burgess saw settlements as useful laboratories for social investigation and for understanding the processes of cultural adaptation and social adjustment. Yet reformers like Addams and McDowell saw settlement houses as much more dynamic and integral features of the communities in which they were situated.[141]

The founding of the University of Chicago Settlement in 1894 symbolized the unification of women's social activism with scientific investigation and municipal reform. The settlement was founded under the auspices of the Philanthropic Committee of the Christian Union at the University of Chicago. Students from a political economy class at the university made a field trip to the Stockyards district in the spring of 1893 and, along with Professors J. Laurence Laughlin and Myra Reynolds, "assessed the needs of the area." At a meeting in December 1893, Laughlin and Hull House founder Jane Addams addressed Christian Union members and discussed the need to bring settlement work to the neighborhood of the Stockyards under the auspices of the university. This meeting helped raise private funds to rent five rooms in the Back of the Yards, the residential area bordering the Chicago Union Stock Yards. Settlement work began there on January 1, 1894, when two of the Chicago students, Max West and William D. Johnson, moved into a flat in back of the Gertrude House Kindergarten, at 4655 South Gross Avenue. During the first year there were five residents from the university and ten other workers, students, and professors, including Mary McDowell, who became head resident. McDowell and the other residents moved to a slightly larger flat over a feed store close by until the larger permanent building at 4630 South Gross was secured.[142]

A settlement, according to the university, was "a body of educated people living in a neighborhood for the purpose of co-operation in social work and for learning the concrete facts of life at first hand." The university wished to promote this activity because "it has been thought that this particular work afforded an opportunity for the members of the University and their friends to give tangible expression to that interest in the welfare of others which modern life suggests and demands."[143] The settlement combined the "fine spirit of idealism" the university sought to foster with the "field work experience" necessary for students in the social sciences.[144] It was a microcosm of the city, allowing students to view urban conditions within a more spatially confined setting. Settlement work offered additional benefits for students, for according to one promoter, "The lives of cultured people are frequently narrow, undignified, useless, and false from exclusiveness. The student of politics, economics and social philosophy can avoid provincial, individualistic and class prejudices only by mingling with people of varied experience."[145]

The settlement fostered a close relationship with the Institute of Social Science and Arts, later the Chicago School of Civics and Philanthropy, another service institution informally associated with the university. The Institute of Social Science and Arts opened in 1903 under the auspices of the University of Chicago Extension Division. The Institute offered lectures by social scientists on local issues at many of the University Extension locations throughout the city. Graham Taylor, professor of sociology at Chicago Theological Seminary and head of the Chicago Commons Settlement, was its director. The Institute was supported by Harper's private funds until his death in 1906. Since he never secured university funding for the program, it was reorganized as part of the Chicago Commons Association and renamed the Chicago Institute of Social Science. Commons trustee Victor Lawson, a local newspaper magnate, as well as the Russell Sage Foundation, contributed money, and in May 1908 the Institute was incorporated as the Chicago School of Civics and Philanthropy (CSCP).[146]

Under the reorganization, the CSCP expanded its programs and created a department of research and investigation, headed first by Hull House resident Julia Lathrop and later by former Chicago graduate students Sophonisba P. Breckinridge and Edith Abbott. They hoped to make the CSCP a professional training ground for educating social scientists by combining an "exceptional ability or experience in social work" with academic courses in "sociology, civics and political economy."[147] Like the settlement, the CSCP sought to break down the emerging barriers between scientific investigation and social reform. The organizations' tenuous relationship with the University of Chicago suggests the university's ambivalence over incorporating social reform into the mainstream of academic life. Nonetheless, many university faculty still maintained close relationships with the organizations, and together they produced some of the most important sociological studies of the early twentieth century.[148]

While the CSCP promoted the scientific basis of social investigation, the University of Chicago Settlement stressed activist civic engagement in shaping social reform. Settlement residents recognized the settlement's role as a training ground for university students in the social sciences but saw it as something more than a laboratory. Jane Addams voiced this perspective when she declared, "I have always objected to the phrase 'sociological laboratory' applied to us, because Settlements should be something much more human and spontaneous than such a phrase connotes."[149] George Herbert Mead, a frequent guest and supporter of Hull House as well as the University of Chicago Settlement, concurred:

> The settlement worker distinguishes himself from either the missionary or the scientific observer by his assumption that he is first of all at home in the community where he lives, and that his attempts at amelioration of the conditions that surround him and his scientific study of these conditions flow from this immediate human relationship, this neighborhood consciousness, from the fact that he is at home there. . . . It is the privilege of the social settlement to be part of its own immediate community, to approach its conditions with no preconceptions, to be the exponents of no fixed dogma or fixed rules of conduct.[150]

Ideally, the settlement was an arena in which active participation in civic life, along with social scientific investigation, fostered a new vision of social democracy that emerged from the ground up. While the settlement residents might direct activities and channel communal needs into concerted efforts for civic improvement, their purpose was not to dictate the needs of the community from above. The main goal of the settlement was to become a dynamic community center whose programs were shaped by the desires and concerns of the neighborhood.

Mary McDowell understood this vision of the interactive basis of the settlement when she accepted the position of head resident at the University of Chicago Settlement in 1894. McDowell grew up in an upper-middle-class household in Cincinnati but did not attend college. Instead, she worked with Frances Willard and the Woman's Christian Temperance Union, an organization devoted to promoting the temperate use of alcohol. In 1887, at age thirty-two, McDowell became the national organizer for the Young Woman's Christian Temperance Union in Evanston, north of Chicago, and began traveling across the nation to promote reform. In 1890 she moved into Jane Addams's Hull House and helped organize the kindergarten there.[151]

McDowell shared with Addams a belief in the mutual exchange that should take place between a settlement and its community. According to McDowell, "Settlement residents do not go to people with a plan, a policy, or a proposition; they go as friends, as neighbors with a keen sense of the commonness of all that is best in all."[152] Like Jane Addams and Ellen Gates Starr at Hull House, McDowell brought the privileges of an upper-middle-class upbringing to an immigrant working-class neighborhood. Yet she recognized that within that neighborhood she was more of a "foreigner" than were the other residents. In a description of her first encounter with the Back of the Yards, she positioned herself as an outsider who must adapt to this "new world" just as recent immigrants must. "As an immigrant from Evanston," she writes, "I landed in the Stockyards district on September 17, 1894—two places as aesthetically and culturally far distant from each other as any in the world. . . . My past, my social position, my family and my religion were unknown to my neighbors, and meant nothing to them."[153]

The tinge of condescension expressed in these comments reflected the constant struggle among settlement workers to overcome the elitism that could color settlement work. Yet McDowell proved her commitment to cross-class coalitions and the promotion of industrial democracy through her continued alliances with the working-class ethnic residents of the Back of the Yards neighborhood.[154]

The Back of the Yards was defined by its spatial relation to the Stockyards district (fig. 26). The neighborhood was bounded by Halsted Street to the east, Western Avenue to the west, Thirty-ninth Street to the north, and Fifty-fifth to the south. The residential area was surrounded by railroad tracks, manufacturing plants, and the stockyards holding the hogs, cattle, and sheep that determined the sensory characteristics of the region. This notorious section of Chicago, which Upton Sinclair immortalized in his 1906 work *The Jungle,* was created in 1865 after the Union Stock Yards and Transit Company was organized to consolidate the city's packinghouses and its livestock yards.

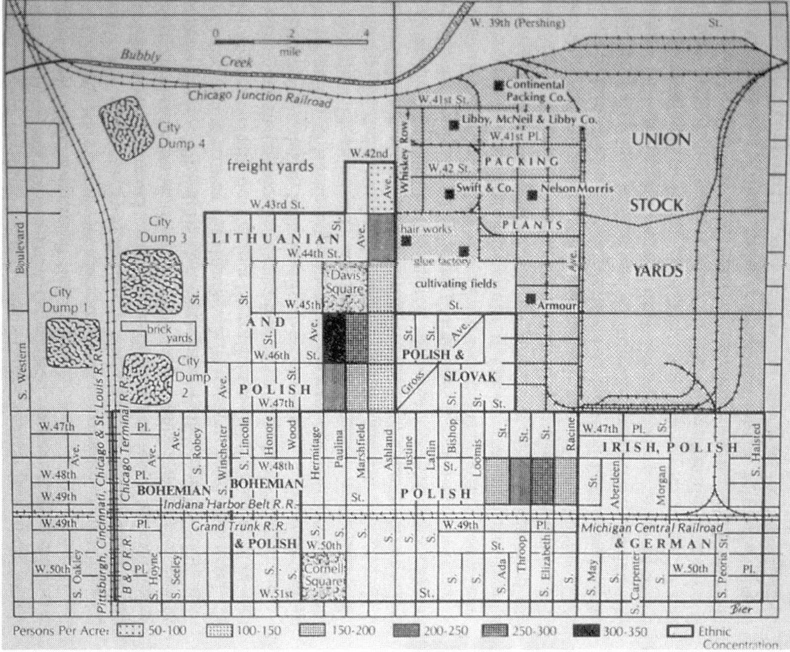

FIGURE 26. Map of the Stockyards District, showing ethnic concentrations and locations of city dumps. The University of Chicago Settlement was at Forty-sixth Street and Gross Avenue. James R. Barrett, *Work and Community in the Jungle* (Urbana: University of Illinois Press, 1987), 80. Copyright by the Board of Trustees of the University of Illinois, 1987. Used with permission of the University of Illinois Press.

Since most livestock entered Chicago from the southwest, company officials secured 320 acres of land from the estate of former mayor "Long John" Wentworth for $100,000. The inexpensive land and the proximity to the south branch of the Chicago River made the location ideal. By its second year of operation, the Yards handled close to 2 million hogs. By the turn of the century, over 4 million hogs, cattle, and sheep passed through the Yards annually.[155]

The most pervasive features of the Back of the Yards were the sights and smells emanating from the stockyards and packinghouses. The more noxious scents included "rotting hair and the scrapings from hides, refuse from the slaughtering houses and stock pens, the stench from 'Bubbly Creek' and the open dumps of putrefying garbage!"[156] Bubbly Creek was the terminus of the fork of the south branch of the Chicago River that wound its way along Western Avenue and settled just south of Forty-third Street. This thin, nearly stagnant stream had the distinction of being the waste deposit site of nineteen packinghouses. The name originated from the bubbles rising to the surface from the decaying carcasses and toxic materials dumped at the bottom. According to McDowell, "So thick was the scum on its surface that cats and gulls were seen to walk over it in safety."[157]

In addition to Bubbly Creek, the neighborhood was plagued with vast excavations used as garbage dumps. The land between Damen and Leavitt, Forty-first and Forty-seventh Streets, owned by Twenty-ninth Ward alderman Thomas Carey, was excavated for the clay that made bricks at his on-site brickyard. After the clay was exhausted, Carey sold the city of Chicago the right to use these pits as garbage dumps, and the packinghouses used one of them to burn waste. These dumps were less than two blocks from working-class residences. An article in the *Chicago Tribune* testified to the public health nuisance they created: "A municipal dump at Forty-seventh and Robey Streets, the largest in the city, according to charges made yesterday, exudes poisonous fumes of such malignant character that babies in the neighborhood are being poisoned to death. . . . Wagon after wagon load of damp and dry garbage is deposited in a hole, day and night. . . . The stench is almost unbearable."[158]

The ethnic composition of the Back of the Yards was changing as McDowell took up residence there. Until the 1880s, the area was 60 percent Irish and 30 thirty percent German. These demographics changed after an 1884 strike in the stockyards, when the packers brought in Polish workers as strikebreakers. Between 1890 and 1900, Poles flooded the area, as did other Eastern Europeans such as Lithuanians, Slovaks, Russians, and Hungarians. By 1920, 80 percent of the Back of the Yards was Polish. As each ethnic group established itself in the district, it built churches that often became the center of its social and cultural life. More than ten churches, most Roman Catholic and each identified with a particular ethnic group, were built in Packingtown, including Saint Joseph's (Polish), Saint John of God (Polish), Saint Michael's (Slovak), and Holy Cross (Lithuanian).[159]

The ethnic businesses and social organizations, along with the churches established by the Irish, Germans, and later Poles and Lithuanians, gave the neighborhood a basis for community organization. Lederer and Oppenheim's general store, Kohr's blacksmith shop, the Lithuanian cooperative "Star," Rosenberg's shoe store, the Teutonia

Turnverein at Heitman Hall, and Schumacher's Hall were some of the anchoring businesses of the neighborhood.[160] Saloons were the most prevalent social institution. The nearly two-block area along Ashland Avenue known as Whiskey Row supposedly had "a saloon for every forty voters," or one saloon in each building. Near the settlement, at Forty-sixth Street and Gross Avenue, was Whiskey Point, a five-point intersection with a saloon on each corner.[161] Unlike many of her colleagues at the university, McDowell recognized the important social function played by the saloons, tying local living conditions directly to labor in the Yards:

> This is an industrial community, not a slum, and the standard of life is influenced by the work and wages "in the yards." . . . The saloon is the most hospitable place in the community to the non–English speaking people. One Slavic saloon has all the Slavic papers. The intelligent saloon keeper is the friend and counselor of his people. They eat in the back of his saloon as they would in a club house. The only place near the Stock Yards which offers a comfortable seat at a table during the lunch hour is the saloon, which is crowded at the noon half-hour.[162]

McDowell's understanding of the role of the saloon in local civic affairs helped her interject the settlement into the neighborhood by working in conjunction with local businesses and community institutions to lobby for municipal reform.

McDowell met resistance from a number of residents, especially from the Catholic parishes. Many were suspicious of the motivations of a "Protestant establishment" in their community that represented the University of Chicago, the home of the rich that received its funding from the likes of the Swifts and Armours, the leading packers of the stockyards. Many residents evidently saw settlement workers as "outsiders," "foreigners" in a working-class community so clearly shaped by ethnic institutions. Historian Robert Slayton argues that the churches in particular saw the settlement as competition, "and it was competition from outsiders who did not understand or really care for the people of the Back of the Yards."[163]

The architecture of the settlement reflected some of these differences for, much like Ida Noyes Hall, it was structured around Victorian notions of propriety and decorum. The new building, opened in 1904, was designed by noted Chicago architect Dwight Heald Perkins. He featured his initial plan in the February 1900 issue of the *Commons,* the social settlement journal (fig. 27). This rendering included a number of prairie

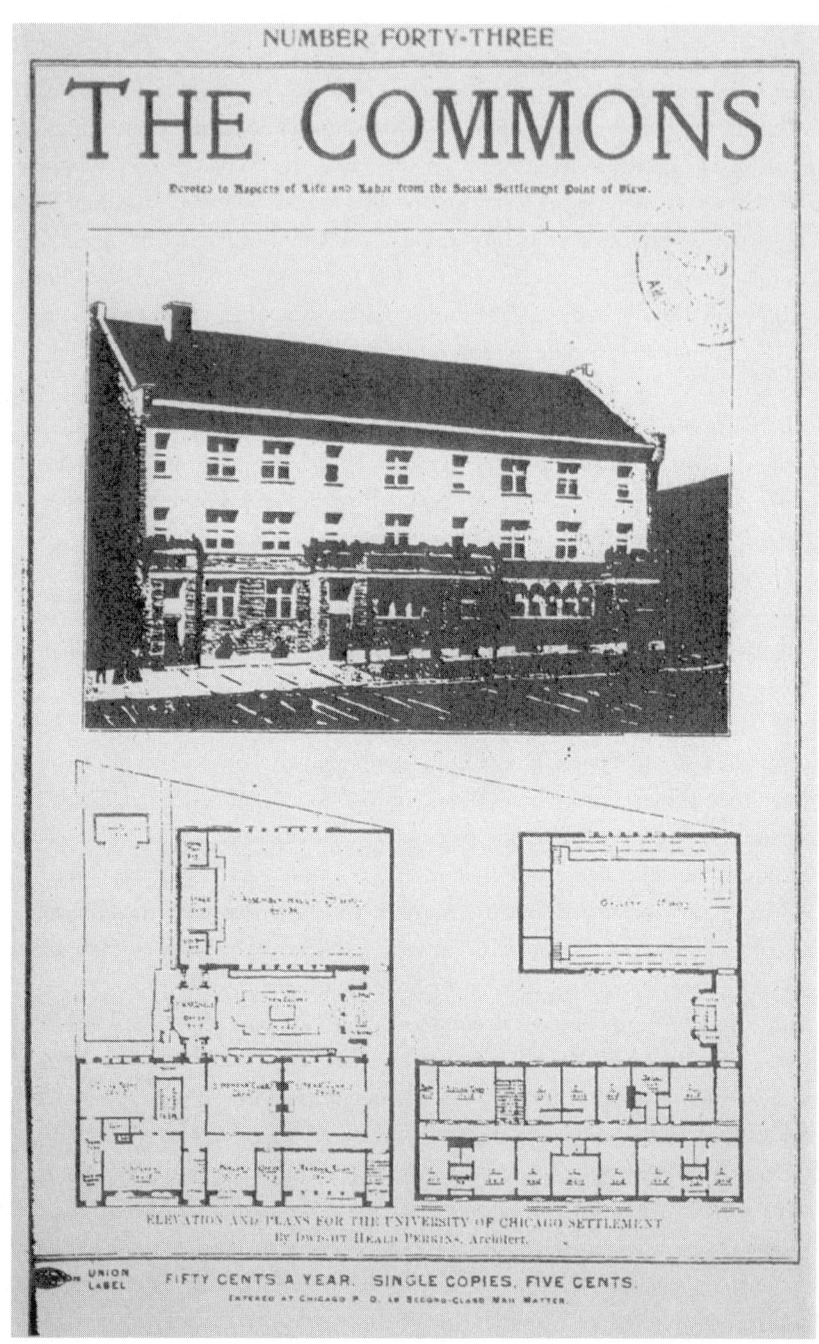

NUMBER FORTY-THREE

THE COMMONS

Devoted to Aspects of Life and Labor from the Social Settlement Point of View.

ELEVATION AND PLANS FOR THE UNIVERSITY OF CHICAGO SETTLEMENT
By Dwight Heald Perkins, Architect.

UNION LABEL

FIFTY CENTS A YEAR. SINGLE COPIES, FIVE CENTS.

ENTERED AT CHICAGO P. O. AS SECOND-CLASS MAIL MATTER.

FIGURE 27. Elevation and plans for University of Chicago Settlement, Dwight Heald Perkins, *Commons* 43 (Feb. 1900).

school motifs on the exterior, including roman bricks creating a horizontal line across the lower tier of the building and flower boxes to emphasize the prairie line. Although some of these elements were removed in the final plan, the building nonetheless reflected changing architectural styles in the Midwest. According the Perkins, a settlement should create an environment that would promote "social communion" and provide opportunities for "the development of the higher life." As such, it should be intimately linked to its environment and community.[164]

The interior of the building featured an open courtyard. Surrounding the courtyard were an assembly hall, a stage and dressing rooms, a dining room, separate rooms for men's and women's clubs, a parlor, a reading room, a sitting room, offices, and sleeping rooms. The common rooms, including the dining room and parlor, bore a striking resemblance to the rooms in Ida Noyes, though they were much less elaborate. Still, they reflected a certain degree of refinement.[165]

At the same time, McDowell tried to make the interior of the settlement reflect the surrounding neighborhood. As a result, she asked the architect's wife, Lucy Fitch Perkins, to create a mural as a backdrop to the stage in the assembly hall. The mural, "May-Pole Dance, Children of All Nations," was modeled directly on children from the neighborhood, and their costumes were designed to suggest the cosmopolitan character of the community (fig. 28). Whereas the mural in the women's building at the University of Chicago depicted an allegory of the educative functions of beauty and medieval honor, this mural symbolized the lived experiences of the settlement residents right outside its doors. The settlement also became an important site for outdoor activity, featuring the first playground in the neighborhood, equipped with its own maypole. In addition, it put into practice many of the pedagogical ideas developed by Dewey, including having kindergarten children tend small garden plots (fig. 29).[166]

The settlement's presence in the Back of the Yards was crucial in linking the expertise developed at the University of Chicago to conditions facing local communities. Like Hull House, the University of Chicago Settlement was an important place for disseminating information from university-affiliated faculty to neighborhood residents. Yet the University Settlement was even more directly involved with addressing issues specific to its own neighborhood than was Hull House. McDowell worked closely with area residents to confront the problems of the community, and in doing so she demonstrated how to achieve some degree of political power even outside traditional electoral politics.

McDowell's efforts at community organizing took place mostly through the Settlement Woman's Club. The club was organized to "associate women of different nation-

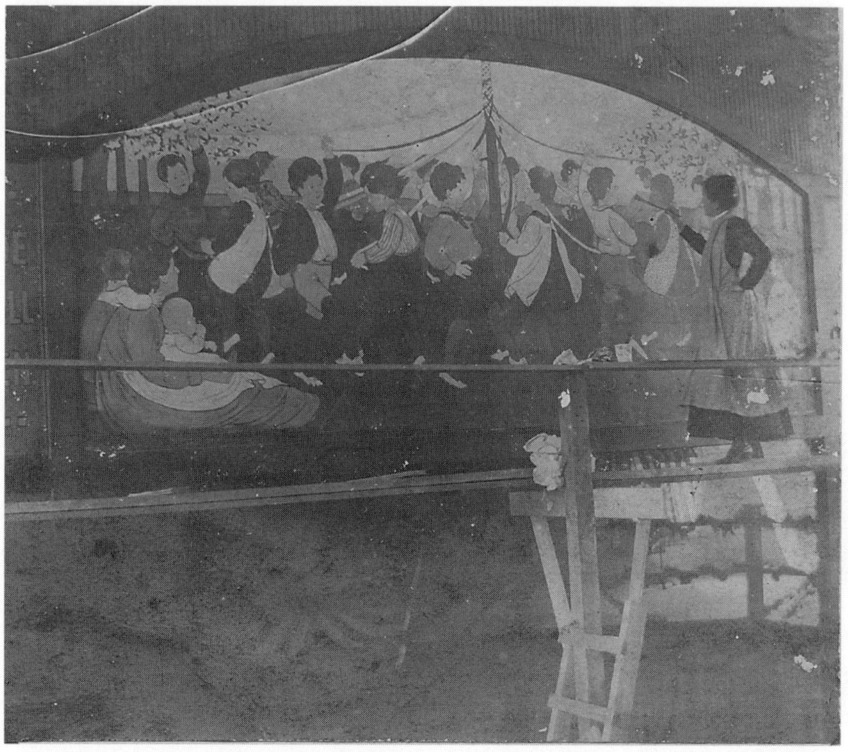

FIGURE 28. "May-Pole Dance, Children of All Nations," Mural by Lucy Fitch Perkins. Courtesy of the Chicago Historical Society.

alities and different creeds together in a fellowship that helps each woman be a better mother, sister, neighbor and citizen." Lectures concerning home and neighborhood sanitation, including evenings where Marion Talbot discussed topics including "scientific cooking" and the dangers of impure food, were common. In addition, the club sponsored social events to raise funds for a library, a settlement garden, and summer picnics for children. It reflected the broader goals of the settlement, such as giving women the information and expertise to empower them to be better mothers and also better citizens.[167]

Very quickly the club became involved in large-scale municipal improvement campaigns. Its first effort at neighborhood improvement related to sanitation, an important issue for this community. McDowell worked with neighborhood residents to petition for a bathhouse. Together they organized neighborhood women and went to city hall to present their petition. This effort led to additional campaigns that expanded the realm of civic activism among the women and got them directly involved in local politics. For example, the club moved from organizing neighborhood children to pick up trash to petitioning city government to address the question of waste disposal so the Back of the Yards no longer would have to bear the burden of the city dump.[168] McDowell, nicknamed "the garbage lady" by local residents, eventually headed the city waste committee of the Woman's City Club and was appointed commissioner of public welfare for the city of Chicago.[169]

These efforts suggested how far the notions of expertise cultivated at the university

FIGURE 29. Kindergarten gardening at playground at University of Chicago Settlement. Courtesy of the Chicago Historical Society.

were put to practical use in the interests of urban communities. Yet sharing information generated new notions of expertise, based more on the lived experiences of neighborhood residents and their understanding of the problems and possibilities of their surroundings. The quotidian basis of local knowledge was then translated into larger political action, opening up new arenas for civic interaction and expression.

UNIVERSITY SETTLEMENT, THE LABOR QUESTION, AND CIVIC CULTURE

Part of the motivation for forming the University of Chicago Settlement came from the recognition that class and labor issues were threatening the city, especially after the World's Columbian Exposition and the subsequent economic depression. The rapid rise of unemployment, along with drastically reduced wages for those who kept their jobs, increased tension between labor and capital. The city had been rocked by dramatic labor upheavals before, including the 1877 railroad strikes and the 1886 Haymarket incident. These class tensions reached a climax during the spring of 1894 in the model town of Pullman, on the Far South Side around 111th Street and Cottage Grove.

Railroad workers who lived in the company town, created by railway sleeping car magnate George Pullman in 1881 in part to quell labor unrest, organized with the newly formed American Railway Union, led by Eugene Debs. After company officials refused to meet with workers' representatives, who complained about wage cuts, indiscriminate firings, and no reduction in rents, workers called a strike that led to a nationwide walkout of railroad employees striking in sympathy with Pullman workers. Despite efforts by progressive Illinois governor John Peter Altgeld to mediate the strike and maintain peace in Chicago, President Grover Cleveland sent federal troops to Chicago, exacerbating the tensions there. As a result of the militia presence (headquartered at Gross Avenue and Forth-seventh Street near the University Settlement), strikebreakers gained easy access to Pullman, allowing the car shops to reopen by late summer 1894. The strike was lost, and the cause of industrial unionism was set back significantly.[170]

Many civic-minded Chicagoans responded to the strike by establishing organizations to address the escalating divisions between labor and capital. The Chicago Civic Federation (CCF) was founded in 1894 after a lecture by British social reformer and minister William T. Stead. In his speech "If Christ Came to Chicago!" he admonished Chicago's civic leaders about the deprivation and decay he found in the city after the

World's Fair. Progressive business leaders, reformers, clergy, professors, and labor leaders responded by forming the Civic Federation, whose purpose was to "gather together in a body for mutual consent, support and combined action all the forces for good, public and private, which are at work in Chicago. It is non-partisan, non-political, and non-sectarian."[171] The Civic Federation developed departments on municipal concerns, politics, industrial relations, and morals. Early members included banker Lyman L. Gage (president), reformer Ralph M. Easley (secretary), Jane Addams, Albion Small, George Herbert Mead, University Extension professor and economist Edward Bemis, and Graham Taylor. The Federation attempted to resolve the dispute between workers and management at Pullman, and it made labor mediation one of its central missions.

While the CCF brought together many progressives in Chicago to promote municipal reform, a number of prominent members became disillusioned with the organization after Easley launched the National Civic Federation (NCF) in 1900. The goals of the new Federation, along with those of the local Federation under Easley, were more conservative and narrow than those set out during the founding of the CCF. While the NCF included many prominent labor leaders, such as Samuel Gompers of the American Federation of Labor (AFL), James Duncan of the Granite Cutters Union, and John Mitchell of the United Mine Workers of America (UMWA), the direction of the organization was toward quelling labor unrest by suppressing radical voices. Easley's orientation toward the national business community, which favored corporate welfare over collective bargaining and labor arbitration, led many reformers like Addams, Mead, Small, and Taylor to look to organizations like the Municipal Voters League (MVL, formed in 1896), an organization focused on promoting good government, and the City Club, established in 1903, to press for broader citywide reform.[172]

Union leaders responded to the violence and bitterness engendered by the Depression and the Pullman strike by forming the Chicago Federation of Labor (CFL) in 1894. The Building Trades Council was the most powerful labor organization in Chicago in the 1890s. It united the numerous unions to which the more than thirty-thousand building trades workers in the city belonged. The Building Trades' unification of all construction workers into one council served as a model for other trades attempting to organize and also for the creation of the Chicago Federation of Labor.[173]

The 1894 Pullman strike illustrated the power workers could generate through the sympathy strike by uniting the goals of all workers in one shared effort. John Fitzpatrick, who became president of the CFL in 1901, called the sympathy strike the best source for the promotion of social justice and industrial democracy. "By engaging in sympathy strikes," he argued, "we prove that the cardinal principle of organized labor (that the injury of one is the concern of all) is not a myth but a reality."[174] Fitzpatrick articulated a vision of labor activism that moved beyond the bread-and-butter issues of more traditional craft unions. In its place, he established a broad-based coalition of workers and sympathizers to fight for public ownership of the means of production, worker participation in management decisions, and the principle of collective bargaining. He carried this emphasis on social solidarity into the public arena, promoting political activism in order to initiate a radical restructuring of civic life through industrial democracy.

The settlements in Chicago sought to bring together these disparate organizations promoting social democracy. Within the walls of the settlement house, academics, labor leaders, and radical political groups could come together not only to promote civic engagement on a wider level, but also to help construct a model of activist social democracy there on the settlement floor. Hull House inaugurated the "Working People's Social Science Club" in 1889, with lectures on Christian socialism, labor, civil service reform, economics, and socialism. Chicago Commons had a Tuesday night "free floor" in which invited speakers introduced topics for open discussion among members of the audience. The lack of censorship encouraged many Chicago radicals to attend the sessions to engage in debate and discussion with academics, university students, and reformers.[175]

Mary McDowell expressed the important role these free exchanges played in cultivating cross-class understanding when she described an encounter between a cattle butcher in the Back of the Yards and a Chicago graduate student. "Another pleasure the settlement offered this intelligent cattle butcher was that of meeting the University students in a genial social atmosphere, giving the working man's point of view with regard to the organization of labor." While the student could argue about labor economics on theoretical grounds, the workers could interject practical experience to force a new understanding of theories of labor and economic policy.[176] Dewey, Mead, Small, Bemis, and Talbot all spoke at the settlements, as did Fitzpatrick and Debs. The settlement provided the kind of interactive intellectual and political engagement Dewey and the Chicago pragmatists advocated and the CFL was so central in fostering. Its physical space created an uninhibited public sphere, at least temporarily, offering a meeting ground for workers, anarchists, scholars, and reformers to engage in civic debate that often was not possible in more "public" settings.[177]

Settlement residents were not just mediators in these confrontations between labor, politicians, and academics. Many settlement leaders, including Addams, Florence Kelley at Hull House, and McDowell, became involved in labor organizing. Kelley articulated this imperative to action in a discussion of working-class philanthropy: "To cast our lot with the workers, to seek to understand the laws of social and industrial development, in the midst of which we live, to spread this enlightenment among the men and women destined to contribute to a change to a higher social order . . . this is the true work for the elevation of the race, the true philanthropy."[178]

Mary McDowell played a crucial role in helping local residents Maggie Condon and Hannah O'Day organize female packinghouse workers into a union in 1903. When male workers in the stockyards organized the Amalgamated Meat Cutters and Butcher Workmen, they did not include women. Yet female workers suffered repeated cuts in their piece rates, largely in the canning and sausage processing departments. Hannah O'Day led a spontaneous strike of female workers to protest the cuts. After receiving little support from the male union, O'Day and Condon met with McDowell to launch a union. The Settlement Woman's Club became an important vehicle for establishing local 183 of the Amalgamated. McDowell again aided strikers during the violent 1904 stockyards strike, offering the settlement as a meeting place for strike organizing.[179]

McDowell's work in forging cross-class alliances at the settlement led to her active involvement in the Women's Trade Union League (WTUL), organized in 1903. McDowell was active in the national WTUL as well as the Chicago branch, serving as president of the latter until 1907. The motto of the WTUL was "The Eight-Hour Day, a Living Wage, to Guard the Home." These goals reflected the merger of feminism and workers' rights that served as the foundation of many reform efforts among both middle-class and working-class women. The WTUL drew on women's organizational networks to forge cross-class alliances and press for the larger principles of democratic social action that shaped much of settlement activity.[180]

At the University of Chicago Settlement, residents worked alongside interested local community members to produce studies of housing conditions, working conditions, child labor, female labor, and local sanitary conditions. Settlement residents used these studies as the basis for labor activism, the promotion of women's suffrage, and campaigns for municipal reform.

McDowell translated her organizing activities and municipal reform campaigns into more overt political activism. In 1903 she joined with University of Chicago graduate students Sophonisba Breckinridge and Edith Abbott to investigate women's and children's labor, leading to the creation of the Department of Commerce and Labor in Washington, D.C. Her first involvement in local politics came during a vote for state university trustees, one of the few offices women could vote for after winning the franchise in Illinois in 1913. McDowell explained, "I always had considered that it was my duty to accept and use this tiny bit of political privilege that the state of Illinois had given to women, also my duty to awaken other women to their public responsibility."[181] McDowell educated neighborhood women about their rights and accompanied interested voters to the polling place during elections. In 1914 she organized the Twenty-ninth Ward Woman's Civic League to inform women of the backgrounds of alderman running for election and provide a forum for political discussion. In 1916 she ran (unsuccessfully) for county office, and in 1924 she was appointed commissioner of the city's Department of Welfare.[182]

McDowell's role in the University of Chicago Settlement, and in the Back of the Yards neighborhood more broadly, suggests how the boundaries between the home and the community, the private and the political, could be transcended. The settlement bridged the divide between the university and the city and brought together neighborhood residents from different nationalities. It joined workers, academics, and reformers in discussions about controversial issues like labor and provided a forum for university women to cultivate their knowledge and expertise for larger civic goals.

Yet the settlement never became a regular part of the university. Harper never secured endowment funds for it, forcing it to rely on philanthropic contributions to remain solvent. Funds collected at the university's Sunday services were devoted to the maintenance of the settlement, and on one Sunday each quarter time was devoted to news about settlement activities and pleas for funds to help with special programs.[183] In addition, in 1895 McDowell helped create the University of Chicago Settlement League to support the work of the settlement. The league became a social and philanthropic organization, with membership open to women on the university faculty and to wives of faculty, students, and alumni. Those women present at the founding meeting included the wives of Harper, sociologist Charles Zueblin, and future university president Harry Pratt Judson.[184] The settlement, then, worked in conjunction with but apart from the university proper, relying instead on ties with university women and their philanthropic activities to continue and develop its programs.

The increasingly distant relationship between the university and the settlement reflected the difficulty in merging academic scholarship with civic activism at Chicago—particularly in relation to labor issues. The Bemis affair illustrated this tension in stark terms. Edward Bemis was an economist and a critic of capitalism who was offered the possibility of a tenured position in the Department of Political Economy along with his lecturing role in the University Extension program. During the 1894 Pullman strike, Bemis publicly criticized Pullman and the railroads for their treatment of workers. When word reached the media that a University of Chicago professor was speaking out against Pullman, intense controversy erupted. Harper was "pounced upon everywhere," leading him to warn Bemis to watch what he said in public while still on faculty at the university. Speaking against the interests of corporate capital eventually did cost Bemis his job, by some accounts. Harper justified Bemis's dismissal on the grounds that he was incompetent and that he had "forgotten that to serve The University we must employ scientific methods and do scientific work."[185]

The Bemis case illustrated how engagement in controversial civic affairs increasingly was off-limits to faculty and came under the purview of institutions like the settlement that had increasingly marginal relationships with the university proper. University administrators posited science and the cultivation of expertise as areas that were at odds with local activism. Rather than linking scientific investigation with social reform, the university erected barriers between the two that curtailed the activities of its faculty and thwarted broader involvement with the surrounding community.

The system of sex segregation, the development of the athletics program, the creation of the Department of Household Administration, and the formation of the University Settlement reflected tensions embodied in the new modern research university. They illustrated the difficulty of merging men and women's intellectual goals, patterns of sociability, and practical career needs into a cohesive educational plan. They also made evident the central role gender played in structuring these divisions. And they exposed the growing tensions between scientific expertise being fostered by the university and the civic activism and coalition building being generated beyond its borders. Educators continued to try to make the structure of the university more fluid and engaged, but they ran up against the rising culture of expertise that segregated knowledge and learning and located their placement inside the campus borders rather than beyond them.

Some university professors, then, transported their scientific theories of knowledge and social structure into the public realm of political engagement. This process was especially important for women. Their academic degrees gave middle-class and upper-middle-class women new authority in the political arena and allowed them to build on urban networks of women's organizations to dominate urban reform and gain a prominent place in civic culture in Chicago. By linking new forms of knowledge and pragmatist philosophy with expertise in fields like hygiene and social welfare, middle-class women worked with male academics and working-class men and women to carve out a new public culture centered on broad-based coalition building and active engagement in civic life.

The University of Chicago Settlement embodied these connections between higher education and social reform. Moreover, the wide variety of participants in settlement activities demonstrated that social reform, and Progressivism more broadly, was not simply a reform agenda imposed from above. Rather, it was a shared—and contested—understanding of the importance of creating social and economic conditions that would foster participatory democracy and a revitalized public sphere. The settlement served as a mediating space, since it provided a model for a new public sphere in which groups like women, immigrants, and workers, whose voices too often had been marginalized in modern industrial America, might foster a dynamic urban civic culture. The settlement transcended the boundaries of the home and the church, the university and the city, and offered the possibility of "the unification of the city's life [and] of the realizing of the city's unity." [186]

Yet within the University of Chicago proper, the emphasis on science and professionalism limited the kinds of public activities available to professors. The rise in specialization and differentiation between university departments was inherent in the design of the institution, with each department occupying separate facilities, with its own libraries and laboratories. This spatial differentiation shaped how the university related to the city. By positing an understanding of civic life in which all institutions served discrete functions, the university staked out a particular role for itself, claiming authority in the realm of thought and knowledge and containing ideas within its boundaries. This spatial differentiation circumscribed the roles academics played in their official capacities as professors. Proponents of more dramatic social restructuring, including Marion Talbot, John Dewey, George Herbert Mead, and Mary McDowell, were ultimately compelled to rely on alliances outside the university to integrate their visions into civic debates.

PART TWO

Parks as Public Space

TO LAY THE FOUNDATIONS FOR GOOD CITIZENSHIP

Neighborhood Parks and Outdoor Recreation

AT THE TURN OF THE TWENTIETH CENTURY, Chicagoans and Americans nationwide embarked on extensive municipal campaigns to improve the physical quality of American cities. Reformers sought to overcome the crowded conditions, poor sanitation, and lack of adequate breathing space that plagued urban America. Planners throughout the country stressed the importance of making parks an integral feature of the landscape. Indeed, according to many proponents, parks were the spaces where democracy and citizenship would be shaped in the modern city. Architect Dwight Heald Perkins, the designer of the University of Chicago Settlement, argued that adding more parks and playgrounds would "lay the foundations for good citizenship" in Chicago.[1] Much like settlement houses, parks were places, according to Perkins and others, where ethnic, class, and even racial difference could be mediated. Within these natural spaces, tensions and divisions plaguing urban industrial society could be surmounted. Park proponents equated natural space with public space and sought ways to infuse nature into the city.

A variety of groups extolled the virtues of parks in urban America. As the Reverend J. A. Rondthaler made clear, parks were more than natural refuges within the crowded, dirty, industrial environment of the city; they would provide the setting for the formation of morality and wholesomeness, integrity and beauty: "The order and harmony and beauty of nature are brought close to us and made visible in the park. Therefore the park brings us into tune with goodness, and so the blessed ministry of the park is to set our feet in right paths, and order our thoughts to things that are true and high and noble and of good report."[2]

This conflation of morality and nature, religious guidance and park design reflected sentiments that served as the impetus for park development in early nineteenth-century America. Combined with additional elements of sanitation and hygiene, environmental conservation, civic boosterism, and science and efficiency, such moral concerns prompted urban residents at the turn of the century to push for a new program of large-scale park development. These themes found their way into arguments for parks made by a variety of proponents, including politicians, industrialists, settlement house workers, physicians, labor leaders, and residents of tenement districts. Quite frequently these varying notions of the proper function of parks clashed, leading to conflict between segments of the city who had competing ideas over the course park development should take.[3]

Uniting these proponents and their competing agendas was the search for a new urban aesthetic, one that combined moralism with scientific management, art with efficiency, and open space with the promotion of democracy and citizenship. Plans for refashioning the urban landscape reflected the attempt by various groups to claim cultural legitimacy and authority by inscribing the city with their visions of order, civility, and democracy.

This new progressive agenda for park development reflected a shift in ideals about parks' function in cultivating a public sphere in the city. Park designers during the Gilded Age emphasized the role of urban parks in creating an arena of civic culture through proper design, which instilled in park users of all classes feelings of harmony and order reflective of bourgeois ideals of respectability. Simply by experiencing the order and tranquillity of properly designed parks, they argued, urban residents would subscribe to an urban vision of civility that transcended the immediate park experience.[4]

By the turn of the century, however, a new generation of park advocates and city boosters looked to scientific models of investigation and problem solving in their quest for an orderly public sphere. They emphasized not only the importance of efficient design and land use, but also the need for expertly supervised urban landscapes to encourage civic stewardship. In the Gilded Age and also the Progressive Era, park planners linked landscape design to both civic boosterism and working-class socialization, hoping to weave these crucial aspects of order and harmony into the fabric of urban life envisioned by the city's economic and cultural elites. Progressive planners, though, used "modern" methods to instill codes of civility, including scientific classification and social investigation, developed at research institutions like the University of Chicago.

At the same time, some park advocates considered leisure and recreation key components in urban reform. Unlike earlier park proponents, many progressive reformers argued that providing adequate space for outdoor recreation was an essential function of the park. Questions surrounding passive versus active use of park space fostered numerous disagreements. Yet the debate also exposed the increasingly important part that leisure and recreation played in shaping ideas about urban citizenship. Parks became a central feature of plans for reform of the urban landscape precisely because they were spaces of leisure, And they reflected the growing belief that the very meaning of urban democracy was shaped and enacted through interactions in leisure sites.

Municipal control of recreation became a prominent feature of efforts at park development. Creating parks went hand in hand with promoting outdoor recreation, and both increasingly came within the purview of municipal government. "The result of this increased leisure of the average man will be good or bad for the community," concluded the Chicago Commission on Recreation, ". . . according as the public—social or civic—provides for control and direction of it."[5]

Women played a central role in linking recreation with municipal control. Women associated with the University of Chicago, especially those whose civic work increasingly was marginalized from the university proper, became active in debates over parks as public space. Female park advocates, especially settlement house workers like Mary McDowell, relocated themselves in relation to urban politics. By occupying positions within the city previously off-limits to them—especially public spaces—women reformulated the relation between public space and civic discourse. In the process they also played leading roles in transforming the urban environment and municipal politics.

In addition, working-class and ethnic groups often had their own views of park use and function. They too called for park development as an essential feature of the modern urban landscape, but they saw parks as places for gathering and recreation. In attempting to claim parks as their own and to use them as staging grounds for everything from ethnic celebrations to strikes, they put forward alternative ideas about the meanings of public space and democracy in the city.

CULTIVATING UNITY: EARLY PARK DESIGN IN CHICAGO

Chicago's first large-scale effort at park building came in 1869 after the state passed legislation calling for a comprehensive park system in the city. This legislation divided the city into three park districts, north (or Lincoln Park), west, and south, each with an independent governing body. The districts had the power to levy taxes for establishing, maintaining, and improving parks and boulevards within the city. By 1870 the city owned 1,887 acres of parkland; by 1880, over 2,000. Only Philadelphia surpassed Chicago in park acreage.[6]

The park proposal came at a time when techniques and ideas in landscape design were being transformed. Many English and American designers reacted against "European excess" and the ornamentation evident in formal, geometric, "artificial" gardens like Versailles. Instead, they called for park designs reflecting the natural landscape. New Englander Andrew Jackson Downing was one of first American proponents of naturalism in landscape design. He advocated the "Modern, Natural or Irregular Style" as opposed to the "Ancient, Formal, of Geometric Style" for design of residential and public grounds.[7] Moreover, Downing believed that strengthening connections to the natural landscape could offer Americans a more cohesive sense of national identity. He argued that if they learned to appreciate the value and beauty of their landscape and cultivate their own artistic expression, "the froth of foreign affectations will work off, and the impurities of vulgar taste settle down, leaving us the pure spirit of a better national taste at last."[8]

This idea of the natural landscape as the basis for American landscape design emerged at a time when many Americans were questioning the meaning of nature and its function in American history. Rural life became romanticized in the middle of the nineteenth century in part because it was disappearing. With the growth of commercial farming, the rise of a market economy, and the movement from farm to factory, agriculture was losing its place as the defining feature of the American economy and culture. Especially in the Northeast, nature no longer was solely associated with hard work and farming. Instead, it was idealized as a lost landscape that reflected the republican values of American society. Landscape painting became a dominant art form in this period, reflecting this nostalgia. Painters like Thomas Cole celebrated "rural nature" as "an unfailing fountain of intellectual enjoyment where all may drink & be awakened to a deeper feeling of the works of genius & a deeper perception of the beauty of our existence."[9]

The writers and intellectuals of the transcendentalist movement articulated this new connection between nature, Americanism, and spiritual renewal. Like Thomas Jefferson, the transcendentalists, especially Ralph Waldo Emerson and Henry David Thoreau, celebrated the virtues of rural life and its connection to republicanism. They believed a return to a more natural landscape would counter the disorder and materialism that they thought plagued American cities.[10] On July 4, 1845, Thoreau moved to a small cabin on Walden Pond in Concord, Massachusetts, to confront "the essential facts of life." For Thoreau, the materialism of the modern world divorced humanity from these essential elements. Only by becoming more fully in tune with the natural world, with the sights, sounds, rhythms, and rhymes of nature, could humanity attain spiritual well-being and gain a sense of purpose.[11] Other writers formed their own rural community in West Roxbury, Massachusetts. There Nathaniel Hawthorne, Emerson, Margaret Fuller, and the family of Louisa May Alcott lived a communal life of simple farming to counter the materialism of the outside world.

This desire among many Americans to escape into the wilderness also led to the fashion for integrating nature into urban spaces. By the 1860s and 1870s, many Americans began to see nature and the city not as antithetical to one another but as complementary features of what David Schuyler calls a "new urban landscape." Park promoters, physicians, religious leaders, and social reformers saw the benefits of combining the morality and spiritual uplift they associated with nature and the refining influence of cultural institutions in cities. These reformers, then, drew a strong connection between morality, social order, and the physical fabric of the city.

Many proponents envisioned the urban park as the antithesis of the surrounding city, showcasing nature and subordinating the man-made to fully achieve moral and spiritual harmony. Frederick Law Olmsted's Central Park in New York City was the first major attempt to bring the natural landscape into the city and remove the "contaminating" influences of the urban environment. Olmsted and Calvert Vaux's 1858 Greensward Plan for Central Park made use of many of these design ideals, including extensive lagoons, curving paths, and native shrubbery and tree plantings. The Greensward Plan brought a piece of the country into the city to serve the spiritual and psychological needs of city residents. For Olmsted, the beauty of the park "should be the beauty of the fields, the meadow, the prairie, of the green pastures and the still waters. What we want to gain is tranquillity and rest to the mind."[12] Olmsted believed that "the restorative qualities of nature" could bring about this harmony. For him, the "contemplation of natural scenes of an impressive character" helped overcome the stresses of modern city life.[13] Whereas the grid plan of New York was designed for efficiency and commercial growth, the curving paths of Central Park defined places for quiet contemplation and reflection.

The design of the park included a wall of trees that screened out surrounding buildings. Sunken reservoirs, paths, and open greens further enhanced the separation of the park from the city. But if Olmsted and Vaux's naturalistic landscape was designed to look as unspoiled and rustic as possible, it was not really natural, since it was all meticulously crafted. So Central Park represented yet another meaning of "the natural," this time denoting the conscious attempts by landscape planners to recreate pastoral scenery in the heart of the city.[14]

When Chicago park commissioners contracted with Olmsted and Vaux for the South Parks, they were confident that the pleasure grounds of Chicago would "imitate the flow, foliage, and apparent casualness of the unspoiled landscapes."[15] The beauty of the natural landscape, however, was less apparent to the park planners. As H. W. S. Cleveland, hired to oversee the South Parks plans of Olmsted and Vaux, remarked, "By what means is it possible to give to areas so utterly devoid of character an expression of natural beauty, and secure enough variety to relieve their monotony?"[16] Olmsted and Vaux had similar doubts: "The fact should be recognized that none of the sites and no part of any one of the sites which have been reserved for parks in Chicago would generally elsewhere be well adapted to the purpose."[17] Indeed, the grounds were swampy, flat, and generally unappealing, but they had the benefit of the lakefront, a naturally picturesque element. According to Olmsted, Lake Michigan "fully compensated for the absence of sublime or picturesque elevations of land," and he and Vaux proposed an elaborate waterway to enhance the beauty and centrality of the lake. In addition, the flat, open grounds were an advantage in constructing the "South Open Green," the largest open space in the country planned for parades and games (one hundred acres). According to Olmsted, the Green achieved the main object of an urban park, which was to create "an antithesis to [the city's] bustling, paved, rectangular, walled-in streets."[18]

Olmsted designed the park to evoke tranquillity through the use of lagoons, open meadows, and winding paths offering picturesque vistas (figs. 30 and 31). He even included sheep in the South Open Green to enhance the naturalism of the park in addition to keeping the grass trimmed. He often used exotic plantings to augment a landscape, but he tried to "make each design unique by basing it on the special qualities of

FIGURE 30. Relaxation and contemplation at Washington Park, 1910. Courtesy of the Chicago Park District, Special Collections.

the individual site."[19] Olmsted's use of exotics, along with other methods for producing "natural" landscapes, illustrates that landscape design for Olmsted was as much about creating nature as preserving it.

Yet for Olmsted and many other park proponents, park design was about more than scenic vistas and naturalist design. In addition to promoting spiritual rejuvenation, Olmsted believed parks could foster interaction among various classes of urban dwellers. This is why the promenade is such a central feature in all his designs (fig. 32).

> [The promenade] is an open-air gathering for the purpose of easy, friendly, unceremonious greetings, for the enjoyment of change of scene, of cheerful and exhilarating sights and sounds, and of various good cheer, to which the people of a town, of all classes, harmoniously resort on equal terms, as to all common property. There is probably no custom which so manifestly displays the advantages of a Christian, civilized, and democratic community. . . . There is nothing more favorable to a healthy civic pride, civic virtue, and civic prosperity.[20]

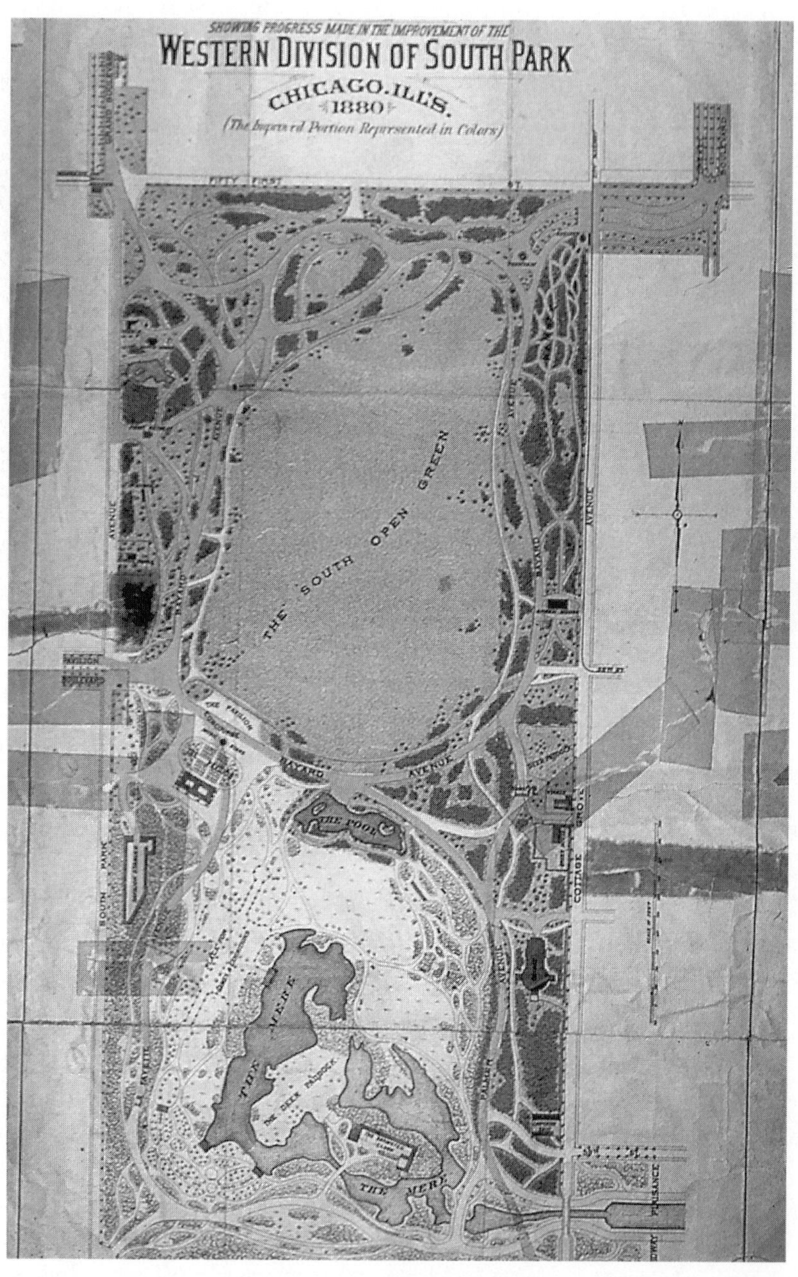

FIGURE 31. Plan for the improvement of Washington Park, 1880. Courtesy of the Chicago Park District.

FIGURE 32. Jackson Park promenade, 1890. Courtesy of the Chicago Historical Society.

Here the inequalities so glaring in other parts of the city could fade away, according to Olmsted. The park provided a shared leisure space around which to structure a vision of urban order and harmony.[21]

Of course this mingling of the classes on public pleasure grounds was not meant to occur on completely equal terms. Olmsted believed in bringing all classes together so that the masses could learn proper deportment from their social superiors.[22] He expressed this view in his comments on the wonders of Central Park. "No one who has closely observed the conduct of the people who visit Central Park can doubt that it exercises a distinctly harmonizing and refining influence upon the most unfortunate and lawless classes of the city—an influence favorable to courtesy, self-control, and temperance."[23]

For Olmsted and other park promoters, the promenade was an idealized space in which rituals of bourgeois respectability and cultural status were affirmed. At the same time, these gestures served as examples for working-class ethnic city residents to emulate. Thus the promenade paradoxically functioned both as social leveler and as promoter of class distinction. All had the opportunity to participate in a public culture of ritual and display within the setting of an urban public sphere. Yet this public display also allowed members of the elite and middle classes to legitimize their claim to cultural authority and social distinction by making visible an accumulation of cultural capital largely unavailable to the working class. In addition, the theatricality of the promenade allowed these classes to enforce norms of civility, self-control, and domesticity through the "policing" of demeanor.[24] The promenade therefore was a place where class difference was reaffirmed rather than eradicated.

Design played a crucial role in enabling a park to fulfill its social function as envisioned by park advocates. These scenic parks were meant to be didactic settings that would mold the characters and values of their users. Nature needed to be properly planned, since uncontrolled wilderness could not alleviate "disorder, indecorum, and indecency, that will be subversive of every good purpose the park should be designed to fulfill."[25]

Formal design reached an apex with the creation of the grounds for the 1893 World's Columbian Exposition in Jackson Park (fig. 33). Here Olmsted's vision of a controlled landscape complemented Daniel Burnham's City Beautiful, even as "nature" seemed antithetical to the control and formalism of Burnham's planned cityscape. As Victoria Post Ranney argues, "Olmsted was more than an artistic arranger of landscape. He was a social and scientific planner on a broad social scale who believed he could change the whole moral and cultural level of our democracy by careful planning of the environment."[26]

In addition to the ordered design of the landscape and the formality of the promenade filled with "crowds of well-dressed people . . . promenading up and down,"[27] there were other features of the large pleasure grounds that were meant to instill gentility and respectability in parkgoers. Signs warning patrons to keep off the grass and forbidding active play reinforced the idea of parkgoing as an exercise in refinement and of leisure as tranquil contemplation. Parkgoers were fined five dollars for playing cricket and baseball in the parks, while walking on the grass warranted a hefty twenty-dollar fine.[28] Only in the mid-1880s, when protests from city residents mounted, were tennis courts installed in Jackson Park and ball games permitted. Still, the rules against spitting, swearing, raising one's voice, and running, along with the prohibition on liquor and speechmaking, underscored the desire to create civic order through park regulation.[29]

Yet the high degree of regulation may have kept away those residents whom Olmsted and others believed would benefit most from the refining influence of scenic parks. The promenade and other features of elite display were so popular with the middle class that many reformers worried about the small percentage of working-class residents visiting the city's large pleasure grounds. Park advocate J. Horace McFarland stated:

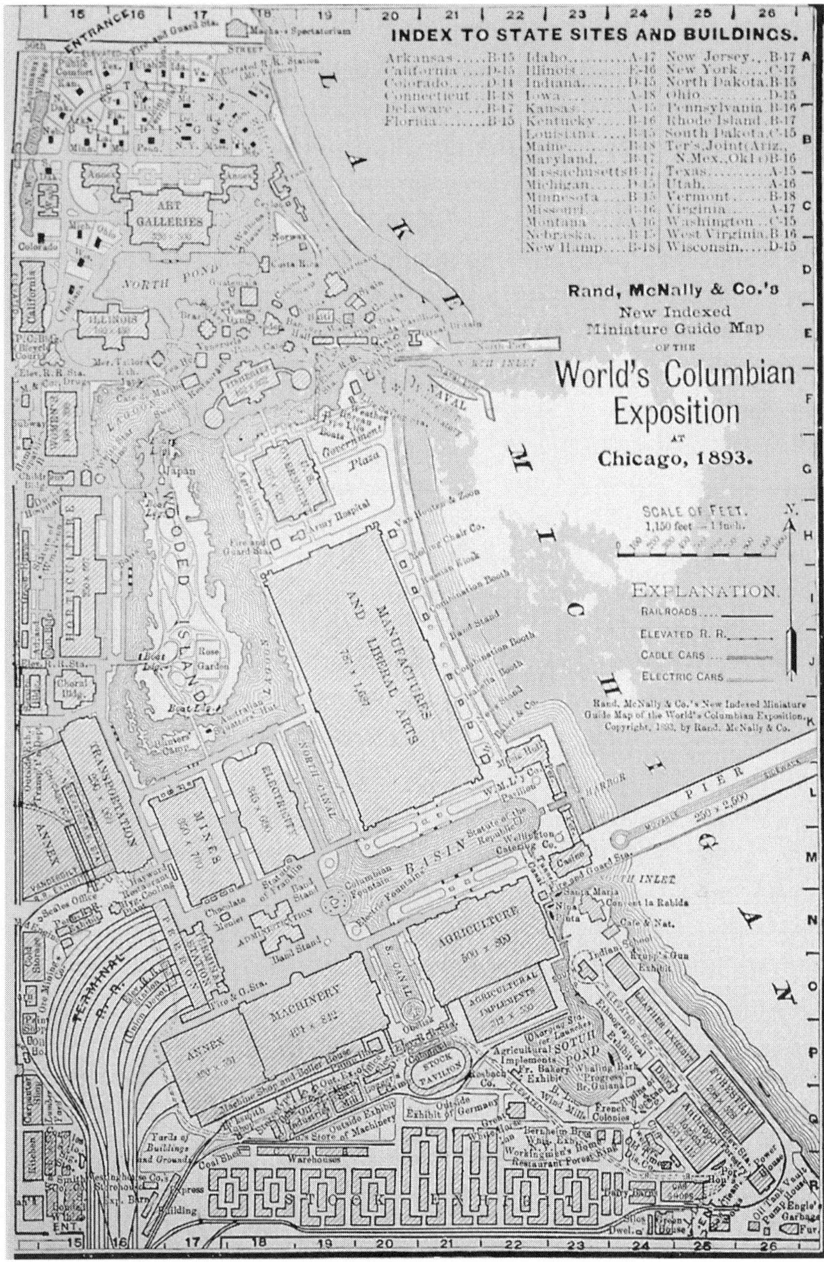

FIGURE 33. Plan of the 1893 World's Columbian Exposition. From Tudor Jenks, *The Century World's Fair Book for Boys and Girls* (New York: Century, 1893).

> In fact, if there is any part of the whole public to which the parks are less importantly related than any other part, it is to the group of well-to-do citizens for whom almost exclusively the earlier [small private] parks were made. . . . I do not in the least object to the use of the parks by the men, women, boys and girls who have homes with park-like surroundings and facilities, but I consider that a mere adjunct to the use of the parks by the vastly greater percentage of the population which cannot so provide itself with recreational facilities.[30]

The definition of a park that emphasized "cultural enlightenment and greater refinement of manners" reflected bourgeois notions of the proper use of leisure and the function of public space.[31] The planning of the large pleasure grounds showed little concern for the recreational and leisure patterns of the urban working class. Yet there were more tangible reasons why working-class urban residents failed to frequent the parks. As Elizabeth Halsey points out in her study of public recreation in Chicago, "The large parks at first were remote from most of the population. . . . They were visited by the fashionable world in handsome carriages or by the less well-to-do who could afford the phaeton trips to the south parks (twenty cents)."[32] Indeed, working-class residents voted against the initial park bills establishing the large pleasure grounds, primarily because the parks would be largely inaccessible to working-class districts.[33] Jane Addams addressed this problem in her *Hull-House Recreation Guide.* She pointed out that "of the five larger parks in the city there are but two—and these not including either of the two chief ones—which a mother of the 19th ward can, without a wearisome walk of half a mile or more each way, visit for less than 20 cents for the round trip."[34] Park commissioners and city residents petitioned the Union Traction Company to issue transfers for park visitors, but the request was "met by a summary refusal."[35]

RECREATION AND THE DEVELOPMENT OF SMALL PARKS AND PLAYGROUNDS

Chicago residents fought on multiple fronts to create neighborhood parks in the city. The multitude of constituents promoting park development coalesced in the last years of the 1890s and forced both city and state government to respond. Residents of crowded wards wanted public parks and playgrounds to meet their social and recreational needs as well as provide open space to relieve crowding and unhealthful conditions. These residents actively petitioned City Council members for park and recreation facilities in their districts. Working-class residents used the language of scientific reform and progressive public policy to stake claims to city spaces, ones that would be designed and used according to their own prescriptions for recreation and relaxation.

In 1895 West Side Germans petitioned park commissioners to build sports areas within West Side municipal parks. They argued that they had built their own "turnvereins" (German gymnasium facilities) but that they needed additional outdoor spaces. A year later, African Americans in the emerging Black Belt worked in conjunction with the Reverend Reverdy Ransom and his Institutional Church and Social Settlement in making "an urgent appeal for a neighborhood park, as the health of the residents would continue to be threatened without it." Similarly, Mary McDowell took the suggestions of members of the University of Chicago Settlement's Bohemian Woman's Club and argued in favor of parkland accessible to the stockyards.[36]

Some businessmen also believed that an expanded park system was in the best interests of the city. In 1898 the Merchants' Club, a group of prominent young business executives, professionals, and social reformers including Graham Taylor, Dwight Perkins, and landscape designer Jens Jensen, invited Jacob Riis, the reform advocate and author of *How the Other Half Lives,* which exposed New York's tenement conditions to the nation, to speak on the subject of municipal parks and plans for park expansion. Before club president Edgar A. Bancroft introduced Riis, he stated, "Business-men, so-called, have the roots of their strength and business in the centers of population. It is . . . a mere matter of intelligent selfishness, or prudence, of wisdom to recognize that they should be interested in improving a city's condition." Indeed, Riis couched park reform in the language of beautifying the city and creating disciplined, moral citizens; he declared, "A boy robbed of his chance to play will not be an honest and effective man—you can't depend on him at the polls."[37] By the end of the talk the club pledged its support for small parks as Bancroft argued, "This is not socialism, not anarchy, not the preaching of a new course of municipal action, but it is common sense applied to actual conditions."[38]

As a result of the Riis meeting, Charles Zueblin, a member of the Municipal Science League and a sociologist at University of Chicago, published an article in the *American Journal of Sociology* titled, "Municipal Playgrounds in Chicago." In it he mapped existing park locations and made correlations between spatial patterns and population figures. He pointed out that "between six and seven hundred thousand people live more than a mile from any large park." The eleven wards of the city containing most of the existing parks had 234 people for each acre of park space, while in twenty-three other wards the figure was 4,720 residents per acre.[39] Zueblin argued that the only way to alleviate these problems was for the city to buy land for the development of more parks.

In 1899 Mayor Carter Harrison Jr. responded to these pleas for parks by calling for an investigation of park conditions in Chicago and recommendations for park expansion based on the findings. He appointed the Special Park Commission to undertake this task.[40] At the same time, the Chicago City Council adopted resolutions advocating increased park space throughout the city. The resolution establishing the Special Park Board stated:

> Whereas, the present park system of the City of Chicago has been and now is a great blessing to our citizens in giving them fresh air and sunshine, which are so difficult to obtain in a crowded and growing city, yet are so valuable in preventing crime and promoting cleanliness and diminishing disease; and Whereas, this system, great and beneficent as it is, fails from lack of small recreation grounds to reach many of our citizens in crowded central wards who most need such opportunities, so that the present system urgently needs to be supplemented in those districts by breathing spaces of various sorts, including small parks and playgrounds for children, swimming places, public baths, parkways and the like.[41]

The resolution also argued that the city should obtain the land necessary for park development immediately rather than waiting until the increase in population density made the need for park space even greater and land that much more expensive. The City Council appropriated $100,000 for developing new parks in the city. The small parks bill also gave the three existing park commissions the authority to issue bonds for creating parks of ten acres or less in each district. The Illinois Park Act of 1869 was amended, and in 1903 the three Chicago park boards were authorized to spend $6,500,000 for new parks.[42]

The *Report of the Special Park Commission to the City Council of Chicago on the Subject of a Metropolitan Park System* became one of the most important documents in the history of park planning in Chicago. Written by architect Dwight Heald Perkins the report traced the history of park building in Chicago and made recommendations for future expansion. It advocated parkland allocation to keep pace with urban population growth. The investigation found that one-third of the population of Chicago lived more than a mile from the nearest park. The slogan adopted by those pressing for more parkland was "Take the parks to the people, if they cannot come to the parks."[43]

The justification for expanded park space was the widely held belief that social and moral degeneration were a direct result of the condition of the urban landscape. Using "modern" tools of scientific problem solving, which included density studies, crime statistics, and moral evaluations, reformers could accurately determine the precise number and location of parks needed to ameliorate the impoverished urban conditions they identified. By mapping the physical geography of the city, park planners could identify areas of "pathology" and try to fix their problems by creating public spaces that conformed to bourgeois codes of respectability. In both tracing the history of park design and pointing to new methods of park planning, Perkins inadvertently highlighted the growing tensions between earlier ideas of civic uplift and modern notions of planning efficiency.[44]

One feature of the report that gave impetus to park expansion was the fear that Chicago was lagging behind other American cities in park development, since it had not added parkland to its original pleasure grounds throughout the latter decades of the nineteenth century. Park advocates pointed to comparisons with other cities to argue for a new phase of extensive park development. Between 1880 and 1903, Chicago's population increased 272.4 percent, but its park area grew by only 58.7 percent. By contrast, New York increased 61.46 percent in population and 701.25 percent in park area, while Boston grew 63.88 percent in population and 5,427 percent in park area.[45]

To be effective in allocating parkland, the Commission had to address sections of the city where population had grown the most dense, and they, of course, were in the ethnic working-class wards. Park proponents and social reformers recognized the need to bring the benefit of parks into the central, crowded wards if the large pleasure grounds remained inaccessible. They also reiterated the link between urban beautification and cleanliness, moral reform, and rational land use. Professor Albion Small of the University of Chicago, for example, argued that all vacant lots should be converted to small parks, which would have the dual effect of providing breathing space for the poor and beautifying the city. "The small park idea is growing. It is found to be the most rational method of giving the poorer residents of a large city at least a taste of rural life and surroundings. It is the most humanizing of all modern methods of counteracting the eternal grind and grime of a city's tenement districts."[46]

The goals of the new parks reflected reformers' faith in the meliorative potential of properly designed public grounds. The park planners hoped "to take children from the streets and alleys and give them a better environment and safer place in which to play," to encourage both children and adults "to give attention to personal hygiene, —exercise and bathing chiefly," and to provide "wholesome amusements for adults and others who do not participate in the activities of gymnasium, athletic and play fields."[47] [48]

The method of selecting sites for park expansion reflected an understanding of the role parks could play not only in instilling moral character but also in preventing crime and disease. According to Fred H. Matthews, Chicago sociologists including Albion Small and Charles Henderson were "eager to create a scientific description of society and driven by a conviction that science not only liberated by giving understanding, but provided the practical tools to realize the just and virtuous society."[49] Park advocates now spoke of the most efficient and "rational" use of parkland instead of merely the most morally uplifting or aesthetically pleasing. These themes of efficiency and scientific investigation were tied to academics' and social reformers' notions of the most effective means to create public spaces that would foster democratic civic engagement and, in turn, moral values.[50]

In its 1902 *Report on Sites and Needs,* the Special Park Commission provided a systematic analysis of conditions throughout Chicago to determine the most rational plan for park development. The conditions that controlled the commissioners' determination of sites were "density of population, bad housing and other unsanitary features, remoteness from parks, excessive mortality, especially among children, destitution of open spaces and recreation grounds, juvenile criminality and delinquency." Given the scientific basis of their findings, they argued, "proper location should not be sacrificed merely for the sake of getting cheaper property."[51]

The Commission's report painted a horrid picture of living conditions in the tenement districts of the city. In one district, near Thirty-ninth and Halsted, the report stated that "there is not a suitable piece of vacant land on which the children can romp or play. Nearly all the men are mechanics or laborers with small incomes. Many wives are forced to work out in support of the family. The little ones are neglected and turned out to shift for themselves and quickly learn the evil lessons of the street." In Bridgeport, the report noted that in 1901 the death rate was 14.49 per thousand, with children under age five making up a large percentage of the deaths. "The inhabitants of this district," the report stated, "are deprived of the enjoyment of the south parks because of distance and for want of money to pay car fares."[52]

In the Thirtieth Ward of the Stockyards district, conditions were similar. "There is a destitution of proper public resorts and places of amusement in the Stock Yards district," the report claimed. The only places for social interaction "are the more than 500 saloons with their attached dance halls and beer gardens." By contrast, Hyde Park, "with its abundance of recreation ground," had only about twenty-five saloons.[53] The commissioners followed their report of conditions with the call for the immediate establishment of neighborhood parks, arguing that "the prevention of disease and of juvenile crime, with its effect upon adult citizenship, follows the establishment of accessible pleasure grounds."[54]

Indeed, numerous supporters of parks argued that increasing the number of accessible parks in working-class districts alleviated crime along with juvenile delinquency. According to an editorial by Charles S. Deneen, who later became governor of Illinois, "Ninety per cent of the criminal class in Chicago is due directly to the environment." He argued that establishing "that environment which produces sound bodies and clean habits" would solve "the crime problem which confronts every large city."[55]

Park promoters emphasized the importance of parks in shaping recreational activities for families. They often juxtaposed the wholesomeness of parks with the "evil" of saloons by arguing that parks brought families together while saloons tore them apart. According to Chicago social worker Amalie Hofer Jerome, "When the family splits up for its recreation, there is danger. When young people take their places apart by themselves without a wholesome influence of family life, there is danger. Only when the family stays together do we have wholesome conditions."[56] Thus, by developing spaces in which women participated in recreational activities alongside men, park planners affirmed the notion of woman as moral influence. Even though parks served as public spaces for women, then, they did not (at least according to prescriptions put forth by reformers) provide arenas in which women's roles as caretakers and embodiments of wholesomeness were overturned. This vision of a circumscribed public role for women would be challenged, though, by the increasing visibility of female social scientists and reformers in the planning of parks.[57]

Women took the lead in advocating parks on behalf of children. Female reformers directly linked the campaign for neighborhood parks with their efforts to curb juvenile delinquency. It was no accident that the campaign for parks came at the same time as the 1889 passage of legislation in Illinois creating the first juvenile court in the nation. For the first time, juvenile offenders had their own court system to address their cases, spurred by the growing belief that youth crimes should be adjudicated based on the particular needs of minors. While the law provided for the creation of the court and the establishment of a system of probation, it failed to allocate salaries for probation officers. As a result, several "public-spirited citizens" organized the Juvenile Court Committee to pay these salaries. In 1907, after years of campaigning to make the court an integral part of municipal government, the committee secured legislation to place probation officers on the county payroll. Members of the committee then shifted their focus and organized the Juvenile Protective Association (JPA) to "make a determined attempt to minimize the wretched conditions which constantly demoralized children."[58]

Of particular concern was the effect that sites of commercial amusement had on children. Louise de Koven Bowen, head of the JPA, argued that the city was "full of dangerous spots for children. The disreputable dance halls, poolrooms and saloons never closed their doors." "The demand for amusement was insistent, the supply of facilities for innocent recreation was inadequate," and so children constantly were exposed to these temptations and eventually ended up in juvenile court.[59] She pointed to an example of a young girl working in a pickle factory who spent money she was given by her employer to buy stamps on a day at the amusement park with a friend. "The temptation was too great," Bowen argued, for "she went to the amusement park and spent there a long and happy day and evening."[60] She especially worried about the protection of young girls in theaters and amusement parks. A 1909 survey of movie houses and theaters identified over 405 five- and ten-cent theaters in Chicago, seating 93,000 people. The survey estimated that 32,000 children a day attended these theaters. Bowen, along with other reformers, worried about the effect the theaters had in drawing children, especially girls, into vice-ridden sections of the city, where rooming houses, gambling dens, and saloons lined the streets.[61]

Reformers such as Bowen and Jane Addams recognized the importance of recreation and mass amusement to urban residents, particularly children, and they sought regulation of these spaces as one means to overcome their association with "vice." According to Addams: "'Going to the show' for thousands of young people in every industrial city is the only possible road to the realms of mystery and romance; the theater is the only place where they can satisfy that craving for a conception of life higher than that which the actual world offers them."[62]

Addams and others stressed the importance of providing alternatives to the cheap theaters that were such an ever-present component of working-class life. Along with Bowen, Edith Abbott, and Sophonisba Breckinridge, she sought to promote "safety" within these settings and "protection" for the city's youth. After offering surveys and investigations into social conditions in "vice" districts, they looked to the state to act on the evidence and provide the appropriate conditions under which these establishments could continue operating. Addams, Abbott, and Breckinridge fought for and won policies that regulated the age of those who could attend the theater, as well as legislation that made school attendance mandatory for youth, thereby keeping youngsters away from illicit entertainment during the day.[63]

These calls for increasing the power of municipal government to regulate leisure activity resulted directly from women's activism. Jane Addams captured the important role women volunteers played in expanding the realm of municipal politics in her praise of the work of the JPA. She argued that the JPA embodied the "new compunction in regard to the civic protection of youth" and that the association "has been able to count upon the cooperation of public-spirited women, when, true to its origin of a voluntary committee supplementing the work of a public court, it has continually induced public authorities to assume new obligations."[64] This redefinition of government function occurred even before women won the right to vote in municipal elections in Illinois in 1913, suggesting how urban politics could be transformed outside the realm of the ballot box and city hall.

Female reformers became vocal proponents of developing parks to counter the lure of the theater and dance hall. Their desire to promote spaces for active recreation, especially for youth, underscored the continued existence of competing notions of the meaning of parks and recreation in progressive reform. Indeed, some park proponents continued to call for pastoral landscapes similar to those in the large parks, while others emphasized the need for children's playgrounds. Charles S. Sargent, editor of *Garden and Forest,* argued, "No mere playground can serve the purpose of recreation in this truer, broader sense—the purpose of refreshment, of renewal of life and strength for body and soul alike. The truest value of public pleasure grounds for large cities is in the rest they give to eyes and mind, to heart and soul, through the soothing charm, the fresh and inspiring influence, the impersonal, unexciting pleasure which nothing but the works of Nature can offer to man."[65]

Jane Addams, Henry C. Foreman, president of the South Park Board, and J. Frank Foster, superintendent of the South Parks system, disagreed. According to Addams, "If there is to be any conflict as to which use shall be made of the land, there is no doubt at all in my mind that it should be decided in favor of the playgrounds. The adults can get almost as much good out of playgrounds as the children, while the children cannot get the good from the parks. If the grass and trees are to be carefully preserved the children must still be made to play in the streets."[66] Foreman said of working-class communities, "This is a population that by heredity requires recreation. By tradition, as well as by instinct, pleasant occupation out of working and sleeping hours is necessary for its physical and moral health, for its happiness and for its contentment."[67] Foster agreed, and he drew up plans for playgrounds with pools, gymnasiums, field houses, ball fields, and tennis courts that were later implemented in the playgrounds.[68]

This call for playgrounds reflected a growing movement among urban residents to recognize the benefits of strenuous activity. Psychologist G. Stanley Hall was extremely influential in the playground movement as he linked the importance of play to advances in social psychology. He stressed the role of play in childhood development in his recapitulation theory, which argued that as children advance through distinct stages of life they recapitulate the evolutionary development of the species. He argued that play enabled children to replicate precivilized activities and therefore aided in cognitive development and moral character formation.[69] Reformers like Jane Addams agreed, arguing that when a boy plays he "unconsciously uses ancient war-cries in his street play."[70] Like advocates of intercollegiate athletics, these reformers tied physical exercise to intellectual growth and social well-being. Moreover, this rhetoric placed most emphasis on children, reflecting the belief in the importance of linking nature and nurture throughout physical and psychological development.

Sophonisba P. Breckinridge and Edith Abbott also emphasized the importance of play in the lives of children, from the perspective of concerns over delinquency. Both women earned doctorates from the University of Chicago (working under the guidance of Marion Talbot), and they headed the Department of Social Investigation at the Chicago School of Civics and Philanthropy. Like Charles S. Deneen, they linked juvenile delinquency directly to the problem of "delinquent neighborhoods." After surveying the variety of environmental factors that contributed to delinquency, from crowding to lack of accessible spaces for wholesome recreation, they mapped the location of homes of all delinquent children who became wards of the Juvenile Court between 1899 and 1909. Their solution, a call for recreational spaces like parks and playgrounds, reflected many of the themes structuring the playground movement. "The essentials of satisfying play suggest themselves at once," they explained. "Muscular effort, giving exercise to a growing body; associated effort, giving facility in social relationships; effort directed towards a purpose demanding preparation and planning, giving scope to the developing human need of consciously seeking an end; the presence of a certain degree of real or apparent risk, giving opportunity to the growing demand for a chance to show his prowess in the case of the boy, or a chance for service in the case of the girl."[71] The need for physical exertion, for association, for conscientious planning, and for different social roles for men and women all captured the progressive ideals of the organized play movement and its larger role in promoting civic culture.

The first American playground was a small sandlot in Boston, created by the Massachusetts Emergency and Hygiene Association after entreaties by Dr. Marie Zakerzewska, who saw similar play spaces in Berlin. In 1894 Hull House opened the first city playground in Chicago, which became a model for playgrounds across the country. It was built after Florence Kelley, leading labor reformer and Hull House resident, wrote an exposé in a local newspaper about a rundown tenement next to Hull House, including the name of the owner, William Kent. Kent came to inspect his property and found conditions so deplorable that he razed the building and donated the space to Hull House for a playground. It included swings, a maypole, and a sandpile, along with spaces for handball and softball.[72] The University of Chicago Settlement, Chicago Commons, and the Northwestern University Settlement soon followed. Along with supervised play activities, the settlement playgrounds also organized traditional ethnic games based on the nationalities of local residents. Settlement playgrounds, then, became spaces where the value of play could be linked both to socialization and to the preservation of ethnic identity.[73]

Settlements clearly linked the social value of recreation directly to the educative value of play. Luther Gulick Jr., head of the Playground Association of America (PAA), founded in 1906, drew a connection between lessons learned on the playground and larger processes of socialization. Much like the proponents of athletics in higher education, Gulick believed that the benefits of structured play transcended the playground and would become valuable life lessons. According to Gulick, "In a well-managed playground . . . the little children playing on the sand pile learn fundamental lessons in mutual rights. . . . They learn that the social unit is larger than the individual unit.[74] University of Chicago sociologist Charles Zueblin agreed with Gulick about the educative role of playgrounds. He argued, "Children's playgrounds are as necessary as schools to the welfare of the modern community. The idea that the public interest in the child ceases at the close of the school session has to be abandoned in the contemporary city."[75]

Proponents of playgrounds also suggested that they should be intimately connected with the public schools, in terms of both supervision and location. To that end, Dwight Perkins and the Special Park Commission proposed making existing schoolyards year-round playgrounds. Perkins encouraged the City Council to join the efforts at creating new parks and playgrounds in Chicago directly to larger efforts at public education. In the *Report of the Special Park Commission* he argued, "Your Commission believes that this practice of depriving school children in the areas of congested population of a healthy and rational outlet for their energies should be stopped. Schools and open-air playgrounds in any enlightened scheme of education should go hand in hand."[76] He suggested that the Board of Education acquire playground sites adjacent to schools wherever possible. He explained, "Playgrounds are essentially educational; in fact they are the basis of the development of children, and should therefore come under the board of education rather than under park supervision."[77] The City Council first appropriated funds for playgrounds in 1898, with $1,000 going to operate six playgrounds under the auspices of the Board of Education. In 1899 the $100,000 City Council appropriation for parks also contributed to purchasing land and equipment for playgrounds.[78]

The success of small playgrounds led to the creation of the PAA, founded by Gulick (a missionary's son and YMCA worker), Henry Curtis (a student of G. Stanley Hall's), and Joseph Lee (the founder of Massachusetts Civic League, which was funded by the Russell Sage Foundation and published the journal *Playground*).[79] When the PAA decided to hold its first annual convention in Chicago in 1907, President Theodore Roosevelt, a proponent of "the strenuous life," issued a public statement suggesting that municipalities send representatives to the conference "to see the magnificent system that Chicago has erected in its South Park district, one of the most notable civic achievements of any American city."[80]

Titles of the papers presented at the meeting illustrated the links between recreation, hygiene, public education, and democracy: "Play as a School of the Citizen," "Public Recreation and Social Morality," "Relation of Play to Juvenile Delinquency," and "Playgrounds and the Prevention of Tuberculosis."[81] One of the central themes of all of these papers was the increasing role played by municipal government in shaping opportunities for recreation in American cities. As Henry Curtis stated, "A notable tendency this year has been the progress toward municipalization."[82] Numerous educators and reformers wanted to bring recreation under the control of municipal government. According to one report, "In devoting public funds to indoor and outdoor playgrounds, parks, lectures . . . civic leaders recognize that the municipality is not only offering its people something of positive value, but is also counteracting influences which are generally detrimental, and against which only the power of the municipality can effectively work."[83] Much like the female reformers who headed the JPA, the leaders of the playground movement drew a direct connection between the educative value of play and the civic responsibilities of municipal government.

The Special Park Commission worked with the Board of Education both to more closely connect public education and recreation and to increase funding. The Commission identified potential playground sites for the board and then secured the leases for the property. Yet the commissioners also argued that leasing properties was not the ultimate goal. They pointed to numerous instances in which some schools, especially parochial ones, withdrew lease options because they needed the land for expansion. The Commission declared that the city should purchase land, rather than lease it, so that these park and playground spaces would remain free and open to the public and not be taken away once schools determined they needed the land. Playground development and land acquisition for parks, the Commission argued, needed to go hand in hand.[84]

THE LOCATION AND DESIGN OF THE SMALL PARKS AND PLAYGROUNDS

By 1900 the Special Park Commission had established five small parks and had assumed the cost of maintaining a sixth (three were on city property and three on property leased from philanthropists). After the City Council's 1901 decision to decrease the Commission's annual budget of $100,000 to a total of $11,500, the Commission began working with the three existing park commissions to use the limited budget more efficiently. The three park boards had already begun establishing neighborhood parks using funding secured from the state of Illinois and its existing parks bill.[85]

The Commission also sought to use its powers of issuing bonds, provided in the 1899 legislation, to capture additional funding. The taxing system for the small parks reflected park planners' belief that these parks benefited the entire city despite their primary function as neighborhood leisure spaces. The Special Park commissioners argued that any bond issue put forward by one of the three existing park commissions would be restricted to use for small parks rather than for maintaining or expanding existing large parks. In addition, the tax would be paid by all residents in the district of the park board, "without the imposition of special assessment on abutting land."[86] The commissioners pointed out that while small parks were intended for use by people living within a radius of one mile, nonetheless all residents in the district were the beneficiaries of these parks in much the same way that all residents supposedly benefited from the existence of the large parks, even if they did not make regular use of them.

In 1903 Henry G. Foreman, president of the South Park Commission, worked in conjunction with aldermen and Chicago newspapers to amend the park bill and appropriate $1,000,000 for additional park sites on the South Side. Newspaper editorials extolling the virtues of parks pointed to a variety of benefits that would result from increased park space. Supporters argued that the new parks would serve as "breathing spots for sweltering humanity." They would "save hundreds of infant lives and the lives of their mothers in the heated spell."[87] At the same time, they would help increase the real estate value of land in the vicinity of the parks. According to one account, buying additional park land was the best investment Chicagoans could make. "There are thousands of vacant acres in the vicinity of Chicago now offered at extremely low prices. To absorb this land for park purposes would add 25 to 50 per cent to all the rest of the land in the vicinity of that taken for parks."[88] The bond issue was approved by the state legislature and won overwhelming voter support, passing with nearly 80 percent of the vote.[89]

Site selection for the new parks was a paramount concern.[90] The Special Park Commission was clear in its guidelines about where parks should be located based on congestion, infant mortality, and lack of access to recreation. In 1902, though, the West Park Commission initially sought alternative sites, and there were charges that these changes in location were the result of bribery and corruption. After several newspaper exposés, it reverted to the suggestions of the Special Park Commission. According to one account, the West Park Commission was being put on notice, since residents reported that "the board tacks better when it is being looked at or even yelped at."[91] South Park commissioner Daniel F. Crilly charged that several prominent real estate men in the city had approached him with bribes to vote in favor of certain park sites. Crilly made these claims in several newspapers, and the state's attorney's office called for a grand jury investigation into the charges. Crilly, however, refused to supply the names, and the matter was dropped before a grand jury was appointed.[92]

These controversies illustrate how park development, despite its support from multiple sectors within Chicago, became a source of political division as well as unity. In designing the parks, the commissioners sought to include amenities for all groups so

FIGURE 34. McKinley Park swimming pool. Courtesy of the Chicago Park District Special Collections.

that controversy could be resolved. Indeed, the proponents of parks believed that the parks alleviated political controversy and corruption and helped create new models of citizenship and civic renewal to which all groups in the city would aspire.

McKinley Park, near the Stockyards district, at Archer and Western, was the first neighborhood park of the South Park Commission (fig. 34). The thirty-four-acre site comprised open prairie and cabbage patches and was previously home to the Brighton Park Race Track. Designers sought to use both playground and park ideals in its design (fig. 34). Henry Foreman emphasized this combination of park and play spaces in his dedication address for the park opening on June 13, 1903. He welcomed residents to the newest "pleasure ground" and listed its many facilities, including a ball field, tennis courts, gymnasium, swimming pool, showers and dressing rooms, and sand beaches, as well as "a dense growth of shrubbery."[93] The placement and planting of the trees and shrubs made parkgoers feel removed from the city's crowding. At the same time, the playground plan reflected an understanding of the contours of urban play and recreation. The final plan for the park represented a merger of the visions of the planners and reformers with the demands of the working-class residents of the neighborhood, who pushed for active play spaces for their children. McKinley Park became a model for other parks, including Sherman Park (fig. 35); it was seen by reformers and politicians as an effective arena of civic culture, since it promoted family leisure and regulated play.

In addition to integrating play facilities with parkland, park advocates pushed for the creation of field houses to serve as neighborhood centers.[94] Mary McDowell stressed the need to provide for adults as well as children and to promote civic pride in both:

> In the neighborhoods where the industrial pressure is hardest, life is apt to be a struggle ten hours every day simply for food, clothes, and shelter. Here people eat and sleep, and the average gain some small relief from the monotony of modern machine driven industry by drinking themselves into another state of being, or by going once a week to the theater, where, for a small outlay, they are helped into another sphere of life at least an hour. . . . The play and social instinct has very little chance in most crowded districts except in the opportunities offered by the saloon or dance hall.[95]

She pointed out that "the social education of a community is a natural and essential department" of the business of park boards. "Would ward politics be cleaner if meetings were held in the field house, or the public school hall? Will they ever be cleaner if kept in the atmosphere of the saloon and the gambling room?" The field house, she argued, was the best setting for reinvigorating civic culture in the city. "Let the field house be the symbol of a civic home of the citizens. Let them go there for refreshment of mind and body, and feel free to discuss under its roof any question of interest to the whole neighborhood, or to the smaller group."[96] Parks and playgrounds, according to McDowell, would replace saloons, ward halls, and even council chambers as sites of democratic politics, thereby linking the physical and the social education of citizens.

Here McDowell articulated the notion of an expanding public sphere with alternative sites of civic participation being keys to creating democratic political culture. The physical setting, she believed, could recast the civic sensibilities of all who entered. While field houses were controlled settings, they nonetheless offered greater public access to the political arena by redefining its physical features.

The planning of the smaller parks conformed to these ideas of a civic landscape. To design the fourteen South Side parks proposed by the Special Park Commission, the

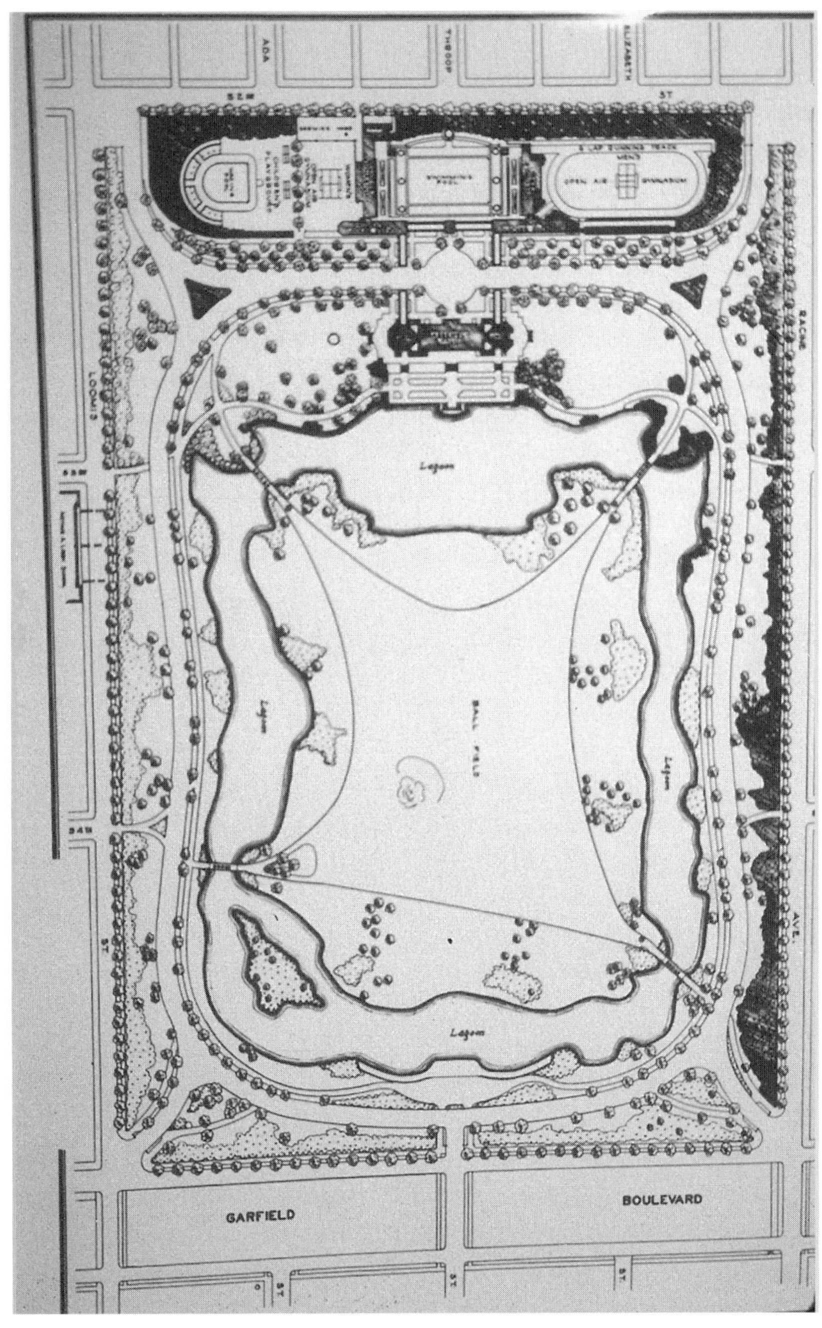

FIGURE 35. South Park Commission design for Sherman Park. Courtesy of the Chicago Park District Special Collections.

South Park Commission hired the firms of Burnham and Olmsted, which had collaborated on the World's Fair. Edward Bennett, a new draftsman in Burnham's firm, would design the field houses, and Olmsted's firm, now run by his son, Frederick Law Jr., and his stepson John, would plan the landscape design. Their contract called for the development of six squares of less than ten acres each and eight small parks, ranging from twenty-eight to fifty-six acres. J. Frank Foster, the superintendent of the South Park system who conceptualized the parks, drew up prototype plans for ten-acre parks and presented them to John C. Olmsted in 1903.[97]

The typical square was rectangular, working with the existing plat plan of the city. The field house was symmetrically placed on one side of the rectangular plot; to one side of the field house was the men's outdoor gym, and on the other side was the women and children's outdoor gym, which often included a wading pool. Davis Square, which opened on May 13, 1905, at Forty-fifth and Marshfield in the Stockyards district, served as a model, with a swimming pool, wading pool, field house, and large tree-ringed play field along the central axis of the six-acre park (fig. 36). The field house contained gymnasiums, bathrooms, reading rooms, a library, a restaurant, and club rooms that could be used by neighborhood residents "for any purpose other than for political or religious meetings," suggesting that the space was meant to transcend party politics and religious difference.[98]

The opening ceremonies at Davis Square illustrated the park's multiple civic roles. Close to four thousand people from the Stockyards district attended the festivities, many of them, especially the children, dressed in patriotic garb. Children from neighborhood schools kicked off the dedication by singing "America" and then "citing the civic creed." Next came the raising of the American flag and a color guard salute. After these patriotic ceremonies, there were athletic drills executed first by the Bohemian Turner Society and then by the Polish Turner Society. In addition, the kindergarten class of Seward School presented a maypole dance. Mary McDowell and the residents of the University of Chicago Settlement oversaw all of the day's activities.[99]

Henry G. Foreman, former president of the South Park Commission, spoke at the evening ceremonies and expressed his hopes for the new park and field house. His speech focused on the civic role of parks that he and other reformers envisioned. He said he understood how hard residents of this district worked to support their families and that they wanted something better for their children. The park would help families help themselves. "Come and take a bath or a swim. Come and see the flowers and trees. . . . . If there is something about this district that you don't like, call a meeting in this big room and come over here and talk about it. Decide what you think is

FIGURE 36. Davis Square swimming area. Courtesy of the Chicago Park District Special Collections.

best and then try to get it."[100] For Foreman and other park advocates, providing the physical spaces for neighborhood interaction simultaneously promoted deliberative democracy and conscientious planning.

The designs of these small parks and squares differed radically from the shape of the large pleasure grounds created during the Gilded Age. Rather than subverting the urban street grid, they conformed to it. Similarly, instead of designing meandering, curved pathways throughout the space, park planners created symmetrical spatial patterns that reinforced the geometry of the city. Paradoxically, while the scale of park planning was much smaller in this design scheme, the urban vision it expressed was more clearly linked to the large-scale, comprehensive urban planning being developed at this time by Burnham and Bennett. The small park planners, then, were more conscious of the park as an integral feature of the urban landscape, embedding it in the layout of the city and blurring the separation between the "natural" and the built environment.

This is not to say that park planners made no attempt to integrate "natural" elements into the park design. In addition to providing athletic facilities, the park commissioners mandated that the small parks leave some room for pastoral plantings. Indeed, arguments over how to do so reflected the continued tension between older ideas about urban landscape design and more recent conceptions of efficient use of space for reform. The Olmsteds, of course, preferred more landscaped areas, but they worked within the perimeters of the park layout to vary the landscape designs. They noted that despite the similarities in size and shape of the playground lots—all between five and nine acres and all but one laid out according to the Chicago grid—each design should be unique. Some variation could come from depressing the ball field where land was generally lower than surrounding streets, leaving off a fence if bordering streets were not highly traveled, centering buildings on sites where ground was higher than surrounding streets, or adding diagonal walkways across fields if there was heavy pedestrian traffic. Using different shrub and tree varieties in plantings also added individuality to the squares.[101]

Edward Bennett's designs for the field houses complemented the symmetry of the landscape design. The field houses and gymnasiums were "symmetrically organized and classically detailed," for Bennett argued that though modern commercial style may be appropriate for the private sector, "classical elements are best for the public realm."[102] The exterior of the buildings was off-white, rough-cast concrete, with green-gray tiled roofs and red-stained eaves. Molded concrete detailing continued on the interior of field houses.[103] For Bennett, classical style in civic architecture redefined the aesthetic sensibilities of urban residents. "The effect of a good building, in which an untrained boy studies or plays, is far more insidious than is that of some imposing, but remote public monuments," argued Bennett. "Such surroundings cannot fail in the long run to make for higher standard of public and private taste."[104]

In order to have the desired civic effects, play and recreation needed to be ordered and controlled. As a result, park and playground developers stressed efficient spatial arrangements in playgrounds. Apparatus had to be in enclosed areas so boys could be properly supervised and to alleviate the influence of gangs (fig. 37).[105] Similarly, all squares originally were enclosed with iron picket fences, while similar barriers separated men's, women's, and children's spaces, making policing the grounds easier.[106] This emphasis on highly structured spaces underscored the park commissioners' belief in order and regulation. It also exposed the tension in reform ideology between a belief in the reforming and restorative power of the physical landscape, which would provide a

FIGURE 37. Mark White Square, showing play apparatus. Courtesy of the Chicago Park District Special Collections.

natural arena of civic pride and political engagement, and the need for more overt supervision to ensure conformity to prescriptions for respectability.

Further evidence of this tension can be seen in the introduction of trained supervisors to control activities in the play spaces. "When the people of the city furnish money for the establishment of a small park or public playground," argued one reformer, "they have done no more than half of a very important civic work."[107] "Parks," said another, "should be managed by wise and public-spirited men who have high ideals and who will strive to gradually and considerably improve the public taste."[108] In addition, letters from E. B. DeGroot, director of recreation, to employees of the South Park District, stressed the role supervisors could play in inculcating loyalty, discipline, and order.[109]

The call for trained play supervisors reflected the increasingly close relationship between progressive ideas about expertise and the centrality of trained experts in shaping municipal government. In the 1910 report of the Special Park Commission, superintendent of playgrounds Theodore A. Gross called for the Civil Service Commission to create the position of "playground attendant" so that play supervisors would come from the "skilled service class" and bring with them the expertise he believed was necessary for the job. He complained that "the laborers employed in the playgrounds are sometimes called upon to act as directors and assume the responsibility of supervision during the absence of the directors." He argued that creating the position of playground attendant through the Civil Service secured "a higher grade of service than is secured from the unskilled labor lists."[110]

Mary McDowell extended the call for supervised recreation to the field house. "To make sure that the field house will be a center for the promotion of the higher civic and social life of the community, it is necessary that the management should be up to the standard at least of the physical directorship. The manager needs to be more than a janitor or a clerk. He or she should be the equal of a head resident of a settlement, or the principal of a school." She stressed the importance of properly trained leaders in creating the most effective public forums and spoke of the need to employ paid, trained social workers chosen by civil service standards of merit in the public parks and field houses.[111]

The call for trained play supervisors at parks and field houses provided an avenue for securing municipal jobs for women trained as social workers in institutions like the University of Chicago. Settlement workers, for example, were models for play supervisors, since they had the training as well as experience to directly engage a variety of neighborhood groups to promote social engagement and civic education. Female reformers also called for women police in a variety of settings throughout the city, including parks. Louise de Koven Bowen argued that female police officers were necessary to safeguard the well-being of women and children in the city. She stated, "We need women police to chaperone the girls in all public places where the danger to young people is great." She made a plea for women police officers in theaters and dance halls, amusement parks, municipal courts, and especially parks and playgrounds.[112] Her call for more female officers reflected the way the new parks and playgrounds necessarily expanded women's public role in the city. It was precisely because these new public spaces of leisure attracted women as well as men that women in positions of authority needed a greater presence.

Many park proponents argued that the viability of the parks largely depended on the skills of their supervisors. Reformers used attendance figures to demonstrate the high level of use of the small parks and playgrounds, thereby suggesting the widespread effectiveness of their programs for civic improvement. During six months in 1906, hundreds of thousands of residents used the amenities of the ten South Side parks: 272,804 people used the indoor gyms; 285,680 the showers; and 416,105 the pools. Close to 1 million visited the outdoor gyms; and 14,403 attended the physical exercise classes. The total population of the South Side was approximately 700,000, and even assuming a high degree of repeat visitors, these figures suggest extensive park use.[113]

An article in the journal *Park and Cemetery* took these high attendance figures as evidence of the success of the parks. "The liberal use of the different facilities as shown by the reports of the Superintendent and Director of Athletics confirms the faith the Commissioners had in the benefits that would come from the installation of neighborhood center buildings, with their accessories, gymnasia, baths, reading rooms, assembly halls and branches of public libraries."[114] Another commissioner's report stated, "One cannot read our statistical records and attempt to measure their relation to the civic problems of the day without a feeling of the most serious responsibility. Such aggregations of people are as represented in the figures given herewith may not be expected to come and go without receiving definite impressions and without acting and reacting upon one another for good or evil. The very nature of the associations makes for positive rather than negative influences."[115]

WORKING-CLASS INITIATIVE AND PARK USE

Yet using the facilities did not necessarily mean people subscribed to all the ideas put forward by park advocates. For example, many working-class park users objected to the high degree of regulation in park spaces. These tensions came to a head in 1905, when the South Park Commission instituted plans to put fences around the large Jackson and Washington Parks. Park commissioners argued that they needed to eliminate improper uses of the parks, including gang activity, fighting, and public drunkenness, and that fences would make the park police more effective. One supporter of fences argued, "The result of [unenclosed parks] is that some of the parks have become worse than useless. Their beautiful recesses, from being places of rest and recreation and aesthetic enjoyment, have become scenes of crime and debauchery." He recognized that some might disagree with his assessment but added, "They are either people who are deficient in common sense or people who wish to visit the parks for indecent or immoral purposes."[116]

Many neighborhood residents felt differently. They presented a petition to the South Park Commission with twelve thousand signatures opposing the fences. Working-class residents joined with ministers, professionals, and reform groups to end the plan. One signer stated, "I appeal to the common sense of the people of Chicago; that this artificial arrangement is an abomination and utterly un-American. For the love of beauty, for the rights of the passer-by and dweller-by, and the freedom of movement of all, spread out the parks like beautiful carpets, unhampered and as open as possible."[117]

Members of the Chicago Woman's Club raised similar objections, arguing, "Our parks belong to the people, and should serve their uses in the most convenient way. . . . The management of these public pleasure grounds should be in a broad and democratic spirit."[118] As a result of these protests, the fence plan was dropped. This confrontation reflected the tension between some reformers' desire to promote well-ordered and regulated public spaces and others' (especially working-class groups and female reformers) notions of parks as arenas of shared civic culture, with all citizens, regardless of ethnic or neighborhood background, entitled to equal access.

One of the park advocates' central themes was the need to create spaces that transcended local antagonisms and ethnic differences, serving as centers of public life and recreation for a broad-based community. The rise of mass industrialization and the resulting large-scale ethnic migration created a heterogeneous urban culture, and with it the potential for ethnic and racial conflict. Ethnic communities formed social organizations like German turners and Bohemian sokols that combined the promotion of religious and cultural heritage with recreation and youth activities. However, separate ethnic athletic clubs often led to ethnic and territorial conflict.

One resident of the Back of the Yards, F. D. Posley, recalled the turf delineations in his community. "If you've ever lived back of the yards, you've heard of Hamburg. And of course, if you've heard of Hamburg, you've heard of Canaryville. Hamburg ran from 31st to 40th. And south of 40th was Canaryville. [S]ometimes—on Saturday nights—there was mutual thirst. And the broken noses and black eyes that were seen the following Sunday were too numerous to count."[119] Both of these groups were Irish, and the sharp divisions between them illustrated the significance of both ethnic difference and spatial separation in creating one's sense of one's place in the urban landscape.

Racial antagonisms were even more violent than ethnic ones and also were tied to spatial relations. White gangs terrorized African Americans who tried to use the parks and recreation facilities on the boundary between the Black Belt east of Wentworth Avenue and the Irish and Polish sections to the west. At Armour Square and Fuller Park, sites of frequent clashes, black youths were assaulted even when accompanied by adults. According to the play director at Armour Square, "I have never gone out to do any promotional work to bring [Negroes] in because I would not choose personally to be responsible for the things that would happen outside my gates if I were responsible for bringing large groups into Armour Square."[120] Similarly, when blacks attempted to use the baseball fields in Washington Park, they were subjected to widespread abuse and often were chased from the fields by white gangs. This violence would culminate in the 1919 race riot, precipitated by members of Ragen's Colts, one of the most infamous athletic clubs in the city.[121]

Reformers like McDowell believed that trained play supervisors in the parks could counter these episodes of racial antagonism. Guiding recreation and maintaining surveillance of the parks, they argued, could overcome gang activity, leading to more harmonious racial relations. The 1909 *Annual Report of the Special Park Commission,* for example, described a relay race in which all the playgrounds entered teams. Playground supervisors oversaw the competition and ensured the participation of blacks and whites alike. An image of the relay races included in the report featured the caption, "A Study in Black and White, with No Color Line Drawn."[122] Despite their best efforts, however, play supervisors could not counter the threats blacks encountered when they attempted to use park facilities on occasions other than officially sponsored events.

This lack of access was the direct result of the absence of parks and field houses in predominantly black areas. A study by the Chicago Commission on Race Relations, the body charged with investigating the 1919 race riot, found that of the 127 places of recreation in the city (excluding the large parks), 37 were in or near black areas (fig. 38). Yet the commission noted that these numbers did not accurately reflect black access to play areas. "Though these figures seem to indicate that the Negro areas are fairly well supplied with recreation facilities," the report noted, "it should be borne in mind that their use by the Negroes in their vicinity is by no means free and undisputed." The report found, for example, that most of the facilities in or near black neighborhoods were playgrounds adjacent to public schools. By contrast, there were no recreation centers (parks with field houses) in black areas. The report argued that the recreation center was "the most unusual and notable feature of Chicago's recreation system but one from which the Negro gets little benefit."[123] These sites, celebrated as arenas of civic engagement and cross-ethnic alliance, were off-limits to blacks. As a result, commercial leisure venues within the boundaries of the narrowly circumscribed Black Belt would become more significant than city parks as places where community identity and civic awareness were forged.

The expression of ethnic identities in the parks did not just take the form of violence against other groups. Rather, parks helped create a sense of community in working-class immigrant districts and provided a place for creation of public spheres. Poles regularly held local meetings in the field house at Sherman Park and staged rallies and celebrations to honor Polish heroes.[124] Members of the Bohemian Women's

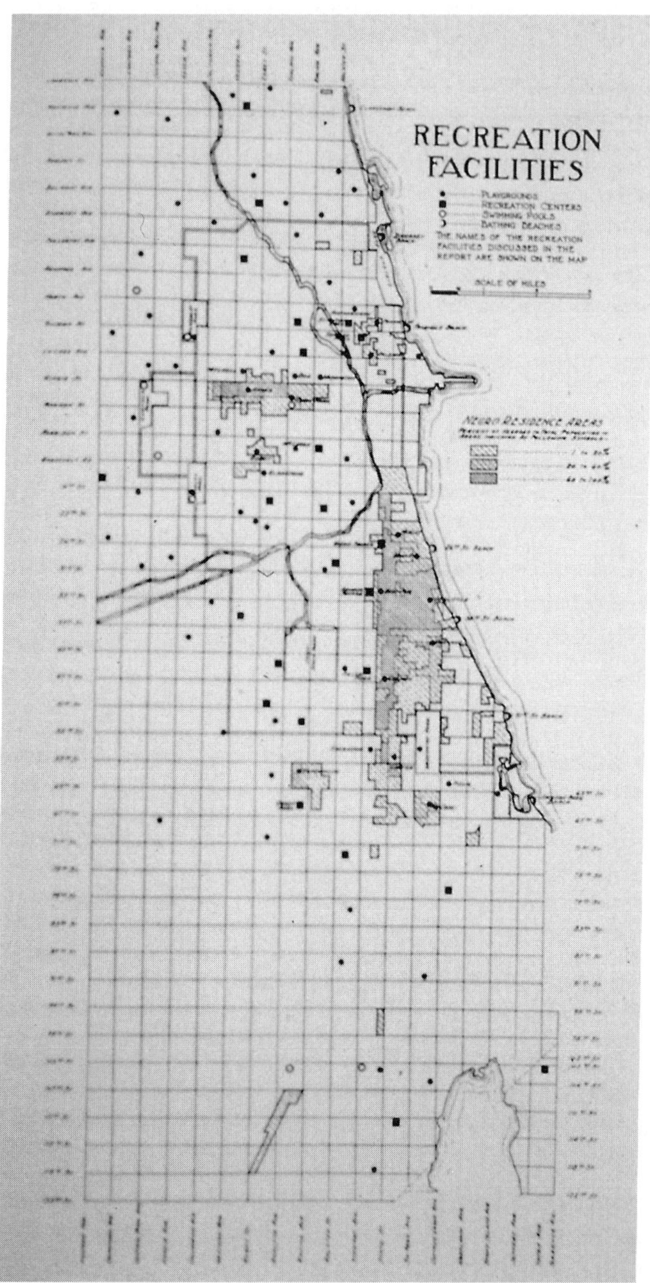

FIGURE 38. "Recreation Facilities." Chicago Commission on Race Relations, *The Negro in Chicago* (Chicago: University of Chicago Press, 1922), facing 272.

Club taught courses in Bohemian culture, history, and the Czech language both at the Davis Square field house and at the University of Chicago Settlement.[125] Similarly, Paul Cressy, a University of Chicago sociologist who studied dance halls and gangs in the Stockyards district, pointed to McKinley Park as a model of civic participation and public spirit. "Here much of the social and recreational life of the area centers. . . . Here meet the various Lithuanian and Polish societies and local associations, while dances are given in the community hall by many different [ethnic] organizations."[126]

Gaelic Park, in the largely Irish section of Bridgeport, became the home of various ethnic displays as well as ethnic intermingling. On Friday and Saturday evenings youths from surrounding communities came to use its dance pavilion. A study of the park indicated that the girls and boys came from a variety of backgrounds. Poles, Bohemians, Lithuanians, and Irish came to the dances and mingled freely. On Sundays, though, "no one save people of Irish lineage is to be found in the grounds." Activities included "Irish jigs and the Irish quadrille" on one side of the park. On the other side, the large pavilion was reserved for "American" dancing. "Here," the study explained, "the young people who are 'Americanized' dance in the 'American' way."[127] Within one space, then, the goals of ethnic mingling, preservation of ethnic tradition, and Americanization could all take place.

Immigrants also sought to infuse their neighborhood parks with a sense of ethnic identity by naming them. The South Park Commission selected park names largely to commemorate the leading lights of Chicago history, politics, and industry. Parks were named for meatpacker Philip D. Armour, Hyde Park developer Paul Cornell, first mayor of Chicago William Ogden, and leading industrialist and philanthropist Potter Palmer, among others. Yet some residents protested "perpetuat[ing] the names of a few local millionaires" for lands that were paid for with public funds. They argued that park names should more closely reflect the neighborhoods where they were situated. Residents in the Sherman Park neighborhood, for example, suggested that the park be named for General Richard Montgomery, an Irishman who distinguished himself in the Revolutionary War. While this campaign ultimately failed, it illustrates how ethnic residents of park districts sought to establish a greater sense of ownership of the parks in their neighborhoods.[128]

Ethnic groups also sought to add statues and memorials to parks as visible symbols of their role in structuring recreation and community activities within immigrant neighborhoods. In 1908, members of the Bohemian community of Pilsen began raising funds for a statue to honor Karel Havilcek, a hero of Czech history. The monument committee requested that the West Park commissioners let them place the monument in Douglas Park, one of the parks run by that board. The permit was granted on condition that the monument would "benefit the public."[129] By 1911 the necessary funds had been raised and the monument was ready for dedication. The ceremony illustrated how neighborhood parks became staging grounds both for expressions of ethnic identity and for celebration of civic unity. The events began with a parade through Pilsen attended by thousands. Leading the parade were the sokols, along with benevolent societies, Bohemian lodges, and the Pilsen district Butchers' Association. Parade attendants were dressed in native costume and sang celebratory songs in Czech to honor the day. Czech speakers emphasized the importance of the day in honoring Havilcek. After the statue was unveiled, Governor Charles Deneen took the platform. Deneen equated Havilcek's struggles with the struggles for freedom that America represented. "When we honor Havilcek, we honor the principles for which he and other patriots of all ages and nations fought." He ended his speech with a plea for all Chicagoans to "learn real patriotism" from a man like Havilcek. "Not only Czechs, but all Americans," Deneen argued, "can learn from Havilcek's examples."[130]

This infusing of parks with elements of ethnic history and culture showed the multiple roles they served in promoting civic culture. Where park promoters often saw parks as vehicles for overcoming ethnic difference, immigrant groups viewed them as spaces to celebrate ethnic affiliation. That these celebrations often took place with the approval and sanction of park authorities further underscored that ethnic identity and Americanization were not at odds. For many ethnic groups, as well as for reformers like Addams and McDowell, celebration of ethnic traditions and Americanization went hand in hand. Parks were spaces where these seemingly contradictory processes could be negotiated.

Public parks became important sites both for expressing ethnic solidarity and for promoting Americanization during World War I. In September 1914 Czechs held a war relief rally in Pilsen Park to raise donations "for our fighting and needy brothers."[131] The same park, and many others, also became home to military drills during the war, along with innumerable parades and patriotic rallies. Field houses incorporated more English classes and civics courses into their programs. Yet the war raised serious questions about how far practices of ethnic solidarity would be acceptable, in urban public parks and elsewhere. Rising nativism and anti-immigrant sentiment led many American leaders to question the loyalty of recent immigrants. Despite pointing out that they had held war bond rallies and Fourth of July celebrations at neighborhood parks, many ethnic groups in Chicago—not just Germans, but also Czechs and Poles—found themselves the targets of slander and intimidation. In response to this rising climate of suspicion, Mary McDowell, for one, defended the practice of using public parks to instill connections to ethnic tradition, history, and language. She argued, "Our efforts should be directed first toward allowing immigrant children to learn to make use of the culture of the native land of their parents, and then, when they are growing up, to acquaint them in their own language with American history and customs. Too hasty Americanization of children makes young rowdies of them, thus creating a more serious danger than is presented by the problem of parents who do not know English."[132] Despite this spirited defense, however, during and after World War I park promoters increasingly staged events promoting "Americanization" rather than celebrating immigrant culture.

Reformers and residents of working-class communities often worked together to alleviate some of the difficult living conditions plaguing these neighborhoods. Frequently, they used the rhetoric of Americanism to push for improved conditions for workers. One Polish worker in the Back of the Yards discussed his frustration with the economic plight of fellow workers and its effect on children. "You know that you can't give your children an American living; you can't send them to school and give them what they ought to have; you can't have a decent American home on fifteen and one-half cents an hour and only forty hours a week the year round."[133] Mary McDowell agreed with this call for fair-minded industrial democracy, and she worked with the unions to promote better conditions and wages. She also argued that the recent child labor law limiting working hours for children had "given the child too much leisure time but nothing to do." Ethnic community leaders and Anglo reformers looked to programs in the parks to alleviate these problems.[134]

Parks became important sites of labor organizing as well. Park workers used the public grounds to stage strikes demanding union recognition and pay increases. In May 1902, five hundred laborers employed in Jackson Park declared a strike after park commissioners refused their demands for pay increases. Police were "held in readiness" to quell any disturbance these strikers might create in the public pleasure grounds.[135] Park employees sent a representative to the meeting of the South Park Board demanding that every department, "even the scrubwomen," be unionized. Led by the teamsters, the park employees demanded higher wages for several departments. The visible presence of strikers in the public parks led the board to settle union appeals and meet all demands.[136]

During the 1904 Stockyards strike, when twenty-two thousand workers walked off the job, strike organizers repeatedly called rallies and organizing drives in neighborhood parks. Chicago Federation of Labor (CFL) president John Fitzpatrick regularly spoke to strikers and their families at rallies in Davis Square. The accessibility of the small neighborhood parks proved essential, giving workers meeting places where all, including family members, could gather daily to plan organizing strategies and generate support for the strikers. By claiming the parks as their own, workers in the Back of the Yards helped forge communal solidarity based on shared notions of class cohesion that, for a time, overcame ethnic differences.

Working-class residents also challenged many of the policies of the park boards when they were at odds with neighborhood needs. For example, the creation of a comprehensive system of outer parks and forest preserves was one of the features of the 1904 report on recommendations. Park advocates argued that conservation and expanding population necessitated linking urban parks with outlying forest areas. John J. Mitchell, president of Illinois Trust and Savings Bank and a member of the Forest Park Commission, challenged those who did not support the park project for financial reasons. "There are other matters which should far outweigh money in the consideration of the forest preserve act—first, civic pride, second, civic duty, third, civic opportunity."[137]

Various labor organizations felt differently. The Chicago Teachers' Federation and the Building Trades Council protested the plan because "this $133,000 per year will be used to maintain pleasure driveways outside of Chicago for rich automobilists, while there are 159 schools in the crowded districts of Chicago having no playgrounds or only insufficient ones."[138] The Building Trades passed a resolution to go on record opposing the forest preserve bill, stating, "Whereas, the great need of Chicago is for small parks in the congested districts, where the children of the poor can come for air and recreation, instead of handsome driveways so far away that they would be accessible only to automobilists, therefore, be it resolved that the Associated Building Trades of Chicago and Cook County hereby condemn the proposed forest preserve act as a scheme in the interest of land speculators and others that wish the handling of the millions of funds."[139] Another laborer wrote, "This is rank injustice, and one of the inevitable results of taxing labor for the benefit of monopoly—a system that everywhere keeps labor poor."[140]

While working-class ethnic residents actively used park programs, they nonetheless maintained a sense of class and ethnic identity that parks and play supervisors could not eradicate. As David Montgomery has noted, "Even where workingmen made extensive use of the language and concepts of middle-class reformers, they infused those concepts with a meaning quite different from what the middle-class had in mind."[141] Working-class city residents sought to create a public sphere that provided beauty, order, and a place for community interaction within an often alienating urban environment. Yet their ideas for the ways to achieve this goal often differed sharply from those of elites and middle-class reformers.

Parks provided public spaces where visible displays of ethnic and working-class visions of a democratic public sphere could be presented. Park workers were able to capitalize on the rhetoric put forth by park proponents as they made their claims for fair treatment and civic recognition. Yet park planners and reformers were curiously silent during these working-class displays. Indeed, many supported the police presence in the parks because union rallies appeared to threaten the "proper and decorous" uses of urban parklands. Others, such as Addams and McDowell, supported the organizing activities of workers through a variety of urban civic and labor organizations like the Women's Trade Union League (WTUL) and the CFL. Indeed, both groups staged several rallies, debates, and lectures in the South Parks, attesting to the ways civic interests could come together in this new arena of political discourse.[142]

Park design went through a transformation, from the early pleasure grounds that emphasized the overall improvement of city life through design of the natural landscape to the Progressive Era program of inscribing city spaces with reformers' ideals for individual improvement through instruction in hygiene and supervised leisure. Urban parks represented a clear manifestation of the progressive faith in science and efficiency as the basis of moral reform that later city planning advocates would draw on. Indeed, park planning was the foundation of the modern city planning emerging in the early twentieth century.[143]

Park planning and park use were integrally linked to public policy, political authority, and urban citizenship. Public displays of political identity, including ethnic rallies, labor organizing, and women's public presence, spoke to the emergence of these groups as central actors on the stage of urban reform. By creating new cultural spaces that acted as public arenas, women and other groups in the city who were traditionally shut out of politics were able to claim new authority in shaping the urban landscape.[144]

Thus, parks were central sites in which contestations over the meanings and uses of public space were played out. Residents had competing visions of the form parks should take and the uses they should be put to. Yet most residents looked to parks as a means of enhancing their neighborhoods and creating accessible public space. By justifying the use of park space for a variety of activities through the language of democracy and citizenship, working-class urban residents, women, ethnic groups, and African Americans could lay claim to their rights as participants in refashioning the urban public sphere.

4

LET YOUR WATCHWORD BE ORDER AND YOUR BEACON BEAUTY

The Burnham Plan and the Civic Lakefront

IN THE SUMMER OF 1909, architect Daniel Burnham and his partner Edward Bennett presented their *Plan of Chicago* to a group of civic and political leaders. Burnham spoke in grandiose terms about the meaning of city planning and its ability to transform the chaos of urban growth into a unified plan of order, rationality, and beauty: "Make no little plans; they have no magic to stir men's blood and probably themselves will not be realized. Make big plans; aim high in hope and work, remembering that a noble diagram once recorded will never die, but long after we are gone will be a living thing. Remember that our sons and grandsons are going to do things that would stagger us. Let your watchword be order and your beacon beauty."[1]

Burnham's call for large-scale design, and the connections between order and beauty, highlighted the central features of the City Beautiful movement in American urban planning. Burnham drew on the design schemes and civic ideals embodied in his plans for the 1893 World's Columbian Exposition to create a model of planning that incorporated all elements of the physical landscape of the modern city into a comprehensive plan (fig. 39). The 1909 Plan codified many of the elements of City Beautiful design that Burnham had begun to articulate during the planning of the White City. It illustrated the links between consolidated planning and urban design, which combined an aesthetic sensibility with practical functionalism. And it stressed the role of the built environment in promoting civic unity and the place of art in shaping civic pride.

FIGURE 39. Court of Honor, World's Columbian Exposition, 1893. Courtesy of the Chicago Historical Society.

Burnham and Bennett drew on the classical imagery of both the Columbian Exposition and the small park field houses for their plan, to create a "well-ordered, convenient, and unified city."[2] By consolidating plans for urban beautification and land use, they argued, civic leaders could use urban lands more efficiently, promote economic growth, and enhance the beauty of the city. The Plan translated the elegance, symmetry, and monumentality of the World's Fair into a realizable plan for an actual city that captured "the progressive spirit of the times."[3]

The Plan also recognized the central role of commercial growth in shaping civic life. The newly consolidated Commercial Club, made up of the older Commercial Club and the Merchants' Club, was the sponsor of the Plan. Both groups comprised the most prominent male businesspeople in Chicago, who saw the creation of comprehensive design schemes for urban development as a means of stimulating commercial growth. Indeed, Burnham assured his sponsors that beauty and financial prosperity went hand in hand. Beautifying the city, he argued, would make Chicago a cosmopolitan city equal to European cities like Paris: "You all know that there is a tendency among our well-to-do people to spend much time and money elsewhere and that this tendency has been rapidly growing in late years. We have been running away to Cairo, Athens, the Riviera, Paris and Vienna, because life at home is not so pleasant as in these fashionable centres."[4] Burnham went on to argue that beautifying Chicago would attract visitors, stimulating the economic growth of the city. "Beauty," he exclaimed, "has always paid better than any other commodity and always will."[5]

This relation between civic design and commercialism would be inscribed on the city through the planning of the City Beautiful. The commodification of art and aesthetics promoted capitalist growth and linked beauty to financial development. According to M. Christine Boyer, planners sought to impose "disciplinary order and ceremonial harmony" on urban growth in order to enhance commercial productivity. The "rational city" of efficiency and technical expertise became a means of expanding the role of the state in order to control land use, and stimulate economic development, and shape urban growth.[6]

At the same time, however, promoters of planning and the City Beautiful movement were uneasy about the relation between beauty, public space, and commerce. While it was clear that the impetus for comprehensive planning came from commercial concerns over real estate values, civic boosterism, and controlled growth, many supporters of the City Beautiful nonetheless were ambivalent about the place commercialism had in the clean, artistic plazas, parks, and squares they hoped to develop. Some urban reform groups saw an inherent contradiction between evidence of commercialism and the civic spirit they wanted to foster in public spaces throughout the city. Like the sponsors of the small parks and playgrounds, promoters of planning and urban beautification argued over the character that public places should take. Should they be devoted to nature and relaxation, or should commercial establishments be allowed to encroach on the space? Was there a way to integrate commercial culture into civic spaces so it would not detract from their overall beauty and aesthetic pleasure? Could reform of the physical landscape be linked to broader social change? Sponsors and supporters of the Plan, as well as its detractors, debated these issues as they tried to make Burnham's vision for a City Beautiful in Chicago one that reflected the interests of all Chicagoans.

CREATING A PUBLIC LAKEFRONT

The lakefront was one of the most significant features of the Chicago landscape. Burnham and Bennett recognized that the shoreline offered numerous opportunities for increased property values, aesthetic enhancement, recreation, and industrial development, and they featured it prominently in their plan. The World's Columbian Exposition, they said, had encouraged Chicagoans to envision future aesthetic improvements throughout the city, including the lakefront: "To the people of Chicago, the dignity, beauty, and convenience of the transitory city in Jackson Park seemed to call for the improvement of the water front of the city."[7] In calling for this enhancement of the lakefront, Burnham and Bennett emphasized preserving the land as a public space, accessible to all people in Chicago:

> The Lake front by right belongs to the people. It affords their one great unobstructed view, stretching away to the horizon, where water and clouds seem to meet. No mountains or high hills enable us to look over broad expanses of the earth's surface; and perforce we must come even to the margin of the Lake for such a survey of nature. These views of a broad expanse are helpful alike to mind and body. They beget calm thoughts and feelings, and afford escape from the petty things in life. . . . Not a foot of its shores should be appropriated by individuals to the exclusion of the people. On the contrary, everything possible should be done to enhance its attractiveness and develop its natural beauties,

> thus fitting it for the part it has to play in the life of the whole city. It should be made so alluring that it will become the fixed habit of the people to seek its restful presence at every opportunity.[8]

This poetic testimonial to the allure of the lake reflects the variety of features that planning proponents articulated as they developed the lakefront pleasure grounds. The opportunity to contemplate the lyric qualities of nature was a central element of plans for the lakefront. Planners like Frederick Law Olmsted believed that peaceful contemplation of natural surroundings helped remove city dwellers from the chaos and disorder of the teeming city, thus contributing to a stable and civilized urban environment. This civilizing effect could be accomplished, though, only if natural spaces were removed from the physical presence of commerce and manufacturing. Like large parks and pleasure grounds, the lakefront became a well-planned natural space that served as an antidote to the stresses of the city. Burnham and Bennett, then, like Olmsted before them, equated nature with the civic realm and sought to make the landscape of the city reflect this division between civic and commercial space.[9]

In creating plans for the lakefront, Burnham and Bennett drew on ideas about the proper uses of lakefront land that had been debated for several decades.[10] As early as 1835 Chicagoans discussed what should be done with the land occupied by Fort Dearborn, the military post established by the federal government during the Blackhawk Indian wars several years earlier. Some prominent Chicago citizens declared that the land, between Lake Michigan and Dearborn Street, and from Madison Street north to the Chicago River, should remain free of commercial development. It should be "reserved in all time to come for a public square, accessible at all times to the people."[11] When the federal government drew up sales maps subdividing the Fort Dearborn land, this block was reserved as public ground, and in 1892 it became the site of the Chicago Public Library.

A second and more important lakefront park south of Madison Street was preserved as public grounds by the three men the state named to construct the shipping canal linking Lake Michigan to the Mississippi River. Gurdon Hubbard, William F. Thornton, and William B. Archer platted the canal in 1836. They declared the strip of land between Michigan Avenue and Lake Michigan and from Madison Street south to Twelfth Street "Public Ground—A Common to Remain Forever Open, Clear and Free of Any Buildings, or other Obstruction Whatever." This land, along with the Fort

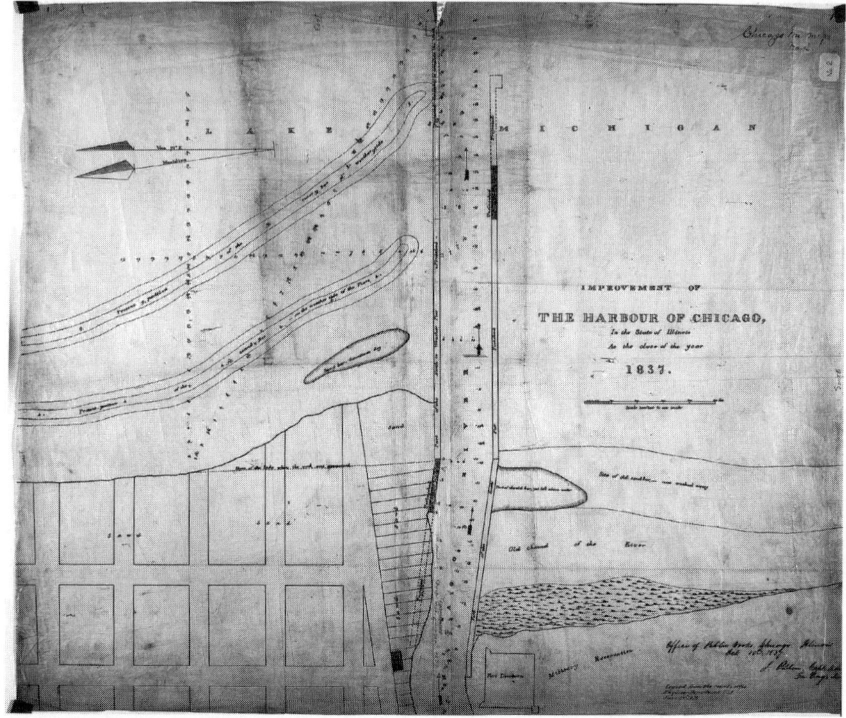

FIGURE 40. Plan for the improvement of the harbor of Chicago, 1837. Courtesy of the Chicago Historical Society.

Dearborn Addition immediately to the north, "had become vested in the city, to be held in trust for the people of the State."[12] Together these two parks made up what came to be known as Lake Park, or Lake Front Park.

The public character of Lake Park was contested almost from its inception. The federal government constructed a harbor in 1833 by digging a channel through a sandbar in Lake Michigan to admit ships to the river (fig. 40). Engineers built a pier extending along the north bank of the Chicago River to the sandbar. While the harbor and pier promoted manufacturing and commercial development, the erosion of the shoreline on the south side of the pier was an unintended outcome. Wealthy property owners building homes on the west side of Michigan Avenue facing Lake Park worried that the lake would wash up on their doorsteps. They joined with the city in pressuring the federal government to fund a breakwater in front of the park, but Washington refused. In 1851 the new Illinois Central Railroad (ICRR) offered a solution—it would build the breakwater in exchange for the right to lay tracks along the Lake Park shoreline.[13]

The sale of lakefront land to the ICRR generated a host of legal and political battles that lasted for decades. They started immediately after the railroad paid the federal government $45,000 on October 14, 1852, for 73,000 square feet of land contiguous to the pier and bounded by the lake. The company soon acquired rights to the shore between Randolph Street and the river and began laying tracks and building a stone masonry breakwater between Randolph and Twenty-second Streets. The railroad also began filling land between the tracks and the lake in order to create a large enough tract for its passenger terminals and train sheds. This process widened the shoreline, which later proved crucial in developing Lake Park. Property owners got their breakwater to protect their investments, but at the cost of a commercial intrusion into their—and the city's—front yard.[14]

The development of the ICRR along the lakefront brought with it further commercial growth. In addition to the railroad terminals and depots growing up along the lake, "two large grain elevators and other costly structures" were built as well.[15] This trend continued through the next several decades. After the opening of the Union Stockyards in 1865, just southwest of Lake Park and the ICRR property, city residents complained about the horrid stench and dreadful health hazards associated with the packer's proclivity for dumping offal and other waste into the river. Businesses related to the packing industry, including glue factories, distilleries, and hide tanneries, grew up along the south branch of the Chicago River, on land near the "park." By the 1890s, a description of the lakefront presented it not as a pleasure ground but as a teeming industrial and manufacturing district:

> A mile of ragged shore broken with piers and small docks; at its northern end tall warehouses and big buildings devoted to the wholesale merchandise trade. A great viaduct runs out here into the waters of Michigan, leading to a little peninsula on which are railroads, saw-mills, and storehouses. . . . From the southern boundary of the old Exposition Building to the southern boundary of the Lake Front itself sweeps away a stretch of green of good width and moderately good sod that is cut up with serpentine walks of gravel.[16]

The article went on to describe the place of the ICRR in the physical and economic growth of the Chicago, with its passenger traffic and freight terminals lining the lakeshore. "And herein lies the disfigurement of this section of Chicago," claimed the author, "which should in all fitness be the most picturesque and inviting part of the city."[17] If Chicago was to reach its fullest potential as a world-class city, planners would have to develop its lakefront into a setting of charm, beauty, and elegance, ridding it of the unsightly features introduced by the railroad.

Several prominent Chicagoans agreed, and in 1890 they launched a campaign to promote lakefront enhancement that combined individual concerns about property values with civic boosterism and arguments over how best to foster the public good. Dry goods merchant Aaron Montgomery Ward headed this effort, along with his friend and attorney George P. Merrick. Ward's mail-order catalog business was housed in an impressive eight-story "skyscraper" on the northwest corner of Michigan Avenue and Madison Street, directly across from Lake Park. He initiated a series of lawsuits against the city in 1890 to preserve the park for public use, free of buildings and other intrusions that detracted from its beauty and accessibility. He admonished the city for allowing commercial interests like the ICRR "to construct a cheap frame building or buildings on said public grounds, and [permitting] same to become a dumping ground for garbage, rubbish, filth, and other materials; and [to construct] certain scaffoldings, supports, and floors upon which said filth, etc., has been placed, thereby obstructing said public grounds, and [to create] a public nuisance thereon to the great loss, injury, detriment, and annoyance of complainants of the public generally."[18]

After additional lawsuits, Ward won his case, and the Chicago City Council turned Lake Park over to the South Park Commission to manage and develop. The Illinois legislature gave the park commission all submerged lands between Randolph and Twelfth Streets stretching out to the Chicago Harbor line.[19]

Part of the impetus behind Ward's numerous lawsuits was concern about the value of his own property. Ward and others with property fronting the lake claimed they had a right to an unobstructed view based on the 1836 canal commissioners' plat and that the value of their real estate depended on that dedication. Ward insisted that owners of lots fronting Michigan Avenue retained all rights, riparian and otherwise, as granted by previous bills upholding the lakefront as public grounds. He argued that "the city ha[d] no right to violate such trust and permit the use of said grounds for any other purpose than that of a street and open public grounds" and that the lots facing the lake had "a largely increased value on account of such dedication, and brought higher prices than they would have brought had not said grounds been so dedicated to be forever vacant and free from encroachments."[20]

The issue of who controlled riparian rights proved crucial in efforts to develop Lake Park. Even after the Illinois legislature granted control of the land to the South Park commissioners, they were engaged in numerous lawsuits with property owners who questioned the validity of their claims to submerged lands and riparian rights. The provision for Commission control was based on the requirement that a majority of owners of abutting land consent to the plan. The commissioners initially had trouble getting this consent. A November 1896 newspaper article claimed they lacked consent for eight feet of frontage that would give them majority consent. Park board attorney James R. Mann launched a swift campaign; just hours before the bill came up for passage, he persuaded the necessary property owners to consent.[21]

Challenges to Commission control of lakefront lands did not end with this consent, though. A series of lawsuits, beginning in 1896 and continuing through 1906, claimed that land added to the lakefront as infill was not part of the park commission's property. In one case a group of claimants argued that 163 acres of lakefront, between Chicago and North Avenues, was technically "vacant" land and therefore could not be claimed by the Commission since it never was under the control of the city, the state, or consenting property owners. These claimants argued that they, and others, should have squatting rights on the land since the land truly was "public." The federal Commission of Public Lands heard this case and ultimately decided in favor of the park commission, but not before requiring amended surveys of the lakefront land in question.[22] In another case, a property owner at Fifty-first Street argued that he had built an L-shaped pier that extended into the lake, and through "natural accretion" lakefront land had been enhanced. He claimed that this property should be his, not the park commission's, because the infill resulted from modifications he made at his own expense.[23] In both cases the courts established park commission ownership, but only after a hard-fought legal battle.

After overcoming these challenges to title of the land, the South Park commissioners began their project of expanding and enhancing the lakefront. The Commission entered into agreements with dredging companies to dump their waste material into the Lake Park basin. When business leaders asked him and other park planners about anticipated costs, Burnham explained that lakefront expansion would be free as a result of the dumping program.[24] The lakefront fill project got a boost in 1899 with the passage of the River and Harbor Act, which called for dredging Chicago's outer basin to a depth of twenty feet, thus providing additional infill material. By 1903 the total area of Grant Park (the park's name was changed in 1901 to honor the late president and Civil War general) was 201.88 acres. Once this land was secured, the Commission worked with the sons of Frederick Law Olmsted (who also designed the grounds for the neighborhood parks) to create a unified plan for the park. The Commission began creating lagoons, planting flower beds, and designing walking paths. In addition, it planted close to five thousand trees and shrubs to begin the beautification of the land.[25]

One of the most important developments that came from the infill, besides the expansion of parkland, was the creation of public beaches along the lakefront. On May 18, 1905, the city obtained the right to acquire "municipal parks, playgrounds, public beaches and bathing places." The South Park Commission then focused on additional dumping at Twenty-second Street and Fifty-First Street for the purpose of creating "recreation and bathing beaches." The justification for creating beaches reflected the same ideas that animated discussions about the need for parks and playgrounds in the city. The scheme devised by the newly created Committee on Bathing Beaches and Recreation Piers called for creating seven public bathing beaches along the lakefront from Montrose Avenue on the Far North Side to Seventy-ninth Street on the South Side. According to the commissioners, "These beaches would, in large measure, give back to the people the right to use the lake front, from which they have been so unwisely and selfishly deprived."[26]

The development of bathing beaches along the lakefront reflects some of the tensions between the commercial and civic ideals of the City Beautiful movement. Members of the Special Park Commission argued that the best way for the city to enhance the lakefront was to pass a $1.2 million bond issue to construct a large-scale recreational beach at Seventy-fifth Street, complete with a restaurant, bathhouse, boardwalk, and parking spaces. Commissioners saw this recreational beach as a vehicle for generating income for the city, both through the profits generated by parking and restaurant facilities and through the possibility of charging user fees. There were additional plans to enhance the recreational pier at Twenty-second Street and include commercial establishments like amusements and boating.[27] Yet many Chicagoans balked at this large expenditure of public funds for commercial recreation along the lakefront. Members of the Woman's City Club, for example, argued that the park commission should devote its funds to developing smaller, more accessible beaches along the lakefront. "We do not need a $50,000 restaurant pavilion at a bathing beach. . . . What Chicago wants is smaller beaches located at more frequent intervals along the lake front, where people can more easily reach them."[28]

The Committee on Bathing Beaches worked in conjunction with the South Park Commission to create these new beaches. They added infill, graded the land, dumped sand from the harbor dredging projects, added changing facilities for men and women, and installed supervisors and lifeguards. Attendance figures attested to the popularity of the beaches. In 1911, for example, over 280,000 people made use of the beaches at Twenty-second Street and Seventy-ninth Street.[29] The South Park commissioners saw the bathing beaches as an integral feature of their plans for creating a cohesive natural landscape on the lakefront. In consultation with Olmsted Brothers, the commissioners hoped to link Jackson Park on the south to Lincoln Park on the north via lakefront improvement. As a result, their plans for Grant Park focused on developing it as the centerpiece of one long public pleasure ground, complete with beaches, lagoons, formal landscaping, and cultural institutions.

THE NATURAL VERSUS THE CULTURAL LAKEFRONT

The relation between nature and culture in Grant Park proved to be one of the most contentious sources of disagreement concerning lakefront development. Various civic and commercial leaders in Chicago continued to express conflicting ideas about the appropriate characteristics of a public lakefront in the city. Once again, Aaron Montgomery Ward was at the center of these debates. Additional battles he waged with the city over the uses of Grant Park illustrated the fierce disagreement over the meaning and function of a public park. They also demonstrated the links made by a variety of groups between aesthetics, nature, and anticommercialism.

Ward's lakefront battle was reignited when Marshall Field sought a new home for the natural history collection he had created, housed in the Palace of Fine Arts from the 1893 Columbian Exposition. Field, working in consultation with South Park Commission president Henry Foreman, eyed the newly refurbished Grant Park as a site for his museum. He wanted to locate it near the recently moved Art Institute, which was given exemption from the court rulings barring buildings on the public grounds because of its civic function. The state legislature aided Field's cause in 1903 by passing a bill allowing park districts to build museums in public parks and levy taxes to maintain them.[30]

In its plan for Grant Park, Olmsted Brothers used this ruling as a vehicle for conceptualizing different areas of land use and function within the park. It divided the park into three large segments, each showcasing a different cultural institution. The northern part would feature the Art Institute; the middle would house the Field Museum; and the lower portion would contain the Crerar Library, a free public library endowed by philanthropist John Crerar.[31] The park plans incorporated formal gardens with statuary, native and exotic shrubs, and shade trees surrounding these neoclassical buildings. In addition, Olmsted Brothers made provision for plazas, playing fields, gymnasiums, and a swimming basin in the park.[32]

Supporters of the Field plan argued that locating the Field Museum and Crerar Library in Grant Park, adjacent to the Art Institute, would create a cultural center in Chicago and augment the city's cosmopolitan appeal. They also declared that museums were an integral part of the public culture of the city and should be situated on public lands where they were accessible to the most people and could stand as a testament to the vibrancy of civic life in Chicago. Harlow N. Higinbotham, department store retailer and president of the Board of Trustees of the Field Museum, argued that museums differed from other structures in that they served a civic function, and that they therefore should be exempted from legislation barring buildings on public land. The Field Museum "must be on the lake front," he exclaimed. "That is the only place for it, and it is entirely proper that it should be in Grant Park. Museums the world over are placed in public parks, whereas armories and other buildings suggested for the lake front are not properly park structures."[33] Field died in 1906, leaving $8 million for the construction of the museum, with the stipulation that the city must provide a site, free of cost, within six years of his death.

The prospect of the construction of additional buildings on parkland lining the lakefront led Montgomery Ward to renew his fight with the legislature. Ward claimed that the proposal to locate the museum in Grant Park violated the 1902 ruling in the Illinois Supreme Court barring the erection of buildings in the lakefront park. He instituted contempt proceedings against the South Park Commission and pushed his case in the courts.[34] Again he argued that his interest reached beyond personal concerns over property values. Like his fight to clean up the rubbish and unsightly railroad shanties, he claimed, this battle against the Field Museum also was about civic pride and public access to lakefront grounds. Merrick, Ward's attorney, contended: "There has been considerable misunderstanding of Mr. Ward's position in this matter. He is not fighting the location of these buildings for the sake of monopolizing any view from his windows, but because he feels impelled to see that the authorities carry out the original intentions of those who gave up the land for this people's park."[35]

Ward faced stiff opposition, since nearly all City Council leaders, civic boosters, and newspapers favored the Field plan. One article accused Ward of having ulterior motives for his opposition to the museum: "There must always remain a very strong suspicion that the opposing forces have something more up their sleeves than the public welfare."[36] Another detractor, a fellow Chicago merchant, claimed that Ward did not care about the welfare of Chicago but merely wanted to protect his property values. Ward shows interest in Chicago, he argued, "only when he wants the police to protect his business from strikers or when a new move is made toward erecting the Field Museum in Grant Park." He maintained that Ward no longer lived in Chicago but spent his summers in Wisconsin and his winters in Florida, and he charged him with a lack of civic spirit. He accused Ward of trying to defraud the city of tax funds by using the sidewalk in front of his office for business purposes, "cumber[ing] the pavement with boxes and bales of merchandise" and not properly compensating the municipality.[37] Henry Foreman threatened to "turn the front yard of the city into a rubbish heap" if he was forced to abandon plans for building the Field Museum in Grant Park.[38]

At issue in this debate was more than protecting property rights. This case exposed deeper divisions over the use of public lands and the relation between natural beauty and cultural promotion in creating spaces designed to foster civic life. Ward and his supporters equated public space with the preservation of natural beauty. "The lake front belongs to the people for a park," they argued, and "it must be kept for a park."[39] Trustees of the Field Museum were incredulous when Ward pressed his point for the conservation of parkland. "Ward expressed the belief that it was better to have this great tract of land as a place for people to go and lie around on the grass," one trustee declared, "than to make it the pivotal point of Chicago's scheme of beautifying the city."[40] The Supreme Court of Illinois upheld Ward's position again in 1909. Though agreeing with civic boosters that a museum was an appropriate building to be housed in the park, the court also accepted Ward's contention that the primary issue in the debate was access to open space and natural beauty. The construction of any building, even civic institutions, threatened to destroy "the city's beautiful water line," thereby detracting from the city's greatest civic resource.[41]

Ward added a class dimension to his fight to preserve the lakefront, claiming that open space was more beneficial to all citizens, especially the poor, than were museums of high culture. He raised the issue of access that promoters of the small park movement emphasized in their campaigns for neighborhood play spaces. In an interview with his leading nemesis, the *Chicago Tribune*, Ward claimed:

> I fought for the people of Chicago, not the millionaires.
>
> In the district bounded by 22nd Street, Chicago Avenue and Halsted live more than 250,000 persons, mostly poor. The city has a magnificent park and boulevard system of some fifty miles, but the poor man's auto is a shank's mare or at best the streetcars. Here is park frontage on the lake, comparing favorably with the Bay of Naples, which city officials would crowd with buildings, transforming the breathing spot for the poor into a showground for the educated rich. I do not think it is right.[42]

Attorney Clarence Darrow, commonly regarded as a devoted friend of labor, agreed with Ward's opposition to the museum plan. Darrow claimed that erecting the building would impose a tax of $100,000 on the people represented by the South Park District for the maintenance and upkeep of the museum. He argued that it was unfair for Chicago citizens to be forced to pay for a building that stood as a monument to the wealth of Marshall Field.[43]

The continued opposition to the museum plan, and the court's ruling against it, forced the South Park Commission to abandon its proposal for a museum in the park. The Crerar Library was built downtown, at Randolph Street and Michigan Avenue. The commission planned to move the Field Museum to Jackson Park, even though it would be far from the center of the city. Ironically, it was the Illinois Central Railroad, the company that had done the most to spoil the natural beauty of the lakefront, that stepped in with a solution. The ICRR offered to give the park commission a two-block tract of land just south of Twelfth Street, adjacent to Grant Park, that it had planned to use for a new train station (fig. 41). Executives at the ICRR saw this offer as a way to shed its image as the leading detractor of city beautification. In late 1911, the railroad proposed the plan and the park commission accepted. Thus it took commercial intervention to accomplish the integration of classically designed cultural institutions with the "natural" beauty of the lakefront, thereby creating a new model for civic space in the city.[44]

THE CITY BEAUTIFUL AND MUNICIPAL REFORM

The ambiguous relation between beauty and commercialism exhibited during the lakefront debates highlighted a central feature of the City Beautiful movement. Promoters

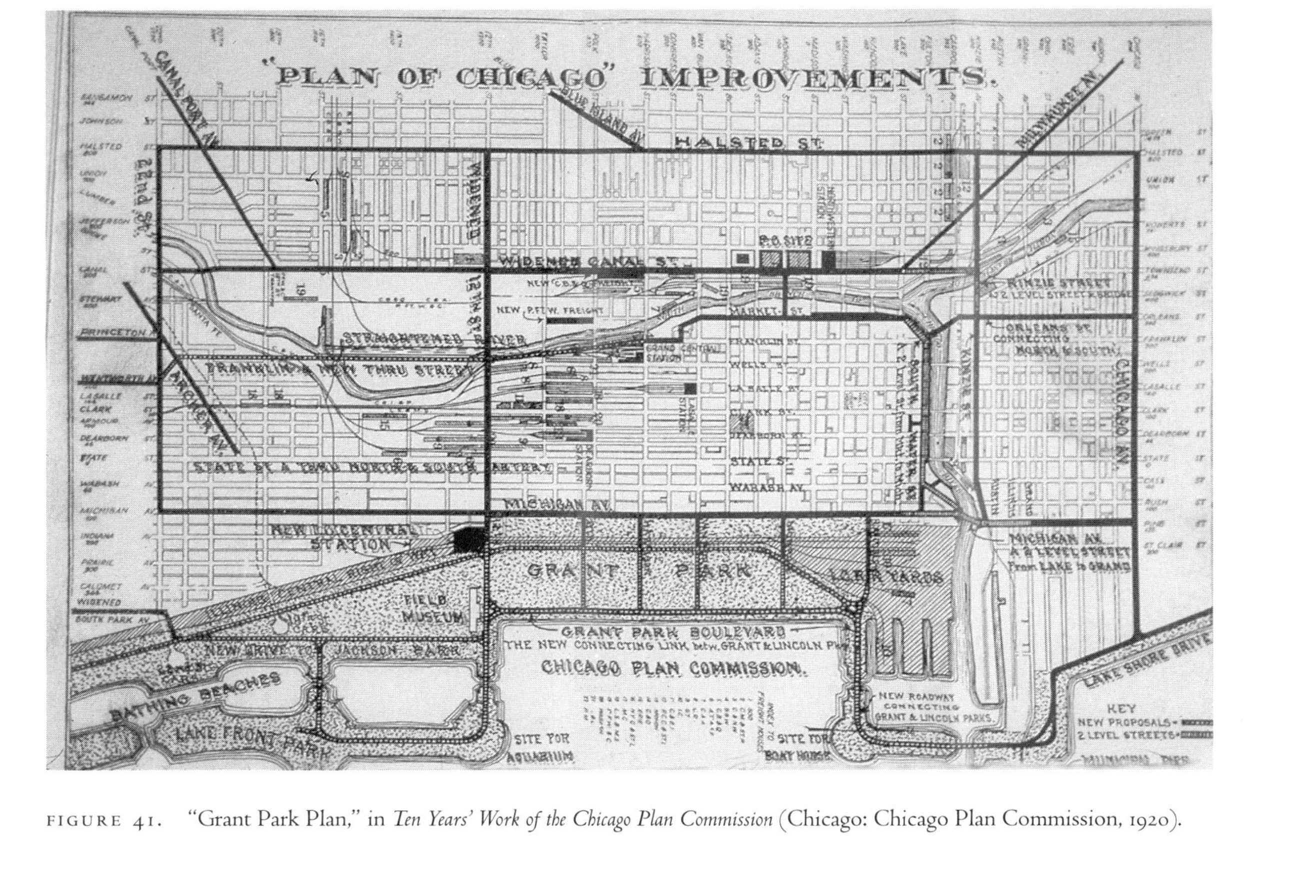

FIGURE 41. "Grant Park Plan," in *Ten Years' Work of the Chicago Plan Commission* (Chicago: Chicago Plan Commission, 1920).

of beautification campaigns clearly recognized that aesthetic enhancement increased property values and helped lure wealthy cosmopolitan tourists to the city. According to one supporter of city beautification, "To every property owner cleaner streets would mean an increased value of his property. For the condition of the streets determines in great measure the selling value of residence property."[45] Yet sponsors of civic improvement nonetheless posited the need for a visual separation of public space and commercial development. Numerous organizations promoted urban beautification as a means to foster civic pride and as a retreat from the world of commerce and industry. Public art and beautification projects not only transcended the grind of daily living, they also instilled civic pride and became sources of urban reform.

Local improvement associations were central in campaigns for the beautification of public spaces throughout the city. The South Park Improvement Association (SPIA) was founded in 1901 by Hyde Park women "to secure and maintain the best possible condition of the streets, alleys, grounds and buildings, and to promote cleanliness, order, and beauty, through the mutual helpfulness of the residents and property owners."[46] The district included the area bounded by Cottage Grove Avenue to the west, the tracks of the ICRR to the east, Fifty-fifth Street to the north, and Fifty-ninth Street to the south. The organization hired African American workers to sweep up garbage and horse droppings, clean streets and alleys, and rake leaves and shovel snow. The Committee on Landscape Architecture bought trees and shrubs for members at wholesale prices and supervised their planting. Several trustees and faculty members of the University of Chicago were members of SPIA, and the university contributed monthly dues to take advantage of its services.[47]

Observers commented on the hopeful image of civic betterment created by the SPIA workers cleaning public spaces with their horse-drawn carts. An article in the *Chicago Record-Herald* commented on the neatness and order of the grounds tended by SPIA workers, as opposed to surrounding areas without the benefit of these services. "The neat cart of the association, propelled by a colored employe [*sic*] arrayed in a tidy white uniform, may be seen daily on its rounds in the district." The workers plowed snow, kept mud off crossings, collected and burned trash, and tended to vacant lots.[48] Members of the SPIA demonstrated how private organizations could supplement the work of municipal government. They also saw their efforts as more than localized attempts to promote cleanliness and order. The SPIA linked neighborhood improvement with large-scale urban beautification. "The City Beautiful is to be realized in Hyde Park through a movement that has already changed dirty streets into models of cleanliness, turned filthy lots into fine grass plots, and created good hygienic conditions where disease had lurked in surroundings that offended the aesthetic sense."[49]

Several other citywide organizations focused on urban beautification as the basis of comprehensive urban reform and civic betterment. These municipal organizations, much like settlement houses, relied heavily on women volunteers. The Women's Outdoor Art League, the Hyde Park Improvement Association, the Hyde Park Betterment League, the Illinois Federation of Women's Clubs, and several citywide reform groups with art committees, including the Chicago Civic Federation, the Chicago City Club, and the Chicago Woman's Club, were leading promoters of urban improvement. One of the most prominent was the Municipal Art League (MAL), a coalition of nearly eighty art societies throughout the city. The MAL, headed by wholesale grocer and philanthropist Franklin MacVeagh, launched numerous campaigns to promote "good taste" by raising funds to purchase art and place it in public buildings in Chicago. Prominent members and supporters included sculptor Max Mauch, University of Chicago professor Charles Zueblin, settlement leaders Jane Addams and Mary McDowell, and architect Louis Sullivan. MacVeagh and other members of the MAL worked closely with the Art Institute to expand their program and lobby for a variety of civic improvements in public places throughout the city.[50]

MacVeagh and his supporters linked the movement for public art with civic cohesion and moral betterment. They saw cultivating an appreciation for art as a corrective to what they perceived as the rising materialism in American society: "The movement for public art is gaining headway everywhere. . . . We should teach the children that there is something in life besides mere wealth. The solidarity of society, of which we talk so much, could be reached in no better way than by having fine public art and plenty of it. The country is money mad and it should become art hungry. Give the men of America something to put in the place of money. Give them the idea of beauty. Art should be part of every great nation's life."[51]

The MAL translated this promotion of civic life into spirited lobbying efforts to remove evidence of commercialism from public grounds. Members labeled anything smacking of commercialism in civic spaces as a threat to artistic sensibilities. Supporters equated commercial billboards with "unsightly school grounds, unclean alleys and inartistic back yards." They waged war on all these symbols of "civic decay" by lobbying the City Council and supporting the veto power of the Municipal Art Commission over objects in public places.[52] When they could not get rid of certain commercial establishments, such as fruit stands under the elevated tracks, the MAL asked the Chicago City Council to submit design plans for the stands to the MAL for approval before the operators could obtain permits.[53]

MAL advocates also admonished the City Council for allowing commercial ventures into public parks. Several city reformers complained that Lincoln Park was "defaced" by the "mill race" concession, the elephant and camel rides, and other amusements that charged fees. They argued that the Lincoln Park board had "recently shown a tendency to turn that place into a site for commercialism by allowing the construction of a most disfiguring concession—the so-called 'old mill and race.'" Critics further warned that the "encroachment of private enterprise upon the parks of Chicago should be watched with zealous interest by the people if these great breathing-places are to be retained in their natural beauty for the enjoyment of the multitude."[54] These detractors of commercial amusement echoed Ward's belief that public park grounds should be preserved as natural spaces, with no place for money-making ventures. An element of elitism underlay many of these arguments against commercial amusements in the parks. Those ventures that were most questionable, according to critics, were those that appealed to the desire for commercial recreation. "The attractions of a Midway are not the attractions of a public park," stated one article, "where peace and grass and foliage are supposed to take precedence, and where a graceful landscape and fragrant flowers should be deemed of more importance than a monstrous, lumbering contrivance whose contortions shake the ground all about."[55] Municipal beautification supporters made arguments about the proper uses of parkland that were similar to those articulated by Frederick Law Olmsted several decades earlier.

Yet MAL supporters were quick to attest to their concern for the urban public and the city's poor as their motive for condemning commercialism in public parks. In his comments on the amusements in Lincoln Park, the park superintendent argued, "To my mind there can be only one way of looking at the matter, as such concessions most decidedly conflict with the idea of a public park, free and accessible to all the people."[56] The debate over amusements uncovered other examples of the public's being taken advantage of in the park. The *Chicago Examiner* exposed the practice of charging children three cents for each fifteen-minute ride on park swings. City residents were outraged. One resident responded, "Surely the great city of Chicago is not so pinched for money that it need take the pennies of pauper babies to replenish its coffers." Mary McDowell added, "I thought the swings and other pleasures of childhood provided in the parks were free to all the children. I cannot understand it at all."[57] This incident represented to many anticommercialism crusaders the dangers of introducing money-making ventures into public spaces. The practice could lead to a violation of the public trust, corrupting the promise of free access to public spaces and undermining civic culture.

The MAL linked its campaigns against commercialism with the promotion of tenement reform and smoke abatement. MacVeagh, like other early advocates of City Beautiful planning, believed art and scientifically based reform should work together to achieve urban beautification. Beauty was directly tied to cleanliness, sanitation, and hygiene, and the various organizations working for civic improvement established a comprehensive movement for the physical and social enhancement of the city. Reform groups worked in conjunction with municipal government and initiated studies of housing problems in Chicago, transportation needs, and suggestions for relieving congestion and pollution and other environmental conditions.

The campaign for smoke abatement became a central issue around which several citywide reform organizations rallied. The smoke abatement effort extended the programs of the local improvement organizations into the wider municipal arena by launching a citywide campaign that joined these groups with local aldermen and city reformers. Cleaning up the smoke nuisance, created largely by the ever-expanding number of railroads passing through Chicago as well as the growing use of furnaces for heating, was the primary feature of many plans for urban beautification. All other measures, including lakefront improvement, were useless, reformers argued, if the smoke issue was ignored. One article questioned the usefulness of spending city dollars to purchase public art when the soot and smoke of the city continued to detract from its beauty:

> What is the use of buying $1,000,000 worth of public works of art annually while our anti-smoke ordinances are violated every hour of the day and our streets are never even half cleaned? As no scheme for beautifying the city can be made effective with our present soot-laden atmosphere and dust and mud-covered streets, let the League go right along and raise $1,000,000 a year if it possibly can, but let the chief object of this fund be to furnish the sinews of war for a relentless prosecution of every violation of the smoke and other ordinances. . . . Following this practical and necessary course the time will come when Chicago shall have pure, clean air and clean streets. Then, and only then, will it be wise to plan

for public statues, fountains, triumphal arches, etc.; then only will it be possible to have these artistic embellishments and to preserve their beauty undefiled.[58]

Other groups, including labor, agreed. Union leaders were some of the most vocal proponents of prosecuting violators of the smoke nuisance ordinances. John Fitzpatrick of the Chicago Federation of Labor lobbied the City Council for stronger punishment of violators. Labor also joined the MAL in efforts to force the electrification of the railroads, a costly prospect for the railroad companies but one that did much to improve public health and enhance the natural beauty of the city. Supporters of smoke abatement linked beauty with environmental cleanliness as the best means to improve living and working conditions. According to a writer in the *Chicago Post,* "Our city beautiful must come through evolutionary, not revolutionary, processes, just as every other city beautiful has come. The basis of all plans in this direction must be cleanliness. Not until we have a thoroughly clean city—clean streets and alleys, and pure air—will it be other than a waste of time to plan a beautiful city.[59]

Daniel Burnham and Edward Bennett confronted these sentiments when they launched their beautification plan for Chicago. They sought to draw on the efforts of the multitude of reform groups fighting a variety of battles to clean up the city and enhance its natural beauty, and at the same time they tried to present a grandiose vision of the modern City Beautiful. They took for granted the natural resources of Chicago, especially the lakefront, and looked to amplify its charm by constructing monumental civic institutions whose clean, elegant classical architecture could be juxtaposed with the clear water and sandy beaches that defined the landscape of the city. The Plan made the lakefront the center of civic and cultural life and offered a comprehensive vision of what could be accomplished by efforts at coordinating transportation, building roads and bridges, and cleaning up air and water. By consolidating these efforts, the Plan's sponsors hoped to realize the City Beautiful as a practical reality. At the same time, they linked beautification and civic promotion directly to commercial growth, putting their goals at odds with those of many reformers in the city.

THE CHICAGO PLAN AND THE LAKEFRONT

Burnham and Bennett received the backing of the Commercial Club to move forward with work on a comprehensive plan of Chicago at the same time that Montgomery Ward was battling to preserve the lakefront for a public park. The Burnham Plan was an unintended beneficiary of Ward's efforts. The Supreme Court rulings barring commercial development on the land between the Chicago River and Twelfth Street, and between Michigan Avenue and the ICRR right of way, allowed Burnham and Bennett to make Grant Park, Chicago's "front yard," the key focal point of their City Beautiful project. Yet Burnham and Bennett, along with the merchants and bushiness people sponsoring the Plan, disagreed with Ward about the role of structures on public grounds. Indeed, the Plan was based on centralizing all civic and cultural institutions right at the heart of Grant Park.

Burnham and Bennett saw the creation of a civic lakefront as the logical result of the movement for small parks throughout the city. In consolidating all these parks into one unified system, the city could appropriate land use more effectively and make Chicago rival great European cities like Paris, London, and Berlin by establishing an encircling band of green space around the city. Burnham and Bennett proposed augmenting Olmsted Brothers' plans by filling in land between Grant Park and Jackson Park, creating a vast system of lagoons, gardens, and forests linked by driveways, outer paths, and an "Outer Drive" that served as a pleasure roadway (fig. 42).[60] They imagined "lagoons, narrow and winding, along the north shore, and wider, with more regular lines, along the south shore. Both margins of these lagoons should be planted with trees and shrubs, so arranged as to leave openings of various sizes, thus making vistas of the water and the life upon it, to be enjoyed by the people passing along the driveways or living in the homes that line park stretches."[61] Burnham and Bennett argued that the primary considerations for park building and design should be the health and enjoyment of an urban population. Careful planning for the proper arrangements of plantings would yield the most beneficial outcome, which would successfully balance concerns over the promotion of health and hygiene, beauty and contemplation, and recreation and enjoyment.

Recognition of the important relation between the "natural" landscape and human design and control of it was a crucial feature of the Plan. This juxtaposition illustrated both the nostalgic look back at nineteenth-century European precedents for the Plan and the treatment of more modern questions concerning transportation and freight circulation (fig. 43). Burnham and Bennett especially looked to Baron Georges-Eugène Haussmann's plans for Parisian parkland, which imprinted rational order and civility on the landscape of the city. Rather than drawing a sharp distinction between nature and culture, they envisioned the two working together. The proper placement of trees and flower beds, rather than just their natural beauty, was the key to creating the modern City Beautiful.[62]

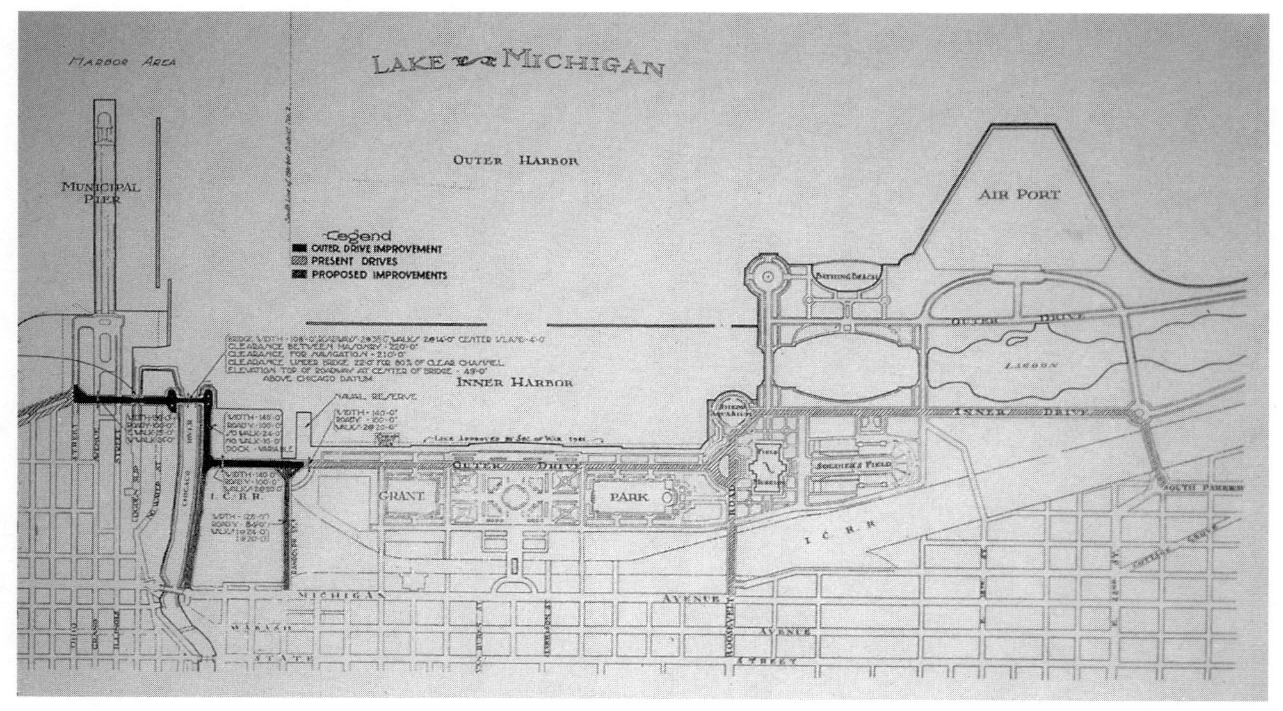

FIGURE 42. "Outer Drive Improvement," in *The Outer Drive along the Lakefront, Chicago* (Chicago: Chicago Plan Commission, 1929).

FIGURE 43. View looking north on the south branch of the Chicago River, showing the proposed arrangement of streets and ways for receiving freight by boat. Daniel H. Burnham and Edward H. Bennett, *Plan of Chicago* (Chicago: Commercial Club, 1909).

The Burnham Plan saw the natural landscape and the built environment as integral features of urban beautification and civic design. Uniting landscape design with classical architecture, Burnham argued, would create a cohesive vision of the artful city that would promote order, harmony, and stability. Burnham agreed with MAL leader Franklin MacVeagh's notion that artistry could and should be promoted in all aspects of city life, regarding the city as "an organic whole," "developing its various units with reference to their relations to one another."[63] Burnham disagreed with Montgomery Ward's contention that introducing buildings into parkland disturbed the beauty and serenity of the scene. Instead, he sought to integrate architecture into the natural landscape to create the unified civic center that would stand as a monument to social harmony and shared civic culture. The chance to form a composition that united natural beauty with architectural design was a wonderful opportunity "for treatment impressive and dignified in the highest degree." Burnham elaborated: "It is such opportunities which when properly utilized give to a city both charm and distinction, because of the satisfaction which the mind obtains in contemplating orderly architectural arrangements of great magnitude both in themselves and in relation to the city of which they must become an integral part."[64]

The Plan proposed a civic center in "the heart of the city," at the intersection of Congress and Halsted, from which all streets and avenues radiated (fig. 44). The civic center was an ensemble of five municipal buildings, all in a classical Beaux-Arts style, that would create a harmonious image inspiring civic pride. This classical monumentality was drawn out from the Civic Center plaza (fig. 45) and linked to Grant Park by the elaborately landscaped park and boulevard system that provided the axial connection to all parts of the city. These streets and boulevards were lined with ornamental statues, fountains, and vista markers that provided a unified civic design. At each end of Grant Park were cultural institutions in the same Beaux-Arts style as the municipal buildings (fig. 46). Burnham, like Olmsted Brothers, envisioned a cultural complex including the Field Museum, the John Crerar Library, and the Art Institute forming the "intellectual center of Chicago." In a statement that could have been addressed directly to Montgomery Ward, Burnham declared, "Public-spirited citizens have left precious legacies by providing for the intellectual and aesthetic needs of the people; and it should be esteemed a high privilege as well as a sacred duty to administer those gifts in such a manner as to accomplish the most effective results from the benefactions." He added that these gifts encouraged others that enhanced the beauty of the city and benefited the whole community.[65]

Artist Jules Guerin's watercolor renderings of the Plan captured its beauty and elegance. His use of pastel colors to show sweeping vistas, monumental civic architecture, and pastoral landscapes created a mythical and idealized image of the city (fig. 47). Guerin's Chicago was an unreal city, an ethereal one, in which all the realties of daily urban life were washed away. Chicago emerged as a tabula rasa, with the Plan presenting a fresh start for city building. People were barely visible in the renderings; instead, architecture, landscape, and rational mapping of urban circulation led to the promised city of the future.

This ideal city would be realized through the cooperation of commercial elites and government leaders. After Burnham presented the Plan, the mayor-appointed Chicago Plan Commission strengthened the role of government, which became the new locus of plans for city growth and economic development. Business and government would

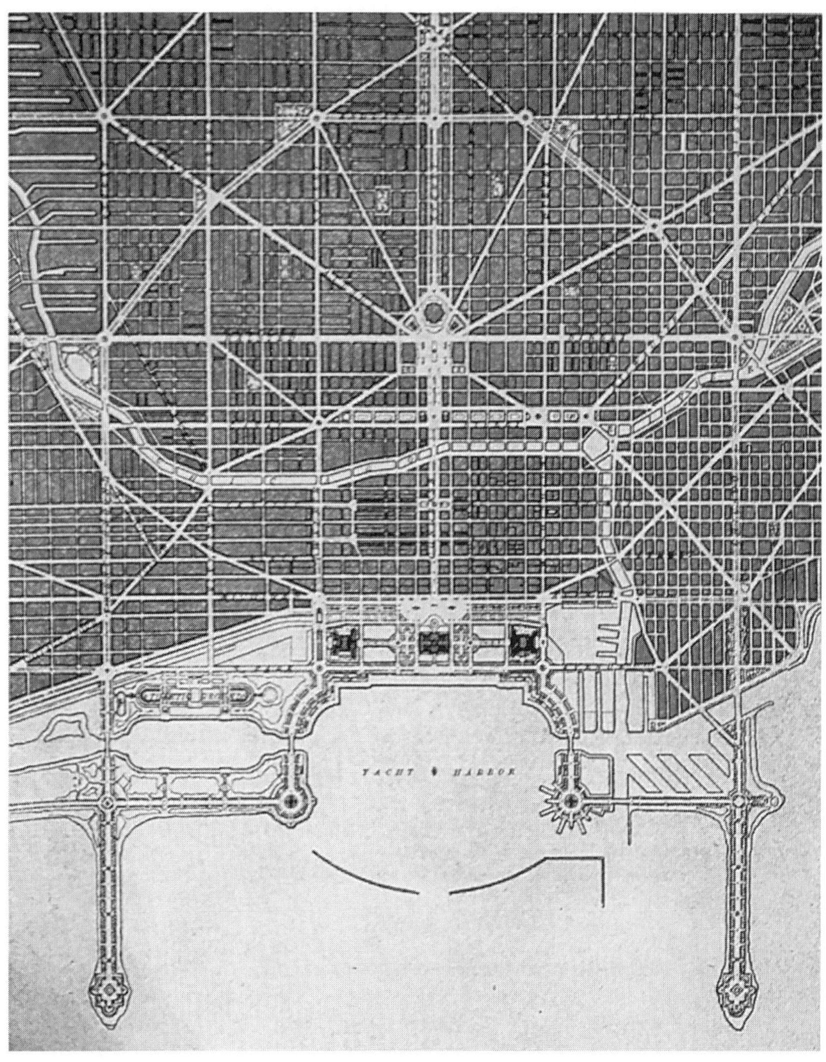

FIGURE 44. Map of the complete system of street circulation, including parks, railway stations, boulevards, recreation piers, the yacht harbor, and the main axis of the Civic Center, "presenting the city as a complete organism." Daniel H. Burnham and Edward H. Bennett, *Plan of Chicago* (Chicago: Commercial Club, 1909).

FIGURE 45. Proposed Civic Center to serve as the central focal point of the lakefront plaza. Daniel H. Burnham and Edward H. Bennett, *Plan of Chicago* (Chicago: Commercial Club, 1909).

FIGURE 46. Proposed boulevard to connect the north and south sides of the river, view looking north from Washington Street. Daniel H. Burnham and Edward H. Bennett, *Plan of Chicago* (Chicago: Commercial Club, 1909).

FIGURE 47. View, looking west, of the proposed civic center, plaza, and buildings. Daniel H. Burnham and Edward H. Bennett, *Plan of Chicago* (Chicago: Commercial Club, 1909).

work together both to promote commercial growth and to regulate and control urban development. Yet this semiofficial body, whose power resided in its twenty-seven-member executive committee, was relatively autonomous and existed outside public control. Moreover, it underscored the role of "experts" in planning urban growth. Rather than working in conjunction with the local municipal reform groups that had initiated urban beautification, the Plan Commission fused the goals of commercial leaders with the professional skills of architects, landscape designers, engineers, and urban planners. The Commission equated science and expertise with efficient commercial development. According the supporters of the Plan, the city needed to "grow to conform to a scientific plan to replace the makeshift that has tried to keep pace with the city's development in the past." Moreover, the Plan Commission linked the "civic patriotism" of the people to the potential for the Plan's success. The "power, growth, and advancement of a city is limited only by the measure of united civic interest of its people. The stronger and more vital the community spirit, the greater and more influential the city."[66] According to the vision, the outcome of civic spirit would be enhanced commercial growth guided by expert planning. As a result grassroots initiatives, led largely by women, lost much of their authority as the Commission sought to consolidate all phases of planning under its control.[67]

Numerous Chicagoans praised the Plan's breadth and vision. Mayor Fred A. Busse, who appointed the first Chicago Plan Commission, lauded the efforts of Burnham and Bennett, as well as those of the Commercial Club. He commended their public spirit and promised to work with Burnham to implement some of the more feasible parts of the Plan as quickly as possible.[68] Alderman Bernard W. Snow, chairman of the finance committee of the City Council, agreed. "The Commercial Club," he stated, "is to be congratulated on its civic pride and energy. The plan it has produced is most valuable, particularly for its educative influence." Alderman and University of Chicago professor Charles Merriam said, "It is an admirable thing to have a plan like this to work toward."[69] Chicago newspapers celebrated Burnham and Bennett's far-ranging vision and their artistry in linking the enhancement of the lakefront with monumental architectural design.

The Plan Commission launched a large-scale effort to educate Chicagoans about the Plan and garner their support. This educational campaign extended to the public schools. The Commission created a guidebook to be incorporated into the school curriculum, highlighting the history of the Plan and its significance for the future of Chicago. The guidebook stated, "Conditions which make for good health, good order and good citizenship must be made clear to our children. The needs and possibilities for expansion and development of community life under proper conditions must be outlined for the young, that effort under the urge of civic patriotism may be properly directed.[70] In addition to providing directions to teachers about how to effectively teach students about the importance of the Plan, the guidebook also included quizzes at the end of each section so that discussion of the Plan could be part of a comprehensive lesson. According to Walter D. Moody, the Plan Commission's managing director, the Chicago Plan was the one issue that "all Chicagoans can and should unite on—a nonpartisan, non-political business plan . . . to make a practical, beautiful piece of finished fabric out of Chicago's crazy quilt."[71]

Not all Chicagoans were so enthusiastic. Of course Ward objected to the proposal to locate any buildings, even cultural institutions, on the lakefront. Yet other groups voiced stronger opposition that reflected competing visions of the role of the built environment in promoting and directing civic culture. Jane Addams, while supporting the general idea of a comprehensive plan for city development, objected to the Plan's centralization and its locating all civic and cultural institutions near downtown, far removed from the neighborhoods where the multitude of Chicagoans lived and worked.[72] Mary McDowell agreed, criticizing the Plan for its lack of attention to the fundamental urban problems of poor housing, bad ventilation, and lack of access to nearby breathing spaces. She pointed out that for the many urban poor living in "dark, unventilated rooms, sometimes in cellars," the Burnham Plan little affected the quality of their daily lives. The University of Chicago Settlement Board averred, "We cannot have a really 'great' Chicago unless there are habitable comfortable dwellings for its wage earner." Urban life for residents of the Twenty-ninth Ward, the Back of the Yards neighborhood near the stockyards, was noted for a lack of trees, parks, or playgrounds; crowded conditions; and high infant mortality. For McDowell, no plan that ignored housing could claim to foster civic pride in Chicago. "Too much emphasis cannot be laid upon the fact that a sense of citizenship can neither be aroused nor maintained among people who cannot be decently housed."[73]

John Fitzpatrick, president of the Chicago Federation of Labor (CFL), declined the offer of membership on the Chicago Plan Commission, questioning the expenditure of public funds for city beautification when so many needs of the city's workers and poor were not being addressed. More fundamentally, though, he objected to the new partnership between the Commercial Club and municipal government. The CFL was pressing for a new municipal charter that placed greater control over civic affairs in the hands of the public. Fitzpatrick lobbied for municipal ownership of transportation; greater control of politics through direct primaries, initiative, and referendum; and reform of municipal taxation. The CFL's version of municipal improvement involved decentralizing political authority rather than consolidating civic reform in the hands of a joint committee of business interests and politicians. The Chicago Plan, according to Fitzpatrick, represented a form of municipal government that numerous reform groups were attempting to overturn.[74]

Fitzpatrick was sharply rebuked by the news media and by the business community. While many observers agreed that there were other issues that Chicago needed to confront, they pointed out that other institutions in the city were addressing them. A comprehensive plan for civic design meant more than mere beautification. Rather, it would play a role in alleviating all other social problems. The *Chicago Record-Herald* explained:

> There are fundamental moral problems, to be sure, before the citizenship of Chicago, as there are in every city in the civilized world. There is the white slavery question, the gambling question, the question of bad housing, vagrancy, unemployment, sweating, and so on. A city moral, clean, healthy, and prosperous is a worthy ideal, and there are in Chicago scores of organizations working for the realization of that ideal. . . . But the Chicago plan, with its outer and inner

> parks, its civic center, its lake front improvements, is necessary and described as a means to the moral ideal as well as for aesthetic and artistic reasons. . . . The poor are as interested in its realization as the rich.[75]

The Chicago Plan served to unite the interests of capital and labor, argued supporters, rather than divide them. The basic principle behind the Plan was the notion that the interests of all Chicagoans could be addressed, and divisions transcended, by fostering a comprehensive vision of the city that stimulated civic harmony and promoted shared public culture.

This celebration of the reforming potential of the civic landscape ignored the growing concern among Addams, Fitzpatrick, and McDowell over the inequity and injustice experienced by immigrants and workers in America's cities. Just as these reformers recognized the need for more fundamental social reconstruction, the Chicago Plan harked back to a nineteenth-century belief in the ability of cultural uplift to alleviate social ills. The Burnham Plan focused on the social values of beauty, order, and dignity that would stimulate "devoted action for the public good." Yet the issues of how that public good was defined, by whom, and in whose interest were not addressed by artistic designs for urban planning.[76]

The realization of some aspects of the Plan, including the "cultural campus" created by the proximity of the Field Museum, the Adler Planetarium, the Shedd Aquarium, and Soldier Field (fig. 48), was a testament to a shared civic vision among many Chicagoans. Yet the piecemeal way elements of the Plan came to fruition reflected the difficulty of uniting the numerous needs and goals of all groups in the city into one complete agenda for reform. The Chicago Plan tried to strike a delicate balance between aesthetic and social reform, a balance that was not sustained as a variety of groups in the city challenged the possibility of one cohesive, unified vision of urban reform and civic culture.

Debates over the Plan also illustrated the contested nature of various groups' understandings of municipal government in Chicago. Numerous groups in Chicago opposed various features of the Burnham Plan because of its promotion of commercial

FIGURE 48. Design for Grant Park Stadium (later Soldier Field), adjacent to the Field Museum and part of the plan for making the lakefront "the foremost recreation spot in the world." From *Chicago, the City Beautiful* (Chicago: S. W. Straus and Co., 1924), 1–2.

and business interests. Many labor leaders, settlement house workers, and reformers argued that municipal government should serve the multitude of urban residents, not the most prominent business leaders. They called for a municipal government that was responsive to needs for improved housing, better sanitation, and affordable transportation. Rather than a plan that focused simply on redesigning the physical environment to renew civic culture, they called for a political system that promoted greater public access to and involvement in the public arena.

By contrast, the Burnham Plan symbolized the trend toward consolidation and centralization in progressive urban reform. It exhibited a corporatist model of planning and reform, similar to the University of Chicago, that understood the city as a complex organism, with functionally interrelated parts. Unlike the movement for small parks and playgrounds, which viewed dispersement and decentralization as the best means to meet the recreational needs of diverse neighborhoods, the Chicago Plan looked to unite all aspects of civic design into a comprehensive scheme for urban growth. The desire to impose disciplinary order on cities signaled a departure from the more localized efforts at reform that had characterized an earlier generation. As a result, the connection between beautification and broader-based urban reform broke down, with planners now emphasizing the need for expertly supervised urban landscapes that would embody the "best" models of civic stewardship.

PART THREE

Commercial Leisure and Civic Culture

BASEBALL PALACE OF THE WORLD

Commercial Recreation and the Building of Comiskey Park

ON A BLUSTERY MARCH DAY IN 1910, architect Zachary Taylor Davis laid a solitary green brick on the lot at Thirty-fifth and Wentworth Streets as the cornerstone of what became the new Comiskey Park. Named for Chicago American League baseball club owner Charles Comiskey, the ceremony attracted a large crowd, for it took place on Saint Patrick's Day in Bridgeport, one of the largest Irish communities in Chicago. No subtlety was wasted in the symbolism of the day's ceremonies: the green brick reflected Comiskey's crystal-clear desire to reach out to Irish fellow community residents. Lest anyone miss the connection between ethnic culture and the new ballpark, Comiskey had had White Sox catcher Billy Sullivan travel to Ireland to bring back a piece of the "auld sod." On this genuine Irish sod Davis laid his cornerstone. Newspaper reporters, local politicians, and area residents celebrated the glory of the day with tributes to Comiskey, the White Sox, and their new neighborhood ballpark, which many both in and outside Chicago came to call the "Baseball Palace of the World."[1]

Yet Comiskey Park was more than just a parochial symbol of urban ethnic working-class culture. It also was an icon of the emerging City Beautiful movement, which sought to unite the street grid of the modern city with green spaces and monumental architecture to create large-scale efforts of urban planning. Like the grandiose museums, parks, and boulevards gracing the pages of Burnham's *Plan of Chicago,* the new ballpark was a site that became a source of civic pride and sociability. Charles Comiskey and other mass-culture entrepreneurs infused their facilities with an aura of respectability in order to justify their business enterprises and establish themselves as legitimate civic leaders. The classically designed physical space of the ballpark pronounced it a place where codes of decorum were observed even as different classes and ethnicities, men and women, mixed with one another. By creating a monumental recreational structure in Chicago, Comiskey could transcend the confines of the immediate neighborhood and make his ballpark an emblem of the emerging links between commercial culture, civic pride, respectability, and Americanism.[2]

At the same time, the rise of commercial mass culture encouraged solidarity among working-class immigrants. Rather than obliterating local, ethnic culture, commercial amusements often grew directly out of that culture. The dance halls, vaudeville theaters, and sporting parks often were sponsored by local businesspeople and drew their support from the localized world of the saloon, the athletic club, and the fraternal lodge. Workers carved out alternative spaces beyond the surveillance of employers and urban reformers, with few restrictions on accessibility (except for race), thereby challenging prevailing notions of appropriate public conduct and social order. By using sites of mass culture as spaces of working-class sociability, new immigrants and their children forged alliances with one another that helped overcome ethnic barriers.[3]

African Americans did not experience this commercial culture in the same way whites did. Often, blacks were excluded from the amusement parks, vaudeville shows, and theaters that welcomed working-class ethnic whites and restructured mass culture, much as they were excluded from public parks. When African Americans were not barred outright, they were segregated into the balconies with the rowdy crowds that gave those spaces their taint of ill repute. In addition, blacks often were the subject of the show. Vaudeville shows and amusement parks mocked black culture, reinforcing negative black stereotypes in the performative space of the minstrel show and the comedy act. As a result, African Americans created their own spaces of commercial amusement, where popular culture could exist comfortably with respectability as the Black Belt grew into one of the most dynamic cultural districts in Chicago.[4]

MASS CULTURE AND THE SPATIALIZATION OF VICE

In many ways the rise of mass amusements represented a sharp contrast between the commercial values of entrepreneurs like Comiskey, seeking to attract large audiences, and the civic elite (like park proponents Frederick Law Olmsted and Henry Foreman) who wished to impose urban social order. Dance halls drew city youth eager to escape the watchful eyes of their Old World parents as well as the instruction of middle-class and elite reformers. Similarly, working-class women often forged what some considered unsavory alliances with men who took them to the new amusement parks, modeled on Luna Park at Coney Island, which allowed men and women to mingle freely on rides that encouraged intimate contact. Yet the emerging importance of mass amusement to the public culture of the city illustrates how commercial considerations and respectability came together as entrepreneurs integrated their facilities into the larger legitimate culture of the city.

Part of this legitimation involved spatial distinction. Promoters of commercial culture followed the lead of planners like Daniel Burnham by clearly differentiating the amusement park from the surrounding culture of the city. Indeed, White City Amusement Park, at Sixty-third Street and South Parkway, replicated the Beaux-Arts style of Burnham's 1893 exposition buildings, from which the amusement park took its name. The owners of White City copied the grandiose entrances and ornamented, brightly lit interiors of Coney Island parks to usher customers into an ethereal, dreamlike space. While the experience of leisure was relatively unstructured once patrons paid their admission fee, the park nonetheless offered a safe zone of adventure marked off from the teeming city beyond. Amusement parks posted regulations for behavior and offered a level of respectability that the city streets seldom offered.

Despite the efforts of amusement park promoters to link commercialism with the culture of respectability, many urban reformers still disapproved of these carnivalesque spaces. Many reformers equated commercial leisure with corruption and vice and saw mass culture entrepreneurs as confidence men who profited from the promotion of "unwholesome" amusements, often targeted specifically to children.[5] The creation of public parks and playgrounds grew out of efforts both to regulate places of mass amusement and to encourage the municipality to develop alternative leisure spaces. These alternative recreation opportunities, reformers hoped, would counter the lure of vice districts and places of ill repute that tempted the young in Chicago and urban Americans in general.

Reformers also recognized that working conditions could lead to immorality and vice, particularly for women, as they were exploited in the factory and department store. Retail sales clerks were especially vulnerable, according to one survey, because they were surrounded by the luxuries they craved but were not paid enough to enjoy them. A 1911 Chicago Women's Trade Union League study showed that between 25 and 30 percent of women employed in department stores did not earn enough "to enable them to procure the necessities of life." A Chicago Vice Commission report pointed to the lure of prostitution for women who could not earn sufficient money elsewhere:

> A former salesgirl in a department store was seen in a fashionable all-night restaurant. She said that four weeks previous she had been earning $8.00 per week. She enumerated different articles of clothing which she was wearing, and gave the prices of each, including her hat. The total amount came to over $200.00. Her eyes had been opened to her earning capacity in the "sporting" life by a man who laughed at her for wasting her good looks and physical charms behind a counter for a boss who was growing rich from her services, and the services of others like her.[6]

Caroline Meeber, Theodore Dreiser's protagonist in *Sister Carrie,* attests to the lure of fashion amid the bustling downtown department store. "Fine clothes to her were a vast persuasion," writes Dreiser. "When she came within earshot of their pleading, desire in her bent a willing ear." Carrie relied on her associations with wealthy men to supply the finery that so enticed her.[7]

In addition, according to many female reformers, the desire to participate in the culture of mass amusement often enticed women into alliances with unsavory men. A Juvenile Protective Association study claimed that amusement parks often posed the most dangerous risks. "In the first place the gates of every park are surrounded by saloons and many of the men are half intoxicated before they enter the part itself. Almost all of the absurd 'amusements' offered require a separate entrance fee and young girls stand about unconsciously offering their chastity in order to be invited to see 'the fat folks' convention,' the 'Kansas cyclone,' or the 'human roulette wheel,' for the man who treats them too often demands a return later in the evening."[8] The lure of commercial amusement, combined with the inadequate wages paid to female workers, together threatened the safety and purity of women in the city, many reformers maintained.[9]

Reformers like Jane Addams sought to use municipal government and labor legislation to counter the influences of both workplace exploitation and the temptations of prostitution. Addams also stressed the need for alternative sites of leisure for children and for working-class men and women. Reiterating her belief in the ability of certain public spaces to promote civic discourse and social engagement, Addams showed how outdoor recreation areas, including parks and playgrounds and also athletic fields, could offer working people recreation and release from the "grind of life." "Well considered public games, easily carried out in a park or athletic field," she explained, "might both fill the mind with imaginative material constantly supplied by the theater, and also afford the activity which the cramped muscles of the town dweller so sorely need." For Addams, the spectacle of neighborhood boys and men eagerly entering the neighborhood baseball field illustrated how public life could be enhanced through play and recreation. "Does not this contain a suggestion of the undoubted power of public recreation to bring together all classes of the community in the modern city unhappily so full of devices for keeping them apart?"[10] Athletics offered an alternative to saloons, amusement parks, and dance halls and a valuable setting for shaping democratic culture and American identity.

BASEBALL AND TEAM SPIRIT

Organized recreation was part of a growing movement among urban residents at the turn of the century to recognize the benefits of strenuous activity. Civic leaders also demonstrated that recreation was important to promoting citizenship in the modern industrial city. Proponents of play, such as the leaders of the Playground Association, stressed the benefits of athletics not only in providing wholesome leisure to the city's youth but also in thwarting the increased inactivity of the growing white-collar population. National leaders, including President Theodore Roosevelt, worried about the effect that office culture had on the physical strength of the nation's workers. As a result, athletics came to be seen as a national imperative, to counter the sedentary character of the American corporate workplace.[11] As historian Daniel T. Rodgers points out, "The cult of strenuosity and the recreation movement grew together, minimizing the distinctions between usefulness and sport, toil and recreation, the work ethic and the spirit of play."[12]

The future of America, according to many proponents of athletics, was linked to citizens' physical prowess, manliness, and loyalty. Roosevelt articulated the integral relation between capitalist culture, American nationalism, and organized athletics: "In a perfectly peaceful and commercial civilization such as ours there is always a danger of laying too little stress upon the more virile virtues—upon the virtues which go to make up a race of statesmen and soldiers. . . . These are the very qualities which are fostered by vigorous, manly out-of-doors sports."[13] Athletics promoted patriotism most effectively, according to Roosevelt and other supporters, when part of the larger realm of team play. Team play became, in William James's words, "the moral equivalent of war."[14]

Like many advocates of athletics at the University of Chicago, Jane Addams and other play proponents emphasized the connections between the values inculcated by sports and those that increased productivity in the workplace. Addams linked team play to the modern industrial work process: "It takes thirty-nine people to make a coat in a modern tailoring establishment, yet those same thirty-nine people might produce a coat in a spirit of 'team work' which would make the entire process as much more exhilarating than the work of the old solitary tailor, as playing in a baseball nine gives more pleasure to a boy than that afforded by a solitary game of handball."[15] The collective experience, according to Addams, was the aspect of athletics that could be most usefully translated to the labor process.

While much of the rhetoric of the play movement related play to industrial capitalism and rising bureaucratic social order, proponents were not merely trying to create efficient industrial workers. Rather, they sought a middle ground between what they perceived as the dangers of the working-class ethnic culture of saloons and the greed and corruption of unregulated capitalism. They tried to strike a balance between advocating individual discipline and skill and encouraging group identification and teamwork. Moreover, for reformers like Addams, the team spirit was the basis for workplace organizing and workers' collective action. The spirit of play also reflected the belief shared by John Dewey and other educational theorists about the best ways to promote learning, shape experiential knowledge, and foster civic engagement.[16]

The most effective game for instilling team spirit, according to play promoters and reformers, was baseball. Many advocates of organized sport objected to the violence often associated with football. Much of this emphasis on baseball resulted from the collegiate football scandals in 1905, in which the increasing brutality of the game led many educators to reassess its place in collegiate sport. University of Chicago professor Shailer Matthews noted, "From the President of the United States to the humblest members of the school and college faculty there arises a general protest against this boy-killing, man-mutilating, money-making, education-prostituting, gladiatorial sport."[17] Instead, sports advocates looked to baseball to promote discipline, order, and self-sacrifice as a means of inculcating nationalism and loyalty. According to sports writer Hugh Fullerton, "Baseball, to my way of thinking, is the greatest single force working for Americanization. No other game appeals so much to the foreign-born youngsters and nothing, not even the schools, teaches the American spirit so quickly, or inculcates the idea of sportsmanship or fair play as thoroughly."[18]

Baseball writers and reformers pointed out that individual skill and success were useful only when used to promote the advancement of the team. Henry Curtis of the Playground Association of America articulated this vision in his discussion of the role of each player in a baseball game:

> A long hit or a daring run may not be what is needed. The judgment of his play is a social judgment. It is estimated not on the basis of its individual excellence, but by its effect on the success of the team. The boy must come out and practice when he wants to go fishing. He must bat out in order that the man on third may run in. Many a time he must sacrifice himself to the team. This type of loyalty is the same thing we call good citizenship as applied to the city, that we call patriotism as applied to the country. The team game is undoubtedly the best training for these civic virtues.[19]

Curtis argued that in baseball the peer group became an instrument of Americanization, as ethnic barriers were overcome in organized team play. Civic culture could be fostered and revitalized by instilling in youth the virtues of cooperation and loyalty as traits to be carried into all phases of public life.

The question whether football or baseball was the most effective vehicle for promoting civic ideals exposed some of the differences in progressive reformers' ideas about civic culture in Chicago. Promoters of football, like Harper, Amos Alonzo Stagg, and Roosevelt, stressed that sport's function in promoting leadership. In many ways the emphasis on football reflected the belief that the best trained, most highly skilled members of the middle class should be leaders in the workplace and in the nation. Indeed, the opportunity to play football was available, for the most part, only to men who had the means to attend college. By contrast, baseball was available to all urban residents through the newly established athletic fields in public parks. Rather than emphasizing leadership and expertise, proponents of baseball stressed team spirit and self-sacrifice as the basis for organized athletics. Equal opportunity to participate, rather than fostering individual prowess, became their motivation for promoting baseball. Similarly, many critics of football agreed with Shailer Matthews's claim that commercialism was corrupting the college game. Amateur baseball, played in the sandlots and ball fields of municipal parks and playgrounds, was free of this money-making taint.

THE POLITICAL ECONOMY OF MAJOR LEAGUE BASEBALL IN CHICAGO

While promoters of baseball stressed that amateur, participatory sports enhanced American culture, they were less clear about the place of professional spectator sports. University of Chicago president William Rainey Harper's praise of athletics linked its moral benefits to its amateur status. Henry Curtis emphasized how team interaction established the values of citizenship that recreation supervisors hoped children would learn. Reformers were more ambivalent about professional sports. Some worried about the potentially illicit connections between owners of professional ball clubs and the world of vice associated with saloons, dance halls, and gambling dens. Others questioned how the links between commerce and recreation would affect players' motivation for engaging in team play. They worried that the values of cooperation and discipline would be corrupted when athletes played for money.

The rise of professional baseball had its roots in the organized athletic clubs of nineteenth-century cities. These clubs sometimes grew out of earlier fraternal organizations and the urban culture of the saloon. Roy Rosenzweig's classic study of the saloon, *Eight Hours for What We Will,* highlighted the increasingly important role spaces of leisure served in promoting community interaction and fostering class solidarity in industrializing cities. With workers exercising less control over the production process, they often looked to leisure sites as the sources of personal and communal identity. By the late nineteenth century, the rituals associated with leisure played a central role in defining and shaping notions of class, community, and masculinity.

Sports as a means for promoting camaraderie grew out of the ethnic athletic clubs many groups started on entering American cities. German turners, Czech sokols, and Scottish Caledonian Clubs all offered alternative spaces for gathering and social activities that helped maintain links to ethnic culture. Baseball clubs followed similar patterns, though they most often comprised skilled craftsmen like carpenters and shipbuilders, clerks, and shopkeepers. In forming organized baseball clubs, they were part of a redefinition of masculinity and male urban culture. Rather than participating in the rough male sports of prizefighting and cockfights, which flouted Victorian prescriptions for gentility, baseball club members created new terms for defining masculinity that reflected the competitive commercial marketplace. These clubs emphasized that baseball helped establish competitiveness, control, and discipline as features of manly virtue.[20] Baseball also allowed men to reclaim part of the world of sports culture as their own at a time when prescriptions for women's participation in certain forms of athletics were blurring the gendered distinctions between male and female leisure and recreation.[21]

As spectatorship grew at games between ball clubs organized by neighborhood, workplace, and church, local businesspeople became active financial supporters of the clubs. Factory owners might provide uniforms, tavern owners could pay for equipment, or booster groups would arrange schedules and charge admission. Before long, ball club sponsors began paying players for their services as the drive to win games led club managers to look beyond the neighborhood, athletic club, or shop floor for the best talent. These practices removed the game from its local social function and placed it in the world of commerce and work culture that many club members initially sought to counter. Baseball thus moved from a world of loosely organized athletic clubs to become a nationally structured professional sport with standardized rules and prescriptions for work discipline. Competitiveness in sports spurred this link to the marketplace. Baseball became a professional enterprise, firmly entrenched in the urban economy. The game established its place in American culture by demonstrating that the character of professional play was congruent with the work ethic of industrial and corporate America.[22]

Yet baseball was not merely an accommodation to industrial work culture and commerce. Just at the time baseball was becoming more clearly linked with the world of the marketplace and urban commercial culture and its popularity was rising, some promoters and former amateur players called for a return to the precommercial era when money was not associated with the game. In issuing this call, they helped create the myth of baseball's pastoral origins. This harking back to a "golden age," when baseball was uncorrupted by commerce, demonstrated their ambivalence toward associating baseball with the marketplace and the city. Indeed, the baseball field, like parks and playgrounds, became a haven within the expanding built-up environment. By juxtaposing rural and urban, preindustrial and modern, professional baseball became a symbol for the complexities of twentieth-century American culture.[23]

This evocation of the rural elements of baseball also contributed to campaigns to recognize it as America's national pastime, directly linking baseball to nationalism. In 1907 Albert G. Spalding, sporting goods magnate and owner of the National League Chicago White Stockings, argued that baseball was undoubtedly a symbol of a distinctive American culture and called for a formal investigation into the national origins of the game: "To enter upon a deliberate argument to prove that Base Ball is our National game; that it has all the attributes of American origin, American character and unbounded public favor in America, seems a work of supererogation. It is to undertake the elucidation of a patent fact; the sober demonstration of an axiom; it is like a solemn declaration that two plus two equals four."[24]

Spalding appointed a committee headed by National League president Abraham G. Mills to conduct the study. Several baseball players and writers pointed to the British games of cricket and rounders as clear sources for baseball's origins. Yet the commission's findings argued that future Civil War general Abner Doubleday "drew the first known diagram of the diamond, indicating positions for the players . . . in Cooperstown, New York in 1839."[25] Thus Spalding and his committee linked baseball, American identity, and agrarian culture in a way that denied the centrality of urban culture and the marketplace in the origins and growth of the game.

Spalding, however, had done more to promote the commercial and professional character of baseball than almost any other sponsor of the game. Cincinnati organized the first professional baseball team in 1869, but Spalding launched baseball as a major commercial venture. He became a pitcher for the Boston Red Stockings the same year the first professional baseball association was formed. In 1871, ten teams met in New York City to form the National Association of Professional Base Ball Players (NAPBBP). During the meeting, players drew up a constitution that set out provisions for players' contracts, admission prices to league games, and ten-dollar fees to establish a franchise. Spalding used this constitution as the basis for his own commercial venture in Chicago just a few years later, establishing baseball as the recreational equivalent of the corporation and the factory. He became a "captain of industry," forging monopolistic control over the game of baseball and promoting skill, efficiency, and productivity.[26] Moreover, he used this promotion of professionalism and expertise to create one of the leading sporting goods businesses in the nation (fig. 49). The ideals of skill, training, and efficiency could be used in the service of advertising and sales, further linking commerce and baseball.[27]

In 1876 Spalding joined with Chicago coal merchant William S. Hulbert to create a new professional league in baseball, the National League of Professional Baseball

FIGURE 49
Advertising for A. G. Spalding Sporting Goods, in *Spalding's Hand Book of Sporting Rules and Training* (Chicago: A. G. Spalding, 1886).

Clubs (NLPBC). One of the central features of the league's constitution was the codification and regulation of play. Following the model put forth by the NAPBBP, Spalding diagrammed the proper measurements of the professional baseball field, along with the position of each player on the field (fig. 50). The strict control of space was matched by specialization among players. Players were assigned specific positions and had clearly mapped-out roles within the ball field.[28] This division of labor, along with the regulation of space, mirrored changes in the modern workplace, where employers looked to gain greater control of production. At the same time, though, the lack of control of time within the ballpark offered an antidote to the factory bell, the pervasive symbol of work discipline in the urban capitalist economy.[29]

Professional baseball's similarities to the modern workplace extended to the control

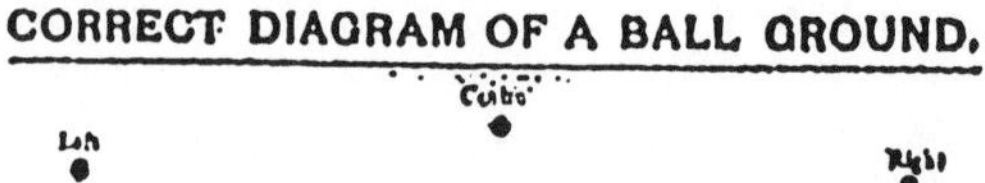

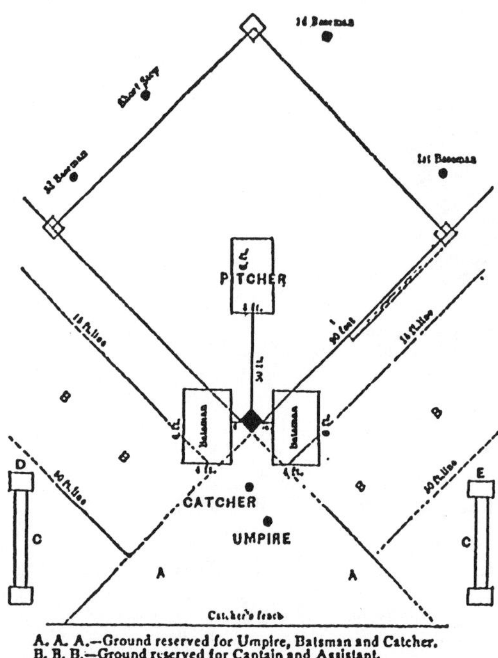

FIGURE 50
"Correct Diagram of a Ball Ground," in A. G. Spalding, *Constitution and Playing Rules of the National League of Professional Base Ball Clubs* (Chicago: A. G. Spalding, 1886).

of the work process by management. The league constitution tightened management's control of players, and one of the rules involved binding players more tightly to their current teams. The National League instituted the "reserve clause" in 1882, whereby a club reserved the right to its players' services indefinitely. Players could be blacklisted if they tried to break their club contracts; owners could be expelled for signing another team's players. Spalding and other promoters of baseball argued that these restrictions were necessary to demonstrate baseball's allegiance to professionalism and expertise. Player contracts, paid referees, and uniform ticket prices all contributed to legitimizing baseball as a reputable and well-managed enterprise. These changes also enabled

Spalding and other owners to codify rules so that leisure activity could be transformed into commerce and labor.[30]

Organized baseball's respectable status also derived from the understanding among all team owners and promoters that the game would be kept white. As early as 1867, when the National Association of Base Ball Players (NABBP) became the first association to codify playing rules and regulations, African Americans were barred from organized baseball. According to a statement from the Nominating Committee of the NABBP: "It is not presumed by your Committee that any club[s] who have applied are composed of persons of color, or any portion of them; and the recommendations of your Committee in this report are based upon this view, and they unanimously report against the admission of any club which may be composed of one or more colored persons."[31]

Once professionalism overtook the game, and the NABBP was supplanted by the NAPBBP, the color bar remained intact. The new professional league had no formal policy statement restricting African American players because it did not need one. Instead, member clubs maintained a "gentlemen's agreement" that no club would sign black players, a ban carried over into the National League.[32]

But the gentlemen's agreement did not prevent African Americans from playing professional baseball. Many black baseball players enjoyed successful careers in semiprofessional baseball, in the various black clubs that barnstormed throughout the nation even before the organization of the Negro National League in 1920. Some also "disguised" themselves as Cubans or Native Americans and played in the major leagues. Numerous contemporary accounts of black baseball teams praised their skill, grace, and respectability. The *Brooklyn Daily Union* commented on the character of two clubs, the Philadelphia Excelsiors and the Brooklyn Uniques: "These organizations are composed of very respectable colored people, well-to-do in the world . . . and include many first-class players. The visitors will receive all due attention from the colored brethren of Brooklyn; and we trust, for the good of the fraternity, that none of the 'white trash' who disgrace white clubs, by following and bawling for them, will be allowed to mar the pleasure of these colored gatherings."[33]

This passage illustrates both the important place of baseball in the black community and the pervasive connections made between baseball and illicit behavior. For members of the African American community, including elite professionals and businesspeople as well as the more recent southern migrants who would enter northern cities in huge numbers after World War I, baseball served as a bridge. It could unite the "old settlers" and the new when tensions over class and respectability in other arenas were growing. At the same time, though, white promoters' desire to professionalize baseball reflected their conflation of respectability with whiteness. The black and white professional leagues thus grew up side by side but rarely intersected.[34]

White club owners also linked professionalism with respectability. Professional baseball still had detractors who complained of its connections to gambling, rowdyism, and saloon culture. Promoters believed they had to overcome this image if baseball was to be a lucrative endeavor. Henry Chadwick, a baseball editor, linked skill, training, and expertise to the professional status of the game. He explained the difference between amateur players and professionals: "[A] professional expert not only requires attentive study to the rules of the game, . . . together with perfect familiarity with each and every rule; but also a regular course of training, to fully develope [*sic*] the physical powers, in order to ensure the highest degree of skill in each and all of the several departments of the game."[35]

The league constitution spelled out rules for behavior among players, both on and off the field. The National League outlawed Sunday games in many cities, barred the sale of alcohol, charged higher admission fees, and fined players for drinking, swearing, arguing with the umpire, and tardiness.[36] Whereas some reformers linked the value of athletics directly to amateurism, then, promoters of professional baseball argued that only through professionalization could players develop the skills and expertise needed to ensure baseball's respectability.

Spalding went beyond promoting expertise to ensure baseball's respectability. He made his players pledge abstinence from liquor, set eleven o'clock curfews, and even hired Pinkerton detectives to report on them. By controlling players' behavior, Spalding believed he could make the sport acceptable to bourgeois urban residents. The baseball park could function as a source of well-regulated leisure, fostering civic pride and team loyalty by creating a mythic space of carefree pastoral recreation. Spalding claimed: "The aim of the Chicago management is to secure the highest standard of baseball efficiency obtainable. In fighting the encroachment of drink . . . we are simply striving to give our patrons the full measure of entertainment and satisfaction to which they are entitled. . . . We don't intend to again insult ladies and gentlemen in this city or any other by allowing men who are full of beer and whiskey to go upon the diamond in the uniform of the Chicago club."[37]

The professionalism of the players would attract respectable patrons and make baseball a legitimate form of cultural entertainment. As a result of his legislating morality, Spalding claimed, the crowds at Chicago White Stocking games were "composed of the best of people in Chicago, and no theater, church, or place of amusement contains a finer class of people than can be found in our grandstands."[38] Between 1882 and 1889, attendance at National League games rapidly increased, and between 1885 and 1889 the National League teams earned close to $750,000, with Spalding's team claiming approximately 20 percent of the total.[39]

Spalding was not solely responsible for the overwhelming popularity of the game, of course. While his regulations certainly helped attract a white-collar, middle-class audience, other factors contributed to the growth of the baseball crowd. In the last decades of the nineteenth century, the admission charges for National League games were fifty cents for standard admission, sixty cents for a bleacher seat, and seventy-five cents for a grandstand seat. By contrast, seats at popular theaters and vaudeville shows were between ten and twenty cents. Average annual income for manufacturing workers in 1890 was $427, which translated to about a $1.50 a day. Some baseball players and promoters saw workers as an untapped potential audience, and they created another league to challenge Spalding's.[40]

In 1882 businessmen in six cities launched the American Association (AA) as a challenge to the monopoly of the National League. The AA specifically catered to working-class fans by underselling National League teams and shedding some of the moral constraints Spalding imposed. American Association teams charged an admission fee of twenty-five cents, adopted Sunday baseball, and sold alcohol in the ballpark. Indeed, many of the club owners responsible for creating the AA were saloonkeepers, brewers, and liquor manufacturers. Their sponsorship of professional baseball teams showed how "legitimate" and "illegitimate" economies and "rough" and "respectable" cultural norms functioned side by side. Tavern owners joined Spalding in becoming local civic leaders. Moreover, they used baseball as an advertising and sales vehicle for their products just as Spalding did for sporting goods. Yet the financial strength of the National League ultimately fueled the collapse of the American Association in 1891. The National League then took over many former American Association teams, creating in essence a corporate monopoly over baseball.[41]

In 1900 another challenge to the dominance of Spalding and the National League emerged, this time from a local Chicago competitor. Charles Comiskey and his friend Byron Bancroft "Ban" Johnson discussed the idea of creating an alternative league to challenge the National League. Comiskey and Johnson had become friends during their days with the Western League, one of the minor leagues formed in the 1890s.

Johnson, a sportswriter for the *Cincinnati Commercial-Gazette,* became president of the Western League, and Charles Comiskey managed the St. Paul team. The successes of the Western League included luring winning teams from major cities and strictly enforcing bans on gambling and rowdiness, striking a delicate balance between excitement and respectability. With fan support and league growth, Johnson and Comiskey changed the name to the American League, giving it a national character. The American League began as a minor league in 1900, and by 1901 it became a second and permanent American major league.[42]

The story of Charles Comiskey's entry into baseball is a highly romanticized one. It helped establish him as a local hero and contributed to the fans' view that baseball club owners were public-spirited citizens, not just entrepreneurs interested only in making money. According to one of many similar accounts, Comiskey got his baseball start by being drawn uncontrollably to a local sandlot game:

> One sunny summer's afternoon in 1876 a gangling, seventeen-year-old from Chicago's teeming West Side was making progress, such as it was, with a horse-drawn truckload of bricks destined for immediate use in reconstruction of the City Hall, a major project of the time. As his plodding span drew near Jackson and Laflin Streets, the youth became aware of a ball game in progress between the Hatfields and the McCoys of Chicago's sandlot ranks. The youth, who had some pretensions as a pitcher, drew up his weary steeds and got down from the driver's seat for a more critical survey of the situation.[43]

Comiskey persuaded the "Hatfields'" manager to put him in and save the game for his team. Comiskey left his load of bricks on the street and eagerly entered the game. In the meantime the workers at the construction site were awaiting their delivery, and it was up to Comiskey's father, "Honest John" Comiskey, alderman for the West Side's Seventh Ward, to take action. He found his son and the load of bricks he had abandoned and was forced to make a quick decision. The story continues, "Honest John made his choice. He took the bricks and drove away. He left his son committed to the game of baseball and thereby set in motion a train of the most interesting events the national pastime has ever recorded."[44]

The story highlights the social geography of the city and illustrates how spaces of leisure played significant roles not just in the daily lives of urban youth but in their potential careers as well. By his driving past the park on that fateful day, Comiskey's own future and his prominent role in the commercial life of the city were set in motion. That he was delivering bricks to build the new city hall further links him to the civic life of the city. Yet his alderman father, "Honest John," decided that Comiskey's potential contribution to the city was better served by playing baseball that day than by completing his delivery. John freed his son to pursue baseball as the vehicle through which he would shape Chicago's future.

Comiskey enjoyed a successful career as a player. He joined a semipro team in Elgin, Illinois, in 1875, and by 1878 he was first baseman and outfielder for the Northwestern League's Dubuque, Iowa, team. In 1882 Comiskey signed with the St. Louis Browns of the newly formed American Association, making $125 a month. By 1884 he became manager and led the team to four consecutive American Association pennants. In 1889 Comiskey joined several other players and managers seeking to challenge the rigid wage scale and reserve clause in the National League to create the Players' League.[45]

The Players' League grew out of players' efforts to take back some control over the game of professional baseball. Initially, these efforts resulted in the first union in baseball. In 1885 New York Giants captain John Montgomery Ward initiated the Brotherhood of Professional Base Ball Players to help raise the status of ballplayers as well as their salaries. In arguing for the necessity of the Brotherhood, Ward used the rhetoric of anticommercialism to challenge owners' treatment of players:

> There was a time when the National League stood for integrity and fair dealing; today it stands for dollars and cents. . . . Players have been bought, sold, or exchanged as though they were sheep, instead of American citizens. . . . By a combination among themselves, stronger than the strongest trusts, owners were able to enforce the most arbitrary measures, and the player had either to submit or get out of the profession in which he had spent years attaining proficiency.[46]

Ward's use of the language of citizenship and professionalism brilliantly captured the hypocrisy in the owners' rhetoric of Americanism. The union sought to improve wages and increase the respect accorded players by linking them to skilled republican artisans of the preindustrial era. In this way the organization was similar to the Knights of Labor, with its emphasis on artisan culture and skill. Ward attempted to demonstrate that the players, not the owners, embodied the values of expertise and integrity. In doing so, he tried to force Americans to recognize the crucial links between sporting culture and labor relations in America. He also exposed the ambivalence many Americans continued to feel over commercialism as a defining feature of American sport and recreation.

Members of the Brotherhood organized the Players' League in 1890 to mount a more serious challenge to managers' and owners' control of the labor force. This new league sought not only to raise players' wages but also to weaken the work rules set forth by the National League. The Players' League was defeated after less than two seasons, but not before Comiskey had a chance to bring a team to the South Side of Chicago. Its defeat resulted from Albert Spalding's "war committee," designed to undermine it by offering its financial backers lucrative opportunities to buy into the National League, in much the same way the National League had swallowed up the American Association teams. This defeat effectively lowered salaries and forestalled unionism for decades. The formation of the American League in 1900 only consolidated the power of management and owners against player-workers.[47]

Ironically, Comiskey was one of the owners who fully exploited this power relationship. Comiskey was forced to return to St. Louis after the collapse of the Players' League, but he had established enough of a base of support in Chicago with the Brotherhood team to return in 1900 and form the Chicago White Sox in the new American League. Comiskey also used his political ties to promote his baseball team. He offered free season tickets to local politicians, including aldermen, the city clerk, the chief of police, and the mayor. He also secured favorable licensing fees and had Chicago police deployed for free, to prevent ticket scalping outside the park and gambling inside.[48]

This arrangement points up the connections between the financial interests of the club owners, the promotion of order and respectability in the ballpark, and local political ties. Comiskey courted local politicians and police and exploited his ties to local working-class residents at the same time that he marked the ballpark as a safe and secure leisure space for middle-class patrons. This was a formula for success. Between 1901 and 1911, Comiskey earned over $700,000, proving how lucrative this model of commercial amusement could be.[49] Comiskey pointed to this success as evidence that sport was gaining legitimacy as a respectable enterprise. "Formerly sport was not regarded as a proper calling for young men," he explained. "It is beginning to assume its rightful place in society. To me baseball is as honorable as any other business. It is the most honest pastime in the world."[50] Comiskey's role as owner of the White Sox also showed how thoroughly the ideals of republicanism and player control that animated the Players' League gave way to a "robber baron" style of management that placed professional baseball more firmly in the ranks of corporate America than among either the sporting underworld or the organized play movement.

THE SOCIAL GEOGRAPHY OF THE BALLPARK

The success of Comiskey's American League White Sox, who won the World Series against their cross-town rivals the Cubs (formerly the White Stockings) in 1906, prompted Comiskey to consider building a modern ballpark for his club. Following the notion that endorsing respectability increased ticket sales, Comiskey set about looking for a site for the park. In planning and building a modern steel and concrete baseball field, Comiskey, like the owners of the other early "baseball palaces," linked the physical control of the game and the crowd to propriety and civic responsibility. By integrating classical design into its structure, Comiskey marked his park as an arena of public gathering and civic pride much like the field houses in the South Parks and the Civic Center in the Burnham Plan.

When Comiskey founded the White Sox in 1900 he secured a site at Thirty-ninth Street and Wentworth Avenue for the team's ballpark. Part of the agreement reached between the new American League and the rival National League was that the Chicago team could not build a park north of Thirty-fifth Street. Spalding had just built his White Stockings a $30,000 park on the West Side, at Polk and Taylor, in a primarily native-born, white middle-class neighborhood across the street from Cook County Hospital and just seven minutes from the Loop on the elevated line. By restricting Comiskey to a park south of Thirty-fifth, the National League hoped the American League team would not lure fans away from its franchise. Indeed, the creation of an American League team on the South Side only increased the number of fans and earnings from gate receipts in Chicago.[51]

The South Side Park at Thirty-ninth and Wentworth had been the home of the Chicago Cricket Club. The Chicago ball club of the small Union Association first used the field as a baseball park in 1884. The Union Association lasted less than a year, and it was not until 1900, when the White Sox moved there, that the field again was used for baseball. Comiskey and Ban Johnson got a loan, reportedly with "only their good names" as collateral, and hired workers to construct a grandstand in time for opening day in 1900. Comiskey's political connections evidently helped him meet this goal, for the construction workers, members of the powerful Building Trades Union, waived labor rules, working overtime and on Sundays in order to have the seats in place by April 21.[52]

The new grandstand held 15,000 spectators, and Comiskey had no trouble filling the seats. The grandstand was wooden, with box seats placed in the front of the stands. The park had no bleachers. Players sat on the bench in front of the stands, with little separation between players and fans. On days when the ballpark was crowded (particularly on Sundays) and spectators exceeded the capacity of the grandstands, fans stood in a roped-off area of the outfield, thereby reducing outfield distances and the space available for play. This hardly was a problem for the White Sox, since their park had one of the largest outfields of any major league team. In 1906, when the White Sox won the World Series, they held opponents to an average of 2.28 runs per game.[53]

The proximity of the fans to the players and umpires, though, threatened the safety Comiskey desired. In numerous turn-of-the-century wooden parks, fans tried to attack umpires after unpopular calls and to fight with players on opposing teams. The leagues issued fines for players' fighting and ejected unruly fans, but their success was limited by the unregulated space of the ballpark. Tommy Leach, a Red Sox player, described the mayhem of a World Series game against the Pirates in 1903: "The fans were *part* of the game in those days. They'd pour right out onto the field and argue with the players and the umpires. Was hard to keep the game going sometimes, to say the least."[54]

The ever-present threat of fire added to the club owners' worries. On August 6, 1894, Spalding's West Side park had a fire in the grandstand, which seated 6,000 fans. Between 1900 and 1911 there were at least five fires in major league parks across the country. In 1903, in one of the biggest tragedies since the 1871 fire, Chicago's Iroquois Theater burned, killing 602 people. After that, many cities rewrote fire codes to make public and semipublic buildings more fire resistant. In 1911 Chicago revised its municipal fire codes and added a specific section for ballparks, requiring that they limit the number of tickets sold to the park's seating capacity, have annual inspections, maintain clear aisles for exiting, and use fire-resistant materials for construction.[55]

Comiskey, however, did not wait for the revised codes to build a new park. His lease at the South Side Park was up in 1909, and that same year there was a fire in the grandstand. Comiskey rebuilt the grandstand but also started scouting other locations for his ball club. Several factors shaped his decision in locating a new park. Proximity to transportation was crucial, so the park could draw fans from throughout the city. Equally important was room for expansion. Baseball's popularity was soaring, and club owners across the country looked for grounds on which additional seating could be added. Perhaps most important was the neighborhood, for club owners wanted their parks to be perceived as safe. Pittsburgh Pirates owner Barney Dreyfuss gave his reasons for building a new park: "The game was growing up, and patrons were no longer willing to put up with nineteenth century conditions. Besides, the park was located in a poor neighborhood, and many of the better class of citizens, especially when accompanied by their womenfolk, were loath to go there."[56]

For these reasons, most of the teams that built the steel-and-concrete stadiums that would launch the "Golden Age of the Baseball Park" located their magnificent parks in "respectable" neighborhoods. These included Pittsburgh's Forbes Field and Philadelphia's Shibe Park, which opened in 1909 and set the standard for modern construction. Comiskey was the exception.[57]

Comiskey chose to build his new park in the working-class neighborhood of Armour Square, just east of largely Irish Bridgeport. Comiskey initially wanted to secure the field used by his former Brotherhood team at Thirty-fifth and Wentworth Avenue because the park was accessible from downtown by the Wentworth streetcar line. The neighborhood also was known for its support of professional baseball. The land where the Brotherhood park stood was unavailable, though. Instead, Comiskey chose the site of a municipal dump and cabbage patch, one block west at Thirty-fifth and Shields. This site happened to be one of the dumps that Mary McDowell worked with University of Chicago Settlement residents to clean up. By buying the property and locating the ballpark there, Comiskey perhaps did as much to clean up the area as McDowell had.

On December 22, 1908, Comiskey purchased the lot from the estate of former Chicago mayor John Wentworth for $100,000. It was being used by Signor Scavado for his truck garden, which supplied fruit and vegetables to South Side residents. Comiskey bought him out for an undisclosed amount and began plans to construct his stadium on the former dump site. He hired local architect Zachary Taylor Davis, who had contributed to the design of neighboring Armour Institute of Technology as well as South Side two-flats and St. Ambrose Roman Catholic Church at Forty-seventh Street and Ellis Avenue. Comiskey wanted his new park to be a pitcher's park, like South Side Park, with a deep outfield that favored pitching over hitting. He sent pitcher Ed Walsh

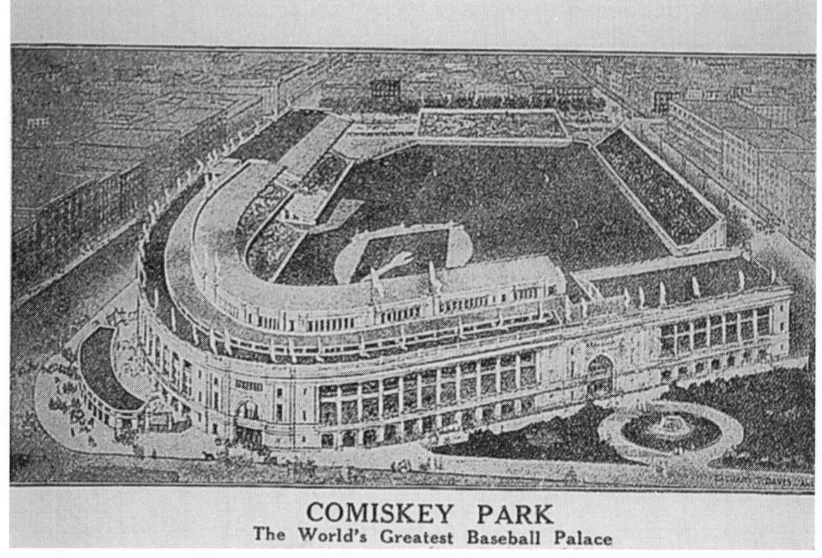

FIGURE 51. Architect Zachary Taylor Davis's design for Comiskey Park, built in 1910. Undated newspaper clipping in author's possession.

and Davis's assistant Karl Vitzhum, who also worked on Daniel Burnham's staff, to tour parks across the country for design ideas.[58]

Davis submitted his first sketch on October 6, 1909. His design was modeled on Forbes Field in Pittsburgh and called for a double-decked grandstand between first and third bases, with detached single-decked pavilions beyond. Separate uncovered wooden bleachers surrounded the outfield. Plans for the outer facade included a Roman-style design (fig. 51) similar to that of ornamental Shibe Park in Philadelphia. Comiskey called for revised plans, however, most likely because of the cost of implementing Davis's design. Instead, Davis created an outer facade of red pressed brick with large archways ringing the stadium. The arcaded masonry exterior with rhythmic archways recalled the Coliseum in Rome. The park embodied the symmetry and grandeur of City Beautiful design even without the more elaborate facade. The design also included Arts and Crafts motifs. Davis had worked as a draftsman in Louis Sullivan's studio, and he incorporated prairie school design elements into the raised geometric detailing running along the middle and sides of the archways. This design was similar to

Allen Pond's prairie motifs in his initial plans for the University of Chicago Settlement. This brick ornamentation subtly blended with the larger facade of the stadium and at the same time provided added decorative detailing.[59]

In addition, the new park's classically inspired design recalled the Armour Square field house immediately to its north, designed by Daniel Burnham (fig. 52) and echoed the design of churches and factories in the surrounding neighborhood. The red brick archways integrated the ballpark into the visual landscape of the Bridgeport community. Surrounding the park were numerous warehouses to the south, including the Chicago Shipping and Storage Company, C. P. Kimball and Company Automobile Factory, and People's Gas. To the west were the tracks of the Illinois Central Railroad, along with railroad warehouses. To the east was the Wentworth streetcar line, as well as the red Romanesque Armour Institute and numerous churches. North of the park, just beyond Armour Square, were several two-flats, workers' cottages, and apartments.[60]

The construction of Comiskey Park also stimulated small businesses along the periphery of the park's grounds. McCuddy's Bar, which became a neighborhood institution, was directly across from the main entrance. The tavern actually opened before the park was built, evidently based on inside information. Other vacant lots surrounding

FIGURE 52. Armour Square Recreation Center, Courtesy of the Chicago Park District Special Collections.

FIGURE 53. Comiskey Park's symmetrical design, 1910. Courtesy of the Chicago Historical Society.

the park were used as parking areas, while a Greek-owned ice-cream parlor opened on the corner of Thirty-fifth Street and Wentworth Avenue. Writer James T. Farrell remembered passing the ice-cream parlor on his way to the park as a youth, always tempted to get a soda and popcorn before he reached Comiskey. The presence of the park sent real estate values in the neighborhood soaring, almost doubling in value between 1900 and 1916. The corner of Thirty-fifth and Wentworth, east of the entrance, experienced the greatest increase, tripling in value between 1910 and 1915.[61]

Davis had to make the park fit within the street grid of the Armour Square neighborhood. Other ballparks built in urban neighborhoods during this period took on irregular shapes as they accommodated the surrounding city. Boston's Fenway Park, for example, had a short left field and much longer right field because of oddly designed street grids. Comiskey was fortunate that he secured a big lot, for he wanted a large, symmetrical outfield to favor pitching. Davis accommodated Comiskey, creating the first symmetrical ballpark in major league baseball. The dimensions of the field were 362 feet down the left and right foul lines and 200 feet to dead center field (fig. 53).[62]

The new ballpark seated 35,000 and, to accommodate working-class fans, had 7,000 twenty-five-cent bleacher seats, the largest number in the major leagues. By contrast, New York's Polo Grounds had only 200 twenty-five-cent seats. Groundbreaking for the stadium took place on February 14, 1910, and, despite a steel strike that delayed the first consignment of beams for five weeks, the park hosted its first game on April 15, 1910. The official opening was on July 1. The park cost a total of $750,000.[63]

A DAY AT THE PARK

The official opening of the new White Sox park was greeted with enormous fanfare. The afternoon's events began with an automobile parade, with Mayor Fred Busse leading the way. The parade commenced at City Hall, and by the time it reached the new grounds, over two hundred vehicles had joined. Decorated with banners, buttons, and emblems, the cars carried Chicago aldermen, police officers, county commissioners, and sportswriters. Once the parade reached the main entrance, five bands joined five marching companies and "marched in to the accompaniment of a storm of cheers that threatened to do damage to Mr. Comiskey's new structure." After the 28,000 fans who came to the opening filed into the park, Mayor Busse offered congratulatory remarks and presented Comiskey with a "shimmering, silken pennant." Comiskey wasted no time in linking patriotism and civic boosterism with professional athletic competition. After the military band raised the Stars and Stripes above the new stadium, he declared, "That flag is with us, they've given us a pennant to-day and we are going out after the other one from this moment."[64] The ceremony recalled the patriotism of the dedication of Davis Square five years earlier and illustrated how both public parks and professional ball fields could be infused with the same rhetoric of civic pride.

Accounts of the opening ceremonies marveled at how easily the unwieldy crowd moved from the parade outside the gates into their seats. The *Chicago Tribune* reported: "Despite the strangeness of it all to everyone concerned and the fact not one in 100 of the visitors had any idea of the location of their seats or the byways and hedges which led to them, the big crowd was handled smoothly and expeditiously. The yawning gates, with their swiftly clicking turnstyles, swallowed the people . . . sweeping them [into] the stands and . . . [toward] the seemingly endless rows of seats."[65]

Indeed, one of the factors that contributed to an atmosphere of refinement and order at the new park was the well-regulated control both of space and of people. New parks like Comiskey introduced crowd-control measures like turnstiles, to slow the surge of entering fans. Color-coded tickets directed spectators to specific gates to avoid a rush at the entrance. For greater safety as spectators entered and left the park, Comiskey installed ramps instead of stairs. Like the public parks and playgrounds, then, the designs of professional sports arenas encompassed ideas about properly ordered space and its ability to control behavior.

Comiskey's prescriptions for crowd control contributed to the segregation of crowds within the ballpark. Of the 35,000 seats, 6,400 were in boxes. In these seats sat local dignitaries. For example, on opening day, several boxes were occupied by friends of Comiskey as well as Chicago politicians. Mayor Busse sat in the "box of honor" above the players' "cage." Accompanying him were the assistant superintendent of police, the commissioner of public works, a Cook County judge, and several alderman. Comiskey's box included his immediate family, while friends both from Chicago and from other cities such as St. Louis and St. Paul occupied nearby boxes. The box seats let Chicago's commercial and political elite gather away from the boisterous crowd.[66]

Comiskey further promoted an atmosphere of respectability by charging different admission fees for various parts of the ballpark. In addition to the 6,400 box seats that sold for a dollar or more, there were 12,600 grandstand seats for seventy-five cents each, 9,000 pavilion seats for fifty cents, and the 7,000 twenty-five-cent bleacher seats. This pricing policy effectively confined working-class fans to the bleachers, reserving the grandstand and pavilion for white-collar and middle-class spectators.[67]

Despite this class segregation and all the pretenses toward refinement, the ballpark still was a male space. Comiskey sought to overcome the association between the park and male sporting culture in a variety of ways. For example, his new park had an inscription emblazoned on the grandstand: "NO BETTING ALLOWED IN THIS PARK" (fig. 54). Paradoxically, this visible reminder of ballpark regulations recalled the historical connections between professional sports and gambling. Yet it marked the park as a space where this link was broken, as police and private detectives patrolled the grounds to enforce club policy. In addition, Comiskey instituted ladies' days, when women were admitted free. While it is unclear what effect this had on behavior inside the park, the policy was effective in encouraging female attendance, for by World War I women made up over 10 percent of baseball crowds.[68]

From the start, Comiskey claimed that the park belonged to the people, and he made it available free of charge for local gatherings, including church picnics, union rallies, and athletic club games. In 1911 Comiskey donated the park to the black Eighth

FIGURE 54. Comiskey Park, showing sign, "NO BETTING ALLOWED IN THIS PARK." Courtesy of the Chicago Historical Society.

Regiment Army for Field Day exercises.[69] The park also was the site of various amusements including boxing matches, football games, and "auto polo" in 1913, a game in which players drove cars around the field and tried to hit a large ball with oversized mallets hung out the car windows (fig. 55). Comiskey hoped to make the park a site of local pride and to make himself a figure of community respect. In 1915, for example, he sponsored a float celebrating American prosperity and linked this prosperity to the success of the White Sox (fig. 56). For Comiskey, civic pride translated into commercial success and popular appeal.

Comiskey also catered to the press, recognizing, as had Spalding, that favorable newspaper coverage boosted fan support and ballpark attendance. Many sportswriters complained that ballparks did not accommodate them in any way, making it difficult for them to do their job adequately, since they were forced to mingle with the fans. Comiskey admitted reporters to his private drinking club on park grounds. The club

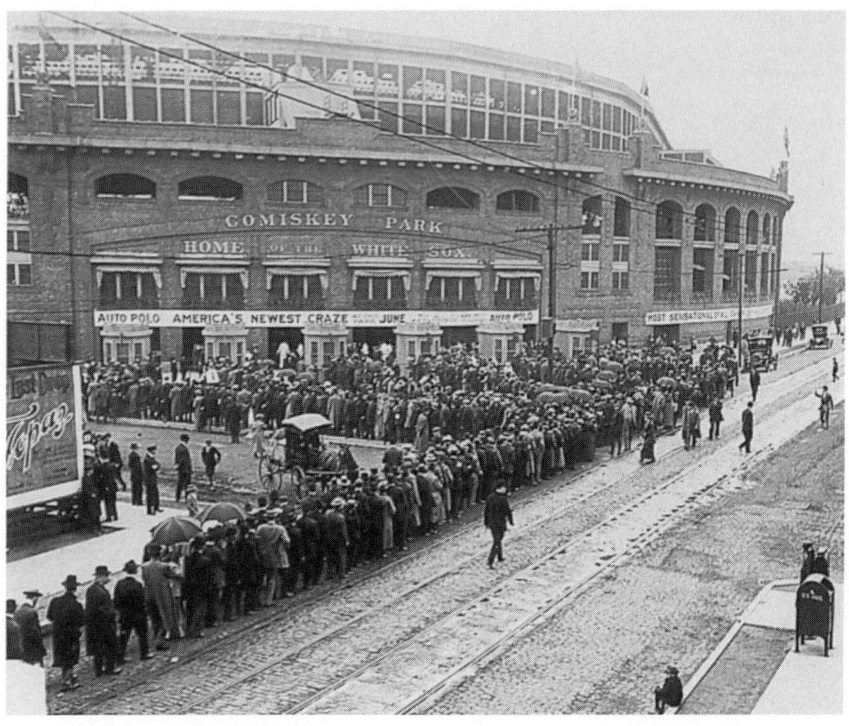

FIGURE 55. Crowds waiting to enter Comiskey Park for "Auto Polo: America's Newest Craze." Courtesy of the Chicago Historical Society.

consisted of politicians, civic leaders, show people, and newsmen. Comiskey called the group the Woodland Bards and invited them all on annual hunting and fishing trips in central Wisconsin. Baseball writing did come to play a large part in increasing the popularity of the game, as reporters like Hugh Fullerton and Ring Lardner, both Bards members, created a unique style of writing that incorporated the street slang of local urban sandlots into sports language and literature.[70]

The rise of baseball writing did much to promote the central place of Comiskey Park in the civic culture of the city. Baseball writers captured the excitement of the ballpark at the same time that they celebrated its atmosphere of civility and comradeship. James T. Farrell, who grew up on the South Side not far from Comiskey Park, remembered nostalgically the prominent part the park had in shaping his sense of local identity:

> I visualized Comiskey Park, with roaring and cheering fans, the players swinging, running to the bases. I imagined myself as a player and also a spectator seeing all of the action. My state of mind was almost describable as one of a walking coma. The sounds around me, the traffic on Grand Boulevard, an occasional horse and wagon, electric car or automobile on Fiftieth Street, of the elevated train, passing one block to the west, these all came to me as though muffled. They might have been the roar of the crowd at Comiskey Park.[71]

For Farrell, the sights and sounds of the ballpark mingled with those of the city around him, structuring his relationship with urban culture. He later discussed his experience of going to the ballpark and camping out overnight to buy bleacher seats for the 1917 World Series. After waiting for dawn to arrive and the ticket office to open, Farrell described his feelings about the crowd of people around him: "This long wait was an adventure rather than a boring experience. These strange men standing in line, sitting on boxes, squatting by a fire, playing poker, chatting intermittently about base-

FIGURE 56. White Sox Prosperity float, 1915. Courtesy of the Chicago Historical Society.

ball, showing the same concern as I did about the weather, shivering a bit as I did—they and I were bound together by a common passion. And those around me were kind and friendly. I felt secure and unafraid and I was like them."[72]

This celebration of democratic spirit, while a bit romanticized, attests to the way the local ballpark brought together diverse groups in the city in the shared project of rooting for the team. Within the ballpark, businesspeople, professionals, and politicians joined with artisans and factory workers to overcome class differences for those few hours and to see each other simply as fans. As sports editor Edward B. Moss put it, "Businessmen and professional men forget their standing in the community and shoulder to shoulder with the street urchin 'root' frantically for the hit needed to win the game."[73] Thus the ballpark functioned in much the same way that park promoters hoped public parks and field houses would, to bring together and even unite diverse groups.

The experience in the ballpark also helped fans transcend ethnic difference. Irish and Germans, especially at Comiskey, celebrated not only their pride in the local team but also their appreciation of fellow ethnic players. Baseball also became popular with the Czech and Polish crowds who came to Comiskey from the neighboring Back of the Yards. Since baseball was a popular sport among ethnic athletic club members, supporters felt a sense of belonging as fans in the major league ballpark. Comiskey even recruited Slavic players from the local sokols to attract fans. Ethnic groups, then, could experience the ballpark both as a site of American civic celebration and as a vehicle of ethnic pride.[74]

Baseball was less popular among Jewish immigrants. Many Jews argued that baseball detracted from the values of study they hoped to instill and that games like chess promoted. Second-generation Jews spoke about having to overcome their parents' hostility to the game. In addition, there were not many Jewish players fans could root for. Historian Steven Riess's calculations of ethnic professional ballplayers from 1901 to 1906 reveal only two Jewish rookies. No more entered the major leagues between 1910 and 1920, in part because of discrimination against Jews among both club owners and fans. This changed for Chicago fans in the 1920s when the White Sox signed catcher Moe Berg. Jewish residents of the South Side and throughout the city came to Comiskey Park to cheer for him. In 1928 Jewish White Sox fans were so enthusiastic about Berg that they offered to put up $25,000 for a special day at the park to honor him. Although Berg declined, the offer demonstrated the important part ethnic players had in generating fan support and creating an arena of ethnic diversity.[75]

African Americans had a more ambiguous relationship with the supposed democracy of the ballpark. The Black Belt, which swelled during the Great Migration during World War I, was just east of Comiskey Park. Wentworth Avenue, just a few blocks west of State Street, formed a solid barrier separating the Black Belt from the white ethnic neighborhoods to the west. White fans often complained because the Black Belt was so close to the park. In his autobiographical novel Farrell described a scene with two friends from the Washington Park area taking the elevated train to the park: "They got off with the crowd at Thirty-fifth Street. Crossing State Street, the sight of so many Negroes . . . talking on the corner made Danny afraid, because at home they always said that niggers would do things to him, and you never could trust a nigger because if you gave him an inch he always took a mile."[76]

African Americans attending games at Comiskey certainly experienced this virulent racism to a certain extent, yet what was more notable for many was that they were welcomed in the park itself. Being spectators at Comiskey Park became a source of pride for many blacks, especially those recently arrived from the South. One migrant from Mississippi exclaimed, "I wish you could have been here to those games. I saw them and believe me they was worth the money I pay to see them."[77] William Everett Samuels, a black musician and officer in Local 208 of the American Federation of Musicians, recalled the proximity of his home in the Black Belt to the new Comiskey Park. "I remember when they built White Sox's Park, that was in 1910. Before that they had a place at 49th [actually 39th] and Wentworth. They leased that to the American Giants, which was a colored ball team, and they moved it. Mr. Cominskey [*sic*], who owned the White Sox's, lived at 3510 Wabash when he built it. I used to see him every day when they built White Sox's Park."[78] Though Samuels was not a baseball fan, his memory of Comiskey walking by his home during the building of the park suggested that some of the neighborhood barriers separating the races on the South Side of Chicago could be crossed.

In addition, the *Chicago Defender,* the largest-selling black newspaper in the nation by World War I, featured regular stories and notices about the White Sox. As sociologists St. Clair Drake and Horace R. Cayton explained, "At ball-parks . . . and other spots where crowds congregate as spectators, Negroes [could] be found sitting where they please, booing and applauding, cheering and 'razzing,' with as little restraint as their white fellows." For many African Americans in Chicago, going to a baseball game was an experience of liberation and a celebration of taking part in the shared culture of Chicago civic life.[79]

At the same time, the African American experience at major league ball games differed from that of white ethnic groups. While blacks attended major league ball games and rooted alongside whites, they did not see fellow blacks on the ball field. The sense of pride and ethnic identification that many immigrants experienced was absent for African American spectators. The exclusion of black players suggested that as much as blacks might enjoy attending games, they were not a part of the complete civic experience embodied in the stadium. The creation of shared American identity in the ballpark, then, contributed to the construction of a civic identity defined, at least in part, by whiteness.[80]

THE BLACK SOX SCANDAL

Comiskey Park illustrated how groups who normally were segregated by the class, racial, and ethnic divisions inscribed in the urban landscape came together in a unified expression of local pride. At the same time, the park experience exposed the fault lines in modern civic culture, laying bare in the stands and on the field the differences in social, economic, and racial status of the city's population. The 1919 "Black Sox" scandal, and the rhetoric used to shape it, demonstrate how commercial leisure sites like baseball parks became battlegrounds in which the meanings of Americanism, democracy, and loyalty were fought out.[81]

On October 1, 1919, the Chicago White Sox played the opening game of the World Series against the Cincinnati Reds and lost nine to one. This was a shocking defeat, for the White Sox were touted as one of the best teams in baseball history. Yet the loss was an omen of things to come, for by the end of the series the White Sox had lost to the Reds five games to three. The larger significance of the loss was not realized for another year, when several White Sox players testified that they had intentionally thrown the series in an arrangement with a nationwide gambling syndicate. The response to the scandal showed how the lines between labor and leisure blurred as Americans looked to commercial amusements like baseball as a source of stability and national identity after World War I.[82]

The prominent place that the Black Sox scandal still holds in American culture testifies to the way it embodies elements of American ideals in the twentieth century. Numerous stories about the scandal are etched in national memory. One involves the reaction of Chicago youth to the news. A crowd of Chicagoans gathered outside the

Cook County courthouse on September 29, 1920, to see the White Sox players who had testified about throwing the 1919 World Series. When outfielder Joe Jackson came out of the court, a newsboy stepped forward and exclaimed, "Say it ain't so, Joe. Say it ain't so." Jackson responded, "It's so, kid."[83]

This story has been repeated in various forms, through a variety of media, for decades. Many baseball reporters claim the story is apocryphal, but others insist it is true.[84] Whether or not the story happened this way, if at all, it is a poignant tale not only about children's love for baseball but also about how the scandal exposed deeper divisions in American culture. According to many observers, it led to the downfall of American youths' faith in the purity of baseball and in the integrity of their heroes. Embedded in these concerns was the idea that baseball represented America as a whole. The game joined leisure and recreation with nationalism and American identity. By 1919, when philosopher Morris Cohen referred to baseball as "the national religion," few argued.[85]

This belief in baseball's Americanness was clear in the rhetoric employed during the 1919 World Series. Sports fans, owners, and writers eagerly anticipated its start.. This would be the first World Series played since the American victory in World War I, adding additional nationalist fervor to the already patriotic event. A *New York Times* article captured this zeal by suggesting that the series had the potential to draw all Americans together despite the contentious events dividing the nation during that summer: "The war against the Bolshevik, the conflict on the Adriatic, the race riots, the struggle between labor and capital, all fade into the background just now; the one topic of transcendent interest, the one great issue, is the struggle now being fought out between the White Guards from that great city which certain of its own poets have hailed as 'hog butcher to the universe' and the warlike Reds from the Metropolis of Malt."[86]

Morris Cohen elaborated his theory of baseball as the national religion by drawing analogies between the game, moralism, and war. "Instead of purifying only fear and pity," he argued, "baseball exercises and purifies all of our emotions, cultivating hope and courage when we are behind, resignation when we are beaten, fairness to the other team when we are ahead, charity for the umpire, and above all the zest for combat and conquest."[87]

Baseball was linked to the war effort in more than just rhetoric. During the 1917 season, the year the White Sox won the World Series, major league baseball teams conducted military drills for one hour each day. In May 1918, with war still raging, Secretary of War Newton Baker issued a "work or fight" order, forcing all eligible men to contribute in some way to the war effort. Over half of the professional baseball players entered the armed forces, while others sought jobs at munitions factories, shipyards, and steel mills. Yet many of the ballplayers who went to work in these factories actually spent more time playing baseball on the company teams. Companies went so far as to recruit big-name players and give them money and fringe benefits for improving the team and drawing crowds.[88]

Many sports writers and fans criticized those players who went to work rather to fight. Charles Comiskey condemned the "disloyal" players as well. His patriotic rhetoric veiled his deeper concern, matched by other club owners, that the company teams who were paying players were subverting the authority of the major league clubs by undermining the reserve clause. The war allowed players to offer their services in an open market and sell to the highest bidder. It was one of the rare instances, aside from strikes and the formation of alternative leagues, in which players enjoyed some control over their labor and work conditions; they made demands and either had them met by one club or threatened to go to another. With the end of the war, players returned to the teams that "owned" them, and despite the owners' threats during the war, most took back all of their players, even those "disloyal" men who had not joined the armed forces.[89] For most owners, winning was the bottom line, and they were loath to threaten their gate receipts and competitive edge by dismissing star players. The reserve clause also ensured that players' relative freedom during the war would revert to owners' complete control over the labor pool. There was no room for negotiating salaries and work conditions.

Both of these issues proved contentious for Chicago White Sox players during the start of the 1919 season. By the end of the season the team was commonly regarded as the one with the most talent, though the players' salaries were often lower than those of mediocre and poor teams, despite their high drawing capacity and gate receipts.[90] These low salaries, combined with a meager daily food allowance, a charge to players to have their uniforms laundered, and the general disdain of the reserve clause, caused a great deal of player dissatisfaction both within the White Sox and throughout the league. When rumors began circulating about a World Series fix, it was not much of a surprise to many journalists closely associated with the game.

Sports writers like Ring Lardner and Hugh Fullerton suspected a fix right from the start. The first game of the series, on October 1, 1919, was enough to fuel these suspicions. The White Sox were touted as easy favorites to win the championship, and the league's leading pitcher, Eddie Cicotte, was pitching in the opening game.[91] Yet the Reds demolished the White Sox, in the first game and in the series. After the series loss, baseball promoters and sports journals did their best to reassert the purity of the game. Sports writers attacked Fullerton as unpatriotic and ignorant of the game.[92] Even the *Chicago Daily News* reported that rumors of a fix were unfair and unfounded:

> Predications on the World Series did not come true in every instance. Some experts who put in many hours figuring out the "dope" gave the White Sox the edge at nearly every position. The Reds upset the predications, and it is an arduous task for the experts who picked the American leaguers to find a suitable alibi. Most of them find it impossible to do so and in order to cover up their mistake cast reflections on the integrity of the national game by insinuating that gambling had something to do with the final results of the battle. Nothing is more absurd.[93]

Reports of a scandal quickly spread, however, and the public was forced to face what many observers had suspected all along. Yet the scandal was confirmed only after a grand jury was called to investigate evidence of corruption involving other clubs, the Chicago Cubs and the Philadelphia Athletics, during the 1920 season. In addition, there were rumors of players from the Yankees, Braves, Red Sox, Indians, and Giants fixing games. Even the great Ty Cobb was suspected. On September 7, 1920, a special Cook County grand jury was established to investigate the rumors surrounding not only the Cubs-Phillies game, but baseball gambling in general. Illinois state's attorney Maclay Hoyne led the investigation and took testimony from a large cast of players and gamblers. The focus, however, soon returned to the White Sox and the 1919 World Series.[94]

On September 27, 1920, the *Philadelphia North American* featured a headline reading, "Gamblers Promised White Sox $100,000 to Lose." The article included an interview with Bill Maharg, a former prize fighter, who related details of how the fix was planned between him, former baseball player William "Sleepy" Burns, first baseman Arnold "Chick" Gandil, and pitcher Eddie Cicotte. Gandil claimed eight White Sox players were willing to go along with the fix, including him, Cicotte, pitcher Claude "Lefty" Williams, third baseman George "Buck" Weaver, outfielder Oscar "Happy" Felsch, shortstop Charles "Swede" Risberg, infielder Fred McMullin, and outfielder "Shoeless Joe" Jackson. By the time the deal was cemented, Maharg said, New Yorker Abe Attel, the former featherweight champion, and Boston gambler Joseph "Sport" Sullivan were involved in raising the necessary money, which they ultimately obtained from Arnold Rothstein, head of one of New York's largest gambling syndicates.[95]

Once the story broke, commentators continued extolling the virtues of the game and its central role in both shaping and reflecting American values. In doing so, they helped recreate the myth of a "golden age of baseball" when it was "pure" and "honest." The language used to discuss the scandal emphasized loyalty, integrity, and Americanism. An article in the *Nation* focused on public belief in the integrity of the game and the reasons behind people's trust in players. "The man at bat, cheer him or hoot at him as we may, is supposed to be doing his best. There is something about the very nature of the game, played in the bright sunlight with nerves at the very edge of tension, that produces the illusion of a cleanliness in the characters of the performers more or less comparable to the sharp, clean movements and instinctive responses of their bodies."[96]

The *North American Review* featured a piece by Walter Camp, director of athletics at Yale University, discussing the links between spectators and baseball players. "Baseball is the true National Game of America. It is a game for the people, played by them and understood by them. . . . Is it any wonder, then, that the public feels a vested interest in this game, and that they are inexpressibly shocked to discover that these players whom they had admired and in whom they had implicit confidence, have been betraying them by selling games?"[97] Camp ended by emphasizing the importance of a player's "loyalty to his uniform" and his "honesty of purpose and . . . single-heartedness in the struggle to win." The *American Review of Reviews* reported that to destroy a boy's faith in "the integrity and honesty" of baseball was to "plant suspicion of all things in his heart."[98]

Throughout the investigation into the fix, reporters portrayed the eight White Sox players as traitors to the game and betrayers of American values. The *Philadelphia Bulletin* compared the indicted players to "the soldier or sailor who would sell out his country and its flag in time of war."[99] The Roosevelt Club of Boston newsboys passed a resolution stating that "the eight White Sox players be condemned and punished for this murderous blow at the kids' game; and be it further resolved that Ray Schalk and Dickie Kerr be commended for their manly stand against the Benedict Arnolds of baseball." Charles Comiskey even offered bonuses of $1,500 to "his honest Sox" in the fall of 1920, when the White Sox were on the verge of capturing the American League pennant once again.[100] Both Comiskey and the press publicly made a sharp distinction between the honest Sox and the disloyal ones and sought to distance themselves and baseball from the latter.

On September 28, one day after the exposé in the *Philadelphia North American,* Charles Comiskey's lawyer Alfred Austrian advised Cicotte, Lefty Williams, and Jackson to confess their roles in the fix before the grand jury. He suggested that by cooperating they would receive immunity, and he told each that the others had already implicated all those involved. In fact, the players signed a waiver of immunity and "confessed" to committing crimes in which they had not played a part. Once the trial got under way, Austrian played a behind-the-scenes part in the players' defense, which was headed by Michael Ahearn (who would later become one of Al Capone's lawyers), partner Thomas Nash, and former state's attorney Ben Short. The eight White Sox and several named gamblers were charged with "conspiracy to defraud the public, . . . conspiracy to commit a confidence game, . . . and conspiracy to injure the business of Charles A. Comiskey."

The district attorney surprised everyone during his opening statements by explaining that the signed confessions of Cicotte, Jackson, and Williams, since retracted, had been lost or stolen. The defense argued that the state now had no case and that the testimonies were obtained under duress and were inadmissible anyway. After fourteen days of questioning, the jury deliberated for two hours before returning a verdict of not guilty, arguing that the state had not proved that "it was the intent of the ballplayers and the gamblers . . . to defraud the public and others and not merely to throw ballgames." The players were cleared of all charges.[101]

During the course of the trial, attention and blame shifted away from the players and toward the gamblers who were named in the indictments. Newspaper accounts referred to the "crooked crooks and gamblers" who were willing to "debase the great national game." During the trial, attended by the accused White Sox but not by the named gamblers, defense attorney Ben Short argued that the state had no case because it was charging the wrong people. "If [the case] wasn't a failure, you'd have the real babies of the conspiracy here—the men who made millions—and not these ballplayers who were reported to get big salaries but most of whom got practically nothing."[102]

Indeed, numerous accounts painted the ballplayers as the victims of the chicanery and furtiveness of the "professional gambler." According to an article in the *Outlook,* "The more the facts become known as regards bribery and game-selling in baseball, the more evident it is that the professional gambler is at the root of the evil." The article went on to express concern over the lack of prosecution of the gamblers. "But what of the sure-thing gamblers? What of those high up, the men who plotted this thing and carried it through, the parasites who preyed on the weakness of character of these unfortunate creatures?"[103] The *Grand Rapids Herald* protested, "When cheap leeches strike at this sport of sports they strike at one of the institutions of the Republic."[104]

Some commentators linked the gambling scandal explicitly to "foreigners," and Jews in particular (specifically gambler Arnold Rothstein, even though he played a minor role in the initial scheme to fix the Series). Commentators linked Jewishness with financial wheeling and dealing, illicit gambling, and un-Americanness. The *Sporting News,* the weekly baseball publication out of St. Louis, issued the harshest indictment of "outsiders" threatening the sanctity of an American institution. "Because a lot of dirty, long-nosed, thick-lipped, and strong-smelling gamblers butted into the World Series —an American event, by the way—and some of said gentlemen got crossed, stories were peddled that there was something wrong with the way the games were played." Henry Ford's *Dearborn Independent* was more straightforward in its anti-Semitic rhetoric. Ford argued that Jews were responsible for all corruption in baseball and scorned them for "soiling the good name of American sports." The *Sporting News* condemned Ford for these "bigoted" statements but proceeded to argue that the best way to clean up baseball was to get the players to inform on one another. It argued that the National Commission, the governing body of baseball, should give medals to players who exposed betrayers among their teammates. "You wouldn't sit down to a poker game with a card player who cheated, would you?" [105] By placing blame squarely on the shoulders of gamblers, and by linking gamblers to the supposed ethnic underworld of vice and corruption, baseball promoters and the popular press could distance the players themselves from the scandal and reassert the purity of the game and its Americanness.

Baseball promoters still feared that the Black Sox scandal would permanently damage the respectability of baseball. The *New York Times* commented, "Professional baseball is in a bad way, not so much because of the Chicago scandal as because that scandal has provoked it to bringing up all the rumors and suspicions of years past." [106] Editorials and cartoons placed baseball back in the same company as horseracing and prizefighting, regarded by many as disreputable underworld pursuits that threatened American values and institutions. The *Kansas City Times* reported, "Owners, managers, and players have got to convince the public the game is square. Unless they can do that baseball must ultimately go the way of horse-racing. The public will not stand for a crooked sport." [107]

Promoters of organized baseball recognized the need to restore faith in the integrity of the game in order to keep the sport popular with the public and thus profitable. The grand jury organized to investigate corruption in baseball took the first step toward meeting this demand. Headlines reported that the investigation "[Found] Baseball Generally Honest," arguing that "the leaders in organized baseball may be relied upon to keep the game above suspicion." [108] Supporters of the game employed the im-

FIGURE 57
Cartoons linking baseball to gambling, mocking the notion that the game ever was "straight and clean." *Literary Digest* 67, no. 2 (Oct. 9, 1920): 12.

agery of cleanliness to sanction its honesty. Articles such as "Making the Black Sox White Again," "The Flaw in the Diamond," and "The Baseball Scandal" featured cartoons depicting baseballs being scrubbed "clean and white" (figs. 57 and 58).[109] The imagery used to describe the scandal, from the term "Black Sox" to the promotion of cleanliness, reflected the overarching concern with labeling anything that potentially threatened American purity as dirty, foreign, and subversive.

To ensure baseball's purity, club owners acted on the grand jury's advice and reorganized the National Commission, putting it solely in the hands of one publicly respected governing official. Club owners put forth several men as possible commissioners, including war hero General John J. "Black Jack" Pershing and Judge William Howard Taft. Ultimately, they chose Judge Kenesaw Mountain Landis, who initially presided over the 1915 Federal League lawsuit that reaffirmed the legality of the reserve clause and exempted baseball from antitrust legislation.[110]

FIGURE 58. Cartoon mocking Judge Kenesaw Mountain Landis's attempts to "clean up baseball." *Literary Digest* 70, no. 8 (Aug. 20, 1921): 13.

Landis immediately worked to "clean up baseball" by expelling all eight White Sox who were acquitted the year before. "Regardless of the verdict of the juries," he argued, "no player who throws a ball game, no player that undertakes or promises to throw a ball game, no player who sits in confidence with a bunch of crooked players and does not promptly tell his club about it, will ever play professional baseball!"[111] Landis evidently agreed with the *New York World*'s contention that "if the crooks who were acquitted try to show their faces in decent sporting circles they should be boycotted and blackballed." While several cartoons and editorials criticized Landis's harsh actions and words, others supported his efforts to save the image of baseball. The *St. Louis Globe-Democrat* linked the integrity of baseball to American morality in general. "If Judge Landis can keep the game of baseball on a high plane of sports ethics, he will do far more for the boys of America than he has ever done or can ever do on the Federal bench. . . . Nor could he do more for the country as a whole, because the standard of integrity of the boy becomes also his standard as a citizen."[112]

The focus on "gamblers" and "outsiders" as responsible for sullying the game allowed baseball promoters, club owners, and fans once again to proclaim their faith in the integrity of America's national pastime. By rooting out the criminals and corrupters of the game, Landis and other supporters of baseball argued for its continued honesty. Moreover, this strategy allowed club owners and the public in general to sidestep issues of labor relations and owner subjugation as the central factors contributing to baseball scandals. Gambling and player involvement provided a way players could assert their autonomy in the face of complete owner authority, best symbolized by the reserve clause and blacklisting. By refusing to confront this long history of the links between gambling and labor disputes in baseball, Landis reasserted the owners' absolute power to impose salaries and work conditions on players who had no recourse.

Charles Comiskey's creating the American League and founding a lucrative baseball franchise on the South Side of Chicago underscored the function of professional sports in linking recreation and mass amusement to the world of respectable business and civic leadership. Comiskey illustrated how baseball club owners straddled the culture of the saloon and ethnic politics and the values of decorum and expertise championed by modern corporate America. His career showed that the connections between the economies of the corporation and of commercial amusement were more fluid and integrated than the critiques of many reformers allowed.

Owners of professional ball clubs tried to overcome the objections of reformers by linking commercial amusement with professionalism and baseball with respectability. They used the language of expertise that dominated the university and the corporation to portray the place of professional sports in the modern marketplace. Club owners codified rules and regulations, statistical measures of talent, and strict prescriptions for training. In doing so, they positioned themselves as "legitimate" businesspeople at the same time that they expanded their spectator base to include a broad spectrum of city residents. Their efforts show that commercial amusements were not programmatically illegitimate or "not respectable." Middle-class reformers were not the only civic leaders promoting Americanization and disciplined leisure. Cultural entrepreneurs like Comiskey were agents of uplift as well, though on their own terms. Professional baseball fields, much like public parks, became arenas where notions of respectability, civic order, and Americanism were refashioned by a wide variety of participants.

Commercial amusements also allowed second-generation immigrants to transcend the cultural world of their parents. Participating in mass culture made them feel more "American" and at the same time forged cross-ethnic alliances that contributed to the class solidarity that ultimately made union organizing easier. Americanization was not simply imposed from above through programs of supervised play or lessons in civics. It also could emerge from below, as immigrants sought to make a place for themselves on their own terms and in spaces of their own choosing. Increasingly those spaces were sites of commercial amusement.[113]

The construction of an elaborate baseball park like Comiskey Park reflected the increasing prominence of commercial leisure in American urban culture. By creating a monumental edifice to house his ball club, Comiskey exemplified the growing belief among turn-of-the-century businesspeople as well as reformers that architectural design and the built environment helped shape respectable behavior and civic engagement. While spectators left the park with a variety of perspectives on its role in simultaneously reflecting and forming American culture, they nonetheless understood that commercial amusement played a significant part. The history of Comiskey Park demonstrates how promoters of commercial culture encouraged social interaction that contributed to Americanization and civic pride.

The Black Sox scandal also showed how popular culture helped shape broader elements of civic identity. It came to stand for themes like respectability, loyalty, and integrity. Baseball players were national heroes who were supposed to represent all that was good about America. When their behavior threatened American values they were labeled as traitors. The scandal, then, illustrates how sites of commercial leisure like Comiskey Park became arenas for negotiating the meanings of Americanism, civic culture, labor, and leisure.

6

A MECCA FOR PLEASURE

Leisure, Work, and Spaces of Race Pride

IN 1918, BLACK AUTHOR AND POET Langston Hughes arrived in Chicago for the first time. In his autobiographical novel *The Big Sea,* he described the thrill of experiencing "the Stroll"—that section of State Street in the Black Belt, between Twenty-sixth and Thirty-ninth Streets. "South State Street was in its glory then," he wrote, "a teeming Negro Street with crowded theaters, restaurants, and cabarets. And excitement from noon to noon. Midnight was like day. The street was full of workers and gamblers, prostitutes and pimps, church folks and sinners."[1] The *Chicago Defender* touted the Stroll as "the popular promenade for the masses and classes." Even the thrill of amusement parks, "with their narrow ideas in the treatment afforded various races," could be ignored when one experienced the Stroll. This "poor man's paradise" was a "Mecca for Pleasure" for local residents as well as visitors, blacks as well as whites.[2]

The excitement Hughes and the *Defender* conveyed in their descriptions of the Stroll embodied the role the district played in shaping ideas about identity, freedom, and race pride in the urban North. In this rigidly defined space, blacks carved out a cultural identity that wedded the traditions of their southern heritage to their hopes and ambitions in industrialized cities of the North. For many African Americans in Chicago, especially the new migrants just making their way from the South in the first decades of the twentieth century, civic pride and community identity were found not in public parks, beaches, or field houses but in the emerging commercial leisure district centered on State Street. This district included both the respectable businesses of "old settlers" and the new sites of commercial amusement that began to proliferate in cities throughout America by 1910.

William Everett Samuels, one of the leaders of the Black Musicians' Union Local 208, described how the Stroll provided blacks a place to display a sense of pride and even flamboyance that was off limits to them in other parts of the city. Referring to his experiences in the 1920s, he said, "You see, you could go from 31st to 35th Street. . . . The stores were open twenty-four hours a day—the barber shops, the haberdasheries, the restaurants; and people would come from all over the world. You could stand at 35th street and see people from any place you wanted to see because they came here to go—just like Times Square."[3] Samuels's comments illustrate the importance for blacks of claiming urban spaces as their own in order to create a sense of belonging. Here, on the Stroll, blacks met friends and relatives, caught up on the day's news, and established communal ties. This was a site of local knowledge, a gathering place where community concerns were discussed, debated, and negotiated. That these activities took place on street corners and sidewalks, in front of saloons and dance halls, attests to the lack of public recreational facilities like parks and field houses in Black Belt neighborhoods. It also shows the difficulties and dangers blacks faced when they attempted to use those so-called public spaces. Public parks and beaches were not just inaccessible to blacks; they also posed grave risks to their safety and security.

Not surprisingly, the race riot of 1919 began at a public beach. On a steamy July afternoon, two African American boys enjoyed a swim in Lake Michigan at the black Twenty-sixth Street beach. But when Eugene Williams drifted past the invisible barrier separating the black beach from the white one farther south, he ignited a deadly battle that remains an enduring legacy in structuring race relations in Chicago. The events of the riot, and the way they unfolded, demonstrate how spatial geography contributed to racial animosity in the city. When Williams inadvertently passed that dividing line on his raft, he crossed a boundary no less well defined than the one separating the two beaches. He challenged the racial boundaries between public spaces in Chicago, which matched the more elusive racial separation in the workplace and in residential areas that contributed to the rising entrenchment of segregation (fig. 59).[4]

Unlike similar episodes of racial brutality that took place in America after World War I and the Great Migration, the Chicago riot was not directly sparked by housing or workplace tensions.[5] Instead, the riot reflected the increasingly important part

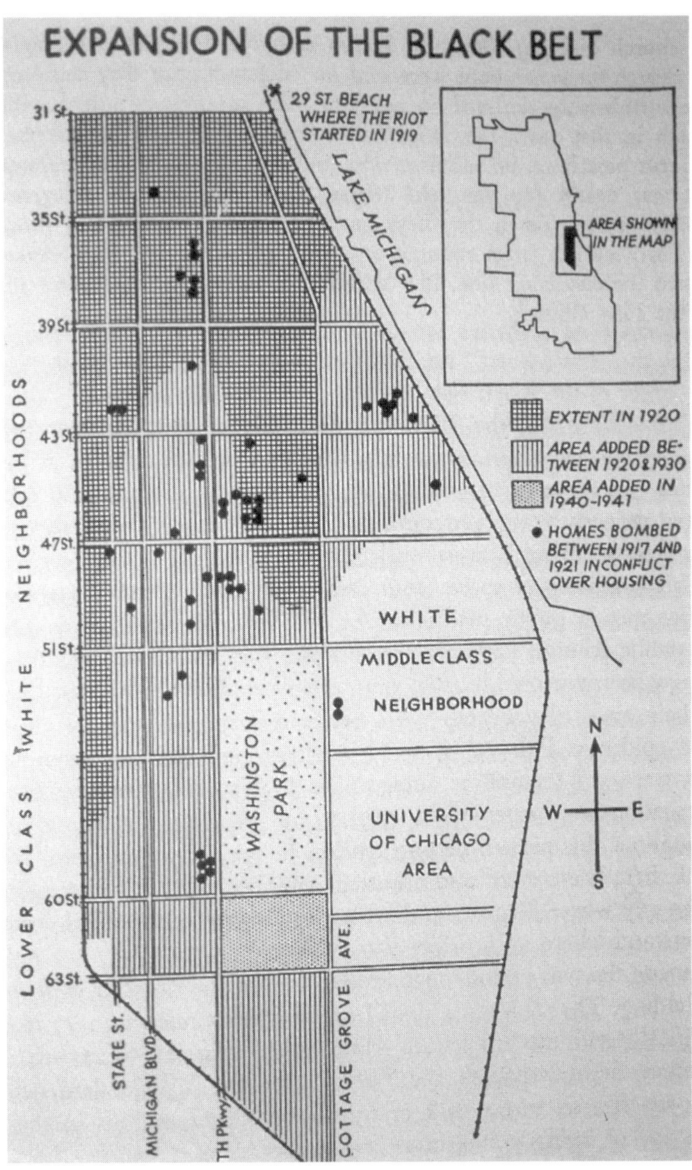

FIGURE 59. "Expansion of the Black Belt," in St. Clair Drake and Horace R. Cayton, *Black Metropolis: A Study of Negro Life in a Northern City* (New York: Harcourt, Brace, 1945), 63.

leisure spaces played in structuring race relations within the city. They also were central in determining how black leaders tried to advance community identity and racial uplift. The theme of race pride was central to discussions of community formation in the emerging Black Belt, as African American club women, local businesspeople, and religious leaders focused on respectability in northern black communities. How to define respectability became a central concern for black civic leaders in large part because of the associations made between commercial leisure and illicit activity, vice and the Black Belt.

A close examination of the social geography of the Black Belt illustrates both the physical and the cultural proximity of spaces of respectability and areas of "vice." Race leaders, like white reformers, often decried the rise of commercialized leisure for its role in promoting vice. Yet efforts at eradicating vice in white areas, and the simultaneous rigidifying of the Black Belt before the Great Migration, meant that the segregation of vice went hand in hand with racial segregation, with "licit" and "illicit" economies and leisure sites moving closer and closer together.[6] The formal and informal economies of the Black Belt often intermingled and made definitions of respectability more permeable than in white communities. This is not to suggest that race leaders promoting respectability accepted the presence of so-called vice in their community. Rather, urban segregation made the sharp lines leaders hoped to draw between licit and illicit spaces in the Black Belt more difficult to maintain, particularly with the increasing importance of commercialized leisure in structuring urban life, both black and white.

THE RACIALIZING OF SPACE IN CHICAGO

The racial boundaries shaping the South Side became increasingly rigid in the years leading up to and following World War I. The Great Migration of blacks from South to North led the black population of Chicago to increase by 148.5 percent between 1910 and 1920. By 1915 the narrow Black Belt, bounded by Twelfth and Thirty-ninth Streets, State and Lake Michigan, solidified and pushed farther south to Forty-seventh Street.[7]

One of the factors fueling the expansion of the Black Belt was the availability of less expensive housing in bordering areas like Hyde Park, Kenwood, and Woodlawn before World War I. Many of the hotels and apartment buildings constructed for the 1893 Columbian Exposition now were vacant, and owners turned them into rooming houses to try to keep them profitable. Many whites in the area also began moving to the North Shore and South Shore, farther from downtown, in areas that were suburban in character. These changes occurred at the start of the Great Migration. At a time when more blacks were coming to Chicago from the South and the Black Belt was increasingly crowded, these neighborhoods provided cheaper housing to help supply the growing population. Both white and black real estate agents rented property to the black migrants in large part because blacks were the only takers. Yet as the boundaries of the Black Belt expanded during and after the war, racial tensions were fueled. Some of the greatest hostility was in the contested neighborhoods like Hyde Park and Kenwood that still were predominantly white.[8]

In part, racial tensions over housing erupted during the war because these years represented the height of the Great Migration, with more blacks coming north in search of wartime employment. At the same time, the suspension of construction during the war created a housing shortage, so there were more blacks coming to Chicago with less housing available. A 1917 realtors' survey showed 664 black applicants for 97 listings. Of those, only 50 secured housing.[9] Increased pressure for housing for blacks was exacerbated after the war by the return of soldiers, both black and white. This homecoming created even greater friction and fostered white homeowners' efforts to keep blacks out of their neighborhoods.

Such efforts were justified by claims about the detrimental effect blacks had on property values. Many neighbors who formed the Hyde Park and Kenwood Property Owners' Association (HPKPOA) argued that blacks had to be kept out to save the neighborhoods from "almost certain destruction." A flyer announcing the October 20, 1918, meeting of the Grand Boulevard district of the HPKPOA asked, "Shall we sacrifice our property for a third of its value and run like rats from a burning ship, or shall we put up a united front and keep Hyde Park desirable for ourselves? It's not too late." The intended goal of this meeting was to create strategies to "make Hyde Park white."[10]

The Association claimed it had no quarrel with blacks and did not wish to harass or intimidate them. The issue simply was one of real estate values. According to one estimate, the property covered by the Association was valued at $50,000,000. Protecting that investment was the goal of the HPKPOA. Yet the *Property Owners' Journal*, the publication of the Association, used more conspicuous racist rhetoric to push its agenda of keeping blacks out. "Any property owner who sells property anywhere in our district to undesirables is an enemy of the white owner and should be discovered and punished," stated one issue. These punitive tactics were not reserved for property owners but were directed at blacks themselves. According to the *Journal,* "every colored man who moves into Hyde Park knows that he is damaging his white neighbor's property. Therefore, he is making war on the white man." The *Journal* suggested that blacks attempting to "invade" white areas should be denied jobs. "If employers should adopt a rule of refusing to employ Negroes who persist in residing in Hyde Park to the damage of the white man's property, it would soon show good results."[11]

Restrictive covenants and threats of unemployment were not the only tactics whites used to keep blacks within the Black Belt. Some residents resorted to violence. Between July 1917 and March 1921 fifty-eight black homes in Chicago were bombed, most of them on the South Side (fig. 60). Victims were blacks who had moved into white neighborhoods and both black and white real estate agents who sold property to blacks in predominantly white areas. These bombings attest to the central role of territoriality and the racializing of urban space in determining white response to black settlement patterns. As the commission appointed to investigate the race riot explained, "Bombing of real estate men's properties appears to have been part of a general scheme to close the channels through which the ["Negro"] invasion proceeded rather than a protest of neighbors."[12] Bombings, like restrictive covenants, served to maintain the color line in housing and neighborhood composition.

Of course, other bombings were aimed directly at residents, attesting to the increasingly virulent racism in cities like Chicago. The bombing at the home of African American S. P. Motley illustrates how racial tensions were rising following World War I. Motley had bought his home at 5230 Maryland Avenue, in the western portion of Hyde Park, in 1913. He and his family lived there with little incident until 1917. On July 1 of that year, with no warning, a bomb exploded in the vestibule of the house, and the front of the building was destroyed. Two years later, after rumors circulated that Motley planned to buy the adjacent building, it too was bombed. Only after the influx of blacks to Chicago and the increasing demand for housing did the issue of a black family's living in a predominantly white neighborhood provoke outright violence.[13]

The most publicized bombing case was the one directed at Jesse Binga. Binga represented the entrepreneurial success story that many "race leaders" like Booker T. Washington extolled. He had come to Chicago in 1893, the year of the Columbian Exposition, and stayed there working as a Pullman porter and then a street vendor. He used his earnings to invest in real estate on the South Side, and by 1908 he had become not only the leading black real estate owner in Chicago but also the city's leading black

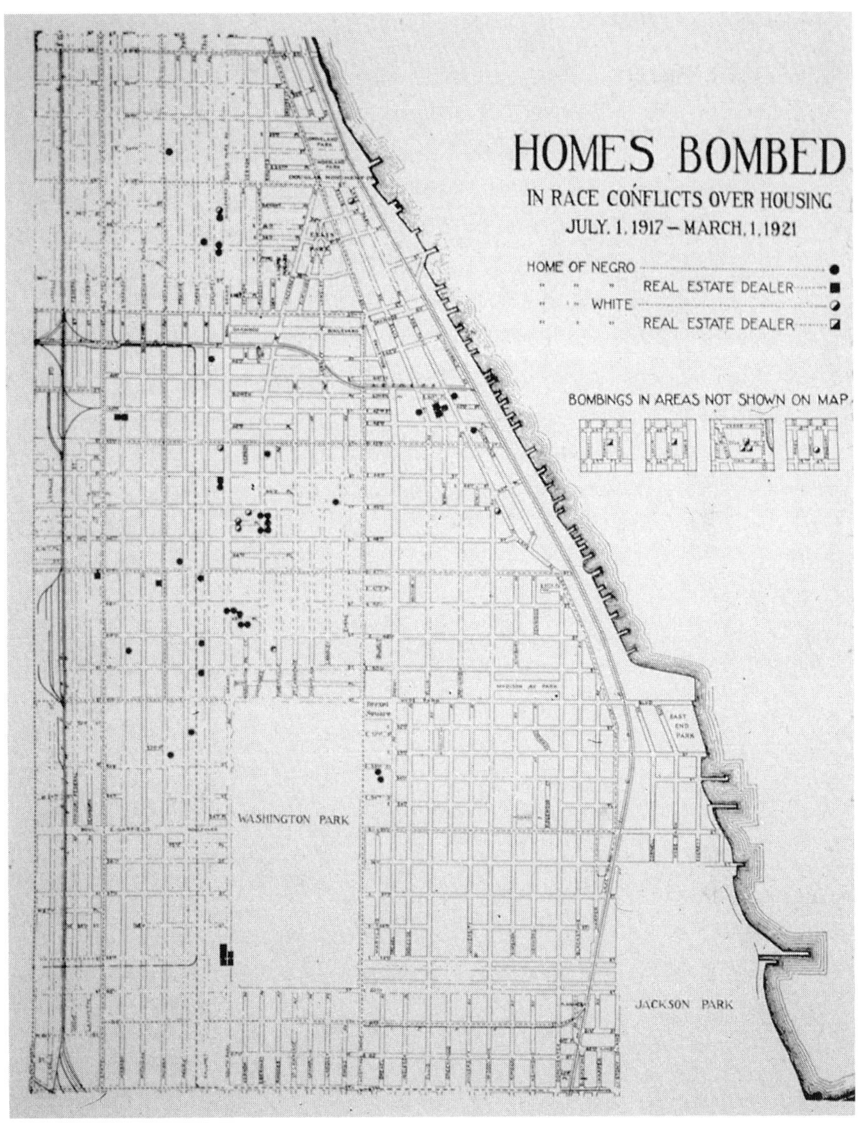

FIGURE 60. "Homes Bombed," in Chicago Commission on Race Relations, *The Negro in Chicago: A Study of Race Relations and a Race Riot* (Chicago: University of Chicago Press, 1922), facing 124.

banker. The *Chicago Defender* lauded his achievements in 1910: "He has been steadily rising from the first day he entered the Real Estate business, not content to stand still and be satisfied with what merely comes his way, like most men."[14] In November 1910 he acquired the block of State Street between Forty-seventh and Forty-eighth Streets, which became known as the "Binga Block." The property included twenty-one stores and fifty-four flats and helped extend the Black Belt farther south.

In March 1919 Binga's real estate office at 4724 South State Street was bombed, along with one of his properties. Nine months later his home at 5922 South Park Avenue was bombed, damaging the porch. After this bombing, police found that the incident was racially motivated, with white men claiming that "Binga rented too many flats to Negroes in high-class residential districts." In a similar bombing episode that occurred in February 1920, the explanation reported by police was that Binga's "$30,000 home is in a white neighborhood." All told, Binga's home was bombed five times, but police made no arrests.[15]

The attacks on Binga's real estate office and on his home demonstrate how concern over expanding black property ownership and the presence of blacks as neighbors were intimately intertwined. Both the symbolic and the real presence of blacks in spaces deemed white strongholds contributed to racial tension and sparked racial violence. Moreover, it was not just black housing that provoked intimidation; even the presence of blacks on streets separating black and white sections of the city fueled antagonism. According to one account, "There are residential parts in Chicago adjacent to those occupied by Negroes in which hostility to Negroes is so marked that they not only find it impossible to live there, but expose themselves to danger even passing through."[16] While there were forces helping to expand the perimeters of the Black Belt, equally strong forces were working to hold them in check.

REFORMING THE "SOCIAL EVIL" IN CHICAGO

The issues that shaped the racial segregation of housing also structured leisure relations between the races. Efforts to promote a culture of respectability and eradicate "vice" exposed the ways race, space, and vice came to be entwined during the Great Migration. These efforts also showed how far it was the intermingling of the races in brothels, saloons, and dance halls that prompted concern among urban reformers about the need to police the boundaries of these districts, so that by the postwar period "vice," and explicitly prostitution, was relocated to African American neighborhoods.

The term "vice" was widespread in reformist rhetoric at the turn of the century, and it often encompassed a variety of activities, both legal and illegal. Under the term, reformers lumped gambling, prostitution, petty theft, the sale of alcohol from unlicensed distributors, "lewd" dancing, and racial mixing. The conflation of illegal activities with legal ones attests to the central role urban space played in structuring ideas about licit and illicit activity. Reformers looked to the physical landscape, and especially commercial leisure districts, for ways to "purify" the city. They argued that containing and regulating spaces of commercial leisure would help eradicate vice. Moreover, even though gambling and prostitution were defined as illegal, they were important in structuring economic relations in black neighborhoods, where participation in the formal economy often was tenuous and unstable. Thus, as recent scholars of prostitution have shown, the distinction between formal and informal economies in black urban communities was ambiguous because the two were dependent on one another for creating employment and stimulating economic exchange.[17]

In the 1870s and 1880s the major center of "vice" in Chicago was the "Black Hole," described by one reformer as "a group of Negro saloons, cribs, and bawdy houses at Washington and Halsted Streets."[18] The first concert saloon, a precursor to the dance hall, was there and served both black and white clients. By the turn of the century, the Levee, on the Near South Side between Jackson and Twelfth Streets, Clark and State Streets, became notorious as the site of saloons, brothels, gambling halls, poolrooms, and bordellos. This was the district that British journalist and reformer William T. Stead made famous in his 1894 plea for urban reform, *If Christ Came to Chicago!*[19] Stead used the practice of mapping the city to expose the supposed prevalence of vice in Chicago and suggest ways to eradicate it.

Stead's analysis of the Levee pointed to the mixture of black and white commercial sex that intermingled to make this district so "depraved." He described the parlor houses, brothels, and saloons that gave the area its character and noted that black "houses of assignation" existed alongside more elite white establishments.[20] According to police detective Clifton Wooldridge, "Here at all hours of the day and night women could be seen at the doors and windows, frequently half-clad, making an exhibition of themselves and using vulgar and obscene language. . . . The habitués of this place embraced every nationality, both black and white, their ages ranging from eighteen to fifty."[21] What struck many observers like Stead was that the culture of the sex trade was not confined to the interior of the brothel or parlor house but made its way into the street. Indeed, this public sexual commerce was one of the features that concerned most reformers.[22]

Within the back room and alley spaces of the Levee, with its concert saloons, burlesque houses, brothels, and gambling dens, there existed a broad spectrum of Chicago's population, from upper-class men seeking sexual pleasures to transients and sailors making their way through the carnivalesque space. Here the rules of decorum that animated behavior in other public spaces of the city were suspended, and a variety of groups could experiment, at least temporarily, with less "respectable" conduct. In the Levee, for example, people of all backgrounds more publicly expressed their sexuality, whether heterosexual or homosexual. Whereas gay men and lesbians were forced into secrecy in other sections of the city, in the Levee they more openly sought out sexual partners. The taboos regarding interracial sex were suspended, and blacks and whites, men and women, could pursue partners who elsewhere were deemed inappropriate. The openness of the sex trade in the Levee allowed for expanded definitions of acceptable public behavior and sexuality. Even as this space was marginal, disreputable, and under constant threat of surveillance, the district offered the lure of risqué and forbidden pursuits that were not found anywhere else in the city.[23]

Official efforts to address the "vicious elements" in the Levee emerged by the late 1890s. Mayor Carter Harrison ordered police to force brothel owners to move their enterprises to other parts of the city. This campaign reflected Harrison's concern that the proximity of the Levee to the central business district would inhibit that district's expansion.[24] Harrison's move to clean up the area was noteworthy for having the vice district moved farther south but not eradicated. At least initially, economic and political decisions, rather than concerns about the moral geography of the city, prompted reform. The Levee thus simply shifted its location, moving south to Twenty-second Street.

This desire to contain vice but not wipe it out was reflected in statements made by Mayor Edward Dunne in 1905. He suggested that districts in Chicago be "mapped out on each side of the city wherein to intern vice," since this tactic would help keep "disreputable women" within these districts.[25] The South Side "vice district" included the area of the new Levee, between Sixteenth and Twenty-second Streets, State and Clark, and stretching south along Wabash to Thirty-ninth Street, placing it right in the heart of the emerging Black Belt.

While Dunne saw this segregation of vice as a compromise between reformers and proprietors of so-called illicit enterprises, many reformers felt differently. The tensions that emerged after the mayor's segregation of vice provoked the creation of the Chicago Vice Commission in 1910. Religious and civic leaders met at the Central YMCA building to discuss "the social evil problem in Chicago." At the conclusion of the meeting, those attending passed a resolution requesting that the mayor appoint a commission "made up of men and women who command the respect and confidence of the public at large . . . to investigate thoroughly the conditions that exist. With such knowledge obtained, let it map out such a course, as in its judgment, will bring about some relief from the frightful conditions that surround us."[26] This emphasis on "mapping out" the course of action is significant, for it reveals that reformers understood vice spatially and suggests the geographic approach they took to eradicate it. Stamping out vice, then, followed the reformers' approaches to other perceived ills of the city, including infant mortality, crowding, and juvenile delinquency. By studying a problem and understanding its spatial dimensions, they attempted to construct solutions based on the reform of the urban landscape.[27]

Members of the Commission, including clergy, University of Chicago professors, settlement house workers, and physicians, led investigators in street-by-street neighborhood canvassing. The investigators sought to identify incidents of prostitution, police corruption, illegal liquor sales, and unsanitary sexual practices. The Commission posited a strong connection between areas of commercialized leisure, "illicit activity," and public health. They investigated behavior in vaudeville houses and dance halls, joint ownership of saloons and gambling dens, drug and alcohol use among prostitutes, and the increasingly commercial nature of the sex business.

Their final report gave case-by-case descriptions of the conditions in what they considered disreputable South Side flats, rooming houses, and saloons. In one case, a two-story frame building owned by a woman had a reception area on the first floor where a white woman played piano. Male guests were escorted to the second floor by "a colored girl . . . [who] has immediate charge and collects the money." There were six "inmates in the house between the ages of 23 and 30. The charge for service is $1.00. The sanitary conditions are very poor."[28] The Commission also chronicled numerous incidents when liquor was secured for flats from neighboring saloons. One report described an investigator at a Dearborn Street saloon who witnessed "a colored maid from a house of ill fame" entering the saloon "with a large shawl over her shoulders. . . . She went to the bar and was given six bottles of beer, which she covered with the shawl and left the saloon. She did not pay for the beer, but the charge was noted down by the bartender." The Commission argued in its recommendations that "one of the most practical moves to reduce the evil effects of this business . . . is to strictly enforce the regulation forbidding the sale of liquor in these places."[29]

Indeed, the report explained that potential customers are lured into a "resort" and forced to drink before "securing one of the girls." At the same time, the commissioners noted, the proprietors of saloons "are using prostitutes as an adjunct to the sale of beer and liquor, and are allowing them to solicit for immoral purposes in their rear rooms."[30] Investigators drew direct connections between the "perniciousness" of the saloon, prostitution, and working-class entertainment. They argued that "vaudeville shows of lewd nature conducted in the rear rooms" of saloons attract unsuspecting men and women, and contribute to general moral degeneracy.[31] Much of the problem, argued the commissioners, was the complicity of the police, who turned the other way in the face of the "social evil."

In its recommendations for eradicating vice, the report pointed to the importance of prosecuting offenders. It also made suggestions for how prostitution could be prevented. Interestingly, the Commission was sympathetic to the lack of adequate jobs for many women. "Is it any wonder that a tempted girl who receives only six dollars per week working with her hands sells her body for $25 per week?" The report went on to list as some causes of prostitution "the economic stress of industrial life on unskilled workers, and the seasonal trades in which women are employed." In addition, though, the report targeted "abnormality, feeble-mindedness, ignorant parents, and love of ease and luxury." Solutions included placing first-time offenders on probation and "under the care of intelligent and sympathetic women" who could advise them in moral instruction and help them find jobs. Those labeled "old and hardened offenders" would be sent to an "industrial farm . . . on an indeterminate sentence."[32]

The result of the Vice Commission investigation was a campaign to clean up vice districts, especially the Levee. In 1912 investigators descended on the district to arrest offenders and shut down the flats and saloons associated with prostitution. The raids led to the demise of many of the establishments, but others scattered into nearby neighborhoods. The growth of the Black Belt after the antivice crusade in the Levee meant that both white and black prostitution moved deeper into African American neighborhoods.

Leaders in the black community were outraged that the vice campaign made brothels, gambling dens, and "sporting taverns" relocate into the Black Belt. The *Chicago Defender* chided black religious and business leaders for not taking a larger part in seeking to control vice. It complained that the efforts of antivice crusaders resulted in "scattering the denizens of the red light district and menacing the residence districts of the race." The paper did not call for the eradication of vice; like reformers on the Vice

Commission, the *Defender* suggested that vice be segregated so that it would not take over the residential districts of the South Side. "Keep them from roaming" was its advice, so that vice areas might be properly regulated.[33]

Ironically, the Vice Commission recognized the problematic connections between "vice" and black neighborhoods in its report, noting that the larger vice districts in the city were always "within or near the settlements of colored people." They explained, "Whenever prostitutes, cadets, and thugs were located among white people and had to be moved for commercial and other reasons, they were driven to undesirable parts of the city, the so-called colored residential sections." According to one former chief of police, "so long as this degenerate group of persons confined their residence [to colored areas] they would not be apprehended."[34] Reformer Louise de Koven Bowen also noted the connections between race and vice, pointing out that black families often were forced to take in lodgers, leading to the potential for "immorality." In addition, she pointed out that "the boys and girls of colored families are often obliged to live near the vice districts."[35] The Vice Commission stressed that the apparent discrimination black residents faced because of the failure to control vice in their districts was unjust, and it argued that all families in Chicago deserved to live in wholesome surroundings. Despite these claims, however, the Commission failed to press for further prosecution of vice within the Black Belt after the closing the Levee in 1912.

With the movement of vice out of more visible white districts and largely dispersed throughout the Black Belt, race and vice were even further conflated. Black leaders recognized the dangers this association held for images of blacks in general. Numerous religious and civic organizations instructed residents and new migrants in appropriate dress and decorum, both to stave off discrimination and to promote a public culture of respectability that would counter the association with vice. The Chicago League on Urban Conditions among Negroes (which would become the Urban League) instructed blacks on how to behave once they arrived in northern cities. Hard work, industriousness, sobriety, and cleanliness led to useful employment, their brochures proclaimed. Staff argued that instruction in public deportment was essential for instilling race pride, since "bad action and conduct are embarrassing to members of the race and reflect not only upon the individual, but react upon the masses." The League warned against crowding in housing because of its associations with immorality and stressed the importance of living among respectable neighbors so that no possibility of illicit behavior might be suspected.[36]

These ideals of self-help and race uplift shaped the black reform organizations in the city. Many "old settlers" looked to the black church as well as to new civic organizations to promote respectability within the black community. Like their white counterparts, these reform organizations searched for ways to instill industriousness among new migrants. Yet unlike most settlement houses, community centers, and other aid societies serving whites, the black organizations often struggled for funds and, at least initially, received little financial backing either from wealthy white philanthropists or from municipal government. That meant the ideology of self-help was particularly important in the black community and influenced ideas about the meaning of race pride.

Black women played a central role in establishing organizations to help blacks find housing, get jobs, and adapt to urban life.[37] Ida B. Wells's efforts at creating clubs to promote respectability for blacks in Chicago illustrate how these efforts became intertwined with calls for racial justice. Wells was the leading antilynching crusader in the nation; she moved to Chicago after being driven out of Memphis because of her exposés of lynching and demands for an end to discrimination. Her marriage to prominent black Chicago publisher and civic activist Ferdinand Barnett made her an even more important leader in efforts to achieve racial justice in the city. Wells-Barnett founded the Negro Fellowship League in 1910. The League was devoted to providing housing for men and helping them get jobs. She pointed to "the problem of the boys," and argued that helping black men find employment was one of the most important factors in shaping family stability and community advancement. The League maintained a reading room to provide wholesome recreation so that young men would not be "idling away their time at saloons or pool rooms."[38] Through her role in founding the League, as well as other clubs, Wells-Barnett worked closely with white reformers like Jane Addams and Mary McDowell to press for a variety of reforms, including an end to police brutality against blacks, reform of the court system, women's suffrage, and of course antilynching legislation.[39]

In addition, black women helped lead programs at several settlements for blacks, including the Frederick Douglass Center and the Emanuel Settlement on the South Side. Both of these settlements included day nurseries and kindergartens for children as well as reading rooms, athletic equipment, and training in domestic arts for young women. Wells-Barnett worked closely with Bethel African Methodist Episcopal (AME) Reverend Reverdy Ransom and his new Institutional Church and Settlement on State Street near Thirty-fifth Street, which included a library, day nursery, and classes in music and business as well as welfare, employment, and educational services.[40] Like their white counterparts, black women sought wholesome spaces of recreation that could counter the lure of vice. This need for alternatives was even more pressing in black communities precisely because of the increasing ties between the geographies of race and vice in the city. Yet black settlements still could not offer the same level of support for "wholesome" recreation that white neighborhoods enjoyed. Black club woman Irene McCoy-Gaines lamented the inadequacy of facilities available for blacks in contrast to "the cozy clubrooms, well-equipped gyms, and swimming pools" of white neighborhoods.[41]

The Phyllis Wheatley Club, named after the noted black poet, was established in 1896 as a women's club. By 1907, though, the group changed its orientation and focused on the needs of newly arrived migrants, providing housing for women to keep newcomers from "going astray by being led into disreputable homes, entertainment, and employment."[42] The club also taught domestic skills and helped young women get jobs. Like Marion Talbot at the University of Chicago, many black female reformers stressed that the domestic arts could be professionalized though scientific study. Recognizing that domestic service was one of the few options available for black women, national leaders like Nannie Helen Burroughs sought to train young women in domestic science.[43] The Phyllis Wheatley Club used the methods and skills Burroughs developed for her school in Washington. The club's motto was "If you can't push, pull, and if you can't pull, please get out of the way," recalling the National Association of Colored Women's motto "lifting as we climb."[44]

One of the goals of these clubs for women was to model respectable behavior and recreation. Black female reformers such as Burroughs and Mary Church Turrell derided the leisure culture of black and tans (clubs that admitted both black and white patrons), saloons, and dance halls, arguing that black women especially needed to overcome immoral patterns of leisure in favor of respectable recreation and employment. In Chicago, Irene McCoy-Gaines and other black reformers cautioned black women to be conscious of their public display. They had to be careful about the hours when they were seen on the street, the way they dressed, and the people they consorted with. McCoy-Gaines also worked with white reformers in the Women's Trade Union League to push for better employment conditions for black women so they were not tempted into prostitution.[45] Black reformers understood the associations made between black women's public presence, crowded living conditions, and immorality, and they sought to distance themselves from these associations as much as possible.

Black reformers received a boost in their efforts to provide wholesome recreation to counter the lure of commercial amusement and illicit activity with the opening of the Wabash YMCA in 1913, in the heart of the Black Belt. The movement for a YMCA in the Black Belt began after a 1909 speech by Wells-Barnett to members of the Congregational Church in Chicago. Wells-Barnett stated that African Americans were denied access to the major sources of wholesome recreation in the city, including YMCAs and other sites of social uplift. After the talk Victor Lawson, the publisher of the *Chicago Daily News,* approached Wells-Barnett and offered to fund the reading room at the Negro Fellowship League until a black YMCA was established on the South Side.[46] In 1911 Julius Rosenwald of Sears, Roebuck, and Company launched a fund-raising campaign to establish a black YMCA. He offered to donate $25,000 if other Chicago philanthropists would make contributions as well. Several followed suit, including Cyrus McCormick, Mrs. Charles F. Swift, and the George Pullman Company. An additional $20,000 was raised from blacks within the Douglas community where the building would be located.[47]

The five-story building was designed by noted YMCA architect Robert C. Berlin. He used the latest techniques of concrete frame construction. The facade was red pressed brick and Bedford limestone and, together with the design of the entrance, recalled both surrounding warehouse buildings and the Gothic motifs of the University of Chicago (fig. 61).[48] The building included dormitory space to temporarily house new migrants, along with a gymnasium, pool, reading room, and assembly hall. The facility also featured a bowling alley, a room for billiards and pool, a restaurant, and a "model kitchen, sanitary." A director of physical culture oversaw all the athletic work, while a director of educational work handled reading and other courses.[49] The Y sponsored glee clubs, baseball leagues, and men's and women's organizations, making it an important site for community activities and the "wholesome" recreation reformers hoped to provide. The *Defender* touted it as source of pride for the entire black community, though others were less excited about a major black institution's being sponsored by white benefactors. Also, many claimed it was elitist. Indeed, Wells-Barnett argued that the membership fees prevented the YMCA from "reaching the boys or men who are farthest down and out."[50]

The establishment of the Chicago branch of the Urban League provided additional services to South Side blacks, both recreation and help with housing and employment. The Chicago chapter was founded in 1916 and promoted interracial reform efforts for the black community. The League's focus was on the "adjustment or assimilation" of recent black migrants to Chicago.[51] The organization sponsored programs in urban

ILLINOIS

Moulding Christian Character In Men and Boys

The Wabash Avenue Department

Young Men's Christian Association

Young men coming to Chicago, register, lodge, or find a home in our thoroughly modern, well kept and convenient dormitory. Special rates and cordial welcome to transients.

Men who know, enjoy their meals in our delightful cafeteria. Home-cooked wholesome food is served at minimum prices. Private dining room for parties.

Complete equipment in gymnasium, natatorium, game rooms, lobby, and class rooms, with a trained staff of secretaries and directors always at the service of the membership.

An attractive, scientific program of all-round activity is promoted throughout the year, varying with the seasons but constant in promoting the "More abundant life."

VISIT! JOIN! BOOST!

Address: 3753 Wabash Ave., Chicago, Ill.

Telephone: Boulevard 9540

FIGURE 61. Wabash Avenue YMCA, 1913. From James N. Simms, *Simms Blue Book and National Negro Business and Professional Directory* (Chicago: J. N. Simms, 1923). Courtesy of the Commission on Chicago Landmarks.

etiquette, helped new migrants find jobs and housing, and provided reading rooms and club spaces for meetings. The board comprised many of the founders of the National Association for the Advancement of Colored People (NAACP) in Chicago in 1910. Members serving on both boards included Jane Addams, Mrs. Emmons Blaine, Sophonisba Breckinridge, Oscar C. Brown, Dr. George Cleveland Hall, Julius Rosenwald, and Reverend Celia Parker Woolley. Woolley, head of the Frederick Douglass Center, offered to allow the League to set up its headquarters there until its permanent office was built. Julius Rosenwald was one of the principal funders of the Chicago branch of the Urban League, leading to his increasingly prominent role as a philanthropist of black causes.[52]

One of the central goals of the Urban League, both in Chicago and nationwide, was to promote respectability among new migrants. The *Chicago Defender* published lists of dos and don'ts put forward by the League. Some of the don'ts included, "Don't use vile language; Don't make yourself a public nuisance; Don't congregate with crowds on the streets . . . ; Don't encourage gamblers, disreputable women or men to ply their business any time or place; Don't leave your job when you have a few dollars in your pocket."[53] The last two warnings were particularly significant, for one of the greatest worries of middle-class black leaders was that new migrants would be drawn into the world of disreputable dance halls, saloons, and gambling dens permeating urban nightlife on the South Side. The Urban League encouraged new migrants to avoid places like the Stroll altogether and instead seek out wholesome recreation within the settlement reading rooms, church facilities, the Wabash YMCA, and the Urban League itself. The Chicago Urban League soon sponsored dances, socials, and athletic teams to counter the attractions of commercial leisure.

SPORT AND COMMERCIAL LEISURE IN BLACK CHICAGO

This emphasis on wholesomeness and respectability was a response to the intimate connections between licit and illicit recreation in the cultural geography of the Black Belt. The economics of black baseball in Chicago reflected the ill-defined boundaries between legal and illegal economies, respectability and vice. Many black civic leaders touted black sports heroes and team owners as symbols of race pride and entrepreneurial success. At the same time, though, the proprietors of athletic teams and sporting venues often maintained closer connections to the "sporting world" than many black leaders wanted to admit. The narrowly confined borders of the Black Belt, and the limited financial resources for black business success, meant that licit and illicit enterprises often existed side by side and were operated by the same entrepreneurs.

In Chicago and other northern cities, baseball played a growing part in the social and economic life of black communities. The *Defender* featured regular coverage of games between clubs in the black church league. Black teams also played in the Chicago City Semi-Pro League, often competing against white teams. As early as 1900, there were five black teams in the city with paid players. Fans flocked to the games, and the *Defender* urged African Americans to support these teams as an expression of race pride.[54]

Chicago was on its way to becoming the center for black baseball after Frank Leland established the city's first black professional club, the Chicago Unions, in 1887. Leland was a former player who had been on the roster of the Washington Capital Citys, one of the teams from the ill-fated League of Colored Base Ball Clubs. After the collapse of the league, Leland moved to Chicago to establish his team. In 1901, after the demise of other upstart black teams, Leland formed the Chicago Union Giants, renamed the Leland Giants, who dominated the Chicago City League.[55]

Coverage of black professional baseball in the *Chicago Defender* testified to its place in the social and economic lives of South Side blacks. The newspaper regularly featured stories about the teams, both in its "Sporting World" column and on the front page. On May 14, 1910, the front page carried a story about a flag raising taking place the following day at the Leland Giants' ball game. The game would be the highlight of daylong events designed to express local pride. A parade starting at Twenty-ninth and State Streets would commence in the afternoon, with "automobiles, tally-hos, carriages, and Chicago Giants Rooters' Club" leading the way. All were invited to attend the parade, wear the colors of the Giants (white and maroon), and make this "the banner day in baseball." The band from the Eighth Regiment, the all-black division of the Illinois National Guard, would begin the festivities at the ballpark with an hour-long concert in the afternoon. The concert would conclude with the playing of the "Star-Spangled Banner," when some of Chicago's favorite black ball players would raise the flag.[56]

When the Giants moved to a new ballpark the *Defender* played a central role in that celebration. The ballpark, at Sixty-first Street and St. Lawrence Avenue, was "part of the most beautiful residence district of the South Side, and an extremely fashionable neighborhood." The new park featured more amenities than the old one, including "4,000 comfortable arm chairs, steel grandstand, reserved seats, [and] boxes with a canopy shade." To encourage fans to attend the opening game, and to point up the close connection between black baseball and black culture on the South Side, the *Defender* offered a year's free subscription to the first fan entering the gates at the new ballpark.[57] Soon after, the club moved nearby, to Sixty-ninth and Halsted where Leland hoped to create an amusement park complex. Here one could find "the most select audiences in the city" and watch "the best talent procurable." The park included box seats that could be reserved in advance for fifty cents, and Leland promised that "special attention" would be paid to accommodating ladies and children. In addition, free ice water was served at all games.[58]

The *Defender* also touted the expansion of professional black baseball in Chicago as a symbol of black entrepreneurial success. In 1907 Andrew "Rube" Foster, a star pitcher in black baseball, joined Leland's team as captain, manager, and booking agent (fig. 62). Foster helped establish the barnstorming system that introduced black baseball to cities and towns across the nation. By 1910 Foster's managerial success prompted him to break off from Leland and establish a partnership with white tavern owner John Schorling, founding the Chicago American Giants. After the White Sox moved out of their South Side Park at Thirty-ninth and Wentworth, Schorling bought the land and refurbished the grounds to house Foster's new team. According to the *Defender*, the new team meant that black Chicagoans now had more opportunities to express race pride. "Now, with two splendid teams playing at the same hour, on the same day, the all-absorbing question is, 'What game shall I go to?'" The *Defender* answered the question by noting that there were more than enough fans to support both teams, and that having the option of which game to attend should be seen as a source of satisfaction.[59]

Frank Leland sought to keep fans coming to his ballpark by stressing its role in promoting race pride. After Foster established his own team, Leland changed his ads to emphasize his team's black ownership. His new ads read, "Upon the success of the Leland Giants this year depends the Negro's continuance as a factor in the baseball arena. The Park is the only Park in the city operated and controlled by Negroes. This should be sufficient for every Negro to attend the games at this Park." The ad also claimed that the Leland Giants played "Genteel, Scientific, and Gentlemanly Ball," suggesting that the ballpark was a space of respectability and decorum for all classes of

FIGURE 62. Andrew "Rube" Foster, Leland Giants, 1909. Courtesy of the Chicago Historical Society.

the race. That sports became such a charged space of demonstrations of race loyalty suggests the central role commercial leisure played in structuring the social and economic life of the Black Belt.[60]

Despite Leland's efforts, Foster's Giants quickly became the dominant black team not only in Chicago but throughout the nation. The Giants joined other black teams in barnstorming tours throughout the East and South, playing white and black teams alike. Foster's ball playing and management skills translated into effective business endeavors. By 1916 Foster had taken over sole proprietorship in the American Giants from Schorling, and after World War I he was central in wresting control of all of black baseball from white owners and placing it in the hands of black entrepreneurs. In 1920 Foster founded the Negro National League and became one of the most respected black businessmen and civic leaders in Chicago and the nation. He demonstrated how, as both players and owners, blacks could promote their race through the culture of leisure and become leaders who could rally the community.[61]

THE STROLL AND THE CONSTRUCTION OF BLACK COMMERCIAL LEISURE

Both Foster's Negro National League and Frank Leland's mass amusement enterprise symbolize the growing role of commercial leisure spaces in African American community life during and after World War I. Like the white middle-class promoters of wholesome recreation, Foster and especially Leland touted baseball parks as appropriate sites for family entertainment. Leland also promoted his skating rink and even his dance hall as family entertainment. The Chateau de la Plaisance, opened in 1907 by Leland and black businessmen Beauregard Mosely and Robert Jackson, featured roller skating from 7:00 to 10:30 p.m. and dancing from 10:30 to midnight. By 1910 the Chateau was under the proprietorship of the Leland Giants Baseball and Amusement Association (LGBBA). Ads for the Chateau exclaimed, "Go where you will. Pay what you may, but the Chateau leads in wholesome, health-giving entertainment. . . . Come away from the stuffy, tubercular, 5¢ death-giving, cheap theater and enjoy the invigorating, health-giving atmosphere of the Chateau." Admission to the Chateau was ten cents, making it accessible for all classes.[62]

The LGBBA acted on its owners' belief in promoting race pride through entrepreneurial success. The Association offered stock options to black investors as a way to build racial solidarity by supporting local enterprises. It also sponsored fund-raising events to benefit institutions in the Black Belt. In August 1910 the Leland Giants staged a benefit baseball game at Comiskey Park with proceeds benefiting Provident Hospital, founded by black surgeon Daniel Hale Williams.[63] Commercial amusement provided employment, business success, and solidarity among blacks in Chicago and also contributed directly to the philanthropic efforts of race leaders.

While Leland's Chateau represented only the most "wholesome entertainment," other attempts by blacks involved in the sporting world ran into the difficulty of creating boundaries between respectable and illicit enterprises in the commercial leisure district of the Black Belt. The case of black prize fighter and world champion Jack Johnson exemplified the precarious nature of the business of recreation on the South Side.

Race leaders across the country eagerly anticipated the boxing match that pitted Jack Johnson against white fighter James J. Jeffries for the heavyweight championship of the world. After the Boxing Federation announced the match, which would take place on the Fourth of July 1910, the *Chicago Defender* began a series of articles on Johnson's prefight activities.. The *Defender* touted Johnson as a hero of the race and a leader in the fight against discrimination. "In the face of opposition, competition and discrimination," declared the *Defender,* "he cleaved his way right through."[64] The paper acknowledged prizefighting's association with unsavory elements of the underworld but suggested that Johnson's skill and perseverance were characteristics essential for all endeavors in life. "While pugilism does not compare favorably with the intellectual forces of mankind," the *Defender* stated, "yet the same pluck, patience, perseverance and stick-to-itiveness characterized by the colored champion is essential to success in all vocations of life." The newspaper asked all "race lovers" to contribute to a welcome fund for greeting Johnson after the bout and promised to print weekly lists of all those "who have faith in Jack's achievements."[65]

After Johnson defeated Jeffries to secure the title, he came back to Chicago amid great fanfare. Moreover, he vowed to stay in Chicago and contribute to the life of the community by establishing a cabaret on the South Side. As early as December 1910 Johnson obtained an option on a property on State Street near Thirty-first, the South Side Turner Hall. The property reportedly was worth $60,000, and there was some question whether the association of German turners that owned it would lease it to Johnson.[66] The deal fell through, though in 1919 the site became home to the grandiose Vendome Theater, one of the largest theaters on the South Side. Johnson instead bought the property at 41 West Thirty-first Street, and on July 12, 1912, he opened the Café de Champion. The grand opening was a huge affair for the South Side. Crowds packed Thirty-first Street for blocks waiting for a chance to view the elaborate interior of the club. The cabaret featured three stories, with the first floor devoted to a large barroom as well as the main cabaret where large orchestras, singers, and dancers performed. The second floor housed a café for private dining and drinking and featured a piano bar, and the top floor was reserved for Johnson's own apartment. Patrons flocking to the club on opening night marveled at the "delicately tinted walls and ceiling, the brilliant chandeliers," and the life-sized oil paintings of Johnson himself that adorned the walls.[67]

Johnson wanted his club to provide respectable entertainment for blacks. He argued that he conducted the club "not only in accordance with the law, but with as much good taste and as strictly as a business of that kind can be conducted."[68] Numerous black Chicagoans attested to the elegance and respectability of Johnson's cabaret. The father of historian Dempsey Travis, for example, claimed that Johnson's cabaret was "the classiest black and tan public club in the country."[69] The *Defender* called it "the most beautiful and elaborately furnished establishment of this kind in the city."[70] The club attracted an interracial clientele, with blacks and whites from all parts of the city, as well as tourists, making frequent stops there.

Still, Johnson faced repeated harassment from local and national authorities as a result of his very public liaisons with white women and his eventual marriage to a white woman. Justice Department officials sent investigators into the Café de Champion to trump up charges against Johnson and undermine his business. Investigators made note of black and white prostitutes who worked in his club in various capacities, including as waitresses and entertainers. Johnson acknowledged that these women were employees in his club, but he claimed he did not in any way profit from their involvement in the illegal sex trade.[71] Johnson's prosecution in 1913 on charges of violating the Mann Act, the law forbidding white slavery, led to the closing of the club and Johnson's exile from the United States.

The case of Café de Champion was somewhat unusual in that the club drew increased attention and surveillance because of its owner's prominence. Yet the club was not unique in the way respectable and "illicit" forms of leisure merged under one roof. Other clubs, cabarets, and theaters in the Black Belt often fought against these associations with "vice" as they attempted to provide respectable entertainment. Yet they also found how difficult it was to draw lines between licit and illicit venues of commercial leisure, in terms of both who frequented these spots and how they were financed.

Efforts to open a black-owned theater catering to blacks illustrated the important role of saloon and gambling interests in promoting black entrepreneurship. In part blacks wanted to open a Black Belt theater because white-owned theaters, especially in the Loop, were off-limits to blacks. The *Defender* recounted the story of Frank D. Donaldson, an African American man who bought tickets for himself and a friend at the Colonial Theater, one of the new ornate motion picture palaces to open in the Loop. Instead of tickets for the balcony, the area usually reserved for blacks, Donaldson bought tickets for the main floor because he was told the balcony was sold out. When Donaldson and his friend went to take their seats, the theater attendant tried to usher them to the balcony. Donaldson refused, saying he had paid full price for floor seats and wanted to sit there. The usher then ordered Donaldson and his friend to leave. Donaldson complied, but he hired an attorney to sue the theater under the state's civil rights laws. During the case, the attorney asked jurors to understand this case not on racial grounds but "as a case of a citizen of the State being refused his rights as a citizen."[72] Donaldson won his case, but the practice of excluding blacks from Loop theaters, as well as other places of amusement, continued.

In 1901 several prominent South Side blacks, including physician George C. Hall (one of the founders of the Urban League), planned to open a theater at Thirty-first and State Streets called Havlin's Theater. Hall agreed to invest $20,000. Since there were no licensed black architects in Chicago, he hired Saint Shuttle, a cakewalk artist, and "Billy" Caldwell, a vaudeville performer, to draw up plans. The venture fell through for unknown reasons, so the dream of a black-owned theater catering to black audiences was put on hold.[73]

The promise of black theater in Chicago was realized in 1905 when Robert T. Motts opened the Pekin Theater (fig. 63). The theater grew out of Mott's popular beer garden and gambling house, the Pekin Inn, opened in 1900 at 2700 South State, in which Motts invested his earnings from his years in the gambling trade. Motts's role in creating the first theater featuring black performances and catering to interracial audiences showed the intimate connections between legitimate business, illicit activity, and race pride on the South Side. Motts first came to Chicago in 1881 and made his money working with John "Mushmouth" Johnson, the leader of black gambling and prostitution in Chicago at the turn of the century. Johnson had worked for several years as a porter in a white gambling house, then he used his money to open his own saloon and gambling house at 464 South State Street. One description of Johnson's gambling den said it was "ornate in the Gay Nineties style," with "glittering incandescent bulbs in rococo chandeliers." It went on to marvel at the "illuminated bar made of polished Honduran mahogany" and the "varicolored cut glassware and many brands of wine, liquor, and cigars."[74] Johnson's establishment attracted black and white, rich and poor, who came to his resort to partake in all levels of gambling, from roulette to five-card poker. He also ran policy games, a lottery in which numbers were drawn randomly and people placed bets on the draw. Johnson's gambling house, along with his interests in crap games and policy throughout the South Side, made his one of the largest gambling syndicates in the city.[75]

FIGURE 63. Pekin Theater, Twenty-seventh and State Streets, 1920. Courtesy of the Chicago Historical Society.

Johnson amassed enough wealth to make him one of the largest owners of real estate on the South Side. He acquired property on State, Dearborn, and Federal Streets, between Harrison and Polk (the heart of the first Levee), worth over $500,000. When he died in 1907, his wealth was estimated at between $250,000 and $750,000. Events following his death also illustrated the hazy divide between respectable and "illegitimate" business in the Black Belt. Johnson's sister Eudora inherited 60 percent of his estate. Five years later Eudora married Jesse Binga, the prominent banker and real estate developer. The wedding was a lavish affair, and the *Defender* called it "the most brilliant ever held in Chicago." The newspaper included details about the attire of the bride and groom as well as their attendants, the variety of gifts, from linens to cut glassware, silver, and china, and the music accompanying the ceremony. The wedding received national attention, including a note of congratulations from Booker T. Washington and his wife.[76] After the marriage, the fortune Eudora inherited from her brother went into Binga's bank, helping to secure its financial footing. Binga's bank, then, the centerpiece of black business in Chicago, owed its success to the entrepreneurial spirits of both Binga and Johnson, to both legitimate and "illegitimate" business.

Johnson's success helped lay a foundation for Robert Motts as well. The money he made working with Johnson allowed Motts first to buy the beer garden and then to refurbish it into a legitimate theater. In 1905 Motts retooled the Pekin Inn and established the "Pekin Temple of Music," featuring sentimental musical performances as well as ragtime, vaudeville acts, popular comedy actors like Bert Williams, and stock theatrical productions. The Pekin was an immediate success, and black newspapers claimed it was a subject of pride for the entire race. The *Chicago Broad Ax* called Motts "the new Moses of the Negro race in the theater world." The article compared him to "those great race heroes" Benjamin Banneker, Toussaint L'Ouverture, and Booker T. Washington. In a July 1910 article the newspaper identified Motts as "full of race pride."[77] Ida B. Wells-Barnett later said that "the race owed Mr. Motts a debt of gratitude for giving us a theater in which we could sit anywhere we chose without any restriction."[78]

The Pekin became a fixture in the black community and served both black and white audiences (fig. 64). The theater's larger civic role became clear in 1906, after Motts renovated the building yet again and added more seating and additional ornamentation. That year Motts offered to host a charity event to raise funds for the Frederick Douglass Center. Ida B. Wells-Barnett coordinated the plans for the evening and thanked Motts for offering his "little gem of a theater." Over one hundred patrons of the Center were invited. Among the attendees were several prominent reformers in the city, both black and white. Jane Addams was joined in her box by leading African American club women, including Wells-Barnett, Mrs. George Hall (wife of the physician), and black physician Fannie Emanuel. The audience witnessed performances by both black and white acting troupes, and the event raised hundreds of dollars for the Center.[79]

Yet the charity event exposed some of the tensions within the black community over the role of commercial leisure spaces, especially cabarets, in the larger civic life of the South Side. Several black ministers protested the event, claiming it was immoral to hold a fund-raiser for a settlement organization in a space that promoted "low morals."

FIGURE 64. "Pekin Rag Intermezzo," showing interior of Pekin Theater. Courtesy of Hogan Jazz Archive, Tulane University.

After Wells-Barnett started her subscription campaign in April 1906, prominent minister Archibald J. Carey of Bethel AME Church (who took over after Reverdy Ransom's departure) criticized the event and attacked Wells-Barnett for associating with owners of dance halls and other places of "illicit amusement." Several black newspapers carried Carey's attack, and it spurred at least one black organization, a South Side theater school, to cancel its participation.[80] Wells-Barnett addressed the attacks head-on after the performance. She thanked the audience for support of the Center, then lambasted the ministers who had criticized the event "upon purely selfish or personal grounds."[81] This criticism drew applause from the crowd, which evidently shared her belief in the importance of the Pekin in the life of the Black Belt.

Reformers such as Addams and Wells-Barnett recognized the centrality of commercial leisure sites in the civic life of the community even as they encouraged alternative forms of recreation. Their support for Motts recognized that so-called illicit activities, business success, and civic responsibility were intertwined. The precarious position of the Pekin after Motts's death in 1911 also reflected the importance of the theater as a symbol of black accomplishment. Motts was mourned by prominent business and civic leaders, both black and white, and Jesse Binga was an honorary pallbearer at his funeral. After Motts's death, his sister Lucy ran the theater with her husband, Dan Jackson. Jackson was the proprietor of an undertaking business next door to the theater and eventually created the Metropolitan Funeral Systems Association, one of the most important black businesses on the South Side. He also was a prominent Second Ward politician and a leading gambler in the city. Jackson used his gambling money to help the Pekin remain viable.[82] Jackson therefore, like Motts and Binga, combined legitimate and illegitimate business to accumulate his wealth.

Black leaders in the city praised Jackson for helping the ailing theater and urged blacks to continue to support the Pekin. The *Chicago Defender* chided blacks for not giving it enough support once white cabaret owners began establishing clubs in the Black Belt after 1909. "It is a sad, sad spectacle," the paper lamented, "to look into the Pekin theater with a good theatrical program in progress, fine music, comfortable seats and surroundings" and see numerous empty seats. The article argued that it was incumbent on the race to support black enterprises and pointed to the injustice of whites' exploiting black business by "catering exclusively to [blacks] in Negro communities and excluding them in white communities."[83] Not supporting a black institution like the Pekin was tantamount to being a race traitor, and the *Defender* and other supporters held the theater up as a symbol of black pride, even if it owed its existence to money made through illicit ventures like gambling. When the theater eventually fell into white hands, the event was mourned not only in Chicago but across the nation. The *Crisis,* the publication of the NAACP, even made note of the change, attesting to the significance of the theater in black civic life nationwide.[84]

The Pekin set the stage for the development of the Stroll on south State Street as the "great light way," the centerpiece of black life in Chicago and the breeding ground for jazz. After the success of the Pekin, several white theater owners who had establishments in the Loop and on the North Side saw how lucrative the Black Belt could be. They opened clubs and theaters such as the Monogram Theater, the Pompeii, and the Panama that became incubators for Chicago jazz. Black entrepreneurs also established cabarets, dance halls, and theaters on State Street, competing for control of the South Side leisure market. Mushmouth Johnson's fortune contributed to the success of this market. On November 6, 1912, Johnson's brother, who inherited the rest of his estate, leased the property directly across the street from Binga's bank and built the Dreamland Café (fig. 65).[85] The Dreamland, at 3518 South State Street, became the hub of black music in the 1910s and 1920s, hosting some of the leading jazz performers of the day: pianist Lil Hardin, cornetist Louis Armstrong (who married Hardin), singer Alberta Hunter, clarinetist Johnny Dodds, and Joe "King" Oliver (fig. 66). Hunter recalled her days at the Dreamland. "That Dreamland was really some place. It was *big* and always packed. And you had to be a singer then—there were no microphones and those bands were marvelous. . . . There were no such things as intermissions and there was never a quiet moment. When you worked at the Dreamland, you worked from about seven thirty in the evening to three or four in the morning—and you didn't move out of there."[86]

The arrival of the Original Creole Jazz Orchestra in Chicago in 1911 signaled the beginning of Chicago's emergence as the capital of jazz. The band, led by Bill Johnson and cornetist Eddie Keppard, immediately secured a spot at the Big Grand Theater at Thirty-first and State Streets. Other New Orleans musicians had played in Chicago before, including pianists Fred "Jelly Roll" Morton and Tony Jackson, who got their start playing at the bawdy houses of the Levee before vice reform.[87] Yet the Creole Jazz Orchestra's success precipitated the migration to Chicago of other jazz musicians, including Joe Oliver and Louis Armstrong, and fueled the transition from the black southern musical tradition of ragtime to the jazz of the urban North.[88]

Black businessmen began opening additional cabarets along the Stroll, further attesting to the strong connections between commercial leisure and the underworld in structuring urban nightlife. Henry "Teenan" Jones was the local businessman who

FIGURE 65. Dreamland Café, 3518 South State Street, 1920s. John Steiner Collection. Courtesy of the Chicago Jazz Archive, University of Chicago Library.

helped Frank Leland establish his first baseball club in Chicago. Jones got his start in the cabaret business when he ran the Senate Buffet and Lakeside Club in Hyde Park before being forced out in the efforts to make the area an all-white residential neighborhood. Jones then moved farther north and joined with white businessmen Art Codozoe and J. H. "Lovie Joe" Whitson to own and run the Elite Café at 3030 South State Street, next door to the Monogram Theater. The Elite was a small music hall with space for dancing that featured such performers as pianists Tony Jackson and Earl Hines. In 1915 Jones decided to open his own club, the Elite #2, at 3445 South State

FIGURE 66. King Oliver's Creole Jazz Band, ca. 1923. Courtesy of Hogan Jazz Archive, Tulane University.

Street. The club featured a white tiled facade and was advertised as the "most elaborate emporium of the Stroll. Fine wines, liquors, and cigars; café and cabaret in connection." Thanks to Jones's opening Elite #2, the *Defender* exclaimed, "the race will have a . . . Mecca for High-Class Amusement."[89] Despite this praise, Jones was best known as the "colored ruler of the underworld district," who controlled much of the gambling and prostitution that took place in cabarets throughout the South Side.[90]

The black and tans along the Stroll contributed to a sense of raw excitement and sensuality in part because of all the doings taking place, as Langston Hughes recalled, "from noon to noon." Despite regulations that required dance halls to close at 1:00 a.m., musicians regularly played though the night and into the morning. According to Earl Hines, musicians on the South Side "worked seven days a week. There was so much going on that nobody paid any attention to the time of day. You'd go to work, get on the stand, play, come off the stand, go outside, get into all sorts of arguments, go back, play again, and so on like that through the night."[91] Trumpeter Joe "King" Oliver, who arrived in Chicago in 1918 to join the Creole Jazz band, regularly played at both the

Royal Gardens (later called Lincoln Gardens) and the Dreamland Café. Other musicians played at the DeLuxe and the Dreamland, which were right across State Street from one another. The Elite #2 fast became known as an after-hours club, with musicians playing their main jobs at clubs like the Dreamland and then moving on to the Elite, and also the Pekin. The *Defender* claimed that going to the Pekin for dancing was better than going to the Loop, for "dancers leave that section and go to the Pekin. . . . Refreshments are served and public dancing is from 11:00 to 5:00 a.m."[92]

By the time of World War I, south State Street was transformed into a mecca of dance halls, theaters, and nightclubs dominated by black musicians and interracial crowds. Black owners opened not only the Royal Gardens (fig. 67), but also the DeLuxe and the Sunset Café, adding to this glorious space of leisure and musical entertainment. The innovation of the musicians, the lure of "suggestive songs," and the thrill of experiencing "indecent" dancing led white customers to frequent these places, contributing to the charged atmosphere of the Stroll. Black and tans fostered an atmo-

FIGURE 67. Vassar's "Scale Steppers" at the Lincoln Gardens (Royal Gardens), 459 East Thirty-first Street, 1921. John Steiner Collection. Courtesy of the Chicago Jazz Archive, University of Chicago Library.

sphere of interracial sensuality that was off-limits in other leisure spaces in the city, thereby making the Stroll a place for experimenting with both racial boundaries and sexual expression.[93]

Many white reformers feared that jazz led directly to objectionable behavior. From Dayton, Ohio, to Des Moines, Iowa, white "dance masters" campaigned to "take the jazz out of music." "If you take the jerk out of the time in music, and make the rhythm smooth and pleasing, you will find very little dancing that is objectionable," claimed one master.[94] White newspapers in Chicago ran a series of attacks on the "immoral" black and tans like this description of the Pekin Café: "'Lawless liquor,' sensuous 'shimmy,' solicitous sirens, wrangling waiters, all the tints of the racial rainbow, black and tan and white, dancing, drinking, singing."[95] The notion that suggestive music and dancing, and race mixing, led to moral degeneration prompted the investigation into dance halls and black and tans by the Juvenile Protective Association in 1917. The Association found "drunkenness, vice, and debauchery," and saw prostitutes plying their trade at places like the Dreamland. But the report also found that the clubs did not provide prostitutes with special rooms for turning tricks.[96]

What one could find in the dance halls were separate spaces reserved for different purposes. Alberta Hunter recounted her experiences in the early days of Chicago jazz and pointed to the variety of performances that took place at the Panama, at Thirty-sixth and State Streets. "Now the downstairs at the Panama was more of a quiet reserved type of entertainment. But upstairs it was rougher. Upstairs, we had Mamie Carter, a dancer, the 'shake' kind, and Twinkle Davis who danced and sang. . . . There, I would really lay the blues on. In fact, it was at the Panama that I introduced the *St. Louis Blues.* Oh yes, I was there a long time and people like Bert Williams and Al Jolson would come to hear me sing."[97] Other musicians recalled how pervasive policy and gambling were in the back rooms of the clubs. Earl Hines, for example, remembered being "sucked into" the gaming room at the Elite #2 on numerous occasions. According to musician Scoville Brown, backstage gambling in South Side clubs "was a ritual. This was part of the night's activities, to have a few games going on."[98]

The proximity between licit and illicit activity in the world of urban nightlife extended out into the street, illustrating that definitions of respectability were fluid and permeable and often spatially determined. Alberta Hunter, for example, argued that she tried to maintain a sense of respectability even as she sang the blues and established a "rough and ready" reputation. She looked down on women who "get on the street and sell [their] wares right out on the corner . . . where's the refinement?" To Hunter, being on stage meant that "you had to enter properly and exit properly," with the theatricality of the performance lending an air of respectability.[99] The *Defender,* at the same time that it praised establishments like the Elite and the Pekin, decried the pool halls that existed along State Street in the heart of the Stroll: "Nightly crowds of men and half-grown boys sit in unsightly positions in front of the [pool hall] or line up along the curb and walls. . . . Vulgarity of the worst is freely used as peaceful women wend their way past the low dives. . . . [N]o section of South State Street is exempt. Around 31st street people to and fro from the various churches and patrons of the theaters are constantly thrown into consternation by these conditions and these dives and their attendant mob of loungers." The *Defender* urged the police to "close up the dives and lock up the loafers."[100]

Significantly, the *Defender* placed churchgoers in the same company as theatergoers, indirectly noting how the respectable and "illicit" elements of cultural life in the Black Belt rubbed up against one another. A survey of the establishments along the Stroll further shows that the boundaries between legal and illegal enterprises were difficult to maintain, contributing to shifting notions of respectability. *Esquire Magazine*'s map of jazz spots on the South Side showcased the multiplicity of spaces that structured the everyday lives of black Chicagoans in this district (fig. 68). The map gives visual evidence of the proximity of spaces of leisure and labor, licit and illicit activity, private and public life. There were enough varied enterprises at Thirty-first and State Streets, for example, that one would not have to leave that corner to meet life's necessities. Rooming houses and apartments were nestled between a music shop and utensil manufacturing company. A few storefronts away there stood drugstores, restaurants, a shoeshine parlor, a barbershop, and a bank. Interspersed throughout were the cabarets and theaters, including the Big Grand Theater and the Vendome Theater, one of the most grandiose on the South Side, which housed Erskine Tate's Orchestra featuring Louis Armstrong.[101]

The map illustrates the specificity of place that animated life in the Black Belt. Each storefront represented a different feature of the South Side economy and was juxtaposed with those that seemingly had little functional relation to it. What united these spaces was their central part in the quotidian lives of black Chicagoans. Unable to find basic services like barbers, restaurants, and theaters that catered to them in other parts of the city, blacks on the South Side made these businesses along the Stroll into symbols of race pride and entrepreneurial success. They constituted the fabric of a rich community life, and the interiors as well as the exteriors of these stores, rooming

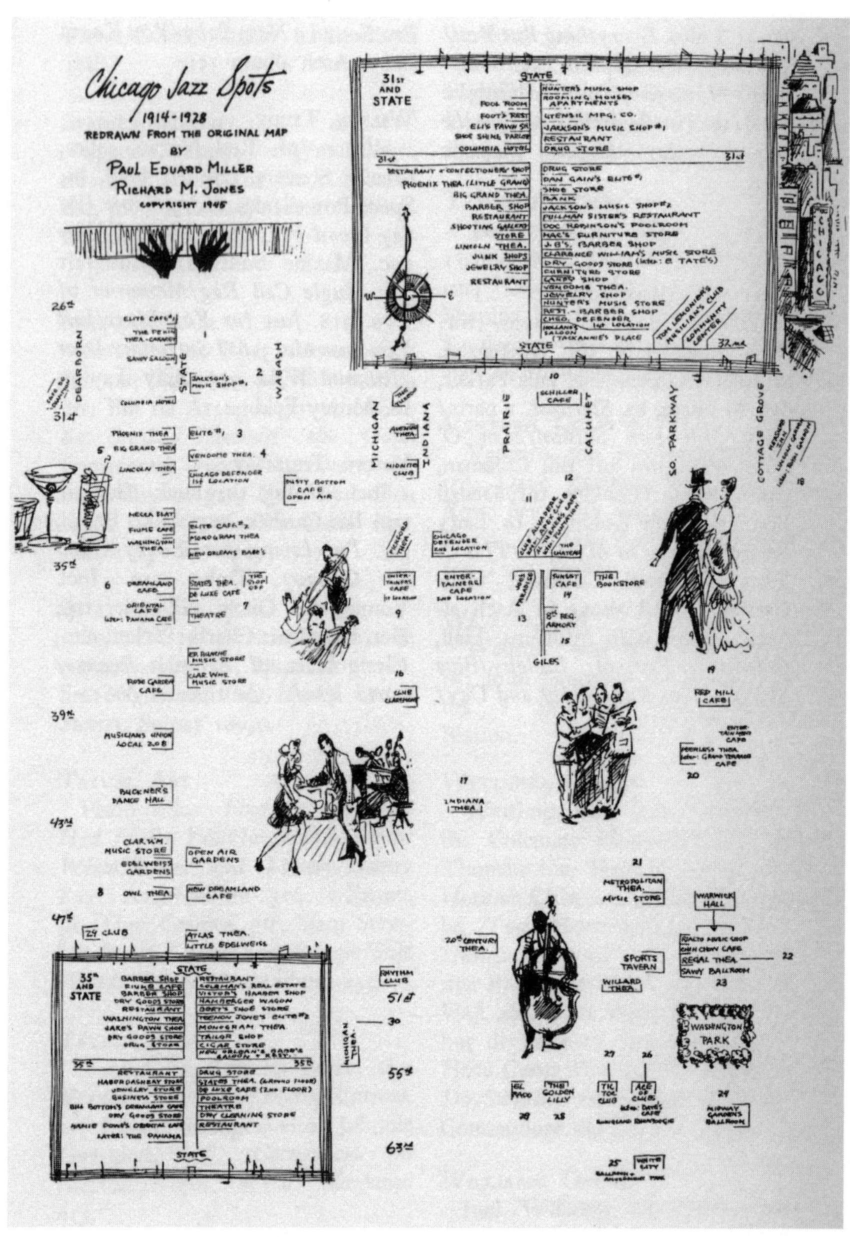

FIGURE 68. "Chicago Jazz Spots, 1914–1928." *Esquire's Jazz Book*, ed. Paul Eduard Miller (New York: Da Capo Press, 1979; originally published New York: A. S. Barnes, 1946). Courtesy of the Chicago Jazz Archive, University of Chicago Library.

houses, and cabarets became critical features. The *Esquire* map accentuates the people who made up this district and showcases the variety of places where they interacted in the course of their daily lives.

SOUTH SIDE POLITICS

The proximity of leisure sites to prominent establishments like banks and insurance companies illustrated the central role commercial amusement played in the political life of the South Side. Indeed, underworld connections were a common way for black politicians to enter city politics in Chicago. Both Mushmouth Johnson and Teenan Jones used their connections with white gambling syndicates to forge alliances with First and Second Ward political machines. Johnson and Jones used their establishments to organize "get out the vote" campaigns to encourage blacks to support candidates sympathetic to their needs. Their roles set the stage for later political leaders, including Dan Jackson, brother-in-law of Robert Motts, to promote the election of the first African American to the City Council: Oscar DePriest, who was elected in 1915. DePriest, like Binga, worked at a variety of jobs before becoming successful in real estate. He eventually got involved in Second Ward politics as secretary to the precinct captain. He quickly learned the ins and outs of ward politics, including the precinct captain's securing of special favors for important constituents. These favors included, among other things, relaxation of zoning ordinances and lack of police enforcement of certain codes, all in exchange for campaign contributions or votes. DePriest effectively negotiated these relationships, particularly those between ward bosses and the purveyors of illegal ventures like prostitution in the Black Belt. He soon gained control of the Republican organization in the Second Ward and was nominated for county commissioner. In the process he helped mediate between the local police and South Side gamblers like Teenan Jones. DePriest won the election and used the political organization he cultivated to win the City Council seat in 1915.[102]

DePriest also had worked among voters in the Black Belt to promote the mayoral candidacy of William "Big Bill" Thompson. Although he was white, Thompson was popular with African American voters because he rewarded black supporters with positions of political power. He launched his support of black politics during his 1900 campaign for alderman in the Second Ward, increasingly dominated by blacks at that point. During that election, he arranged for local black politician Adelbert H. Roberts to make one of his nominating speeches. He also established friendships with prominent civic leaders like Robert Abbott, editor of the *Chicago Defender,* and Reverend Archibald J. Carey, the minister at Quinn and later Bethel AME Church—Ida B. Wells-Barnett's nemesis. Despite their history of tense relations, though, both Carey and Wells-Barnett supported Thompson, in large part because they recognized that he had done more for the black community than any other candidate. Thompson eventually appointed several black leaders to political posts in his administration, and he also supported Oscar DePriest during his bid to become the city's first black alderman. At a 1915 gathering commemorating black progress since the Civil War, Carey praised Thompson for his support of black causes: "Whatever Mayor Thompson has done, whatever he will do, he will not do out of sympathy for the descendants of a race once enslaved, but for American citizens who have earned their position. . . . There are three names which will stand high in American history—Abraham Lincoln, William McKinley, and William Hale Thompson."[103] This overwhelming praise served Thompson well in his election bids, as black voters gave him the margin he needed to win.[104]

Yet while Carey supported Thompson, he objected to DePriest's candidacy for alderman because of his association with saloon and cabaret interests and with people like Robert Motts. Wells-Barnett, by contrast, backed DePriest and worked hard to secure the support of Chicago's black club women for his 1915 election.[105] Yet this faith in DePriest was tested after he became a leading candidate for investigation into vice in the Black Belt. In 1917 he was arrested for his alleged role in gambling, vice, and political corruption. DePriest, along with Teenan Jones and several others, was indicted for "conspiracy to allow gambling houses and houses of prostitution to operate" and "for bribery of police officers in connection with the protection of these houses."[106] Jones turned state's evidence and admitted to leading a gambling ring and making payments to both DePriest and police captain Stephen K. Healy. DePriest denied taking money to protect gambling, and his attorney, the legendary Clarence Darrow, argued that any money DePriest might have received from Jones and other gamblers was a campaign contribution, not protection money. The grand jury found him not guilty.

The political career of DePriest illustrates how closely connected black politics was to commercial leisure and the informal economy of "vice," and how the relationship between the two continued to breed suspicion among black and white civic leaders alike. Yet it was no accident that the world of black urban nightlife incubated black politics in Chicago. It was one arena in which blacks could succeed financially. Even legitimate businesspeople, like banker Jesse Binga and funeral parlor director Dan Jackson, had close ties to the underworld. These connections attest to the fluid boundaries between respectability and vice in the Black Belt. Moreover, the dance halls, gambling dens, and saloons became important sources of employment for South Side blacks. As the *Esquire* map illustrates, the spaces of the Stroll were significant not just for the leisure they offered, but for the jobs they provided.

LABOR STRIFE AND RACIAL UNREST IN POSTWAR CHICAGO

Blacks' efforts to attain secure positions in the city's labor market illustrate how important these alternative options for work proved to be. Wartime industry brought large numbers of African American men and women into the workforce. Most newcomers found work in the meatpacking industry and steel mills, or as porters, janitors, and waiters. A survey of African American employment found increasing opportunities for blacks during the war in industries such as steelworks, building trades, and laundries (for women). Yet the postwar recession led to widespread layoffs of black workers. Illinois Steel, for example, employed 35 black workers in 1916 and 1,209 in 1919, but only 338 in 1920.[107] The frequency of layoffs and the dangerous and unsanitary working conditions led blacks to move between the licit and illicit economies. They recognized that they did not have the same opportunities for more skilled jobs or promotions as their white counterparts in major industries and usually were the first to lose jobs during industry layoffs. They also understood the precarious place they held within organized labor.

Progressive white unionists like John Fitzpatrick of the Chicago Federation of Labor recognized the advantages of industrywide organizing campaigns to present a united labor front to employers. In large-scale industries like meatpacking and steel, Fitzpatrick, together with William Z. Foster, helped create industrial unions with broad-based coalitions and far-reaching agendas.[108] These campaigns allowed the Chicago labor movement to craft a definition of industrial democracy that included not only wage issues but the creation of a class-conscious unionism that might bridge ethnic and racial difference and redefine American democracy. Workers thus became "Americanized" through their participation in organizing campaigns. Yet a large part of this Americanizing entailed immigrants' ability to construct their own sense of "whiteness." The large influx of black workers complicated this process. While the prosperity of wartime allowed workers to partially set aside racial hostilities and organize for the benefit of labor as a whole, conditions in postwar America threatened to destroy this fragile coalition.[109] Much as with housing, blacks also saw more expressions of racial animosity on the shop floor following the war.

The Chicago Federation of Labor (CFL) was central in articulating a theory of industrial democracy based on cross-ethnic and cross-racial coalition building during World War I. The Stockyards Labor Council (SLC) and the National Committee for the Organization of Iron and Steel Workers illustrated the fruits of this progressive vision. Fitzpatrick and Foster organized the SLC under the auspices of the CFL. They built on Michael Donnelly's efforts to organize the Amalgamated Meat Cutters and Butcher Workmen as a broad-based union, a project cut short by the failure of the 1904 strike. The wartime labor shortage provided impetus for workers to use their strength to launch a new organizing drive and press for higher wages and improved work conditions. The SLC was created on July 23, 1917, determined to join together various international craft unions with common laborers of all ethnic and racial groups, creating a united front of packinghouse workers.[110]

Organizing African American workers was one of the greatest challenges of the SLC. By 1918, nearly 12,000 blacks were employed in the yards, or about 22 percent of the stockyards workforce. SLC organizers knew they must bring black workers into the fold of unionism if they were to make significant gains. To do so they had to overcome hostility within white craft unions and African Americans' suspicion of white unions. Many of the craft unions within the Council had policies excluding blacks from their international unions. White unionists barred blacks for a variety of reasons. The racist union policies derived from an ideology that equated black labor with lack of skill or independence, symbolized by slave labor, which many whites believed undermined the autonomy of craft labor. In addition, employers often recruited black workers from the South to break strikes led by white workers, subverting the strength of the union. To overcome many white workers' objections to admitting blacks to the unions, the SLC created neighborhood-based locals. This solution gave blacks representation within the Council while avoiding the appearance of creating racially or ethnically defined locals. In effect, though, this arrangement did just that, since Local 651 in the Black Belt was primarily African American while other locals in the Back of the Yards were mostly Polish and Lithuanian. Local ethnic leaders like John Kikulski, a Polish organizer, were crucial to the success of the coalition. Addressing a crowd of workers in Polish, Kikulski celebrated this "great campaign" in which "Polish, Irish, Lithuanian, and in fact every race, color, creed, and nationality is to be included."[111]

The SLC was able to gain the support of African American workers largely because of backing from the Chicago Urban League. League executive director T. Arnold Hill made it clear to SLC organizers that if black workers joined Local 651, they expected "union men themselves to be fair to colored workers."[112] The SLC incorporated black workers' concerns into their demands, which included substantial wage increases in all departments, for skilled and common laborers, equal pay for men and women doing the same work, and an eight-hour day. African Americans who joined the union recognized its potential to improve work conditions for them and also saw the benefits of creating an interracial coalition to challenge the power of the packers. Others argued that joining the SLC was a good opportunity for blacks to "show that they are not natural born strikebreakers."[113] All members of the SLC saw in the wartime economy a chance to refashion industrial relations along lines more favorable to workers by uniting across ethnic, racial, and gender lines to forge a concerted challenge to the packers' power.

The strength of workers' bargaining power in the wartime economy was made clear in 1917, after members of the SLC threatened a strike. Judge Samuel Alschuler, a federal administrator, took over control of the packinghouses to prevent strikes and ensure their continued productivity. At Fitzpatrick's instigation, Alschuler granted stockyards workers many of their initial demands, including the eight-hour day, double pay for overtime, a wage increase (though minimal), and a five-day workweek. Workers celebrated their gains at a rally at Davis Square, at which John Fitzpatrick exclaimed, "It's a new day, and out in God's sunshine, you men and you women, Black and White, have not only an eight-hour day, but you are on an equality."[114] This celebration of union victory, and the broad-based support it enjoyed, led the CFL to launch an Independent Labor Party, adopting labor's "Fourteen Point" platform that included many of the concessions won during the Alschuler ruling. The formation of the party illustrated Fitzpatrick's faith in the ability of cross-ethnic and interracial coalitions to translate shop floor concerns into a broad-based political program designed to make postwar American society more equitable, both materially and culturally.

Postwar conditions, both in the packinghouses and in workers' communities, contributed to the breakdown of this hopeful coalition. Returning white soldiers added to the oversupply of labor after the armistice. So did returning black soldiers, many of them from the South, who were mustered out in or near Chicago. The slackening of the economy, along with the rising cost of living, increased tensions between workers and employers and between whites and blacks, in Chicago and throughout the nation. Between December 1914 and June 1919, the cost of living in Chicago increased by close to 75 percent.[115] Employers exacerbated difficult economic conditions by reducing wage gains made during the war and refusing to bargain collectively. By the spring of 1919 a massive strike wave rocked the city and the nation. Packinghouse workers staged wildcat strikes throughout the summer of 1919 to try to secure "100 percent unionism" in each shop. In May 1919 there were at least 388 strikes across the country. Chicago was the most strike-prone city in the nation, partially because of the high level of organization. By July 1919 over 250,000 workers were on strike or locked out.[116]

Racial tensions were fueled by policies designed to divide workers and generate racial hostility to forestall union gains. Packers targeted many of their welfare capitalism programs to black workers. They gave financial support to black churches and organizations, sponsored club activities at the black Wabash Avenue YMCA, and guaranteed jobs to members of the American Unity Welfare Labor League (AUWLL). The AUWLL was founded by black labor agent Richard Parker, who urged black workers to bypass the "white man's union" and join his organization instead. He argued that African Americans needed to save their jobs and that they could not accomplish this by associating with a white union. Parker claimed that a card from his "union" would get blacks employment in the stockyards, building trades, and steel mills. "Get together and stick together . . . make your own way," stated one of his ads. "Make a union of your own race."[117] Although Parker's organization did not attract substantial numbers of African Americans, it illustrated black workers' persistent distrust of white unions. Though the SLC was more successful than almost any other union in attracting black workers, it was able to organize only about one-third of the African American stockyards workers.[118]

The CFL was less successful in forging interracial coalitions in the steel industry. Fitzpatrick and Foster launched a nationwide organizing campaign in the steel mills in the spring of 1918, and by August they had established the National Committee for the Organization of Iron and Steel Workers under the auspices of the American Federation of Labor (AFL). The organization was a coalition of twenty-four AFL craft unions, which backed the effort after seeing overwhelming evidence of support for unionization among rank-and-file workers throughout the country. Yet the leaders of the craft unions were less enthusiastic about promoting industrial unionism than were Fitzpatrick and Foster. They felt that industrial unionism undermined the ability of craft-based unions to negotiate wages and control of their work by bringing unskilled workers into the fold.[119]

Adding to the difficulty of forging a nationwide program of industrial unionism in the steel industry was the employers' success at fostering ethnic and racial division. Workers in steel mills, like those in packinghouses, often were divided into different departments based on ethnicity. Employers attempted to generate further hostility by hiring detectives to "stir up as much bad feeling" as they could among ethnic workers trying to organize.[120] Recent immigrants such as Poles, Lithuanians, and Serbs often worked in the least skilled, lowest-wage jobs and were eager to overcome ethnic difference. Yet many native-born workers were hostile to these workers and attempts at coalition building. According to Foster, "Everywhere American-born workingmen, unfortunately, are prone to look with some suspicion, if not contempt and hatred, upon foreigners, whom they have been taught to believe are injuring their standard of living."[121]

Racial animosity further hindered organizing efforts. While African Americans made up over 10 percent of the steel workforce in Chicago by 1919, they did not play an active role in organizing. The same factors that contributed to difficulties in cross-racial alliances in the packinghouses also plagued steel organizing campaigns. The conservatism of the craft unions in the mills made such alliances more difficult there than in the packinghouses. Organizing nationwide also made efforts to include black workers more difficult, since locals in cities across the country had different notions of the role African Americans could play in the union movement. Organizers focused less energy on overcoming racial hostility in the steel industry than they had in the packinghouses.[122] African American steel workers joined the 350,000 steel workers nationwide—and 90,000 in Chicago—in the September 22, 1919, strike protesting U.S. Steel's refusal to recognize the union. Yet part of the reason the strike ended in defeat several months later was the organizers' inability to promote class solidarity that transcended ethnic and racial difference.[123]

The continuing suspicion and hostility between white and black workers on the shop floor carried over into the community and set the conditions for the brutal race riot in July 1919. The riot exposed the deep fissures between African Americans and whites, whether native-born or immigrants. While most of the violence was attributed to second- and third-generation white American youths, distrust among the races permeated all groups after the riot. This racial hostility was difficult to transcend, and it shaped labor and political relations in Chicago for years to come.

THE RACE RIOT AND CHALLENGES TO WORKING-CLASS SOLIDARITY

The riot exposed how deeply intertwined were the issues of public space, leisure, and labor in shaping race relations in Chicago (fig. 69). Blacks experienced threats, hostility, and intimidation at public beaches long before the 1919 riot erupted. The Twenty-sixth Street beach was informally designated as the black beach, but reaching it was difficult and dangerous, since one had to cross a railroad embankment to get there. Police routinely warned black bathers not to enter the water by way of "white" beaches. In the summer of 1919 racial tensions grew as blacks were increasingly intimidated by white gangs at public parks and beaches. The *Chicago Defender* chastised local police for failing to protect African Americans attempting to use South Side parks and beaches: "The parks are public property, open to all citizens, black and white alike. The law exercises no discrimination in the matter of levying taxes for the maintenance of these breathing spots. They exact from us our measure for their upkeep, and those charged with the protection of citizens who frequent such places are derelict in their duty if they do not see to it that ruffianism is put down with the strong arm of the law."[124] This warning went unheeded, though, and the lack of official response set the stage for the riot.

The rapidity with which Eugene Williams's drowning ignited a large-scale riot demonstrates the level of tension on the South Side. Most of the violence during the several days of rioting took place in the Black Belt itself, as armed white youths attacked African Americans on public transportation, on street corners, and in front of their homes. The most contested area was the district on either side of Wentworth Avenue that separated the Black Belt from Bridgeport, the primarily Irish neighborhood. Attacks spilled over into Packingtown, west of Bridgeport, when members of Bridgeport's Hamburgs and Ragen's Colts street gangs provoked black workers going to the stockyards.[125]

Rumors in the press and on the streets about the brutality of the riot fueled further violence. The *Defender* reported how a young black woman who attempted to board a streetcar at Forth-seventh and Wentworth and was beaten and stabbed, while her three-month-old baby was mauled, all in front of several police officers.[126] The *Chicago Daily News* reported that carloads of colored men passed through Thirty-fifth Street at Wallace "shouting and shooting," hitting a white woman and a little boy who stood

FIGURE 69. Scene of the start of the race riot at Twenty-ninth Street Beach. From Chicago Commission on Race Relations, *The Negro in Chicago* (Chicago: University of Chicago Press, 1922).

close by.[127] These stories sparked more violence, which by the end of the week left fifteen whites and twenty-three blacks dead and over five hundred injured (fig. 70).

The importance of the racial segregation of leisure sites in structuring the riot emerged immediately. It was not just that the riot started at a contested bathing beach. Rather, the subsequent explosion of violence most often took place on streets and sidewalks, in parks and on streetcars. Williams's drowning, for example, appeared to be the consequence rather than the cause of racial tension and violence at the beach, as blacks experienced violence and intimidation by members of the Ragen's Colts for several months before the riot.[128] As Mary McDowell explained, "It was evident during the riot that . . . it was committed by the second and third generations of American born young men from the 'athletic clubs' which had grown under the protection of political leaders in this district, themselves mostly American born."[129] Most athletic clubs, of course, were not perpetrators of violence and gang warfare. But the fact that Ragen's Colts and other less notorious athletic clubs largely fueled the racial violence in Chi-

FIGURE 70. Whites chasing a black man and stoning him to death. From Chicago Commission on Race Relations, *The Negro in Chicago* (Chicago: University of Chicago Press, 1922), facing 12.

cago attests to the significant role recreational organizations played in delimiting racial boundaries in the city.

Significantly, most of violence took place on streetcars, street corners, "thoroughfares and natural highways between the job and the home."[130] In these liminal places, the contested public spaces of the South Side, the bloodiest disputes erupted. An account of the riot in the *Chicago Daily Tribune* stated, "Riots are increasing in violence and frequency, not alone because of neighborhood friction, but because of conflicts in interests which are extensions of neighborhood life, such as bathing beaches and on street cars."[131] According to the report on the events leading up to the riot, for years "there had been clashes over baseball grounds, swimming-pools in the parks, the right to walk on certain streets" that defined the racial geography of public space in Chicago. When workers, both black and white, had to travel the streets and sidewalks of South Side neighborhoods coming to and from work, their safety was in jeopardy.

The Chicago Federation of Labor tried to alleviate racial tensions by urging union members to make every effort to protect fellow workers from race prejudice. The *New Majority,* the newspaper of the CFL, issued a statement "For White Union Members to Read" in the midst of the riot. The article compared the fear of union members on the picket line, when employers and police terrorized strikers, to conditions blacks were experiencing during the riot. The CFL urged white union members to come to the forefront of the movement for easing tensions by doing all they could to suppress violence:

> This responsibility rests particularly heavy upon the white men and women of organized labor, not because they had anything to do with starting the present trouble, but because of their advantageous position to help end it. Right now it is going to decide whether the colored workers are to continue to come into the labor movement or whether they are going to feel that they have been abandoned by it and lose confidence in it.
>
> It is a critical time for Chicago.
>
> It is a critical time for organized labor.[132]

Despite pleas like this one, and attempts to foster interracial solidarity, the CFL was unable to fully alleviate racial tensions in the workplace. Labor leaders failed to persuade many African Americans of the continued benefits of "white" unions. While union officials promoted class solidarity, their counterparts in the black community argued for racial solidarity. Efforts on the shop floor were not enough to overcome the intensified racial strife that plagued public spaces, housing, schools, and transportation in Chicago. As a result, organizations like the American Unity Welfare Labor League gained greater credibility among black workers, and concerns with promoting racial solidarity became more pronounced. According to one African American, "The recent race riots have done at least one thing for the colored race. In the past we Negroes have failed to appreciate what solidarity means. We have, on the contrary, been much divided. Since the riot we are getting together and devising ways and means of protecting our interests."[133]

This movement toward racial solidarity among African Americans was matched by increased nativism on the part of native-born and second-generation whites. The end of the war, along with the advent of the Bolshevik revolution in Russia, led many "Americans" to question the loyalty and patriotism of workers fighting for industrial unionism through organizations like the Industrial Workers of the World (IWW), the radical labor movement organized in Chicago in 1905. Conservative leaders of the AFL accused IWW members of being dangerous foreigners, intent on provoking wildcat strikes and disrupting the advantages gained by craft unions during the war.

Some conservative unionists also accused progressive organizations like the CFL of being unpatriotic. One worker who testified before the Senate Investigating Committee during the steel strike estimated that "at least 99% [of the strikers] were foreigners." He argued that strike leaders did not represent workers and that "they should be sent out of the country, and if necessary, some of them ought to be shot." Judge Joseph Buffington of the U.S. Court of Appeals was more specific about who was guilty of causing unrest. "[William] Foster is the type of man who is causing all this unrest among the foreign born. . . . He is a most dangerous leader and a dangerous domestic enemy."[134]

To many Americans, anyone associated with labor organizing, but particularly with industrial unionism, was dangerous and subversive. Groups like the American Legion and the Ku Klux Klan gained new authority in shaping national definitions of Americanism. More important, Attorney General A. Mitchell Palmer translated this rising nativist ideology into public policy by indiscriminately persecuting any individuals or groups affiliated with radicalism, labor activism, or even ethnic clubs and associations. Class, labor activism, and ethnicity were intertwined and often conflated as the definitions of Americanism were circumscribed during the Red Scare of 1919.[135]

African Americans sought to obtain permanent status in the workplace and in politics by demonstrating their loyalty and Americanness. After the riot, many placed unionism among black workers behind efforts for race progress and saw cooperation with employers in the face of strikes as a way to secure jobs and better wages. T. Arnold Hill, head of the Chicago Urban League, explained the benefits to employers of hiring black workers and promoting black progress. "Failure to educate, utilize and appreciate a loyal and dependable racial group within our borders," he argued, "while we hazard our future by making it comfortable for others whom some day we may have to deport, is bad economics."[136]

The animosity felt after the riot made the hope of interracial organizing in the stockyards untenable. Black workers showed their hostility toward the white Amalgamated Meat Cutters Union during the 1921 strike. Instead of joining fellow workers on the picket line, the AUWLL issued a statement to the packers attesting to their continued loyalty and willingness to accept employers' terms, which included wage cuts as well as concessions for hours and overtime. In a letter to President Warren G. Harding, Robert E. Parker, president of the AUWLL, stated: "We are an independent union with all colored members as we have found that the American Federation, and the Amalgamated Meat Cutters Union, is just as unfair to colored labor, as it is in settling this question with the packers. We will refuse to co-operate with them in any way and will not strike as we believe the packers will meet [our demands]."[137]

The *Chicago Defender* repeatedly denounced Bolshevism and linked foreign labor with threats to American institutions. In 1919 it published a cartoon labeled "Birds of a Feather," with four vultures sitting on a perch. The birds were the "Lyncher," the "Bomber of Our Homes," "Segregation," and "Bolshevism."[138] By equating racism with anti-Americanism, African Americans staked their claim as loyal citizens working against threats of foreign Bolshevism to protect American interests.

At the same time that blacks attempted to assert their Americanness, white ethnic workers helped construct their own identity as Americans through their understanding and acceptance of racism in America. As St. Clair Drake and Horace R. Cayton explained: "On the whole, Negroes regarded foreigners with a certain amount of understandable condescension. The foreign-born, in turn, were not slow to adopt the prevailing stereotypes about Negroes. 'Foreigners learn how to cuss, count and say nigger as soon as they get here,' grumbled the Negroes. Not until the First World War, however, were masses of Negroes thrown into direct competition with the foreign-born in industry."[139]

Part of Americanization for foreign-born workers, then, was accepting American ideologies of race. This equation of Americanism and whiteness was complicated during the postwar period as suspicions over contested nationalist loyalties among immigrants transcended the benefits of whiteness they accrued in social, political, and economic life. Employers played on this divisiveness to thwart unionizing efforts. As a result, the development of company unionism and welfare capitalism gained new prominence and success as employers "bought off" some workers to undercut more radical worker demands. Americanism came to be defined by worker loyalty and complacency, nativism, and corporate control.[140]

Spaces of leisure such as ballparks, dance halls, and cabarets epitomized how the commercial leisure economy broke down some of the barriers between respectability and vice. This was especially true in African American communities like Chicago's Black Belt. The desire to promote black entrepreneurship and the importance of business leaders' supporting more traditional sites of race uplift—including churches and civic organizations—redefined the meaning of race uplift and made it more expansive. At the same time, leisure spaces, perhaps more than workplaces or neighborhoods, blurred the lines of segregation in urban America. Within ballparks, saloons, and dance halls, blacks and whites crossed the boundaries that divided the races, at least temporarily redrawing the mental maps that delimited community and neighborhood.

Indeed, while the shop floor became a space that divided the races after the war, the dance halls and cabarets of the South Side increasingly brought them together. After World War I, with the advent of the Vitaphone and jazz recording, more white audiences were introduced to South Side jazz. Many white youths, especially young musicians, began making excursions into the Black Belt to experience firsthand the thrill of the new music they heard on their radios and record players. The most famous of these white interlopers was the Austin High Gang, a group of musicians from the Austin neighborhood on Chicago's West Side who forged close relationships with Chicago's black jazz impresarios and developed their own jazz sound. By the interwar period, white musicians had adapted many of the musical styles and improvisational techniques of black jazz musicians and, together with black orchestras, helped cultivate the Big Band sound. If leisure spaces of urban nightlife were places where much of the code of decorum could be relaxed and rewritten, they also were places where racial divisions could be transcended.[141]

In addition, the relative freedom of spaces along the Stroll allowed for new black identities. The luxurious theaters and dance halls, the sophisticated dress of the musicians, and the excitement of urban nightlife created a new sense of identity for blacks, one shaped by their encounters with this variegated urban landscape. Claiming these spaces as their own, infusing them with race pride, and celebrating their role in fostering the entrepreneurial spirit showed the way culture influenced notions of citizenship. The Stroll offered a chance to express oneself in public though dress, speech, and performance, contributing to an emerging sense of racial autonomy that eventually would be translated into political power. Identity, power, and notions of citizenship were enacted and displayed within sites of commercial leisure. Blacks felt a sense of safety and even ownership in this space that was absent from other areas of the city, especially public parks and beaches along the lakefront.

The social geography of leisure in the Black Belt, and the increasing importance of black ownership of commercial leisure spaces in promoting race uplift, illustrates the shifting relation between leisure and civic culture in America by the 1920s. Rather than seeing commercial leisure as antithetical to civic culture, more and more reformers—especially within the Black Belt—understood the importance of leisure spaces to community relations, social engagement, and economic success. The economics of leisure in the Black Belt, in addition to conditions of labor, served as a model for understanding the shifting meanings of American identity throughout the nation as Americanness came to be defined more and more through patterns of leisure and consumption. This process also helped recast the meaning of public space as sites of commercial leisure served as the focal points of community interaction, local identity, and civic debate.

CONCLUSION

Chicago in 1919

THE YEAR 1919 WAS A WATERSHED for Chicago and the nation. The steel strikes, race riots, and Red Scare hysteria that plagued major cities across the country exposed the fault lines of the postwar era. They illustrated how delicate and fragile were the wartime coalitions between interracial and interethnic unions, workers and reformers, government and industry. Making the world safe for democracy abroad seemed to many to translate into unrest and upheaval at home. Industrial and political anarchy appeared to be the price of democracy on the domestic front. As a result, campaigns to rein in democracy and circumscribe its meaning took on new force. The nativism that blanketed America after wartime victory demonstrated the variety of forms the meanings of Americanism and citizenship could take and that they could be exclusive rather than inclusive. The promotion of "one hundred percent Americanism" translated into the repression and persecution of voices of alternative forms of democracy, including the promotion of industrial unionism and activist participatory democracy. Instead, progressive coalitions seeking to construct a cooperative and interactive model of the public sphere were coopted by the forces of welfare capitalism and state policies of exclusion, embodied in the Palmer Raids and the Immigration Restriction Acts.

Despite these tremendous factors working against cross-class and interethnic alliances, however, 1919 did not represent a total defeat for this brand of coalition-based reform. Rather, events showed the volatility of progressivism and the ability of a variety of groups, including academically trained social scientists, female settlement house workers, labor leaders, employers, and politicians, to use the language of progressivism to cultivate their own agendas. These alliances, forged in a variety of settings, from universities to arenas of popular culture, helped translate city building into state building. While the corporatist model of progressive urbanism appeared to win out with the rise of welfare capitalism and the increased power of the federal government, the coalition model of civic culture maintained an influence over political life and multiplied the number of constituents who had a voice in the political arena.[1]

The creation of the Chicago Commission on Race Relations to investigate the events leading up to the riot, identify its causes, and propose solutions epitomized the role of progressive reform methods in shaping urban public policy. Commission members used the language and techniques of the social sciences to investigate patterns of migration, ethnic settlement, racial segregation, and crime and vice. They hoped to better understand urban "pathologies" and establish a theoretical basis for reform decisions to reshape the built environment and ameliorate the city's ills.

Many of the ideas structuring the Commission's approach to the study of the riot, and to race relations more broadly, grew out of the theories of the emerging Chicago school of sociology. Understanding the meaning of Americanism, and the roles of ethnicity and race in shaping American identity, was a central concern of the Chicago sociologists. They pioneered studies in ethnic and race relations that shaped scholarly opinions for decades. William I. Thomas, Ernest W. Burgess, Robert E. Park, and Louis Wirth developed their theories of assimilation and identity just at the time when America experienced these upheavals in domestic relations. In part the Chicago sociologists sought to reconceptualize race and ethnicity as a way to understand these upheavals. They demonstrated the place of ethnic cultural identity in the broader process of creating American identity. In doing so, they helped denaturalize ethnic difference and began to understand race as a sociological construct rather than a biological fact.[2]

One of the central contributions of the Chicago sociologists was their sociological theory of race. According to their theories of the "race relations cycle," ethnicity and race functioned in the same way and should be understood in similar terms. Park in particular challenged biological arguments and theories of racial difference. By developing scientific theories of society, the sociologists argued, they could examine society, not the individual, for the causes of disorganization and social discord. By grouping all immigrants and races together with little differentiation in their discussions, they further downplayed inherent racial or ethnic difference.[3]

Sociologists looked to the geography of the city as a model for understanding race relations. The Chicago school drew a connection between environment, spatial relations, and racial and ethnic identity. In doing so, they envisioned a science of society from which scientific understandings of human relations could be drawn. As Ernest W. Burgess put it, "If neighborhood work can have a scientific basis, it is because there are social forces in community life—forces like geographical conditions, human wishes, community consciousness—that can be studied, described, analyzed, and ultimately measured." Contacts between groups in the urban environment, argued Burgess, Park, and Wirth, explained both the geographical development of the city and the social and cultural relations among residents.[4] The Chicago school based its understanding of the urban environment on the theories of Durkheim and Tönnies and their ideas of "human ecology." According to these theories, society was an organism that experienced both decay and reorganization. Chicago sociologists applied the same model to ethnic groups in the United States. Immigrants' entry into the New World disrupted their previous social and communal order, and it was not adequately replaced. In describing this type of disruption of social control, Ernest Burgess and Donald Bogue noted, "On the one hand, individuals are incompletely or differentially socialized and on the other hand social solidarity and social control are weakened, so that both personal and social disorganization results."[5]

Chicago sociologists' conceptualization of human ecology rested on the notion of social disorganization that ultimately led to integration and reorganization. This pattern could be applied to all racial and ethnic groups without regard to nationality. The "race relations cycle" included competition, conflict, accommodation, and assimilation. They posited an evolutionary understanding of the role that migration would play in creating order from differentiation.[6] Their faith in the inevitable cycle of integration and assimilation to smooth over social conflict in America led many critics to charge them with conservatism in the face of increasing prejudice and intolerance. By focusing on gradual, evolutionary change as the basis of social organization and human understanding, the Chicago school deemphasized the role individuals played in challenging discrimination and promoting racial equality.[7] For equality and pluralism to exist in America, argued scholars like W. E. B. Du Bois, minorities had to actively combat discrimination in order to increase the pace of progress. Du Bois articulated the theory of the "double consciousness" of African Americans, who developed a feeling of dual identity from living as blacks in an American culture that privileged whiteness. The African American "ever feels his two-ness—an American, a Negro; two souls, two thoughts, two unreconciled strivings. . . . The history of the American Negro is the history of this strife—this longing to attain self-conscious manhood, to merge his double self into a better and truer self."[8]

For Du Bois, the liminal space of marginality represented a chasm African Americans confronted in their everyday experiences. Yet marginality did not have to lead to alienation from both worlds. Du Bois agreed with social theorist Georg Simmel's idea of the "stranger" who had the freedom to negotiate between two separate worlds because he lacked deep attachment to either. Simmel believed that marginality had the potential to foster greater respect and appreciation between worlds, leading to new models of understanding among different groups.[9]

Du Bois believed that active engagement with urban issues fostered this mutual understanding. Indeed, while Park and other members of the Chicago school established the model of the scientific observer as the ideal position for the objective social scientist, Du Bois pointed to the role of the community observer in shaping urban reform.[10] He drew on the settlement house model of using data from urban investigation to generate plans for addressing urban ills. Du Bois pioneered the study of black community formation in the city with the publication of *The Philadelphia Negro* in 1899. He used census data, interviews, participant observation, and social and economic analysis of the geography of the neighborhood to understand conditions facing the black community. *The Philadelphia Negro* also illustrated the tensions in twentieth-century urban sociology over the proper relationship between social scientists and reformers. To what extent should sociologists become detached observers? When should they employ the collected data to implement change? In addition, Du Bois's study focused on another lasting tension within African American reform, and urban reform more broadly—the recognition that economic and social inequality shaped conditions faced by blacks, coupled with the lingering concern among elite and middle-class race leaders that members of the community engaged in the illicit economy were a threat to efforts at race uplift. This tension, though, obscured the increasing proximity of legitimate and illegitimate commerce within the segregated black communities of the early twentieth century.[11]

The Chicago Commission on Race Relations bridged the divide between detached social science and activist reform. The investigation used the tools of the social scientific observer, but it did so in the service of reform and public policy. The membership on the Commission attested to this new model of urban politics. The interracial board included *Chicago Defender* publisher Robert Abbott, black physician George C. Hall, white newspaper editor Victor Lawson, Jewish merchant and philanthropist Julius Rosenwald, and black attorney Edgar Addison Bancroft, among others. The Commission, along with its field investigators, addressed a multiplicity of issues in its exhaustive report. The researchers investigated the history of racial conflict in Chicago as well as in the United States; the roles of housing, jobs, and public spaces in fostering racial interactions; the opinions of members of both races in structuring race relations; and the importance of recreation and leisure sites in promoting racial contact.[12]

The Commission's recommendations reflected the belief in progressive urbanism, whereby urban ills were ameliorated through proper control of the urban environment. The conditions of blacks would be improved, and race relations made more harmonious, if the city offered better housing in nonsegregated areas, proper sanitation, and enough recreation space for both races. The Commission also called for the enforcement of laws aimed at promoting equal rights in public places so that racial contacts would be encouraged. Finally, they mandated the creation of a "permanent race relations body" in the city to investigate racial conflicts, disseminate information, and promote "the spirit of interracial tolerance and co-operation."[13] The Commission, then, appeared to represent a victory for the forces of Progressivism in the city.

The Chicago mayoral election of 1919 seemed to indicate the opposite, a defeat for the interests of progressive reform. Yet the election exposes how new coalitions on the South Side, especially those shaped by the economy of commercial leisure, also fostered interracial unity and expanded definitions of urban citizenship. In the 1919 election, five individuals ran on distinct platforms and demonstrated the wide variety of forms and meanings of citizenship and municipal reform. Incumbent Republican William "Big Bill" Thompson, first elected mayor in 1915, faced a contested primary election when University of Chicago political scientist Charles Merriam entered the race. Merriam, an alderman and a Hyde Park resident, ran on a platform of "good government" that would create public agencies administered by trained experts. Merriam labeled the system of political patronage and spoils represented by Big Bill Thompson the "Big Fix":

> What is the Big Fix? It is the combination of influences and agencies designed to control the political situation, and to be able to give immunity from the law. Never quite complete, it strives for completion, reaching out constantly for new

> connections and protections. Prosecuting officials, police, sheriffs, judges, mayors, governors, were among the many meshes in the great net, recently designed to entwine and entangle the law. It was presumed that the Big Fix could fix anything sought by the hordes of fixers, little and otherwise.[14]

Merriam complained that the "Underworld" of "grafters and gunmen, gangsters and thugs" was intimately connected to the "Upperworld" of urban politics. Only through civil service reform and "enlightened" government, he argued, could the needs of the public be properly served. Merriam advocated a program of centralized planning and bureaucratic control as a means to civic engagement and responsible public leadership.[15]

Thompson won the primary largely because Judge Harry Olson, another proponent of civil service reform and an opponent of partisan government, split the reformist vote with Merriam. Yet the election also illustrated Thompson's ability to incorporate elements of progressive reformist rhetoric into his campaign platform. Thompson had honed these tactics during the 1915 mayoral campaign, when he beat Democratic rival Robert Sweitzer. Sweitzer had soundly defeated incumbent Carter Harrison II in the primary partially as a result of ethnic hostility to Harrison's antivice crusade. Sweitzer, a Catholic, formed a coalition of ethnic voters to help make him the Democratic candidate for mayor in 1915. Yet these ethnic associations also contributed to his downfall. The wartime climate of anti-German sentiment made itself apparent upon his election bid. Though he was an Irish American, many voters mistook him for a German.[16] This mistake affected not only Anglo voters caught up in anti-German zeal but also Polish voters, who brought to America their resentment of Germany's imperialist policies toward Poland. The day before the election, the Polish National Alliance published an article stating: "The Germans wish to make the election of the Mayor of Chicago a matter of nationality politics, since they are openly declaring that Germans must, through the election of their candidate as mayor of Chicago, prove that the name of German is not so defiled as the American press would wish it to be. It is fortunate that Sweitzer will not reach the City Hall so easily, for the people of Chicago will not buy the Catholicism of Sweitzer and Poles will stand as one man for W. H. Thompson, the Republican candidate for Mayor of Chicago."[17]

Thompson capitalized on these sentiments by forging a broad-based coalition of Protestants, new immigrants, and most important, African Americans. He beat Sweitzer by a margin of close to 150,000 votes.[18]

As mayor, Thompson at first emphasized the need for responsive, respectable government and an end to patronage and corruption. He successfully dealt with middle-class residents' demand for vice reform, ethnic voters' desire for cultural autonomy, and political supporters' pressure for jobs and contracts. He initially followed Carter Harrison's policy of strictly policing and shutting down saloons, but he soon looked the other way as police made agreements with saloon keepers. He argued that he paid "experts" to consult on public works projects in order to ensure fiscal responsibility, but he gave contracts to political insiders. Finally, he rallied against American involvement in World War I and argued in favor of independence for Ireland, thereby garnering the German and Irish vote. His continued appeals to voters in the Black Belt ensured his popularity even as many of his constituents were at odds with one another.[19]

The 1919 election revealed a number of these divisions in the social and cultural fabric of Chicago politics. The campaign against Thompson exposed the racial and ethnic animosity that boiled beneath the surface of Chicago life and erupted during the July race riot. Many white immigrants on the South Side, particularly the Irish in the Bridgeport neighborhood, resented antipapal slurs Thompson had made in the past. They also saw the increased political power his policies gave to African Americans as a threat to white Democrats who represented the working-class ethnic wards on the South Side. According to one report, Thompson's foes "[painted him as' a nigger lover who kissed black babies, and his black cohorts were blamed for the decline of South Side real estate values, for putting white men out of jobs, and for the deterioration of South Side schools."[20] State's attorney and mayoral candidate Maclay Hoyne assailed Thompson for what he called his exploitation of the black vote, while he accused Sweitzer of playing on the fears of immigrants in order to garner the Catholic vote. Ironically, Sweitzer's campaign material challenged Thompson's national loyalty because of his stance against World War I. John Fitzpatrick, the fifth candidate in the election, attempted to appeal to workers based on class and to all Chicagoans based on a model of responsive municipal government.[21]

The variety of challengers in 1919 ultimately led to Thompson's re-reelection. On April 1, over 700,000 voters went to the polls in what the *New York Times* called "the wildest mayoral campaign in Chicago's history."[22] Thompson won by only 21,622 votes, largely because of Black Belt support. His campaign drew from a number of the platforms of his rivals, including municipal ownership of utilities, nickel fares on streetcars, and opposition to Prohibition. At the same time, he expressed concern over housing reform and municipal beautification and lobbied for more rigid building ordinances and zoning codes. His ability to draw constituents from a wide range of political positions, as well as the growing political power of the Black Belt, allowed him to win the election.[23]

Many critics commenting on the ramifications of the 1919 election saw it as a defeat for progressive reform in Chicago. St. Clair Drake and Horace R. Cayton argued that Thompson's win symbolized Chicago's disillusion with progressive reform.[24] The *Chicago Tribune* linked Thompson with all the forces of corruption in the city: "For Chicago, Thompson has meant filth, corruption, obscenity, idiocy and bankruptcy. He has given the city an international reputation for moronic buffoonery, barbaric crime, triumphant hoodlumism, unchecked graft and dejected citizenship. . . . He [has] made Chicago a byword of the collapse of American civilization."[25]

Political scientist Harold F. Gosnell captured some of the complexities of Thompson's rule when he stated, "As mayor of the city . . . he was hailed as 'Big Bill, the Builder,' Chicago's greatest booster, the defender of the weak, the champion of the people, while at the same time in certain newspapers the word 'Thompsonism' began to be a symbol for spoils politics, police scandals, school-board scandals, padded payrolls, gangster alliances, . . . and buffoonery in public office."[26]

Yet the scandal and corruption associated with Thompson's tenure obscure his ability to forge coalitions among groups that often had competing political agendas. While his election represented in part the defeat of activist participatory democracy advocated by people such as Jane Addams, Mary McDowell, John Dewey, and John Fitzpatrick and the politics of expertise championed by Merriam, his election nonetheless brought about a new model of government that combined machine-style patronage with the rhetoric of reform as the means to construct cross-class, interracial coalitions. The language of progressivism, which was very malleable, along with many progressive platforms, made its way into his campaigns and his mayoral policies. As Charles Merriam stated, "[Chicago's] politicians have been forced to use the language of public service, and to carry through a program of expenditure, with improvement incidental in motive perhaps but not unsubstantial in fact. 'Bill the Builder' was from one point of view a pathetic spectacle as was his 'Eight Years of Progress' with its elaborate charts and diagrams, but unintentionally this was a recognition of the triumph of the planning spirit in the city."[27]

Ethnic machine-style politics and progressive reform were not merely competing political alternatives, perpetually at odds, but aspects of an emerging political culture that saw these components function together to build new forms of political power.

Moreover, the issues of planning and the ability to reshape the urban landscape in the interest of reform became fixtures of this new municipal politics.

The political culture of Chicago in 1919 calls for a reinterpretation of progressivism and its role in forging a new model of urban government. Rather than pitting the ethnic machine politician against the progressive civil service reformer, or working-class labor leaders against settlement house workers, the events of 1919 and earlier reveal how these groups fostered alliances that bridged these artificial divides. Indeed, one of the salient features of this era was the difficulty of categorizing certain individuals like philosophers John Dewey and George Herbert Mead, settlement house workers Jane Addams and Mary McDowell, labor leaders like John Fitzpatrick and Margaret Haley, and black civic leaders like Ida B. Wells-Barnett and Robert Abbott. New coalitions that united these people in common projects of reform were built by negotiating the terrain of urban public culture.[28]

What emerged after 1919 was a new understanding of municipal government in which all these groups staked their claims as proponents of urban reform and sought to fashion a municipal state corresponding to their vision of civic culture. They saw local government as a vehicle for meeting specific needs of particular groups, but also for forging broad-based coalitions out of which new forms of public culture would emerge. Thus progressivism was not the property of one group or another. Rather, it laid the foundation for a new kind of political culture that joined the state with reform organizations, labor leaders, women's groups, and mass culture entrepreneurs to challenge the parochialism of partisan politics and promote public interest in civic engagement. All of these groups played central roles in reformulating the state and attempting to define and promote new models of urban citizenship.[29]

The four sites studied here—the university, the public park, the professional baseball field, and the Black Belt—offered different and often competing meanings of the broader civic culture of the city. These visions were reflected in the physical design of the space. Yet the blueprint for civic engagement could be read in a number of ways, since it often communicated multiple meanings through its design. The imposing Gothic towers of the university suggested isolation and exclusion yet also connoted serious scholarly investigation and a deep monastic concern for the human condition. The naturalistic landscape elements of the public parks and playgrounds, with their meandering paths and pastoral plantings, suggested free, open spaces accessible to all for any form of recreational enjoyment. But the symmetry of the design, and the introduction of fences and rules for use also demonstrated that comprehensive planning could impose order on an urban populace. The ethereal visions of a grand civic lakefront promoted unity and civic cohesion, both physically and socially, while exposing the inequalities in Chicagoans' access to public space. Similarly, the grand archways of Comiskey Park could signify localized ethnic culture, while the classically inspired facade might symbolize order and decorum. And amusement and "vice" within the Black Belt could undermine efforts at race uplift yet at the same time reflect the central role of leisure spaces in shaping economic success and race pride. Through their use of these spaces, a variety of urban residents gave them new meanings and functions and made them crucial fixtures in the development of the urban landscape and civic culture in Chicago.

The linkages I have highlighted throughout this book between negotiations over urban space, the progressive culture of expertise and reform, and the fashioning of public parks and recreational spaces as new arenas of democracy illustrate how urbanism was an open and contested process. The line separating the state and society was blurred, and new visions of urban citizenship were put forward. Elements of society deemed to be outside the perimeters of political culture, including academia and commercial recreation, contributed to refashioning the public sphere. Exploring the interstices of a variety of visions of urban culture and politics allows us to see spaces like universities, parks, baseball fields, and cabarets as potential terrain for a new civic culture that linked prescriptions for shaping the built environment with the transformation of urban politics.

NOTES

ABBREVIATIONS USED IN NOTES

AAS Papers	Amos Alonzo Stagg Papers, Special Collections Research Center, University of Chicago Library
BPCA Minutes	Minutes of the Board of Physical Culture and Athletics, University of Chicago, Joseph Regenstein Library, Special Collections
CCRR	Chicago Commission on Race Relations
CFA	Correspondence of the Founder and His Associates, University of Chicago, Joseph Regenstein Library, Special Collections
CFLM	Minutes of the Chicago Federation of Labor, Chicago Historical Society, Special Collections
CFLPS	*Chicago Foreign Language Press Survey*, Chicago Public Library Omnibus Project (Chicago: The Project, 1942)
CPD	Chicago Park District, Special Collections

CSCPP	Chicago School of Civics and Philanthropy Papers, University of Chicago, Joseph Regenstein Library, Special Collections
HPCC	Hyde Park Community Collection, Chicago Public Library Special Collections
HPHS	Hyde Park Historical Society Collection, University of Chicago, Joseph Regenstein Library, Special Collections
MBG-1	Minutes of the Committee on Buildings and Grounds, vol. 1, 1890–1916, University of Chicago, Joseph Regenstein Library, Special Collections
MBT	Minutes of the Board of Trustees, various years, University of Chicago, Joseph Regenstein Library, Special Collections
MBT-1	Minutes of the Board of Trustees, vol. 1, 1890–96, University of Chicago, Joseph Regenstein Library, Special Collections
MBT-2	Minutes of the Board of Trustees, vol. 2, 1896–1900, University of Chicago, Joseph Regenstein Library, Special Collections
MMP	Mary McDowell Papers, Chicago Historical Society, Special Collections
MTP	Marion Talbot Papers, University of Chicago, Joseph Regenstein Library, Special Collections
RFA, RG2	Rockefeller Family Archives, Pocantico Hills, New York, Record Group 2
SPCC	South Park Commission Collection, Chicago Park District, Special Collections
SPCNC	South Park Commission Newspaper Clippings, Chicago Park District, Special Collections
UCSL	University of Chicago Service League Papers, University of Chicago, Joseph Regenstein Library, Special Collections
UPP	University Presidents' Papers, Special Collections Research Center, University of Chicago Library
WRHP	William Rainey Harper Papers, Special Collections Research Center, University of Chicago Library

INTRODUCTION

1. John Coleman Adams, "What a Great City Might Be—a Lesson from the White City," *New England Magazine* 14 (March 1896): 3.
2. For further discussion of the World's Columbian Exposition, see David F. Burg, *Chicago's White City of 1893* (Lexington: University of Kentucky Press, 1976); James Gilbert, *Perfect Cities: Chicago's Utopias of 1893* (Chicago: University of Chicago Press, 1991); Peter Bacon Hales, *Constructing the Fair: Platinum Photographs by C. D. Arnold of the World's Columbian Exposition* (Chicago: Art Institute of Chicago, 1993); Neil Harris, *Cultural Excursions: Marketing Appetites and Cultural Tastes in Modern America* (Chicago: University of Chicago Press, 1990), chap. 6; Neil Harris et al., *Grand Illusions: Chicago's World Fair of 1893* (Chicago: Chicago Historical Society, 1993); David Nasaw, *Going Out: The Rise and Fall of Public Amusements* (New York: Basic Books, 1993), 62–79; and Robert Rydell, *All the World's a Fair: Visions of Empire at American International Expositions, 1876–1916* (Chicago: University of Chicago Press, 1984). For the variety of ways urban historians have analyzed the fair, see Timothy J. Gilfoyle, "White Cities, Linguistic Turns, and Disneylands: The New Paradigms of Urban History," *Reviews in American History* 26 (1998): 175–204, esp. 175–76.
3. For a discussion of this notion of exhibiting "exotic" cultures, and the relation between natural history and museums, see Steven Conn, *Museums and American Intellectual Life, 1876–1926* (Chicago: University of Chicago Press, 1998), 32–114, and Gilbert, *Perfect Cities,* 75–130.
4. *Dial,* no. 173 (Sept. 1, 1893): n.p.
5. Nancy Fraser, "Rethinking the Public Sphere: A Contribution to the Critique of Actually Existing Democracy," *Social Text* 25–26 (1990): 57.
6. For an overview of this notion of "inventing" these categories of identity see Werner Sollors, ed., *The Invention of Ethnicity* (New York: Oxford University Press, 1989). See also John Bodnar, *Remaking America: Public Memory, Commemoration, and Patriotism in the Twentieth Century* (Princeton: Princeton University Press, 1992); Lizabeth Cohen, *Making a New Deal: Industrial Workers in Chicago, 1919–1939* (Cambridge: Yale University Press, 1990); Benjamin B. Ringer and Elinor R. Lawless, *Race-Ethnicity and Society* (New York: Routledge, 1989); and Jeffrey Ross, "Urban Development and the Politics of Ethnicity: A Conceptual Approach," *Ethnic and Racial Studies* 5 (Oct. 1982): 440–56.
7. David Harvey, *The Condition of Postmodernity: An Enquiry into the Origins of Cultural Change* (Oxford: Basil Blackwell, 1989), 233.
8. Dolores Hayden, *The Power of Place: Urban Landscapes as Public History* (Cambridge: MIT Press, 1995). For further discussion of space, politics, and urban identities, see Mark

Gottdiener, *The Social Production of Urban Space,* 2d ed. (Austin: University of Texas Press, 1985); Harvey, *Condition of Postmodernity;* Michael Keith and Steve Pile, eds., *Place and the Politics of Identity* (New York: Routledge, 1993); Lynn Hollen Lees, "Urban Public Space and Imagined Communities in the 1980s and 1990s," *Journal of Urban History* 20 (August 1994): 443–65; Henri Lefebvre, *The Production of Space,* trans. Donald Nicholson-Smith (Cambridge, Mass.: Blackwell, 1991); Robert Rotenberg and Gary McDonogh, eds., *The Cultural Meaning of Urban Space* (Westport, Conn.: Bergin and Garvey, 1993); and Edward Soja, *Postmodern Geographies: The Reassertion of Space in Critical Social Theory* (London: Verso, 1988).

9. William M. Sullivan, "Making Society Work: Democracy as a Problem of Civic Cooperation," in *Civil Society, Democracy, and Civic Renewal,* ed. Robert K. Fullinwider (Lanham, Md.: Rowman and Littlefield, 1999), 31–54, quotation on 41.

10. Iris Marion Young, "Impartiality and the Civic Public: Some Implications of Feminist Critiques of Moral and Political Theory," in *Feminism as Critique,* ed. Seyla Benhabib and Drucilla Cornell (Minneapolis: University of Minnesota Press, 1987), 56–76. On democracy and public spheres, see Craig Calhoun, ed., *Habermas and the Public Sphere* (Cambridge: MIT Press, 1992); Jürgen Habermas, *The Structural Transformation of the Public Sphere: An Inquiry into a Category of Bourgeois Society,* trans. Thomas Burger with assistance from Frederick Lawrence (Cambridge: MIT Press, 1989); and Robert C. Holub, *Jürgen Habermas: Critic in the Public Sphere* (London: Routledge, 1991). For further discussion of gender, public spheres, and social science, see, see Linda Martin Alcoff, "Feminist Theory and Social Science: New Knowledges, New Epistemologies," in *BodySpace: Destabalizing Geographies of Gender and Sexuality,* ed. Nancy Duncan (New York: Routledge, 1996), 13–27, esp. 17; Seyla Benhabib, "Models of Public Space: Hannah Arendt, the Liberal Tradition, and Jürgen Habermas," in *Habermas and the Public Sphere,* ed. Craig Calhoun (Cambridge: MIT Press, 1992); Fraser, "Rethinking the Public Sphere," 56–80; Nancy Fraser, *Unruly Practices: Power, Discourse, and Gender in Contemporary Social Theory* (Minneapolis: University of Minnesota Press, 1989); E. A. Grosz, *Volatile Bodies: Toward a Corporeal Feminism* (Bloomington: Indiana University Press, 1994), esp. chaps. 1 and 4; Elizabeth Lunbeck, *The Psychiatric Persuasion: Knowledge, Gender, and Power in Modern America* (Princeton: Princeton University Press, 1994), esp. chap. 2; Mary P. Ryan, *Civic Wars: Democracy and Public Life in the American City during the Nineteenth Century* (Berkeley: University of California Press, 1997), esp. 1–18; and Iris Marion Young, *Justice and the Politics of Difference* (Princeton: Princeton University Press, 1990).

11. Linda McDowell, *Gender, Identity and Place: Understanding Feminist Geographies* (Minneapolis: University of Minnesota Press, 1999). For examples of this spatial analysis and its rela-

tion to gender, see also Sarah Deutsch, *Women and the City: Gender, Power, and Space in Boston, 1870–1940* (New York: Oxford University Press, 2000); Mona Domosh and Joni Seager, *Putting Women in Place: Feminist Geographers Make Sense of the World* (New York: Guilford Press, 2001); Elizabeth Teather, ed., *Embodied Geographies: Spaces, Bodies, and Rites of Passage* (London: Routledge, 1999); Kristine B. Miranne and Alma H. Young, eds., *Gendering the City: Women, Boundaries, and Visions of Urban Life* (Lanham, Md.: Rowman and Littlefield, 2000); David Bell and Gill Valentine, eds., *Mapping Desire: Geographies of Sexualities* (London: Routledge, 1995); Doreen Massey, *Gender, Place, and Space* (Minneapolis: University of Minnesota Press, 1994); Daphne Spain, *Gendered Spaces* (Chapel Hill: University of North Carolina Press, 1992); and Daphne Spain, *How Women Saved the City* (Minneapolis: University of Minnesota Press, 2001).

12. James Holston and Arjun Appadurai, "Cities and Citizenship," *Public Culture* 8 (1996):, 187–204, esp. 188.
13. Philip J. Ethington, *The Public City: The Political Construction of Urban Life in San Francisco, 1850–1900* (Cambridge: Cambridge University Press, 1994), 346, 407.
14. Mary P. Ryan, *Civic Wars: Democracy and Public Life in the American City during the Nineteenth Century* (Berkeley: University of California Press, 1997).
15. Roy Rosenzweig and Elizabeth Blackmar, *The Park and the People: A History of Central Park* (Ithaca: Cornell University Press, 1992).
16. Jean-Christophe Agnew, "Times Square: Secularization and Sacralization," in *Inventing Times Square: Commerce and Culture at the Crossroads of the World,* ed. William R. Taylor (Baltimore: Johns Hopkins University Press, 1991), 2–13, quotation on 3.
17. Robin D. G. Kelley, "'We Are Not What We Seem': The Politics and Pleasures of Community," in *Race Rebels: Culture, Politics, and the Black Working Class* (New York: Free Press, 1994), 35–53, quotation on 52.
18. See John Street, "Political Culture: From Civic Culture to Mass Culture," *British Journal of Political Science* 24, no. 1 (Jan. 1994): 95–113, for further discussion of the relationship between culture and politics.
19. See, for example, the essays in Michael H. Ebner and Eugene M. Tobin, eds., *The Age of Urban Reform: New Perspectives on the Progressive Era* (Port Washington, N.Y.: Kennikat Press, 1977); Richard Hofstadter, *The Age of Reform: From Bryan to F.D.R.* (New York: Vintage Books, 1955), Daniel T. Rodgers, "In Search of Progressivism," *Reviews in American History* 10, no. 4 (Dec. 1982): 113–31; and Robert H. Wiebe, *The Search for Order, 1877–1920* (New York: Hill and Wang, 1967). Other scholars have emphasized the role of Progressivism in establishing the "organizational synthesis" that led to greater government bureaucracy.

See especially Louis Galambos, "The Emerging Organizational Synthesis in Modern American History," *Business History Review* 44 (1970); Samuel P. Hays, "The New Organizational Society," in *American Political History as Social Analysis* (Knoxville: University of Tennessee Press, 1980); and Stephen Skowronek, *Building the New American State: The Expansion of National Administrative Capacities, 1877–1920* (New York: Cambridge University Press, 1982). Still others point to the conservative nature of Progressive reform, including Gabriel Kolko, *The Triumph of Conservatism: A Reinterpretation of American History* (New York: Alfred A. Knopf, 1963), and James Weinstein, *The Corporate Ideal in the Liberal State, 1900–1918* (Boston: Beacon Press, 1968).

20. For further discussion of Progressive reform in general, see Mina Carson, *Settlement Folk: Social Thought and the American Settlement Movement, 1885–1930* (Chicago: University of Chicago Press, 1990); Robert Crunden, *Ministers of Reform: The Progressives' Achievement in American Civilization, 1889–1920* (New York: Basic Books, 1982); Allen F. Davis, *Spearheads for Reform: The Social Settlements and the Progressives, 1890–1914* (New York: Oxford University Press, 1967); Rivka Shpak Lissak, *Pluralism and Progressives: Hull-House and the New Immigrants, 1890–1919* (Chicago: University of Chicago Press 1989); and Kathleen D. McCarthy, *Noblesse Oblige: Charity and Cultural Philanthropy in Chicago, 1849–1929* (Chicago: University of Chicago Press, 1982). While the books above take different approaches to their interpretations, they all share an emphasis on the role of elites in shaping and defining Progressivism. Few address the roles of working-class city residents in providing alternative visions of urban growth. One notable exception is Kevin Mattson's *Creating a Democratic Public: The Struggle for Urban Participatory Democracy during the Progressive Era* (University Park: Pennsylvania State University Press, 1998). Mattson discusses the changes in political culture during the Progressive Era and stresses the opportunities for forging a democratic public sphere based on participatory democracy. He focuses on the "social centers" movement in which reformers opened up public schools in the evening for broad-based public debate, and he argues that a variety of reformers, including Charles Zueblin, Frederick Howe, and Mary Park Follett, sought a genuine transformation of urban democracy until these ideals were eclipsed by World War I and new conceptions of public opinion.

21. See, for example, Thomas Bender, *Toward an Urban Vision: Ideas and Institutions in Nineteenth-Century America* (Lexington: University of Kentucky Press, 1975); Stanley Buder, *Visionaries and Planners: The Garden City Movement and the Modern Community* (New York: Oxford University Press, 1990); Robert Fishman, *Urban Utopias in the Twentieth Century: Ebenezer Howard, Frank Lloyd Wright, and Le Corbusier* (New York: Basic Books, 1977); John Reps, *The Making*

of Urban America: A History of City Planning in the United States (Princeton: Princeton University Press, 1965); David Schuyler, *The New Urban Landscape: The Redefinition of City Form in Nineteenth-Century America* (Baltimore: Johns Hopkins University Press, 1986); and Mel Scott, *American Planning since 1890* (Berkeley: University of California Press, 1969).

22. See, for example, M. Christine Boyer, *Dreaming the Rational City: The Myth of American City Planning* (Cambridge: MIT Press, 1983); Richard E. Foglesong, *Planning the Capitalist City: The Colonial Era to the 1920s* (Princeton: Princeton University Press, 1986); and Stanley K. Schultz, *Constructing Urban Culture: American Cities and City Planning, 1800–1920* (Philadelphia: Temple University Press, 1989).

23. Patricia Burgess, *Planning for the Private Interest: Land Use Controls and Residential Patterns in Columbus, Ohio, 1900–1970* (Columbus: Ohio State University Press, 1994); Greg Hise, *Magnetic Los Angeles: Planning the Twentieth-Century Metropolis* (Baltimore: Johns Hopkins University Press, 1997); Eric Sandweiss, *St. Louis: The Evolution of an American Urban Landscape* (Philadelphia: Temple University Press, 2001); Marc Weiss, *The Rise of the Community Builders: The American Real Estate Industry and Urban Land Planning* (New York: Columbia University Press, 1987); and William H. Wilson, *The City Beautiful Movement* (Baltimore: Johns Hopkins University Press, 1989).

24. Recent works in planning history that emphasize the contested nature of urban development include Peter Baldwin, *Domesticating the Street: The Reform of Public Space in Hartford, 1850–1930* (Columbus: Ohio State University Press, 1999); John Fairfield, *The Mysteries of the Great City: The Politics of Urban Design, 1877–1937* (Columbus: Ohio State University Press, 1995); Max Page, *The Creative Destruction of Manhattan, 1900–1940* (Chicago: University of Chicago Press, 1999); David Ward and Olivier Zunz, eds., *The Landscape of Modernity: Essays on New York City* (New York: Russell Sage Foundation, 1992); John N. Mollenkopf, *The Contested City* (Princeton: Princeton University Press, 1983); and David M. Scobey, *Empire City: The Making and Meaning of the New York City Landscape* (Philadelphia: Temple University Press, 2001).

25. See Richard D. Butsch, *For Fun and Profit: The Transformation of Leisure into Consumption* (Philadelphia: Temple University Press, 1990); Lewis Erenberg, *Steppin' Out: New York Nightlife and the Transformation of American Culture, 1890–1930* (Westport, Conn.: Greenwood Press, 1981); John F. Kasson, *Amusing the Million: Coney Island at the Turn of the Century* (New York: Hill and Wang, 1978); William Leach, *Land of Desire: Merchants, Power, and the Rise of a New American Culture* (New York: Vintage Books, 1993); Nasaw, *Going Out;* Kathy Peiss, *Cheap Amusements: Working Women and Leisure in Turn-of-the-Century New York* (Philadelphia: Temple University Press, 1986); Roy Rosenzweig, *Eight Hours for What We Will: Workers and Leisure*

in an Industrial City (Cambridge: Cambridge University Press, 1983); and William R. Taylor, ed., *Inventing Times Square: Commerce and Culture at the Crossroads of the World* (Baltimore: Johns Hopkins University Press, 1991).

26. For discussions of commercial growth of Chicago and the role of downtown construction in putting forth one civic image of the city, see Daniel Bluestone, *Constructing Chicago* (New Haven: Yale University Press, 1991), especially chap. 4; Carl Condit, *The Chicago School of Architecture: A History of Commercial and Public Building in the City Area, 1875–1925* (Chicago: University of Chicago Press, 1964); Carl Condit, *The Rise of the Skyscraper* (Chicago: University of Chicago Press, 1952); and John Zukowsky, ed., *Chicago Architecture, 1872–1922* (Chicago: University of Chicago Press, 1990). For general discussions of American downtowns see Robert M. Fogelson, *Downtown: Its Rise and Fall, 1880–1950* (New Haven: Yale University Press, 2001); Alison Isenberg, "Downtown Democracy: Rebuilding Main Street Ideals in the Twentieth-Century American City" (Ph.D. diss., University of Pennsylvania, 1995); and Jon C. Teaford, *The Rough Road to Renaissance: Urban Revitalization in America, 1940–1985* (Baltimore: Johns Hopkins University Press, 1990).

27. United States Bureau of the Census, *Ninth Census*, 1870, Part 1 "Population"; *Eleventh Census*, 1890, "Population"; Bessie Louise Pierce's classic work, *A History of Chicago*, vol. 3, *The Rise of the Modern City* (New York: Alfred A. Knopf, 1957), 343; and Frank A. Randall, *History of the Development of Building Construction in Chicago* (Urbana: University of Illinois Press, 1949), 4.

28. See William Cronon, *Nature's Metropolis: Chicago and the Great West* (New York: W. W. Norton, 1991), for further discussion of the changes in the Chicago landscape throughout the nineteenth century. Cronon points to the importance of studying regions rather than cities if we are to fully understand patterns of urban growth. As he convincingly argues, the growth of cities cannot be understood apart from the interconnectedness between rural and urban economies, markets, natural landscapes, and human interactions with those landscapes. Cronon's work calls for an urban history that sees city and country as a tightly bound system, in which natural and built environments are integrally linked. See especially 23–54. For further discussion of changes in Chicago during the early to mid-nineteenth century, see Alfred T. A. Andreas, *A History of Chicago*, 3 vols. (Chicago: A. T. Andreas, 1887); Perry R. Duis, *Challenging Chicago: Coping with Everyday Life, 1837–1920* (Urbana: University of Illinois Press, 1998); Harold M. Mayer and Richard C. Wade, *Chicago: Growth of a Metropolis* (Chicago: University of Chicago Press, 1969); Donald L. Miller, *City of the Century: The Epic of Chicago and the Making of America* (New York: Simon and Schuster, 1996); Dominic A. Pacyga and Ellen Skerrett, *Chicago, City of Neighborhoods: His-*

tories and Tours (Chicago: University of Chicago Press, 1986); and Pierce, *History of Chicago,* vol. 3.

29. Carl Sandburg, *Chicago Poems* (New York: Henry Holt, 1916), 3.
30. Ibid., 4.
31. For more on Chicago cultural institutions, see Harris, *Cultural Excursions,* esp. chap. 6, and Helen Lefkowitz Horowitz, *Culture and the City: Cultural Philanthropy in Chicago from the 1880s to 1917* (Chicago: University of Chicago Press, 1976).
32. George M. Pullman was the sleeping-car magnate who founded the Pullman Palace Car Company; Gustavus Swift and Philip Armour were the founders of Chicago's largest meatpacking companies; Martin Ryerson acquired his initial wealth in the lumber industry and became director of the Corn Exchange Bank, of which Charles L. Hutchinson was president; and Marshall Field established one of Chicago's first department stores. See *The Book of Chicagoans* (Chicago: A. N. Marquis, 1905), and Thomas Wakefield Goodspeed, *The University of Chicago Biographical Sketches,* 2 vols. (Chicago: University of Chicago Press, 1925).
33. For further discussion of middle-class and white-collar professions, see Cindy Sondik Aron, *Ladies and Gentleman of the Civil Service: Middle Class Workers in Victorian America* (Oxford: Oxford University Press, 1987); Burton J. Bledstein, *The Culture of Professionalism: The Middle Class and the Development of Higher Education in America* (New York: W. W. Norton, 1976); Stuart Blumin, "Black Coats to White Collars: Economic Change, Nonmanual Work, and the Social Structure of Industrializing America," in *Small Business in American Life,* ed. Stuart W. Bruchey (New York: Columbia University Press, 1980), 100–121; and Stuart Blumin, *The Emergence of the Middle Class: Social Experience in the American City, 1760–1900* (Cambridge: Cambridge University Press, 1989).
34. For further discussion of notions of disorder in the city, see Paul S. Boyer, *Urban Masses and Moral Order in America, 1820–1920* (Cambridge: Harvard University Press, 1978), esp. 1–7; Carl Smith, *Urban Disorder and the Shape of Belief: The Great Chicago Fire, the Haymarket Bomb, and the Model Town of Pullman* (Chicago: University of Chicago Press, 1995); and Wiebe, *Search for Order.*
35. For an excellent analysis of these political cleavages in Chicago at the time of the fire, see Karen Sawislak, *Smoldering City: Chicagoans and the Great Fire, 1871–1874* (Chicago: University of Chicago Press, 1995). See also Smith, *Urban Disorder;* Ross Miller, *American Apocalypse: The Great Fire and the Myth of Chicago* (Chicago: University of Chicago Press, 1990); and Christine Meisner Rosen, *The Limits of Power: Great Fires and the Process of City Growth in America* (New York: Cambridge University Press, 1986).

36. See Sawislak, *Smoldering City*, 79, 139–48, for further discussion of the hardships experienced by working-class immigrants who were left homeless in the wake of the fire and had difficulty rebuilding because of fire codes and lack of insurance money. See also Robin L. Einhorn, *Property Rules: Political Economy in Chicago, 1833–1872* (Chicago: University of Chicago Press, 1991), 104–43, for a discussion of nineteenth-century Chicago's "segmented system" of government, in which city improvements were paid for by special assessment of property owners, thereby creating a limited role for city government.
37. United States Bureau of the Census, *Ninth Census*, 1870, Part 1, "Population"; *Eleventh Census*, 1890, "Population"; Pierce, *History of Chicago*, 3:343; and Frank A. Randall, *History of the Development of Building Construction in Chicago* (Urbana: University of Illinois Press, 1949), 4.
38. Sam Bass Warner Jr., "Foreword," in Susan Hirsch and Robert I. Goler, *A City Comes of Age: Chicago in the 1890s* (Chicago: Chicago Historical Society, 1990), 8–23, 22.

CHAPTER ONE

1. For further discussion of the changing role of universities, see Roger L. Geiger, *To Advance Knowledge: The Growth of American Research Universities, 1900–1940* (New York: Oxford University Press, 1986); Thomas L. Haskell, *The Emergence of Professional Social Science: The American Social Science Association and the Nineteenth Century Crisis of Authority* (Urbana: University of Illinois Press, 1977); Bruce Kuklick, *The Rise of American Philosophy: Cambridge, Massachusetts, 1860–1930* (New Haven: Yale University Press, 1977),230–53; W. Bruce Leslie, *Gentlemen and Scholars: College and Community in the "Age of the University," 1865–1917* (University Park: Pennsylvania State University Press, 1992); Julie A. Reuben, *The Making of the Modern University: Intellectual Transformation and the Marginalization of Morality* (Chicago: University of Chicago Press, 1996); and Laurence R. Veysey, *The Emergence of the American University* (Chicago: University of Chicago Press, 1965).
2. Robert Herrick, "The University of Chicago," *Scribner's Magazine* 18 (October 1895): 399–417, esp. 404, 417.
3. Neil Harris, "Foreword," in Jean F. Block, *The Uses of Gothic: Planning and Building the University of Chicago, 1892–1932* (Chicago: University of Chicago Press, 1983), xii.
4. William Rainey Harper to John D. Rockefeller, May 7, 1892, Correspondence of the Founder and His Associates (hereafter cited as CFA), box 3, folder 4, Special Collections Research Center, University of Chicago Library. For further discussion of Rockefeller's commitment to Baptist causes, and especially the University of Chicago, see Ron Chernow, *Titan: The Life of John D. Rockefeller, Sr.* (New York: Random House, 1998), 299–329.

5. Quoted in Thomas Wakefield Goodspeed, *A History of the University of Chicago: The First Quarter-Century* (Chicago: University of Chicago Press, 1916), 224.
6. For further discussion of the ideas surrounding the founding of the University of Chicago, see Chauncey Samuel Boucher, *The Chicago College Plan* (Chicago: University of Chicago Press, 1935); Steven J. Diner, *A City and Its Universities: Public Policy in Chicago, 1892–1919* (Chapel Hill: University of North Carolina Press, 1980); Goodspeed, *History;* and Richard J. Storr, *Harper's University: The Beginnings* (Chicago: University of Chicago Press, 1966).
7. See Diner, *City and Its Universities,* 22–25. See also Reuben, *Making of the Modern University.*
8. Quoted in *The University and the City: A Centennial View of the University of Chicago* (Chicago: University of Chicago Library, 1992), ix.
9. For further discussion of the World's Columbian Exposition and its role in introducing visitors to the University of Chicago, see David F. Burg, *Chicago's White City of 1893* (Lexington: University of Kentucky Press, 1976); James Gilbert, *Perfect Cities: Chicago's Utopias of 1893* (Chicago: University of Chicago Press, 1991); Neil Harris et al., *Grand Illusions: Chicago's World Fair of 1893* (Chicago: Chicago Historical Society, 1993); Horowitz, *Culture and the City;* and Robert Rydell, *All the World's a Fair: Visions of Empire at American International Expositions, 1876–1916* (Chicago: University of Chicago Press, 1984).
10. Thomas Wakefield Goodspeed to John D. Rockefeller, Jan. 7, 1887, CFA, box 1, folder 1. See also the handwritten version of this letter at the Rockefeller Family Archives, Record Group 2 (hereafter cited as RFA, RG 2), Pocantico Hills, New York, Educational Interests, box 100, unprocessed materials.
11. Frederick T. Gates to Henry L. Morehouse, Oct. 23, 1888, CFA, box 1, folder 3; Frederick T. Gates, "The Need of a Baptist University in Chicago, as Illustrated by a Study of Baptist Collegiate Education in the West," paper read before the Baptist Ministers' Conference, Chicago, Oct. 15, 1888, Papers of Frederick Taylor Gates, box 1, folder 2, Special Collections Research Center, University of Chicago Library.
12. Gates, "Need of a Baptist University in Chicago."
13. Papers of the American Baptist Education Society, box 1, folder 1, Special Collections Research Center, University of Chicago Library.
14. Augustus H. Strong to William Rainey Harper, Nov. 18, 1888, CFA, box 1, folder 4. See also the correspondence in the Rockefeller Family Archives between Strong and Rockefeller. Strong was a close friend of Rockefeller; he was the pastor of the First Baptist Church of Cleveland where Rockefeller was a parishioner. Rockefeller's oldest daughter Bessie married Strong's son Charles, so the two men became even more intimately connected. Still, the correspondence suggests that a chilly relationship developed as Strong

tried to make his case for the new institution in New York, an institution that he presumably would head. At one point Rockefeller declared a moratorium on further discussion of the university idea by Strong. See correspondence between Strong and Rockefeller in RFA, RG2, Educational Interests, box 100, unprocessed materials. See also Chernow, *Titan,* 309–17.

15. Thomas Wakefield Goodspeed to John D. Rockefeller, Jan. 7, 1887, CFA, box 1, folder 1.
16. Thomas Wakefield Goodspeed, *William Rainey Harper: First President of the University of Chicago* (Chicago: University of Chicago Press, 1928), chap. 1. See also Chernow, *Titan,* 307–9; Diner, *City and Its Universities,* 15–16.
17. See John E. Tapia, *Circuit Chautauqua: From Rural Education to Popular Entertainment in Early Twentieth Century America* (Jefferson, N.C.: McFarland, 1997).
18. William Rainey Harper to Dr. Henry L. Morehouse, Dec. 28, 1888, CFA, box 1, folder 4.
19. Harper's ideas were not shared by some Baptist theologians, including Augustus Strong. Strong used his criticism of Harper's theology to further dissuade Rockefeller from endowing the university in Chicago. Strong based this criticism on lectures Harper gave at Vassar College. After gaining national prominence for his work with the Chautauqua movement, Harper joined the faculty at Yale as a professor of Semitic languages at the Divinity School. On Sundays he traveled to Vassar College in southeastern New York to teach Bible classes. One of his students was Strong's daughter, Kate. After looking over her notes from one of Harper's lectures, Strong accused Harper of heretical teaching and threatened to have him removed from the program at Vassar, where Strong served on the Board of Trustees. In a stinging letter to Rockefeller, Strong wrote that he believed Harper departed from "the sound faith as to inspiration and prophecy, and is no longer to be trusted in his teachings." Strong to Rockefeller, Dec. 25, 1888, RFA, RG2, Educational Interests, box 100, unprocessed materials. A typewritten copy can be found in CFA, box 1, folder 4.
20. Dr. P. S. Henson, quoted in Goodspeed, *History,*93–94. See also Henson to Rockefeller, June 4, 1888, CFA, box 1, folder 3.
21. William Rainey Harper, *The Trend in Higher Education* (Chicago: University of Chicago Press, 1905), 49–50. For further discussion of the emergence of professionalism in large-scale research universities see Andrew Abbott, *The System of Professions: An Essay on the Division of Expert Labor* (Chicago: University of Chicago Press, 1988); Burton J. Bledstein, *The Culture of Professionalism: The Middle Class and the Development of Higher Education in America* (New York: W. W. Norton, 1976); Thomas L. Haskell, *The Emergence of Professional Social Science: The American Social Science Association and the Nineteenth-Century Crisis of Authority* (Urbana: Uni-

versity of Illinois Press, 1977); and Dorothy Ross, *The Origins of American Social Science* (Cambridge: Cambridge University Press, 1991).

22. Martin A. Ryerson, quoted in *Quarterly Calendar,* 1892–96, Aug. 1894, 31.

23. Rockefeller to Gates, May 15, 1889, CFA, box 2, folder 1; Minutes of the Board of Trustees, vol. 1, 1890–96 (hereafter cited as MBT-1), Sept. 10, 1890, Special Collections Research Center, University of Chicago Library; Storr, *Harper's University,* 32–33; Goodspeed, *History,*55, 66, 91. The charter stipulated that the American Baptist Education Society was the organization charged with securing support for a Baptist institution of higher education in Chicago. Yet it said that its immediate goal was to create a college, not a university. "It need only to be remarked here that it has never been the purpose of the Society to seek to limit the institution to the work of a College. It has been hoped and believed that a good college located in this city would naturally and inevitably develop into a great university. . . . But from the first, it has been believed that the enlargement would be affected naturally by the inherent life of the institution and would by no means require the fostering care of the Society." See MBT-1,12–12K, and "Notes from Sept. 18, 1890 Board of Trustees Meeting, CFA, box 1, folder 11.

24. Storr, *Harper's University,* 35; Goodspeed, *History,* 69–74.

25. Frederick T. Gates in *Standard,* Dec. 1889, 1.

26. MBT-1, Sept. 10, 1890; Storr, *Harper's University,* 38–42; Goodspeed, *History,* 85–92. Gates to Rockefeller, Apr. 28, 1890, CFA, box 1, folder 9. Pullman did become a donor.

27. Gates to Harper, Feb. 17, 1890, CFA, box 1, folder 9.

28. Goodspeed to his sons, Feb. 23, 1890, CFA, box 1, folder 9.

29. See also Goodspeed to his sons, Feb. 23, 1890, CFA, box 1, folder 9.

30. Charter of the University of Chicago, Sept. 18, 1890, CFA, box 1, folder 11, 1–2. At its May 15, 1917, meeting, the Board of Trustees of the university determined that "the unexpected present magnitude of the University and its increasing importance in the educational world make these conditions in the title [the requirement that two-thirds of the board members be Baptists] to what is now but a small part of the campus unbecoming to the dignity of the institution." See MBT, vol. 10, May 15, 1917; On June 14, 1923, the Board of Trustees amended the charter to stipulate that three-fifths of the trustees should be members of Baptist churches. MBT, vol. 13, June 14, 1923. The Baptist provision was amended again in 1930 and 1944, with the latter stating, "The Board of Trustees of the Baptist Theological Union (whose charter requires that all of the members of its Board of Trustees shall be members of regular Baptist churches) shall always be represented on the Board of Trustees of The University of Chicago." See "Amendment to the Articles

of Incorporation of the University of Chicago," July 13, 1944, Special Collections Research Center, University of Chicago Library.

31. Charter of the University of Chicago, Sept. 18, 1890, CFA, box 1, folder 11, 1–2; Rockefeller to Gates, Apr. 26, 1890, CFA, box 2, folder 3.

32. The other original trustees were George A. Pillsbury, Ferdinand W. Peck, Herman H. Kohlsaat, Edward Goodman, Alonzo K. Parker, John W. Midgely, George C. Walker, C. C. Bowen, Judge J. W. Bailey, Fred A. Smith, Francis Hinckley, Elmer L. Corthell, and W. B. Brayton. See MBT-1, 4–5; Block, *Uses of Gothic,* 232n. For background on trustees see Diner, *City and Its Universities,* 61.

33. Field to Gates, May 26, 1890, quoted in Horowitz, *University and the City,* 5.

34. MBT-1, 12c; Goodspeed, *History,* 92–96; University of Chicago *Official Bulletin,* no. 1, Jan. 1891, 6.

35. Goodspeed to Harper, Jan. 6, 1891, William Rainey Harper Papers (hereafter cited as WRHP), Special Collections Research Center, University of Chicago Library.

36. Goodspeed, *History,* 171.

37. Gates to Morehouse, Jan. 17, 1890, CFA, box 1, folder 9.

38. "Examination of Title," Hyde Park Community Collection (hereafter cited as HPCC), Chicago Public Library, Special Collections, box 3, folder 11; A. T. Andreas, *History of Chicago* (Chicago: A. T. Andreas, 1884), 2:479.

39. For example, George Kimbark bought land between Fifty-first and Fifty-fifth Streets, Woodlawn and Dorchester. John Kennicot bought property and built a home at Forty-eighth and Dorchester in an area he would call Kenwood. A. T. Andreas, *History of Cook County* (Chicago: A. T. Andreas, 1884), 555; Jean Block, *Hyde Park Houses: An Informal History, 1865–1910* (Chicago: University of Chicago Press, 1978), 6–8.

40. Janet Ayer, "Old Hyde Park," in *Chicago Yesterdays: A Sheaf of Reminiscences,* ed. Cardine Kirkland (Chicago: Daughaday, 1919), 187. For further discussion of suburbanization in Chicago see Michael Ebner, *Creating Chicago's North Shore: A Suburban History* (Chicago: University of Chicago Press, 1988); Everett Chamberlin, *Chicago and Its Suburbs* (Chicago: T. A. Hungerford, 1874); Ann Durkin Keating, *Building Chicago: Suburban Developers and the Creation of the Divided Metropolis* (Columbus: Ohio State University Press, 1988); and Harold M. Mayer and Richard C. Wade, *Chicago: Growth of a Metropolis* (Chicago: University of Chicago Press, 1969).

41. Andreas, *Cook County,* 557; Block, *Hyde Park Houses,* 12; Bluestone, *Constructing Chicago,* 39–44; Chamberlin, *Chicago and Its Suburbs,* 314; Homer Hoyt, *One Hundred Years of Land Values in Chicago: The Relationship of the Growth of Chicago to the Rise of Its Land Values, 1830–1933* (Chicago: University of Chicago Press, 1933), 99.

42. *Real Estate and Building Journal,* Aug. 19, 1871; Hoyt, *One Hundred Years,* 100.

43. Chamberlin, *Chicago and Its Suburbs,* 309, 353; Hoyt, *One Hundred Years,* 107, 113.

44. *Real Estate and Building Journal,* Aug. 19, 1871; Hoyt, *One Hundred Years,* 100. For further discussion of the effects of the fire on suburban development and land speculation see Thomas Knudtson, *Chicago, The Rising City: A Historical View of Chicago, One Hundred Years after the Great Fire* (Chicago: Chicago Publishing, 1975); Christine Meisner Rosen, *The Limits of Power: Great Fires and the Process of City Growth in America* (New York: Cambridge University Press, 1986); and Karen Sawislak, *Smoldering City: Chicagoans and the Great Fire, 1871–1874* (Chicago: University of Chicago Press, 1995).

45. Hoyt, *One Hundred Years,* 104. Although wages for skilled workers in the building trades and for mechanics rose to five and often ten dollars a day in 1872, the financial panic of 1873 caused a rapid decrease in wages, to as low as two to three dollars a day as a result of the halt in building. Many of those workers who bought cottages in outlying areas of the city were forced to give up their homes and become renters. Ibid., 118.

46. Block, *Hyde Park Houses,* 10. The population of Hyde Park skyrocketed in the 1870s and 1880s, from 3,644 in 1870 to 15,724 in 1880 to over 45,000 in 1883. See *Chicago Tribune,* Jan. 6, 1884; U.S. Census, *Population Census,* 1870, 1880.

47. *Chicago Tribune,* Mar. 18, 1874; Mar. 12, 1876; Feb. 24, 1878; Mar. 28, 1880; *Rascher's Atlas of the North Half of Hyde Park,* 1890, Chicago Historical Society; Block, *Hyde Park Houses,* 10, 40–44. Hyde Park Center was by far the most densely populated section of Hyde Park–Kenwood. In 1886 there were 4,570 people in Hyde Park Center, 750 in Kenwood (including North Kenwood, between Thirty-ninth and Forty-ninth Streets), and about 500 in South Park (between Fifty-fifth and Fifty-ninth Streets). The total population of Hyde Park Township was 50,000. *Hyde Park Herald,* Aug. 26, 1886.

48. U.S. Census, *Population Census,* 1870, 1880, 1900.

49. Developers began building apartments on the periphery of Kenwood, but not without protest. Charles Hutchinson and other residents took builders Russell Ulrich and W. I. Beman to court to fight their construction of an apartment house on the southwest corner of Forty-fourth and Greenwood. In 1893 the Illinois Supreme Court upheld the ruling of a lower court in favor of the builders. Despite this ruling, there were relatively few apartment houses built in Kenwood owing to the overwhelming disapproval of the residents. *Economist,* Apr. 8, 1893; Block, *Hyde Park Houses,* 38, 40, 75–76.

50. The town of Pullman in the southern portion of Hyde Park was the model for this development. Buckingham had Pullman architect Solon S. Beman design the homes as well as a business block with a café, club, reading room, public hall, grocery, and drugstore. "Some Residential Structures of Historical and Architectural Significance in Hyde

Park and Kenwood," Hyde Park Historical Society Collection (hereafter cited as HPHS), box 1, folder 1, Special Collections Research Center, University of Chicago Library; *Chicago Tribune,* Dec. 23, 1883; *Hyde Park Herald,* May 18, 1884; Feb. 14, 1885; *Inland Architect,* 3 (1884), 51.

51. See City of Chicago, Board of Elections Commissioners, *Record of Index of Persons Registered,* 1888, Newberry Library, along with the *Lakeside Directory of Hyde Park,* 1887, 1889, 1889, and the U.S. Census, *Manuscript Census for the Tenth Census,* 1880.

52. *Town of Hyde Park Annual Report* (Chicago: Rand McNally, 1882, 1884); *Hyde Park Herald,* Feb. 4, 1882; Jan. 10, Feb. 7, 1885; *Chicago Tribune,* Mar. 1, 4, 15, 29, 1885). For further discussion of Rosalie Villas, see Gwendolyn Wright, *Moralism and the Model Home: Domestic Architecture and Cultural Conflict in Chicago, 1873–1913* (Chicago: University of Chicago Press, 1980), 74–78.

53. *Memorial Volume: An Account of the Tri-centennial Class Meeting of 1854, Union College* (Hyde Park, Ill.: Hyde Park Publishing, 1884), 41–42.

54. *Proceedings of the Board of Trustees, Village of Hyde Park* (1887), HPCC; *Hyde Park Herald,* Nov. 9, 1887; *Chicago Tribune,* Nov. 10, 13, 17, 1887; *Chicago Herald,* Nov. 6, 1887; *Chicago Daily News,* Nov. 9, 1887.

55. *Chicago Herald,* Jan. 13, 1889; *Chicago Tribune,* Jan. 13, July 14, 1889; *Chicago Daily News,* July 2, 1889.

56. *Chicago Tribune,* May 15, 1892, quoted in Block, *Hyde Park Houses,* 28.

57. Another resident of Hyde Park expressed her grief over the changes wrought by annexation in her unfinished master's thesis at the University of Chicago. Laura Willard wrote, "The outlying village may have been quite independent in its beginnings; it may have epitomized within itself the political struggles, the mistakes and successes of a nation. But when swallowed by the hungry city, it has practically ceased to live. Like the human life which is said to have vanished, it has been absorbed by a larger whole." Laura Willard, "The History of Hyde Park: A Study in Local Government," unpublished manuscript, Chicago Historical Society, 1896.

58. Hoyt, *One Hundred Years,* 146.

59. *Chicago Tribune,* June 15, 1890.

60. *Chicago Tribune,* May 25, 1890.

61. Hoyt, *One Hundred Years,* 156–57, 173, 177; *Economist,* Sept. 17, 1892.

62. *Chicago Tribune,* May 8, 1892, quoted in Block, *Hyde Park Houses,* 47.

63. Block, *Hyde Park Houses,* 82–83.

64. U.S. Census, *Populations at the Twelfth Census,* 1900.

65. The university later rented rooms in many of these hotels to accommodate the growing number of students for whom sufficient dorm space was not yet available. Faculty members also rented rooms there until their homes were built. The university bought the land these buildings stood on after many of them were razed. See "A Review of Planning at the University of Chicago," *University of Chicago Record* 12, no. 4 (Apr. 28, 1973): 47–49.
66. *Chicago Tribune,* Aug. 18, 1879.
67. *Chicago Tribune,* Sept. 27, 1903; see also MBT-1, 12–12F; Block, *Hyde Park Houses,* 82.
68. *Chicago Record Herald,* Oct. 22, 1903.
69. *Chicago Tribune,* Oct. 30, 1892.
70. MBT-1, Sept. 29, 1891.
71. Rockefeller donated an additional $1 million in 1892, and Marshall Field pledged $100,000. Sidney A. Kent, a Chicago grain speculator and member of the Board of Trade, donated $250,000 to establish the Kent Chemical Laboratory. Elizabeth Kelly contributed $50,000 for a women's dormitory, as did Mary Beecher and Nancy S. Foster. Henrietta Snell gave $50,000 to build a men's dormitory. Silas B. Cobb, one of the earliest settlers of Chicago, pledged $150,000 for a recitation building, while Martin Ryerson gave the same amount for the Ryerson Physical Laboratory. In addition, George C. Walker provided $130,000 for a museum. MBT-1, 39–52, 60–68, 367–84; Goodspeed, *History,* 183–86.
72. Goodspeed to Harper, Sept. 7, 1890, CFA, box 1, folder 1; Goodspeed to Harper, Oct. 7, 1890, Harper Papers, box 9, folder 7; Minutes of the Committee on Buildings and Grounds, vol. 1, 1890–1916 (hereafter cited as MBG-1), Oct. 15, 1890, Apr. 25, 1891, Special Collections Research Center, University of Chicago Library; Goodspeed, *History,* 219.
73. MBG-1, May 19, 1891. The firms solicited by the Board of Trustees were Adler and Sullivan, Burling and Whitehouse, Flanders and Zimmerman, Solon S. Beman, Patton and Fischer, and Henry Ives Cobb.
74. Frank Hurburt O'Hara, *The University of Chicago: An Official Guide* (Chicago: University of Chicago Press, 1928), 17.
75. Hutchinson to Harper, Mar. 2, 1891, WRHP.
76. Harper, *Trend,* 23–24.
77. Goodspeed to Harper, Sept. 9, 1890, CFA, box 1, folder 11.
78. MBG-1, July 13, Sept. 29, 1891.
79. Once Cobb and the committee agreed on design and materials the university secured bids for the three buildings from nine local contractors. On November 23, 1891, committee

members chose the firm of Grace and Hyde, who offered the lowest bid. Ibid., Nov. 13, 18, 1891; July 9, 1892. See also Jean F. Block, *The Uses of Gothic: Planning and Building the University of Chicago, 1892–1932* (Chicago: University of Chicago Press, 1983), 15.

80. Block, *Uses of Gothic,*17.

81. MBG-1, Nov. 6, 1891. In *Uses of Gothic,* Block provides an extremely useful building-by-building discussion of the planning of the university, along with numerous illustrations and architectural descriptions.

82. MBG-1, Nov. 23, 26, 1891.

83. Block, *Uses of Gothic,* 25.

84. *President's Report* (1892–1902), 393.

85. Cobb to Harper, Jan. 7, 1895, WRHP, 7:8.

86. MBT-1, Dec. 27, 1895.

87. Thomas Chrowder Chamberlin to Harper, Nov. 26, 1896, Thomas Chrowder Chamberlin Papers, box 2, folder 2, Special Collections Research Center, University of Chicago Library.

88. Frank Lloyd Wright, "The Art and Craft of the Machine," in *Eighty Years at Hull House,* ed. Allen F. Davis and Mary Lynn McCree (Chicago: Quadrangle Books, 1969), 85–88, 86.

89. Montgomery Schuyler, "The Evolution of the Sky-Scraper," *Scribner's Magazine* 46 (Sept. 1909): 257–71. See also Daniel Bluestone, *Constructing Chicago,* chap 4. The classic text on the history of Chicago architecture is Carl W. Condit, *The Chicago School of Architecture: A History of Commercial and Public Building in the Chicago Area, 1875–1925* (Chicago: University of Chicago Press, 1964). For a discussion of Jenney, see 79–94.

90. Louis H. Sullivan, "Characteristics and Tendencies of American Architecture," in *Kindergarten Chats and Other Writings* (New York: George Wittenborn, 1947), 177–181, esp. 180.

91. Louis H. Sullivan, "The Tall Office Building Artistically Considered," in *Kindergarten Chats and Other Writings* (New York: George Wittenborn, Inc., 1947), 202–213, quotation on 208.

92. Ibid., 181.

93. For further discussion of architecture in Chicago see Bluestone, *Constructing Chicago;* H. Allen Brooks, *The Prairie School* (Toronto: University of Toronto Press, 1972); Condit, *Chicago School of Architecture;* John Drury, *Old Chicago Houses* (Chicago: University of Chicago Press, 1941); Carol Willis, *Form Follows Finance: Skyscrapers and Skylines in New York and Chicago* (New York: Princeton Architectural Press, 1995); and John Zukowsky, ed., *Chicago Architecture, 1872–1922: Birth of a Metropolis* (Munich: Prestel-Verlag, 1987).

94. Charles Richmond Henderson, *The Social Spirit in America* (Chicago: Scott, Foresman, 1902), 27. The phrase "domestic vernacular" comes from Wendy Kaplan, *Leading the Simple Life: The Arts and Crafts Movement in Britain, 1880–1910* (Miami Beach: Wolfsonian-Florida International University, 1999), 12. For further discussion of the Arts and Crafts movement see Wendy Kaplan and Elizabeth Cumming, *The Arts and Crafts Movement* (London: Thames and Hudson, 1991), and Peter Stansky, *Redesigning the World: William Morris, the 1880s, and the Arts and Crafts Movement* (Princeton: Princeton University Press, 1985).
95. See Claude Bragdon, *Architecture and Democracy* (New York: Alfred A. Knopf, 1918); Leonard Eaton, *Two Chicago Architects and Their Clients: Frank Lloyd Wright and Howard Van Doren Shaw* (Cambridge: MIT Press, 1969); Donald Hoffman, *Frank Lloyd Wright, Architecture and Nature* (New York; Dover, 1986); James F. O'Gorman, *Three American Architects: Richardson, Sullivan, and Wright, 1865–1915* (Chicago: University of Chicago Press, 1991); and Louis H. Sullivan, *The Autobiography of an Idea* (New York: Press of the American Institute of Architects, 1924).
96. See Block, *Hyde Park Houses*, 82–88, for detailed descriptions of the homes built near the university in South Park in the 1890s.
97. See Paul Venable Turner, *Campus: The American Planning Tradition* (Cambridge: MIT Press, 1984), 34, 80.
98. Charles E. Jenkins, "The University of Chicago," *Architectural Record* 4 (Oct.–Dec., 1894), 229–46, 240.
99. Ernest D. Burton to President Harry Pratt Judson, Sept. 27, 1910, Correspondence of the Board of Trustees, box 5, folder 3, Special Collections Research Center, University of Chicago Library.
100. The Gothic symbolized the implicit linkages the university constructed between Gothic design and Anglo-Saxon heritage. As T. J. Jackson Lears put it, the celebration of Gothic in America at the turn of the century reflected the growing discomfort of urban elites with the transitions taking place in American culture, especially the influx of immigrants whose traditions, religious beliefs, and languages seemed to challenge the social, political, and cultural foundations of Victorian society in America. The use of Gothic was one way to reimpose the Anglo-Saxon tradition onto a space like the South Side of Chicago that increasingly was defined by the new immigrants seeking work in the surrounding steel mills, stockyards, and foundries. T. J. Jackson Lears, *No Place of Grace: Antimodernism and the Transformation of American Culture, 1880–1920* (New York: Pantheon Books, 1981).
101. Letter to Chicago Pastors concerning the University of Chicago, June 1888, RFA, RG 2, Educational Interests, box 102, unprocessed materials.

102. Hutchinson to Gates, Aug. 27, 1892, RFA, RG 2, Educational Interests, box 103, unprocessed materials. This property was at LaSalle and Jackson Streets and was purchased for $265,000. The university later would buy the rest of the block, along with property on Indiana Avenue, for $290,000. Mrs. Gallup donated $30,000 of the price to the university for a memorial to her late husband, Benjamin E. Gallup. The LaSalle block was the first piece of downtown property the university bought, and it would set an important precedent for later buying. Minutes of the Board of Trustees, vol. 2, 1896–1900 (hereafter cited as MBT-2), Apr. 17, 1900, 366, 372, 382, 385, Special Collections Research Center, University of Chicago Library.
103. JDR to Gates, Sept. 2, 1892, RFA, RG 2, Educational Interests, box 103, unprocessed materials.
104. See Harper to Gates, Mar. 21, 1893, and Harper to JDR, May 13, 1893, RFA, RG 2, Educational Interests, box 103, unprocessed materials
105. William H. Holden, Esq., to Board of Trustees, Dec. 5, 1892, General Education Board, series 1, subseries 4, box 657, and Felsenthal to Board of Trustees, Dec. 6, 1892, Correspondence of the Board of Trustees, 1890–1913, box 1, folder 1, Special Collections Research Center, University of Chicago Library.
106. Harper to Gates, Dec. 11, 1895, RFA, RG 2, Educational Interests, box 103, unprocessed materials.
107. Ibid.
108. See MBT-1 384; MBT-2, 221.
109. MBT-2, *Report of the Comptroller,* Mar. 31, 1899, 248.
110. Minutes of the Board of Trustees, vol. 9, 1915–16 (hereafter cited as MBT plus volume number and dates), May 11, 1916, Special Collections Research Center, University of Chicago Library. In 1917 Berwyn residents asked if they might use vacant university property for neighborhood gardens, and the board gave approval. MBT, vol. 10, 1917–18, Apr. 21, Apr. 25, 1917. By contrast, the downtown commercial properties generated $572,624 in rent, an annual rate of return of, on average, 6.45 percent.
111. Heckman to Board of Trustees, June 26, 1912, Board of Trustees, Correspondence of the Secretary, 1890–1913, Special Collections Research Center, University of Chicago Library. The university also bought commercial buildings to finance the institution. Some of the best income-producing properties included the Tacoma Building, the Security Building, the Lees Building, and the Great Lakes Building, all downtown. Between 1915 and 1922 these buildings underwent dramatic increases in rental value, with the rent from

the Tacoma rising 90.6 percent, from the Security 70.4 percent, from the Lees 57.5 percent, and from the Great Lakes 72.1 percent. Heckman to Board of Trustees, Apr. 11, 1922, MBT, vol. 14, 1922–24.

112. Heckman to Board of Trustees, July 16, 1918, MBT, vol. 10, 1917–18, 548–49.

113. MBT, vol. 14, 1922–24, Feb. 14, 1924, 110–16.

114. Chicago Commission on Race Relations (hereafter cited as CCRR), *The Negro in Chicago* (Chicago: University of Chicago Press, 1922), 79–80; James R. Grossman, *Land of Hope: Chicago, Black Southerners, and the Great Migration* (Chicago: University of Chicago Press, 1989), 3–4; Allan H. Spear, *Black Chicago: The Making of a Negro Ghetto* (Chicago: University of Chicago Press, 1967), 11–12; and William M. Tuttle Jr., *Race Riot: Chicago in the Red Summer of 1919* (New York: Atheneum, 1970), 74–76.

115. St. Clair Drake and Horace R. Cayton, *Black Metropolis: A Study of Negro Life in a Northern City,* 2 vols. (New York: Harcourt, Brace, 1945), 1:178–211; Otis D. Duncan and Beverly Duncan, *The Negro Population of Chicago* (Chicago: University of Chicago Press, 1957), 89; Spear, *Black Chicago,* 20–21.

116. MBT-1 Feb. 20, 1894; MBT, vol. 5, 1906–8, Oct. 16, 1906; MBT, vol. 7, 1911–12, Aug. 8, 1911; MBT, vol. 9, 1915–16, June 13, 1916.

117. MBT, vol. 11, 1919–20, Aug. 12, 1919.

118. *Broad Ax,* Aug. 28, 1909.

119. *Chicago Tribune,* Jan. 10, 1920.

120. *Chicago Tribune,* May 21, 1921. Also quoted in St. Clair Drake and Horace R. Cayton, *Black Metropolis: A Study of Negro Life in a Northern City* (1945; Chicago: University of Chicago Press, 1993), 179. See also Grossman, *Land of Hope,* 174.

121. *Chicago Defender,* May 7, 1927. See also Drake and Cayton, *Black Metropolis,* 184.

122. *Chicago Defender,* Sept. 25, 1937.

123. *Chicago Record Herald,* Oct. 22, 1903.

124. MBT, vol. 14, 1922–24. Feb. 14, 1924, 39–44.

125. By the 1940s the connection between the university's need for more land and its fears of declining real estate values because of the growth of the Black Belt became further intertwined. A graduate of Chicago wrote to John D. Rockefeller Jr. suggesting that the university help support the Masonic lodges in Hyde Park and Woodlawn so that they could remain there and help maintain the "white island" around the university. He wrote, "Masons do not admit Negroes to membership, and as long as these organizations remain in Woodlawn they will fight to keep colored out. . . . The day the colored cross Cottage

Grove Ave. that day the University's holdings will lose half their value this side of the Midway, and the University itself will be endangered." Clarence A. Bales to JDR Jr., Dec. 18, 1945, RFA, RG 2, Educational Interests, box 104.

126. Thomas Wakefield Goodspeed to Frederick T. Gates, Mar. 1889, quoted in Goodspeed, *History,* 165.

127. Harper to Gates, Aug. 5, 1890, RFA, RG 2, Educational Interests, box 101; and Goodspeed, *History,* 164–68.

128. The university eventually agreed to rent space to the YMCA but not make it an official part of the university.

129. See Storr, *Harper's University,* 184–85.

130. Charles R. Henderson, "The Religious Work of the University," *President's Report* (1892–1902), 371.

131. Harper, University of Chicago *Quarterly Calendar* 4, no. 3 (1891): 17

132. Ibid.

133. See Storr, *Harper's University,* 216–17, 219.

134. Gates to Harper, WRHP, May 2, 1892.

135. Rush would become part of the University of Chicago Medical Schools in 1916, along with Sprague Memorial Institute and the Memorial Institute of Infectious Disease. That year the university launched a campaign to endow the medical school, bringing in some of the largest donations it had received to date. "Subscriptions to University of Chicago Medical School, 1917. RFA, General Education Board, series 1, subseries 4, box 657, folder 7188.

136. Frederick T. Gates, *Chapters in My Life* (New York: Free Press, 1977), 265; also quoted in Chernow, *Titan,* 328–29.

137. Harper, *Decennial Report,* quoted in Goodspeed, *History,* 358.

138. See Harper to Gates, Aug. 5, 1890, RFA, RG 2, Educational Interests, box 101; Gates to Franklin Winslow Johnson, principal of Morgan Park Academy, Mar. 12, 1907, RFA, RG 2, Educational Interests, box 105; and Goodspeed, *History,* 357–60. Part of the reason for declining enrollment was that during the 1899–1900 school year, the academy changed its status from being coeducational to admitting boys only. I have not found any explanation in the records for this shift, though clearly it was part of a broader rethinking of coeducation that would affect university policy a couple of years later.

139. Secondary schools could enter into either of two relationships with the university. They could become affiliated academies, which were functionally similar to a university de-

partment and governed jointly by the university and the local school board. Otherwise, they could be "connected schools," meaning they remained separate institutions, with the university responsible for conducting examinations, making teaching appointments, and publishing school announcements alongside those of the university. By 1891 the university was affiliated with nine academies. Other less formal options for secondary schools included entering into cooperative agreements whereby the university helped train the teachers, visited the schools to investigate their methods, and accepted students whose work had been certified by the teacher. In 1902 there were 129 cooperating institutions. See *Official Bulletin*, no. 3 (June 1891): 5–6; Harper, *President's Report* (1892–1902), lxvi–lxvii; Albion W. Small, "The Department of Affiliations," *President's Report*, 1897–98, 195; and Storr, *Harper's University*, 212, 218–19.

140. *Chicago Tribune*, July 16, 1893.

141. MBT-1, June 29, 1897; Goodspeed, *History*, 326–27.

142. MBT-1, Jan. 12, 1897, 50; Harper to Gates, May 28, 1897, RFA, RG 2, Educational Interests, box 100; Gates to Harper, June 1, 1897, WRHP.

143. MBT-1, May 16, 1897, 96; Goodspeed, *History*, 281; and Storr, *Harper's University*, 134–35. Harper also sought to establish a professional school of technology and proposed a merger between the university and Armour Institute. As early as 1897, the Board of Trustees of Armour Institute wanted to affiliate with the University of Chicago, and Philip Armour pledged to provide the money necessary to bring about the affiliation. The project stalled for several years, though, and after Armour's death in 1901 his widow and son were less enthusiastic, as were Gates and Rockefeller. The proposed merger never gained the support of Mrs. Philip Armour or Rockefeller, and the plan was aborted. See Goodspeed to Gates, Apr. 15, 1897, RFA, RG 2, Educational Interests, box 103, and Storr, *Harper's University*, 286.

144. Kathleen D. McCarthy, *Noblesse Oblige: Charity and Cultural Philanthropy in Chicago, 1849–1929* (Chicago: University of Chicago Press, 1982), 114–16; Goodspeed, *History*, 327–28; and Storr, *Harper's University*, 300–302. Blaine also contributed to teacher education at the university in 1898 by providing $5,000 a year for five years to the University of Chicago College for Teachers, incorporated in 1900 as the University College. This school, in downtown Chicago, allowed public school teachers in Chicago to take university courses taught by regular university faculty. It grew to include classes for railway employees, training courses for social work, and lectures for Sunday school teachers. The college was so successful that if became self-supporting after the Blaine subscription ended. See Goodspeed, *History*, 324–25; Harper, *President's Report*, 1892–1902, lxvi; Edmund J. James,

"University of Chicago College for Teachers," *University Record* 3, no. 31 (Oct. 28, 1898): 189; and Storr, *Harper's University,* 200–201.

145. The establishment of the School of Education was complete after the university secured the Scammon block in order to build new facilities. Mrs. Jonathan Young Scammon, widow of a prominent Chicago banker, deeded three acres of the Scammon homestead, which fronted south on the Midway Plaisance between Kimbark and Kenwood, two blocks from the main campus. The university soon secured the entire Scammon block and broke ground for the new School of Education in the autumn of 1901, with the dedication taking place on May 1, 1904. The building was named Emmons Blaine Hall in memory of the donor's husband. See Jean F. Block, *The Uses of Gothic: Planning and Building the Campus of the University of Chicago, 1892–1932* (Chicago: University of Chicago Press, 1983), 80–85; Goodspeed, *History,* 352–54; and James Gamble Rogers, "The Architecture of the School of Education Building," *University Record* 8, no. 7 (Nov. 1903): 183–86.

146. For more on John Dewey's life see Alan Ryan, *John Dewey and the High Tide of American Liberalism* (New York: W. W. Norton, 1995), and Robert Westbrook, *John Dewey and American Democracy* (Ithaca: Cornell University Press, 1991).

147. *Annual Register,* 1894–95, 49.

148. For further discussion of the founding of the University of Chicago Laboratory School, see Lawrence Cremin, *The Transformation of the School: Progressivism and American Education, 1876–1957* (New York: Alfred A. Knopf, 1961), 135–42; Steven J. Diner, *A City and Its Universities: Public Policy in Chicago, 1892–1919* (Chapel Hill: University of North Carolina Press, 1980), 77–80; George Dykhuizen, *The Life and Mind of John Dewey* (Carbondale: Southern Illinois University Press, 1973), 74–81; Andrew Feffer, *The Chicago Pragmatists and American Progressivism* (Ithaca: Cornell University Press, 1993), 117–23; Goodspeed, *History,* 326–30; and Storr, *Harper's University,* 296–302.

149. John Dewey, "Christianity and Democracy: An Address to the University of Michigan Christian Association" (Mar. 27, 1892), in John Dewey, *The Early Works, 1882–1898,* ed. Jo Ann Boydston et al., 5 vols. (Carbondale: Southern Illinois University Press, 1967–72), 4:7. For further discussion of the links between religion and pragmatic philosophy at Chicago, see Feffer, *Chicago Pragmatists,* 76–78; James T. Kloppenberg, *Uncertain Victory: Social Democracy and Progressivism in European and American Thought, 1870–1920* (New York: Oxford University Press, 1986), 43–46; Bruce Kuklick, *The Rise of American Philosophy: Cambridge, Massachusetts, 1860–1930* (New Haven: Yale University Press, 1977), 230–53; George M. Marsden, *The Soul of the American University: From Protestant Establishment to Established Nonbelief* (New York: Oxford University Press, 1994), 175; Stephen C. Rockefeller, *John Dewey: Religious Faith and Democratic Humanism* (New York: Columbia University Press,

1991), esp. 129–30; and Darnell Tucker, *The Chicago Pragmatists* (Minneapolis: University of Minnesota Press, 1969), 10–26.

150. While Peirce, James, and Dewey all articulated a version of radical empiricism and emphasized the experimental qualities of knowledge, Peirce differed from the others in maintaining a belief in the possibility of absolute truth, which could be found through unending inquiry and investigation. James challenged this idea, arguing instead for the individual's lived experience as the basis of contingent and ever-changing knowledge. Dewey took James's belief in the primacy of lived experience as the basis for knowledge, but instead of placing primary emphasis on the personal construction of truth, Dewey tied truth and lived experience directly to social engagement, positing community interaction as the basis of knowledge and truth. See David A. Hollinger, "William James and the Culture of Inquiry," and idem, "The Problem of Pragmatism in American History," in *In the American Province: Studies in the History and Historiography of Ideas,* ed David A. Hollinger (Baltimore: Johns Hopkins University Press, 1985), 3–22 and 23–43; Kloppenberg, *Uncertain Victory,* 95–99; Kuklick, *Rise of American Philosophy,* 269n; and H. S Thayer, *Meaning and Action: A Critical History of Pragmatism* (Indianapolis: Bobbs-Merrill, 1968), 442. Kloppenberg argues that the difference between James's pragmatism and Dewey's instrumentalism is one of emphasis, since both regarded social interaction as a central element of lived experience and knowledge.

151. Dewey, *Democracy and Education,* 10.

152. Ibid., 99.

153. John Dewey, *Experience and Education* (New York: Collier Books, 1938), 82–86. See also Cremin, *Transformation,* chaps. 2–4; Feffer, *Chicago Pragmatists,* 118–23; and Kloppenberg, *Uncertain Victory,* 375. Not everyone supported progressive education. One parent of a student attending the University Elementary School complained, "One year at the University Preparatory Laboratory, otherwise known as the D—— School (supply the proper word, not on Sunday, please!) nearly ruined [our son]. We have to teach him how to study. He learned to 'observe' last year." Quoted in Storr, *Harper's University,* 298.

154. See Sullivan, *Autobiography of an Idea,* and Frank Lloyd Wright, "The Art and Craft of the Machine" (1900), in *Frank Lloyd Wright, Collected Writings,* vol. 1, ed. Bruce Brooks Pfeiffer (New York: Rizzoli, 1994), 58. See also Casey Nelson Blake, *Beloved Community: The Cultural Criticism of Randolph Bourne, Van Wyck Brooks, Waldo Frank, and Lewis Mumford* (Chapel Hill: University of North Carolina Press, 1990); and Condit, *Chicago School of Architecture,* 1–13.

155. Jane Addams, *Twenty Years at Hull-House* (1910; New York: Signet Books, 1960), 172. See also Ellen Christensen, "A Vision of Urban Social Reform: Wright, Perkins, Jones, and

the Abraham Lincoln Center," *Chicago History* 22 (Mar. 1993): 50–61; Feffer, *Chicago Pragmatists,* 138; and Rivka Shpak Lissak, *Pluralism and Progressives: Hull House and the New Immigrants, 1890–1919* (Chicago: University of Chicago Press, 1989), chap. 2. For additional contemporary discussions, see Ellen Gates Starr, "Art and Labor," in *Hull-House Maps and Papers,* ed. Jane Addams (New York: Crowell, 1895), 165, and Thorstein Veblen, *The Vested Interests and the State of Industrial Arts* (New York: B. W. Huebsch, 1919).

156. Storr, *Harper's University,* 301.

157. Harper to Gates, June 24, 1895, RFA, RG 2, Educational Interests, box 100.

158. William Rainey Harper, *The Report of the Chicago Educational Commission* (Chicago, 1899).

159. For further discussion of the Harper Report and school reform in Chicago, see Cremin, *Transformation,* 3–176; Feffer, *Chicago,* 181–86; Marjorie Murphy, *Blackboard Unions: The AFT and the NEA* (Ithaca: Cornell University Press, 1990), 26–29; John Christian Pennoyer, "The Harper Report of 1899: Administrative Progress and the Chicago Public Schools" (Ph.D. diss., University of Denver, 1978); and Julia Wrigley, *Class Politics and Public Schools: Chicago, 1900–1950* (New Brunswick: Rutgers University Press, 1982), 83–104.

160. See Margaret Haley, *Battleground: The Autobiography of Margaret Haley,* ed. Robert Reid (Urbana: University of Illinois Press, 1982), 35–36; Feffer, *Chicago Pragmatists,* 183–84; Murphy, *Blackboard Unions,* 26–29; and Wrigley, *Class Politics,* 92–94.

161. Margaret Haley, quoted in Feffer, *Chicago Pragmatists,* 185–86.

162. Feffer, *Chicago Pragmatists,* 185.

163. These differences, in part, led to his departure from Chicago in 1904. For further discussion of Dewey's resignation from Chicago, see Dykhuizen, *Life and Mind of John Dewey,* 107–15; Feffer, *Chicago Pragmatists,* 194–95; and Robert B. Westbrook, *John Dewey and American Democracy* (Ithaca: Cornell University Press, 1991), 112–13.

164. For further discussion of Gothic design and Chicago's elite, see Richard P. Doper, *Campus Design* (New York: John Wiley, 1992), 75.

CHAPTER TWO

1. "The Projected Women's Building for the University," Feb. 11, 1913, Archival Buildings Files, Ida Noyes Hall 1, Special Collections Research Center, University of Chicago Library.

2. "'The Gift': A Masque on the Occasion of the Dedication of Ida Noyes Hall," written by Lucine Finch, June 1916. Archival Buildings Files, Ida Noyes Hall 1, Special Collections Research Center, University of Chicago Library.

3. Richard J. Storr, *Harper's University: The Beginnings* (Chicago: University of Chicago Press, 1966), 109.
4. Margaret W. Rossiter, *Women Scientists in America: Struggles and Strategies to 1940* (Baltimore: Johns Hopkins University Press, 1982), 35. See also Walter Crosby Ealls, "Earned Doctorates for Women in the Nineteenth Century," *Bulletin of the American Association of University Professors* 42 (1956): 646, 648; Barbara Miller Solomon, *In the Company of Educated Women: A History of Women and Higher Education in America* (New Haven: Yale University Press, 1985), 57, and Rosalind Rosenberg, "The Limits of Access: the History of Coeducation in America," in *Women and Higher Education in American History*, ed. John Mack Faragher and Florence Howe (New York: W. W. Norton, 1988), 115.
5. Harper, *Convocation Address*, December 1901, quoted in Thomas Wakefield Goodspeed, *A History of the University of Chicago: The First Quarter-Century* (Chicago: University of Chicago Press, 1916), 406.
6. Albion Small to William Rainey Harper, Mar. 13, 1902, Rockefeller Family Archives, Pocantico Hills, New York, Record Group 2 (hereafter cited as RFA, RG 2), Educational Interests, box 103, unprocessed materials. For additional arguments in favor of sex segregation, see Harry Pratt Judson to the University Recorder, June 30, 1902, University Presidents' Papers, 1889–1925 (hereafter cited as UPP), box 60, folder 11, Special Collections Research Center, University of Chicago Library; and "Segregation of the Sexes at the University of Chicago," UPP, box 60, folder 11.
7. For further discussion of women's higher education, see Lynn D. Gordon, *Gender and Higher Education in the Progressive Era* (New Haven: Yale University Press, 1990); John Mack Faragher and Florence Howe, eds., *Women and Higher Education in American History* (New York: W. W. Norton, 1988); Mabel Newcomer, *A Century of Higher Education for American Women* (New York: Harper, 1959); Rosalind Rosenberg, *Beyond Separate Spheres: Intellectual Roots of Modern Feminism* (New Haven: Yale University Press, 1982); Solomon, *In the Company of Educated Women;* and Thomas Woody, *A History of Women's Education in the United States*, 2 vols. (New York: Octagon Books, 1966). For discussion of gender, space, and the body, see Rosa Ainley, ed., *New Frontiers of Space, Bodies, and Gender* (New York: Routledge, 1998); Nancy Duncan, ed., *BodySpace: Destabalizing Geographies of Gender and Sexuality* (New York: Routledge, 1996); Doreen Massey, *Space, Place, and Gender* (Minneapolis: University of Minnesota Press 1994); and Daphne Spain, *Gendered Spaces* (Chapel Hill: University of North Carolina Press, 1992).
8. Several scholars of women's history have stressed the important role that university training played in expanding women's opportunities for public engagement and municipal reform. See especially Ellen Fitzpatrick, *Endless Crusade: Women Social Scientists and Progressive*

Reform (New York: Oxford University Press, 1990); Maureen A. Flanagan, *Seeing with Their Hearts: Chicago Women and the Vision of the Good City, 1871–1933* (Princeton: Princeton University Press, 2002); Joanne L. Goodwin, *Gender and the Politics of Welfare Reform: Mother's Pensions in Chicago, 1911–1929* (Chicago: University of Chicago Press, 1997); Robyn Muncy, *Creating a Female Dominion in American Reform, 1890–1995* (New York: Oxford University Press, 1991); and Daphne Spain, *How Women Saved the City* (Minneapolis: University of Minnesota Press, 2001).

9. The percentage of college-age men attending college continued to double in nearly every subsequent decade. In 1920, 8 percent attended college, in 1940, 16 percent, and by 1970 the number climbed to 48 percent. See Helen Lefkowitz Horowitz, *Campus Life: Undergraduate Cultures from the End of the Eighteenth Century to the Present* (Chicago: University of Chicago Press, 1987), 5. See also Colin B. Burke, *American Collegiate Populations: A Test of the Traditional View* (New York: New York University Press, 1982), 90–136; Seymour E. Harris, *A Statistical Portrait of Higher Education: A Report for the Carnegie Commission on Higher Education* (New York: McGraw-Hill, 1972), 924; and United States Bureau of the Census, *Historical Statistics of the United States: Colonial Times to 1957* (Washington, D.C.: Government Printing Office, 1960), 210–11.

10. For further discussion of land-grant colleges, see J. B. Edmond, *The Magnificent Charter: The Origins and Role of the Morrill Land-Grant Colleges and Universities* (Hicksville, N.Y.: Exposition Press, 1978), 6–13, 27, and Laurence K. Veysey, *The Emergence of the American University* (Chicago: University of Chicago Press, 1965), 180–251.

11. For further discussion of the changing curriculum, see Burton J. Bledstein, *The Culture of Professionalism: The Middle Classes and the Development of Higher Education in America* (New York: W. W. Norton, 1976), chap. 1.

12. For further discussion of planning women's colleges, see Horowitz, *Campus Life,* chap. 1; Helen Lefkowitz Horowitz, *Alma Mater: Design and Experience in the Women's Colleges from Their Nineteenth-Century Beginnings to the 1930s* (New York: Alfred A. Knopf, 1984); and Paul Venable Turner, *Campus: The American Planning Tradition* (Cambridge: MIT Press, 1984), chap. 2.

13. See Newcomer, *Century,* 35–51; Solomon, *In the Company of Educated Women,* 43–61; and Woody, *History of Women's Education,* 2:137–303.

14. Storr, *Harper's University,* 109.

15. The University of Chicago Annual Register (1892–93), 96–110. Hereafter cited as *Annual Register.*

16. *University of Chicago Maroon,* June 12, 1903, 1.

17. See United States Census, 1890, *Population,* part 1, 708, 714, 720, 726, 728. See also Michael F. Funchion, "Irish Chicago: Church, Homeland, Politics, and Class—the Shaping of an Ethnic Group, 1870–1900," in *Ethnic Chicago: A Multicultural Portrait,* ed. Melvin G. Holli and Peter d'A. Jones (Grand Rapids: William B. Eerdmans, 1995), 59.

18. Even though the university and residents of neighborhoods like Washington Park clashed over real estate and other issues, they served each others' interests in their efforts to keep blacks from moving into the neighborhoods. See John T. McGreevy, *Parish Boundaries* (Chicago: University of Chicago Press, 1996), 33–38.

19. James T. Farrell, *My Days of Anger* (New York: Vanguard Press, 1943), 193. See also "Family Recollections" and "Memoir Notes," 285, 290, James T. Farrell Papers, box 68, Research Notes, Department of Special Collections, Van Pelt-Dietrich Library Center, University of Pennsylvania. Most of these papers were burned in a house fire, though some charred pages remain.

20. In 1921 Monsignor Thomas Shannon commissioned a new building across the street at Fifty-fourth Street and Kimbark Avenue, designed by Frank Lloyd Wright's associate Barry Byrne. Architectural historians called that church the "first modern Catholic church in the United States" because it expressed in built form many of the liturgical reforms being implemented at the time. The building has been described as a modern example of Spanish mission architecture and is listed on the National Register of Historic Places. See "St. Thomas the Apostle Catholic Church: God's People in Extraordinary Variety" (Chicago: St. Thomas the Apostle Catholic Church, n.d.), 2–3.

21. St. Thomas served Washington Park, Hyde Park, and surrounding Catholic communities, and it experienced rapid growth by the turn of the century. Indeed, although the numbers of Roman Catholics at the university remained small for decades, St. Thomas played an important role in ministering to their needs. Initially, most Catholic students maintained close ties to their home parishes. They also established a campus organization to address their interests and concerns. In 1902, students formed the Catholic Club of the University of Chicago. The club formally reorganized in 1904 as the "Brownson Club," named for noted author and Catholic convert Orestes Brownson. Club activities included discussions of liturgy, lectures, charity dances, and other socials. Yet despite early interest, the club soon folded—in large part, according to the club's official history, because of the difficulties of being a Catholic at the University of Chicago. According to one account, "The University's teachings seemed to have indirectly promoted a vigorous agnosticism. The accent placed on modernity and being at the forefront of research, made something so ancient as the Catholic Church seem out of place by com-

parison." *Calvert House: An Informal History* (Chicago: University of Chicago Catholic Campus Ministry, 1982), 1. See also Elbert C. Cole, "A Critical Analysis and Evaluation of the Religious Ministry to Students at the University of Chicago" (Ph.D. diss., University of Chicago, 1942), 38–41.

22. George T. Mundelein, Archbishop of Chicago, to P. J. Mode, Department of Church History, University of Chicago, Sept. 16, 1916, Madaj Collection, Archives of the Archdiocese of Chicago.

23. Archbishop George Mundelein, "Discourse to Priests in Retreat," 1919, Madaj Collection, Archives of the Archdiocese of Chicago.

24. In addition, Mundelein believed that the university represented the interests of industrial elites in the city, not the ethnic working class that constituted much of Catholic Church membership. One local industrialist appealed to Mundelein in 1919 during the nationwide steel strike, asking him to "use his influence with the workers" to quell labor tension. Mundelein responded by asking, "Will you kindly tell me what your company has ever done for the Catholic Church that we should act as the policemen for you now?" Chicago industrialists, explained Mundelein, had given large sums of money to the Young Men's Christian Association and the University of Chicago, which housed a local chapter. For Mundelein, these contributions suggested that industrialists cared little for the plight of workers and even less for the conditions faced by immigrant Catholics. By contrast, Mundelein stated, "We are with the laboring man, with the worker, with the striker." Ibid.

25. Jewish support would grow over the next decades as Sears president Julius Rosenwald, an active Chicago philanthropist, gave extensive aid to the university and its programs. See Goodspeed, *History,* 87; Storr, *Harper's University,* 40, 234; and Irving Cutler, "The Jews of Chicago," in *Ethnic Chicago: A Multicultural Portrait,* ed. Melvin G. Holli and Peter d'A. Jones (Grand Rapids: William B. Eerdmans, 1995), 128–29, 142–43.

26. Cutler, "Jews," 127–28.

27. For further discussion of ethnicity and university admissions policies, see Horowitz, *Campus Life,* 76; Stephen Steinberg, *The Ethnic Myth: Race, Ethnicity, and Class in America* (New York: Atheneum, 1981); Martha Graham Synnott, *The Half-Opened Door: Discrimination and Admissions at Harvard, Yale, and Princeton,* 1900–1970 (Westport, Conn.: Greenwood Press, 1979), 16; and Veysey, *Emergence,* chap. 7.

28. Vincent Sheean, *Personal History* (Garden City, N.Y.: Doubleday, Doran, 1934), 12–13.

29. Hillel, the national Jewish student organization, established a chapter at the University of Chicago in 1941. Chicago's Hillel was an outgrowth of an informal Jewish organiza-

tion established by Rabbi George Fox in the previous decade. See Cole, "Critical Analysis," 33–37.

30. William Rainey Harper to Frederick T. Gates, July 22, 1899, quoted in Storr, *Harper's University,* 110.

31. Robert Herrick, "The University of Chicago," *Scribner's Magazine* 18, no. 4 (October 1895): 403. Though both Harper and Herrick celebrated the university's role in offering higher education to the working class, a dean's survey of the graduating class of 1902 suggested that most students were not working class but middle class. Forty percent of graduating seniors had parents who worked in business; 14 percent, in trades; 11 percent, in farming; 5 percent, unknown; and the rest, in the professions and government.

32. Harper, quoted in Goodspeed, *History,* 144.

33. Poor students also could take part in work-study programs in exchange for a waiver of part or all of their tuition. In 1897, for example, sixteen students in the student service choir received their tuition fees for performing at daily chapel services and the Sunday vesper service. Another group of students worked in the "Student Service," answering phones and attending to the university post office, messenger service, libraries, and laboratories. See "1897 Report of Budget and Expenses," RFA, RG 2, Educational Interests, box 101, unprocessed materials.

34. Frederick T. Gates to Harper, Dec. 29, 1905, William Rainey Harper Papers (hereafter cited as WRHP), box 9, folder 4, Special Collections Research Center, University of Chicago Library.

35. Harper, quoted in Goodspeed, *History,* 144–45.

36. Goodspeed, *History,* 248; Storr, *Harper's University,* 164–67. Many eastern colleges, including Harvard and Yale, adopted the house system in the 1920s in an effort to democratize student life by replacing the private halls and dining clubs that had previously characterized college residence patterns. For Harper, the house system had less to do with democratization than with the desire to foster collegiate spirit and fraternalism.

37. Harper, "The Antagonism of Fraternities to the Democratic Spirit of Scholarship," *University Magazine* 7 (Dec. 1892): 441.

38. Minutes of the Faculty of Arts, Literature, and Science, Oct. 14, 1892, quoted in Storr, *Harper's University,* 168.

39. Goodspeed, *History,* 254; Harper, University of Chicago *President's Report* (1892–1902), cxxxi–cxxxii (hereafter cited as *President's Report*); and Storr, *Harper's University,* 170–171.

40. One survey of Chicago students suggested that fraternity culture was antithetical to the goals of intellectual development, much as Harper had feared. The study revealed that

students spent more time on extracurricular activities, both formal and informal, than they did on their studies. *Report of the Faculty-Student Committee on the Distribution of Students' Time at the University of Chicago* (Chicago, 1925), cited in Paula Fass, *The Damned and the Beautiful: American Youth in the 1920s* (New York: Oxford University Press, 1977), 173.

41. By 1928 there were thirty-three fraternities but only twelve women's clubs. *Life on the Quads: A Centennial View of the Student Experience at the University of Chicago* (Chicago: University of Chicago Library, 1992), 34.

42. Marion Talbot, *More Than Lore: Reminiscences of Marion Talbot* (Chicago: University of Chicago Press, 1936), 6, 31.

43. Marion Talbot to Harper, Mar. 5, 1896, WRHP. See also Talbot to Harper, Nov. 19, 1894, Marion Talbot Papers (hereafter cited as MTP), box 18, "Women's Clubs" folder, Special Collections Research Center, University of Chicago Library. Alice Mary Baldwin, who received her Ph.D. from the University of Chicago at the turn of the century, became dean of the women's college at Duke. While there she commented on the conditions female students faced at coeducational institutions. "The interests of the women students, always in the minority, tend to be submerged in those of the men. . . . Perhaps the most serious loss is in the part played by the women themselves; in their sense of unity, of belonging to a college which is peculiarly their own and for which they are in large part responsible." Talbot sought to rectify this situation by establishing a cohesive body of students who could together make a place for women on campus. Baldwin is quoted in Linda K, Kerber, "'Why Should Girls be Learn'd and Wise?': Two Centuries of Higher Education for Women as Seen through the Unfinished Work of Alice Mary Baldwin," in Faragher and Howe, *Women and Higher Education,* 40.

44. See Dolores Hayden, *The Grand Domestic Revolution: A History of Feminist Designs for Homes, Neighborhoods, and Cities* (Cambridge: MIT Press, 1981), for further discussion of Richards.

45. See Virginia Kemp Fish, "'More Than Lore': Marion Talbot and Her Role in the Founding Years of the University of Chicago," *International Journal of Women's Studies* 8, no. 3 (1985): 231.

46. See Marion Talbot to Harper, Mar. 5, 1896, WRHP, for a discussion of her concerns regarding female sociability. See also Talbot to Harper, Nov. 19, 1894, MTP, box 18, "Women's Clubs" folder.

47. Marion Talbot to her parents, Sept. 25, 1892, MTP, box 1, folder 11. See also Horowitz, *Campus Life,* 111.

48. Quoted in Rosenberg, "Limits of Access," 116.

49. In the early years of the twentieth century, numerous institutions refashioned their policies on coeducation. The widow of Leland Stanford, founder of Stanford University, froze the admission of women at five hundred for fear of the university's becoming a "female seminary." Wesleyan abandoned coeducation altogether, and Boston University launched a "More Men Movement." On this backlash against coeducation, see Jill Ker Conway, *True North* (New York: Alfred A. Knopf, 1994), 238; W. Bruce Leslie, *Gentlemen and Scholars: College and Community Life in the "Age of the University,"* 1865–1917 (University Park: Pennsylvania State University Press, 1992), 206; Lynn D. Gordon, *Gender and Higher Education in the Progressive Era* (New Haven: Yale University Press, 1990); Rosenberg, "Limits of Access," 116; and Solomon, *Educated Women,* 60.
50. See Rossiter, *Women Scientists,* 13–22, and Solomon, *Educated Women,* 56–60. G. Stanley Hall, *Adolescence: Its Psychology and Its Relation to Physiology, Anthropology, Sociology, Sex, Crime, Religion, and Education* (New York: Appleton, 1904), chap. 2, quoted in Solomon, *Educated Women,* 60.
51. Albion W. Small to Harper, Mar. 13, 1902, RFA, RG 2, Educational Interests, box 103, unprocessed materials.
52. Harper, *Convocation Address,* December 1901, quoted in Goodspeed, *History,* 406.
53. Talbot to Mrs. John D. Rockefeller, June 24, 1902, UPP, box 60, folder 11.
54. John Dewey, quoted in Solomon, *Educated Women,* 59, and in Rosenberg, *Beyond Separate Spheres,* 46. See also "Memorial to President W. R. Harper and the Board of Trustees of the University of Chicago," in UPP, box 60, folder 11, for the list of faculty who opposed the policy. For further discussion of the sex segregation controversy at Chicago, see Goodspeed, *History,* 405–8; Gordon, *Gender and Higher Education,* chaps. 1–2; Harper, *President's Report* (1903); "Segregated Chicago," *Independent* 61 (October 1906); and Storr, *Harper's University,* 323–27.
55. Gates to Rockefeller, August 25, 1902, RFA, RG 2, Educational Interests, box 103, unprocessed materials.
56. JDR to Board of Trustees, Oct. 21, 1902, RFA, RG 2, Educational Interests, box 103, unprocessed materials. See also John D. Rockefeller Jr., "Memorandum on Dr. Harper's Plan for a Woman's Quadrangle at the University of Chicago, Mar. 5, 1902, RFA, RG 2, Educational Interests, box 103, unprocessed materials.
57. Harper, "Quarterly Statement," *University Record* 10 (Oct. 1905): 69; Goodspeed, *History,* 408; Storr, *Harper's University,* 326–27.
58. Harry Pratt Judson to the University Recorder, June 30, 1902, UPP, box 60, folder 11; and "Segregation of the Sexes at the University of Chicago," UPP, box 60, folder 11.

59. For further discussion of the rise of college athletic programs, see Robin Lester, *Stagg's University: The Rise, Decline, and Fall of Big-Time Football at Chicago* (Urbana: University of Illinois Press, 1995); Benjamin G. Rader, *American Sports: From the Age of Folk Games to the Age of Spectators* (Englewood Cliffs, N.J.: Prentice-Hall, 1983), 75–86; and Ronald A. Smith, *Sports and Freedom: The Rise of Big-Time Athletics* (New York: Oxford University Press, 1988), esp. chaps. 9 and 10.

60. William Rainey Harper, "Convocation Address, July 1, 1896," in *The Idea of the University of Chicago: Selections from the Papers of the First Eight Chief Executives of the University of Chicago from 1891 to 1975*, ed. William Michael Murphy and D. J. R. Bruckner (Chicago: University of Chicago Press, 1976), 211–12.

61. William Rainey Harper, "Convocation Address, July 1, 1896," in *Idea of the University*, 212.

62. Albion Small, *University of Chicago Record* 5, no. 4 (Apr. 27, 1900): 42.

63. See Clifford Putney, *Muscular Christianity: Manhood and Sports in Protestant America, 1880–1920* (Cambridge: Harvard University Press, 2001). See also Linda J. Borish, "The Robust Woman and the Muscular Christian: Catherine Beecher, Thomas Higginson, and Their Vision of American Society, Health, and Physical Activities," *International Journal of the History of Sport* 4, no. 2 (Sept. 1987): 139–54.

64. Stagg to his family, Jan. 20, 1891, quoted in Storr, *Harper's University*, 179.

65. For further discussion of the history of intercollegiate sport and the emergence of football as its centerpiece at the turn of the century, see Lester, *Stagg's University;* Patrick B. Miller, *The Playing Fields of American Culture: Athletics and Higher Education, 1850–1945* (New York: Oxford University Press, forthcoming); Michael Oriard, *Reading Football: How the Popular Press Created an American Spectacle* (Chapel Hill: University of North Carolina Press, 1993); Ronald A. Smith, *Sports and Freedom: The Rise of Big-Time College Athletics* (New York: Oxford University Press, 1988); Murray Sperber, *Shake Down the Thunder: The Creation of Notre Dame Football* (New York: Henry Holt, 1993).

66. Herrick, "University of Chicago," 416. See Horowitz, *Campus Life*, 119, for further discussion of athletics, male collegiate culture, and their role in corporate American life.

67. *New York Times*, Aug. 28, 1869, quoted in Melvin L. Adelman, *A Sporting Time: New York City and the Rise of Modern Athletics, 1820–1870* (Urbana: University of Illinois Press, 1990), 284.

68. T. J. Jackson Lears, *No Place of Grace: Antimodernism and the Transformation of American Culture, 1880–1920* (New York: Pantheon Books, 1981), 32, 108–9.

69. William I. Thomas, *Sex and Society: Studies in the Social Psychology of Sex* (Chicago: University of Chicago Press, 1907). For further discussion of gender, sexuality, and science, see Paul Atkinson, "The Feminist Physique: Physical Education and the Medicalization of

Women's Education," in *From "Fair Sex" to Feminism,* ed. J. A. Mangan and Roberta J. Park (London: Frank Cass, 1987), 38–57; Anita Clair Fellman and Michael Fellman, *Making Sense of Self: Medical Advice Literature in Late Nineteenth-Century America* (Philadelphia: University of Pennsylvania Press, 1981); Mabel Lee, *A History of Physical Education and Sports in the U.S.A.* (New York: John Wiley, 1983); Helen Lenskyj, *Out of Bounds: Women, Sport, and Sexuality* (Toronto: Women's Press, 1986), chaps. 1–2; Elizabeth Lunbeck, *The Psychiatric Persuasion: Knowledge, Gender, and Power in Modern America* (Princeton: Princeton University Press, 1994); Regina Markle Morantz-Sanchez, *Sympathy and Science: Women Physicians in American Medicine* (New York: Oxford University Press, 1985); and Martha H. Verbrugge, *Able-Bodied Womanhood: Personal Health and Social Change in Nineteenth-Century Boston* (New York: Oxford University Press, 1988).

70. Dudley A. Sargent, "Are Athletics Making Girls Masculine? A Practical Answer to a Question Every Girl Asks," *Ladies' Home Journal* 29 (Mar. 1912): 72. Women's prescriptive literature also called on women to exercise, since it would improve their health, make them better and stronger mothers, and lead to greater feelings of freedom and independence. See Catharine Beecher, *Educational Reminiscences and Suggestions* (New York: J. B. Ford, 1874), esp. chaps. 3 and 7; Catharine Beecher, *Physiology and Calisthenics for Schools and Families* (New York: Harper, 1856); and Frances E. Willard, *How I Learned to Ride the Bicycle* (Sunnyvale, Calif.: Fair Oaks, 1991); reprint of *A Wheel within a Wheel* (1895).

71. Catharine E. Beecher and Harriet Beecher Stowe, *The American Woman's Home, or Principles of Domestic Science; Being a Guide to the Formation and Maintenance of Economical, Healthful, Beautiful, and Christian Homes* (New York: J. B. Ford, 1869), 117.

72. For further discussion of female scientists and their role in promoting physical activity for women, see Lynn Gordon, *Gender and Higher Education in the Progressive Era* (New Haven: Yale University Press, 1990); Rosenberg, *Beyond Separate Spheres,* 54–83; Margaret W. Rossiter, *Women Scientists in America: Struggles and Strategies to 1940* (Baltimore: Johns Hopkins University Press, 1982), 51–72; and Solomon, *In the Company of Educated Women,* 103; and Verbrugge, *Able-Bodied Womanhood.* For further discussion of college women and athletics, see Susan K. Cahn, *Coming on Strong: Gender and Sexuality in Twentieth-Century Women's Sport* (New York: Free Press, 1994), esp. chaps. 1–3; George Eisen, "Sport, Recreation and Gender: Jewish Immigrant Women in Turn-of-the-Century America (1880–1920)," *Journal of Sport History* 18 (Spring 1991): 103–20; Allen Guttmann, *Women's Sports: A History* (New York: Columbia University Press, 1991); Horowitz, *Alma Mater;* Horowitz, *Campus Life;* Morantz-Sanchez, *Sympathy and Science;* Gregory Kent Stanley, *The Rise and Fall of the Sportswoman: Women's Health, Fitness, and Athletics, 1860–1940* (New York: Peter Lang, 1996);

Stephanie L. Twin, *Out of the Bleachers: Writing on Women and Sport* (Old Westbury, N.Y.: Feminist Press, 1979); Twin, "Women and Sport," in *Sport in America: New Historical Perspectives,* ed. Donald Spivey (Westport, Conn.: Greenwood Press, 1985), 193–217; and Patricia A. Vertinsky, *The Eternally Wounded Woman: Women, Doctors, and Exercise in the Late Nineteenth Century* (Manchester: Manchester University Press, 1990).

73. Edith Rickert, "What Has College Done for Girls: How Can the Woman's College Be Bettered?" *Ladies' Home Journal* 29 (Apr. 1912): 23.

74. Sargent, "Are Athletics Making Girls Masculine?" 11.

75. Ibid., 72.

76. "Division of Physical Culture and Athletics," typed history, 2, Amos Alonzo Stagg Papers (hereafter cited as AAS Papers), box 18, folder 10, Special Collections Research Center, University of Chicago Library.

77. "Statement concerning the Women's Division of the Department of Physical Education," 8; AAS Papers, box 18, folder 10.

78. Oct. 6, 1894, Minutes of the Board of Physical Culture and Athletics (hereafter cited as BPCA Minutes), box 1, folder 1, Special Collections Research Center, University of Chicago Library.

79. "Statement concerning the Women's Division of the Department of Physical Education," 8, 9; AAS Papers, box 18, folder 10.

80. June 1894, BPCA Minutes.

81. "The Women's Department, 1904–5 Physical Culture Report," 12–13; AAS Papers, box 18, folder 12.

82. Ibid., 9.

83. Historian Susan Cahn discusses the process by which women's rules were codified. Smith College athletic director Senda Berenson sought to draw up single set of rules of play for women's basketball, since in the 1880s and 1890s there were numerous variations, with rules set by each school's athletic directors. In 1899 Berenson organized the National Women's Basketball Committee under the auspices of the American Physical Education Association. Through the Spalding Sporting Goods Company, the committee issued the first women's rule book in 1901. The rules called for six players per side and three regions of the court. Players were designated as forwards, centers, or guards and were confined to their own sections of the court. No physical contact was allowed, and players could dribble only once. Female physical educators tried to thwart attempts by local businesspeople to sponsor competition among women's teams, seeing a threat to the amateur ideal and femininity of sport. See Cahn, *Coming on Strong,* 86–87. See also Senda Berenson, ed., *Line Basket Ball, or Basket Ball for Women* (New York: American Sports Publishing, 1901).

84. Jan. 8, 1909, letter from Stagg to Ortmayer, with her response; AAS Papers, box 12, folder 22.
85. See "Resolutions III and IV, Adopted by the Conference of Deans of Women," Correspondence of the Board of Trustees of the University of Chicago, 1890–1913, Nov. 3–4, 1903, box 3, folder 6, Special Collections Research Center, University of Chicago Library. For further discussion of this lack of support for women's intercollegiate competition, see Cahn, *Coming on Strong,* chap. 3.
86. See William Scott Bond, "Summer Baseball," *University of Chicago Magazine* 4, no. 2 (Jan. 1912): 70–71; Gerald R. Gems, *Windy City Wars: Labor, Leisure, and Sport in the Making of Chicago* (Lanham, Md.: Scarecrow Press, 1997), 101; Lester, *Stagg's University,* 72–91; Miller, *Playing Fields of American Culture;* and Michael Oriard, *Reading Football: How the Popular Press Created an American Spectacle* (Chapel Hill: University of North Carolina Press, 1993), 96.
87. John S. Watterson, "Chicago's City Championship: Northwestern University versus the University of Chicago, 1892–1905," *Chicago History* 11, no. 3 (Fall and Winter 1982): 163.
88. For further discussion of the popularity of athletics among college students, see Burton Bledstein, *The Culture of Professionalism: The Middle Class and the Development of Higher Education* (New York: W. W. Norton, 1976), 83–85; Lester, *Stagg's University,* especially chaps. 1–2; Storr, *Harper's University,* 178–81; *University of Chicago Maroon,* esp. Nov. 17, 1904; and Watterson, "City Championship." For a description of Stagg Field, see Jean Block, *The Uses of Gothic: Planning and Building the University of Chicago, 1892–1932* (Chicago: University of Chicago Press, 1983), 85, 87.
89. Oct. 8, 10, 17, 1892 entries, Diary of Demia Butler, Special Collections Research Center, University of Chicago Library. The women could attend the football game only if they went "in a body, accompanied by the Dean," and watched from the sidelines. See Marion Talbot, "Women's Houses at the University of Chicago: Their Origin and Meaning," 1933, typescript in MTP, box 4, folder 13.
90. Talbot quoted in the *Chicago Inter-Ocean,* Oct. 8, 1902.
91. For further discussion of these incidents, see Lester, *Stagg's University,* 36–37. Lester suggests that this cheer competition illustrated how "women were working out their peculiar role as major athletic advocates on the American campus" (36). For further discussion of women's roles as cheerleaders, see Mary Ellen Hanson, *Go! Fight! Win! Cheerleading in American Culture* (Bowling Green, Ohio: Bowling Green University Popular Press, 1995), esp. chap. 1.
92. Stagg to Dudley, May 9, 1913, AAS Papers, box 11, folder 8.
93. Stagg to Dr. Dudley B. Reed, May 9, 1913, AAS Papers, box 12, folder 9.
94. Dudley to Stagg, May 27, 1913, AAS Papers, box 11, folder 8.

95. Stagg to Reed, May 9, 1913, AAS Papers, box 12, folder 9. Dudley says she wants to help in any way possible and to show the loyalty of the female students to the athletic program, but only if their participation does not detract from their preparations for Woman's Day events. Dudley to Stagg, May 27, 1913, AAS Papers, box 11, folder 8.

96. A series of letters over several years shows that there was no clearly designated amount set aside for women's athletics. In a 1910 letter to Stagg, for example, Dudley states that in the past year the women have used only $98.13 from the athletics fund, and that amount was on requisition. She asks, "Do you not think we might arrange to have at least one quarter of [the athletic funds] for the use of the women?" Dudley to Stagg, Apr. 17, 1910, AAS Papers, box 11, folder 8. In 1905 Stagg had urged Harper to create a separate fund for women's athletics by using a one-time contribution of $500 from the General Athletic Fund along with an additional $500 that the Women's Athletic Association would raise. That money would be invested, with the income from it used to support women's athletics. See Stagg to Gertrude Dudley, Feb. 18, 1905. AAS Papers, box 11, folder 8. Apparently this plan was never implemented, since Dudley continually had to ask Stagg for funds to help pay the female coaches, whose salaries came from fund-raisers sponsored by the Women's Athletic Fund, the General Athletic Fund, and the General Appropriations Fund of the university. See Stagg to Trevor Arnett, vice president and business manager of the University of Chicago, Feb. 23, 1907, AAS Papers, box 8, folder 4.

97. "A Permanent Building for the Women of the University," *University of Chicago Magazine* 4 (May 1912): 207.

98. See also "Report of the Department of Physical Culture, Women's Department, 1892," AAS Papers, box 18, folder 10; Dudley to Stagg, May 29, 1905, AAS Papers, box 11, folder 8. Letters from Dudley to Stagg recount the lack of field space for women's outdoor sports, including hockey. In a 1905 letter Dudley writes, "Once again I have to trouble you about space." In another letter she questions why the athletic fund provides for the upkeep of Marshall Field, the main athletic field that hosted intercollegiate football games, but not for any spaces used by women, and asks that someone from Buildings and Grounds be assigned to the women's field. By June 1910, the superintendent of buildings and grounds agrees to turn over vacant ground (south of Greenwood Hall, between Sixtieth and Sixty-first Streets) for women's use but cannot guarantee upkeep. See M. H. MacLean, Superintendent of Buildings and Grounds, to Stagg, June 10, 1910, AAS Papers, box 11, folder 8.

99. Feb. 2, 1901, BPCA Minutes, vol. 1, 1893–1908.

100. President William Rainey Harper, Sept. 18, 1900, Convocation Address, quoted in Goodspeed, *History*, 348. The dedication is above the door of the gymnasium facing the front entrance. The building included a swimming pool, professors' exercise room, general gymnasium and running track, and lockers and showers. The total cost of the building was $238,000, the rest coming from a Rockefeller subscription of 1895. Goodspeed, *History*, 249.
101. See Linda Seidel and Katherine Taylor, *Looking to Learn: Visual Pedagogy at the University of Chicago* (Chicago: David and Alfred Smart Museum of Art, 1998), 43. For further discussion of the use of medieval imagery and Gothic design in countering the perceived feminization of American culture at the turn of the century, see Lears, *No Place of Grace*, 103, 116, 132.
102. Stagg to Harper, May 12, 1904, AAS Papers, box 9, folder 8; and "The Women's Department, 1904–05 Physical Culture Report," 12–13, AAS Papers, box 18, folder 12.
103. "A Permanent Building for the Women of the University," 204–7; quotation on 207.
104. Stagg to Dudley, July 17, 1913, AAS Papers, box 11, folder 8.
105. Letter enclosed with Stagg's letter to Dudley, ibid.
106. Goodspeed, *History*, 441–42.
107. Harry Pratt Judson, in Block, *Uses of Gothic*, 123.
108. Marion Talbot, Ida Noyes Hall Cornerstone Ceremony, Apr. 18, 1915, quoted in Goodspeed, *History*, 441.
109. For further discussion of alternative models of athletics and female sociability on college campuses, see Cahn, *Coming on Strong;* Horowitz, *Alma Mater;* Horowitz, *Campus Life*, 110–20; Leslie, *Gentlemen and Scholars*, 105–11; Ann Palmieri, *In Adamless Eden: The Community of Women Faculty at Wellesley* (New Haven: Yale University Press, 1995); and Solomon, *Educated Women*, 103.
110. Robert Herrick to Robert M. Lovett, Dec. 13, 1895, quoted in Storr, *Harper's University*, 336
111. John Dewey, "Academic Freedom," *Educational Review* 23, no. 1 (Jan. 1902): 9–13.
112. Storr, *Harper's University*, 336–37.
113. *University of Chicago Register*, 1892–93 (Chicago: University of Chicago Press, 1893), v.
114. Dewey, "Academic Freedom."
115. Rosenberg, *Beyond Separate Spheres*, 49.
116. Marion Talbot, *The Education of Women* (Chicago: University of Chicago Press, 1910), viii.
117. Marion Talbot, "The Women of the University," *President's Report* (1901–2), 122–45. For further discussion of the introduction of scientific method into the college curriculum and the rise of specialized courses in domestic science, see Mary O. Furner, *Advocacy and*

Objectivity: A Crisis in the Professionalization of American Social Science, 1865–1905 (Lexington: University of Kentucky Press, 1977), 1–34; Victoria Lyn Getis, "A Disciplined Society: The Juvenile Court, Reform, and the Social Sciences in Chicago, 1890–1930" (Ph.D. diss., University of Michigan, 1994); Thomas L. Haskell, *The Emergence of Professional Social Science: The American Social Science Association and the Nineteenth-Century Crisis of Authority* (Urbana: University of Illinois Press, 1977), 24–47; Rosenberg, *Separate Spheres*, 47–53; and Solomon, *Educated Women*, 80–85.

118. Talbot, *Education*, 244–46. See also Rossiter, *Women Scientists*, 109.

119. Edith Rickert, "What Has College Done for Girls: Has the College Really Helped Girls?" *Ladies' Home Journal* 29 (Feb. 1912): 9, 52.

120. Edith Rickert, "What Has College Done for Girls: Where the College Has Failed with Girls," *Ladies' Home Journal* 29 (Mar. 1912): 15.

121. Talbot, *Education*, viii. See also her discussion of "Hygienic Training," 205; Mina Carson, *Settlement Folk: Social Thought and the American Settlement Movement, 1885–1930* (Chicago: University of Chicago Press, 1990), 23; and Solomon, *Educated Women*, 56–57.

122. Talbot to Harper, n.d., 1902, WRHP; Talbot to Harper, Feb, 18, 1904, WRHP.

123. Mary N. Wilmarth to Talbot, July 1894, UPP, box 39, folder 7.

124. Marion Talbot, "Sanitary Science and Its Place in the University," *University Record* 1, no. 36 (Dec. 4, 1896): 1. See also Talbot, "Sanitation and Sociology," *American Journal of Sociology* 2 (July 1896): 74–81.

125. Talbot to Albion Small, Nov. 24, 1894, UPP, box 39, folder 7.

126. Harper to Talbot, Mar. 28, 1904, WRHP.

127. Marion Talbot, "First Draft of a Plan for a Department of Household Technology in the University of Chicago," Feb. 1902, UPP, box 39, folder 7.

128. "Women's Education: The Lack of Domestic Science in Women's Colleges," newspaper clipping, n.d., UPP, box 39, folder 7.

129. Rosenberg, *Beyond Separate Spheres*, 49. See also Furner, *Advocacy*, 33–34; Roger L. Geiger, *To Advance Knowledge: The Growth of American Research Universities, 1900–1940* (New York: Oxford University Press, 1986), 3–20; Haskell, *Emergence*, 24–47; and Henrika Kuklick, "Boundary Maintenance in American Sociology: Limits to Academic 'Professionalization,'" *Journal of the History of the Behavioral Sciences* 16 (July 1980): 201–19.

130. For further discussion of the Social Gospel, see Carson, *Settlement Folk*, 17; Crunden, *Ministers*, 88; Arthur A. Ekirch Jr., *Progressivism in America: A Study of the Era from Theodore Roosevelt to Woodrow Wilson* (New York: New Viewpoints, 1974), 54–58; Andrew Feffer, *The Chicago Pragmatists and American Progressivism* (Ithaca: Cornell University Press, 1993), 71;

Haskell, *Emergence,* 100; and James T. Kloppenberg, *Uncertain Victory: Social Democracy and Progressivism in European and American Thought, 1870–1920* (New York: Oxford University Press, 1986), 297.

131. See Mary McDowell, "Social Reformers: A Descriptive Definition," *Commons* 5 (Aug. 1900): 5–6; and Graham Taylor, "A Social Center for Civic Cooperation: Chicago Commons," *Commons* 9 (Dec. 1904): 585–94. For further discussion of women's roles in social reform during the Progressive Era, see Helen Lefkowitz Horowitz, "Hull-House as a Women's Space," *Chicago History* 12, no. 4 (1984): 40–50; Rosenberg, *Beyond Separate Spheres,* 51; Solomon, *Educated Women,* 113, 123–24; Barbara Sicherman, "College and Careers: Historical Perspectives on the Lives and Work Patterns of Women College Graduates," in Faragher and Howe, *Women and Higher Education,* 155; and Gwendolyn Wright, *Moralism and the Model Home: Domestic Architecture and Cultural Conflict in Chicago, 1873–1913* (Chicago: University of Chicago Press, 1985). See also Florence Kelley's discussion of the need for a scientific basis for philanthropy in "My Novitiate," an article addressed in part to women college graduates, in the *Notes of Sixty Years: The Autobiography of Florence Kelley,* ed. Kathryn Kish Sklar (Chicago: Charles Kerr for the Illinois Labor History Society, 1986), 9, 92.

132. Louise de Koven Bowen, quoted in Wright, *Moralism,* 109. See also Louise de Koven Bowen, *Growing Up with a City* (New York: Macmillan, 1926).

133. Harper lured a number of prominent scholars from their posts elsewhere, not only with the promise of together creating a model for the modern research university but also through high salaries. He offered salaries of $7,000 to senior scholars previously earning about $4,000, and $5,000 to younger scholars. Albion Small and History Department chair Edward Von Holst, for example, earned $7,000 at Chicago, while the younger Dewey earned $5,000. This generosity did not cut across gender lines, however, as professor of history and dean of women Alice Freeman Palmer earned only $3,000. For additional information on salaries, see MBT-1, Dec. 29, 1891; "Report of Budget and Expenses," 1897, RFA, RG 2, Educational Interests, box 101, unprocessed materials; Goodspeed, *History,* 206–14; Storr, *Harper's University,* 72–74, 82–83. For further discussion of female scholars' roles in social reform, see especially Marion Talbot's contributions in "The Women of the University," *President's Report,* 1892–1925; Steven J. Diner, *A City and Its Universities: Public Policy in Chicago, 1892–1919* (Chapel Hill: University of North Carolina Press, 1980), 52–75; and Rosenberg, *Beyond Separate Spheres,* 34.

134. Kloppenberg, *Uncertain Victory,* 3.

135. For further discussion of Dewey, pragmatism, and the formation of a democratic public sphere, see Feffer, *Chicago Pragmatists,* 88–90; Kloppenberg, "Democracy and Disen-

chantment: From Weber and Dewey to Habermas and Rorty," in *Modernist Impulses in the Human Sciences, 1870–1930,* ed. Dorothy Ross (Baltimore: Johns Hopkins University Press, 1994), 69–90; Kloppenberg, *Uncertain Victory,* 352; Alan Ryan, *John Dewey and the High Tide of American Liberalism* (New York: W. W. Norton, 1995); and especially Robert B. Westbrook, *John Dewey and American Democracy* (Ithaca: Cornell university Press, 1991). Both Kloppenberg and Westbrook stress Dewey's role as a leading theorist of participatory democracy, and Kloppenberg compares Dewey's ideas about democracy and collective experience with Jürgen Habermas's discussion of a participatory democratic public sphere (see Kloppenberg, "Democracy and Disenchantment," 86–88). While these ideas seem to be grounded in American conceptions of democracy, some historians also focus on the broader transcontinental scope of pragmatist theories of democracy. Kloppenberg stresses the importance of seeing pragmatism as part of a larger tradition in European thought, while Ryan highlights the links between American pragmatism and British social thought. For discussion of the shortcomings of pragmatic philosophy, see John Patrick Diggins, *The Promise of Pragmatism: Modernism and the Crisis of Knowledge and Authority* (Chicago: University of Chicago Press, 1994), and Feffer, *Chicago Pragmatists,* 265–67.

136. Of the many discussions of Chicago sociology, I found the most useful to be Robert C. Bannister, *Sociology and Scientism: The American Quest for Objectivity, 1880–1940* (Chapel Hill: University of North Carolina Press, 1987), 34–60; Martin Bulmer, *The Chicago School of Sociology* (Chicago: University of Chicago Press, 1984), 1–11, 34–36; and Dorothy Ross, *The Origins of American Social Science* (Cambridge: Cambridge University Press, 1991), chap. 1.

137. Albion W. Small, *The Meaning of Sociology* (Chicago: University of Sociology Press, 1910), 61.

138. See Rosenberg, *Beyond Separate Spheres,* 126.

139. Frank. L. Tolman, "Study of Sociology in Institutions of Learning in the United States," part 2, *American Journal of Sociology* 7 (July 1902): 116. See also Edward Shils, "The University, the City, and the World: Chicago and the University of Chicago," in *The University and the City: From Medieval Origins to the Present,* ed. Thomas Bender (New York: Oxford University Press, 1988), 210–30.

140. "Recent Community Studies at the University of Chicago," Laura Spelman Rockefeller Memorial Papers, RFA, series 3, box 70, folder 749; Lester R. Kurtz, *Evaluating Chicago Sociology: A Guide to the Literature, with an Annotated Bibliography* (Chicago: University of Chicago Press, 1984), 21; and Stow Persons, *Ethnic Studies at Chicago, 1905–45* (Urbana: University of Illinois Press, 1987), 54, 62.

141. The first settlement in America opened on the Lower East Side of New York City in 1885. It was funded by Stanton Coit, who modeled the settlement on Toynbee Hall in

East London. Soon similar institutions opened in other major cities, including Boston and Philadelphia, but Chicago became a leader in the settlement house movement. Jane Addams and Ellen Gates Starr, two graduates of Rockford Seminary in Illinois, started Hull House on Chicago's Near West Side (1889), the settlement that would play a major role in shaping reform activities throughout the city and eventually the nation. Other settlements quickly followed Hull House in Chicago, including the Northwestern University Settlement (1891), started by Chicago sociologist Charles Zueblin; Chicago Commons (1894), founded by Graham Taylor, a Dutch Reformed minister and professor at the Chicago Theological Seminary; and the University of Chicago Settlement (1894), headed by Mary McDowell, a former resident at Hull House.

142. For further discussion of the founding of the University of Chicago Settlement, see Goodspeed, *History,* 447–48; Charles R. Henderson, "The University Settlement," *President's Report* (1897–1898), 208–16; Eleanor Kroll, "The History of the University of Chicago Settlement," Mary McDowell Papers, Chicago Historical Society, Special Collections, box 1, folder 3a (hereafter cited as MMP); Mary McDowell, "Beginnings: Reminiscing on the Stock Yards Area," MMP, box 1, folder 1; McDowell, "The Activities of the University of Chicago Settlement," MMP, box 1, folder 36; Storr, *Harper's University,* 186–87; and Howard E. Wilson, *Mary McDowell, Neighbor* (Chicago: University of Chicago Press, 1928), 22–24.

143. *Annual Register* (1893–94), 302, and *University Record* 1 (1896–97): 6.

144. "University of Chicago Settlement Survey (1929)," MMP, box 2, folder 7.

145. *Annual Register* (1893–94), 302.

146. "Institute of Social Science and Art" (1903), Chicago School of Civics and Philanthropy Papers (hereafter cited as CSCPP), box 1, folder 7, Special Collections Research Center, University of Chicago Library; Chicago Commons Finding Aid, Chicago Commons Papers, Chicago Historical Society, Special Collections; and "Chicago School of Civics and Philanthropy," *Charities and Commons* 21 (Oct. 1908): 83–84. See also Carson, *Settlement Folk,* 130; Fitzpatrick, *Endless Crusade,* 196–200; Rivka Shpak Lissak, *Pluralism and Progressives: Hull House and the New Immigrants, 1890–1919* (Chicago: University of Chicago Press, 1989), 21; and Louise Carroll Wade, *Graham Taylor: Pioneer for Social Justice, 1851–1938* (Chicago: University of Chicago Press, 1964), 4.

147. *Chicago School of Civics and Philanthropy Bulletin* 1 (July 1914), CSCPP, box 1, folder 15.

148. Some of the publications produced by the school include *The Housing Problem in Chicago* (1910–15), *The Delinquent Child and the Home* (1912), and *The Charity Visitor: A Handbook for Beginners* (1913). The CSCP eventually merged with the Philanthropic Science Division of

the university's School of Commerce and Administration to form the School of Social Service Administration, the first graduate school of social work to be affiliated with a major research university. See MBT-2, Aug. 10, 1920, and Fitzpatrick, *Endless Crusade,* 196–200.

149. Jane Addams, *Twenty Years at Hull-House* (1910; New York: Signet Books, 1960), 217.

150. George Herbert Mead, "The Social Settlement: Its Basis and Function (1927)," MMP, box 1, folder 36.

151. For more on McDowell, see Karen M. Mason, "Testing the Boundaries: Women, Politics, and Gender Roles in Chicago, 1890–1930" (Ph.D. diss., University of Michigan, 1991).

152. McDowell, quoted in Wilson, *McDowell,* 45.

153. McDowell, "Beginnings."

154. For further discussion of Mary McDowell's role in the neighborhood, and the Back of the Yards as a "laboratory" for social scientists, see James R. Barrett, *Work and Community in the Jungle: Chicago's Packinghouse Workers, 1894–1922* (Urbana: University of Illinois Press, 1987), 66–67, 85–86.

155. See Thomas J. Jablonsky, *Pride in The Jungle: Community and Everyday Life in Back of the Yards Chicago* (Baltimore: Johns Hopkins University Press, 1993), 1–4, and Louise Carroll Wade, *Chicago's Pride: The Stockyards, Packingtown, and Environs in the Nineteenth Century* (Urbana: University of Illinois Press, 1987), 11–15, 25–33, 47–57.

156. Wilson, *McDowell,* 27.

157. McDowell, "Beginnings," 3.

158. *Chicago Tribune,* Oct. 27, 1909.

159. Jablonsky, *Pride,* 29–39; Ernest Burgess and Charles Newcomb, *Census Data of the City of Chicago, 1920* (Chicago: University of Chicago Press, 1931), 451–52; Wade, *Chicago's Pride,* 158–59; and Edward R. Kantowitcz, "Polish Chicago: Survival through Solidarity," in Holli and Jones, *Ethnic Chicago,* 173–98.

160. Jablonsky, *Pride,* 30; Kroll, "History," 2; and "University of Chicago Settlement," 2.

161. Jablonsky, *Pride,* 41, 45; Kroll, "History," 2; "Prohibition Survey of the Stock Yards Community," 4, MMP, box 2, folder 7; Robert A. Slayton, *Back of the Yards: The Making of a Local Democracy* (Chicago: University of Chicago Press, 1986), 175–77; and Wilson, *McDowell,* 26.

162. "University of Chicago Settlement," 2–3.

163. Slayton, *Back of the Yards,* 175–77. While Slayton is correct in pointing to the hostility generated by the settlement presence in the neighborhood, he ignores the coalitions formed

as a result of its existence. The settlement was about more than addressing direct needs of local residents and imposing social control. It helped forge cross-class alliances that played central roles in bringing state attention to living and working conditions in the Yards. See below for further discussion of these coalitions.

164. Dwight H. Perkins and Howell Taylor, "The Functions and Plan-Types of Community Buildings," *Architectural Record* 56 (1924): 289–90.

165. See *Commons* 43 (Feb. 1900), cover. See also Guy Szuberla, "Three Chicago Settlements: Their Architectural Form and Social Meaning," *Journal of the Illinois State Historical Society* 70 (May 1077): 114–29.

166. Szuberla, "Three Chicago Settlements."

167. University of Chicago Settlement Women's Club Minutes, 1896–1922, box 4, Chicago Historical Society.

168. Ibid.

169. See Carolyn Hill, ed., *Mary McDowell and Municipal Housekeeping: A Symposium* (Chicago: University of Chicago Settlement, 1938).

170. For further discussion of the Pullman strike, see Stanley Buder, *Pullman: An Experiment in Industrial Order and Community Planning, 1880–1930* (New York: Oxford University Press, 1967); James Gilbert, *Perfect Cities: Chicago's Utopias of 1893* (Chicago: University of Chicago Press, 1991); Almont Lindsey, *The Pullman Strike: The Story of a Unique Experiment and of a Great Labor Upheaval* (Chicago: University of Chicago Press, 1942); and Carl Smith, *Urban Disorder and the Shape of Belief: The Great Chicago Fire, the Haymarket Bomb, and the Model Town of Pullman* (Chicago: University of Chicago Press, 1995).

171. The Civic Federation of Chicago, *First Annual Report of the Central Council, May 1895* (Chicago: R. R. Donnelly, 1895), 7. See also William T. Stead, *If Christ Came to Chicago! A Plea for the Union of All Who Love in the Service of All Who Suffer* (Chicago: Laird and Lee, 1894). For further discussion of the Civic Federation, see Diner, *City and Its Universities;* Maureen A. Flanagan, *Charter Reform in Chicago* (Carbondale: Southern Illinois University Press, 1987); Donald D. Marks, "Polishing the Gem of the Prairie: The Evolution of Civic Reform Consciousness in Chicago, 1874–1900" (Ph.D. diss., University of Wisconsin, 1974); David Montgomery, *Workers' Control in America: Studies in the History of Work, Technology, and Labor Struggles* (Cambridge: Cambridge University Press, 1979); Douglas Sutherland, *Fifty Years on the Civic Front* (Chicago: Chicago Civic Federation, 1943); and James Weinstein, *The Corporate Ideal in the Liberal State, 1900–1918* (Boston: Beacon Press, 1968).

172. For further discussion of the National Civic Federation, and disillusionment with its conservatism, see Foster Rhea Dulles and Melvyn Dubofsky, *Labor in America: A History*

(Arlington Heights, Ill.: Harlan Davidson, 1984), 177–78, 182; Feffer, *Chicago Pragmatists,* 98; Flanagan, *Charter Reform,* 34–36; James R. Green, *The World of the Worker: Labor in Twentieth-Century America* (New York: Hill and Wang, 1980), 53–55; and Marguerite Green, *The National Civic Federation and the American Labor Movement* (Washington, D.C.: Catholic University Press, 1956).

173. For further discussion of the Building Trades Council and the Chicago Federation of Labor, see Georg Leidenberger, "Working-Class Progressivism and the Politics of Transportation in Chicago, 1895–1907" (Ph.D. diss., University of North Carolina, 1995), 45–52, and Richard Schneirov and Thomas J. Suhrbur, *Union Brotherhood, Union Town: The History of the Carpenters' Union of Chicago, 1863–1987* (Carbondale: Southern Illinois University Press, 1988), esp. 75–76.

174. Minutes of the Chicago Federation of Labor (hereafter cited as CFLM), Sept. 20, 1903, Chicago Historical Society, Special Collections. For further discussions of Fitzpatrick and the CFL, see Feffer, *Chicago Pragmatists,* 104; John Fitzpatrick Papers, Chicago Historical Society, Special Collections; and "John Fitzpatrick," in *Biographical Dictionary of American Labor,* ed. Gary M. Fink (Westport, Conn.: Greenwood Press, 1984).

175. See Jane Addams, "Hull-House: A Social Settlement," in *Hull-House Maps and Papers,* 215–18; Feffer, *Chicago Pragmatists,* 112; and Wade, *Graham Taylor,* 127.

176. McDowell, "Quarter Century," 4.

177. Additional volunteers included prominent Chicagoans in other fields, such as Oak Park physician Clarence E. Hemingway, father of Ernest Hemingway, who started the Agassiz Club for a group of boys interested in nature; Hester P. Stowe, niece of Harriet Beecher Stowe, who directed the girls' clubs, and Alice Masaryk, daughter of Professor Thomas Masaryk, who led the independence movement and became the first president of Czechoslovakia.

178. Kelley, *Notes of Sixty Years,* 104. See also Kathryn Kish Sklar, *Florence Kelley and the Nation's Work: The Rise of Women's Political Culture, 1830–1900* (New Haven: Yale University Press, 1995).

179. See Elizabeth Anne Payne, *Reform, Labor, and Feminism: Margaret Dreier Robbins and the Women's Trade Union League* (Urbana: University of Illinois Press, 1988), 47. See also Nancy Shrom Dye, *As Equals and as Sisters: Feminism, the Labor Movement, and the Women's Trade Union League* (Columbia: University of Missouri Press, 1980).

180. Payne, *Reform, Labor, and Feminism,* 4. See also Maureen A. Flanagan, *Seeing with Their Hearts: Chicago Women and the Vision of the Good City* (Princeton: Princeton University Press, 2001), 77–79.

181. Mary McDowell, "Civic Experiences—1914," MMP, box 3, folder 19.
182. Mason, "Testing the Boundaries," 42.
183. Goodspeed, *History,* 448; Carolyn M. Hill, "Forty Years Back of the Yards," *Unity,* Dec. 7, 1936, 128, MMP, box 1, folder 2; Storr, *Harper's University,* 186.
184. "Constitution and By-Laws of the University of Chicago Settlement League," University of Chicago Service League Papers, box 1, folder 1, Special Collections Research Center, University of Chicago Library. The League changed its name to the University of Chicago Service League after a reorganization in 1957. During the previous year the name of the University Settlement was changed to the Mary McDowell Settlement to honor the first head resident and to clarify the lack of formal association between the settlement and the university.
185. See Harper to Edward W. Bemis, Jan. 15, 1894, WRHP; Harper, "Quarterly Statement," *Calendar* 4, no. 1 (Aug. 1895); Furner, *Advocacy and Objectivity,* 151–78; and Bari Jane Watkins, "The Professors and the Unions: American Academic Social Theory and Labor Reform, 1882–1915" (Ph.D. diss., Yale University, 1976).
186. John Dewey to Alice Dewey, 1894, quoted in Feffer, *Chicago Pragmatists,* 113. See also Mead, "The Social Settlement: Its Basis and Function," *University Record* 12 (1907–8): 114.

CHAPTER THREE

1. Dwight Heald Perkins, *Report of the Special Park Commission to the City Council of Chicago on the Subject of a Metropolitan Park System* (Chicago: City of Chicago, 1904), 31.
2. J. A. Rondthaler, "The Moral Influence of Parks," *American Park and Outdoor Art Association.* 4, no. 2 (1900): 78–84, quotation on 80.
3. For general discussions of park design in the Progressive Era, see *A Breath of Fresh Air: Chicago's Neighborhood Parks of the Progressive Reform Era, 1900–1925* (Chicago: Chicago Park District, 1989); Paul Boyer, *Urban Masses and Moral Order in America, 1820–1920* (Cambridge: Harvard University Press, 1978); Galen Cranz, *The Politics of Park Design: A History of Urban Parks in America* (Cambridge: MIT Press, 1982); Marian Lorena Osborn, "The Development of Recreation in the South Park System of Chicago" (Ph.D. diss., University of Chicago, 1928); *Prairie in the City: Naturalism in Chicago's Parks, 1870–1940* (Chicago: Chicago Historical Society, 1991); Roy Rosenzweig, *Eight Hours for What We Will: Workers and Leisure in an Industrial City, 1870–1920* (Cambridge: Cambridge University Press, 1983); Roy Rosenzweig and Elizabeth Blackmar, *The Park and the People: A History of Central Park*

(Ithaca: Cornell University Press, 1992); Stanley K. Schultz, *Constructing Urban Culture: American Cities and City Planning, 1800–1920* (Philadelphia: Temple University Press, 1989); Christopher Silver and Mary Corbin Sies, eds., *Planning the Twentieth-Century American City* (Baltimore: Johns Hopkins University Press, 1995); William W. Tippens, "Synthesis of Reform: The Development of the Small Parks in Chicago's South and West Park Commissions" (M.A. thesis, Columbia University, 1988); Robert Weyeneth, "Moral Spaces: Reforming the Landscape of Leisure in Urban America, 1850–1920" (Ph.D. diss., University of California, Berkeley, 1984); Lois Wille, *Forever Open, Clear and Free: The Historic Struggle for Chicago's Lakefront* (Chicago: Henry Regnery, 1972); and William H. Wilson, *The City Beautiful Movement* (Baltimore: Johns Hopkins University Press, 1989).

4. For further discussion of Victorian notions of park design and moral uplift, see Thomas Bender, *Toward an Urban Vision: Ideas and Institutions in Nineteenth-Century America* (Baltimore: Johns Hopkins University Press, 1975); Boyer, *Urban Masses and Moral Order;* Cranz, *Politics of Park Design;* Rosenzweig and Blackmar, *Park and the People;* David Schuyler, *The New Urban Landscape: The Redefinition of City Form in Nineteenth-Century America* (Baltimore: Johns Hopkins University Press, 1986); and David M. Scobey, *Empire City: The Making and Meaning of the New York City Landscape* (Philadelphia: Temple University Press, 2002).

5. *The Chicago Recreation Survey 1937*, vol. 1, *Public Recreation* (Chicago: Chicago Recreation Commission, 1937), 3.

6. Perkins, *Report of the Special Park Commission* (1904), 89–106. See also H. W. S. Cleveland, *The Public Grounds of Chicago: How to Give Them Character and Expression* (Chicago: Charles D. Lakey, 1869); and *Chicago Recreation Survey 1937*, 1:18. The legislation stipulated that the commissioners of the West Park and Lincoln Park districts be appointed by the governor and the South Park commissioners appointed by the circuit court judges of Cook County. Many critics claimed that the West Park and Lincoln Park boards were ineffective as a result, since they were subject to the whims of shifting political concerns of the statehouse. As a result, the South Park board was touted as the most successful in securing park sites and developing them.

7. See Andrew Jackson Downing, *A Treatise on the Theory and Practice of Landscape Gardening Adapted to North America; with a View toward the Improvement of Country Residences* (Boston: C. C. Little, 1841). For more on Downing see Judith A. Major, *To Live in a New World: A. J. Downing and American Landscape Gardening* (Cambridge: MIT Press, 1997), and David A. Schuyler, *Apostle of Taste: Andrew Jackson Downing, 1815–1852* (Baltimore: Johns Hopkins University Press, 1996).

8. Andrew Jackson Downing, "A Few Words on Our Progress in Building," *Horticulturalist* 6 (June 1851): 250–51, quoted in Major, *To Live in a New World,* 133. For further discussion of changes in ideas about park design, see Francis R. Kowsky, *Country, Park and City: The Architecture and Life of Calvert Vaux* (Oxford: Oxford University Press, 1998); Major, *To Live in a New World;* Witold Rybczynski, *A Clearing in the Distance: Frederick Law Olmsted and America in the Nineteenth Century* (New York: Scribner's, 1999); Schuyler, *Apostle of Taste;* and Schuyler, *New Urban Landscape.*
9. Thomas Cole, quoted in Schuyler, *New Urban Landscape,* 32.
10. Ralph Waldo Emerson, "Self-Reliance," in *The Collected Works of Ralph Waldo Emerson,* vol. 2, ed. Joseph Slater and Douglas Emory Wilson (Cambridge, Mass.: Belknap Press, 1979), 25–51.
11. Charles Capper and Conrad Edick Wright, eds., *Transient and Permanent: The Transcendental Movement and Its Contexts* (Boston: Massachusetts Historical Society, 1999); Henry David Thoreau, *Walden,* ed. Bill McKibben (Boston: Beacon Press, 1997), 85.
12. Frederick Law Olmsted, "Public Parks and the Enlargement of Towns," *Journal of Social Science,* no. 3 (1871): 1–36, quotation on 23.
13. Quoted in Anne Whiston Spirn, "Constructing Nature: The Legacy of Frederick Law Olmsted," in *Uncommon Ground: Rethinking the Human Place in Nature,* ed. William Cronon (New York: W. W. Norton, 1996), 91–113, 93.
14. See Frederick Law Olmsted Sr., *Forty Years of Landscape Architecture: Early Years and Experiences, 1822–1903* (New York: G. P. Putnam's Sons, 1922), 88–93, for further discussion of Olmsted's relationship with Downing. On Olmsted's design aesthetic, see Charles E. Beveridge, "Frederick Law Olmsted's Theory of Landscape Design," *Nineteenth Century* 3, no. 2 (Summer 1977): 38–43; Charles E. Beveridge and David Schuyler, eds., *The Papers of Frederick Law Olmsted,* vol. 3, *Creating Central Park, 1857–1861* (Baltimore: Johns Hopkins University Press, 1989); Geoffrey Blodgett, "Frederick Law Olmsted: Landscape Architecture as Conservative Reform," *Journal of American History* 62, no. 4 (Mar. 1976): 869–89; Albert Fein, ed., *Landscape into Cityscape: Frederick Law Olmsted's Plan for a Greater New York City* (Ithaca: Cornell University Press, 1968); Irving D. Fisher, *Frederick Law Olmsted and the City Planning Movement* (Ann Arbor: University of Michigan Research Press, 1986); Melvin Kalfus, *Frederick Law Olmsted: The Passion of a Public Artist* (Cambridge: Harvard University Press, 1990); Victoria Post Ranney, *Olmsted in Chicago* (Chicago: R. R. Donnelly, 1972); Rosenzweig and Blackmar, *Park and the People;* Schuyler, *New Urban Landscape,* 59–195; Rybczynski, *Clearing in the Distance,* 165–77; and Scobey, *Empire City.*

15. Quoted in Julia Sniderman, "Bringing the Prairie Vision into Focus," in *Prairie in the City: Naturalism in Chicago's Parks, 1879–1920*, ed. Julia Sniderman, William Tippens, et al. (Chicago: Chicago Historical Society, 1991), 19. Also, see Ranney, *Olmsted in Chicago,* 16.
16. H. W. S. Cleveland, *The Public Grounds of Chicago: How to Give Them Character and Expression* (Chicago: Charles D. Lakey, 1869), 13, quoted in Daniel Bluestone, *Constructing Chicago* (New Haven: Yale University Press, 1991) 37.
17. Quoted in Ranney, *Olmsted in Chicago,* 26.
18. Olmsted, Vaux and Co., *Report Accompanying Plan for Laying out the South Park* (Chicago: South Park Commission, 1871), 17. See also Ranney, *Olmsted in Chicago,* 21, 27.
19. Beveridge, "Frederick Law Olmsted's Theory of Landscape Design," 43. For discussions of these elements in the Greensward Plan of Central Park, see Rosenzweig and Blackmar, *Park and the People,* 294–95.
20. Olmsted, Vaux and Company, *Preliminary Report upon the Proposed Suburban Village of Riverside, near Chicago* (New York: Sutton, Browne, 1868), 12.
21. Bluestone, *Constructing Chicago,* 18. See also David Scobey, "Anatomy of the Promenade: The Politics of Bourgeois Sociability in Nineteenth-Century New York," *Social History* 17 (May 1992): 203–27. Scobey argues that the promenade "served as a site where elite Americans negotiated the tension between class hierarchies and civic fellowship in a capitalist democracy" (203). In addition, the promenade and parks in general were spaces where the very definition of civic culture was negotiated, through discussions of proper designs, locations, and uses of parks.
22. Blodgett, "Frederick Law Olmsted, 875.
23. Frederick Law Olmsted Jr. and Theodore Kimball, eds., *Frederick Law Olmsted: Landscape Architect, 1822–1903,* 2 vols. (New York: Putnam, 1922), 2:171; quoted in John F. Kasson, *Amusing the Million: Coney Island at the Turn of the Century* (Toronto: McGraw-Hill, 1978), 15, and Rosenzweig, *Eight Hours for What We Will,* 127.
24. Pierre Bourdieu discusses the links between cultural authority and capital accumulation in *Distinction,* trans. Richard Nice (Cambridge: Harvard University Press, 1984), 480–96. He argues that taste represents an arena of struggle and that those who can demonstrate their control of taste have both cultural and political power. Thus cultural capital can function in the same way as economic capital, with those in the process of acquiring it wanting to display it publicly at the same time that they want to claim it as their own. See also Neil Harris, *Cultural Excursions: Marketing Appetites and Cultural Tastes in Modern America* (Chicago: University of Chicago Press, 1990), for further discussion of the links between commerce and culture.

25. Olmsted, "Public Parks and the Enlargement of Towns," 23. See also Weyeneth, "Moral Spaces," 41.
26. Ranney, *Olmsted in Chicago*, 7.
27. See *Gem of the Prairie*, June 30, 1849, quoted in Bluestone, *Constructing Chicago*, 18.
28. Elizabeth Halsey, *The Development of Public Recreation in Metropolitan Chicago* (Chicago: Chicago Recreation Commission, 1940), 8, 115. See also Benjamin McArthur, "The Chicago Playground Movement: A Neglected Feature of Social Justice," *Social Science Review* 49 (Sept. 1975): 376–95, and Tippens, "Synthesis of Reform, 7.
29. Cranz, *Politics of Park Design*, 19.
30. J. Horace McFarland, "Parks and the Public," *Parks and Recreation* 6 (Sept.–Oct. 1922): 12.
31. John Brinckerhoff Jackson, *American Space: The Centennial Years, 1865–1876* (New York: W. W. Norton, 1972), 214–15.
32. Halsey, *Development of Public Recreation*, 145.
33. *Chicago Times*, Apr. 17, 1867, Mar. 24, 1869.
34. Jane Addams, *Hull-House Recreation Guide* (Chicago: Hull-House, 1897).
35. *Chicago Tribune*, July 29, 1901.
36. *Abendpost*, June 26, 1895, WPA translation, *Chicago Foreign Language Press Survey*, Chicago Public Library Omnibus Project (Chicago: The Project, 1942) (hereafter CFLPS). City of Chicago, *Special Park District Report on Conditions*, 1902, 9–10; Eleanor Kroll, "The History of the University of Chicago Settlement," Mary McDowell Papers (hereafter cited as MMP), Chicago Historical Society, Special Collections, box 1, folder 3a.
37. Michael P. McCarthy, "Politics and the Parks: Chicago Businessmen and the Recreation Movement," *Journal of the Illinois State Historical Society* 65 (1972): 158–72, quotation on 161.
38. *Chicago Daily Tribune*, Nov. 12, 1899.
39. Charles Zueblin, "Municipal Playgrounds in Chicago," *American Journal of Sociology* 4 (Sept. 1898): 145–58; Charles Zueblin, *A Decade of Civic Development* (Chicago: University of Chicago Press, 1905); and Joan E. Draper, "The Art and Science of Park Planning in the United States: Chicago's Small Parks, 1902 to 1905," in *Planning the Twentieth-Century American City*, ed. Mary Corbin Sies and Christopher Silver (Baltimore: Johns Hopkins University Press, 1996), 98–119, esp. 108–13.
40. Unidentified newspaper, Sept. 1901, Lincoln Park Commission Newspaper Clippings, Chicago Park District, Special Collections (hereafter cited as CPD), and Benjamin McArthur, "Parks, Playgrounds, and Progressivism," 10.
41. "Resolutions Establishing the Special Park Commission," *Chicago City Council, Proceedings* (Chicago: 1899), 1536. The resolutions were adopted by City Council on November 6,

1899. See also Dwight Heald Perkins, *Report of the Special Park Commission to the City Council of Chicago on the Subject of a Metropolitan Park System* (Chicago: City of Chicago, 1901), 22, and Halsey, *Development of Public Recreation,* appendix, 303.

42. *Chicago Recreation Survey 1937,* 22.
43. Dwight Heald Perkins, *Report of the Special Park Commission* (1904), 89–106.
44. One of the elements discussed in the report was the importance of conservation, for Jens Jensen (who contributed to the report) recognized the toll that rapid growth was taking on the land and called for efforts to preserve it. Through these efforts to save the native forests and vegetation, Jensen hoped to teach midwesterners to appreciate the regional landscape. He pointed to a lack of appreciation of the prairie landscape as one factor that had allowed it to deteriorate since the city's first pleasure grounds were built, and he looked to this earlier period for inspiration. Indeed, Jensen became a leader in efforts to use only native planting to preserve and enhance the "natural landscape" of Chicago. Robert E. Grese, *Jens Jensen: Maker of Natural Parks and Gardens* (Baltimore: Johns Hopkins University Press, 1992).
45. Perkins, *Report of the Special Park Commission* (1904), 40.
46. *Chicago American,* June 4, 1902, South Park Commission Newspaper Clippings (hereafter cited as SPCNC), Chicago Park District, Special Collections. The South Park Board put a bond issue for small parks on the ballot, and it passed overwhelmingly on November 2, 1902 (*Chicago Record,* June 12, 1902, CPD). The total area of the South Park system doubled as a result of the vote, as nearly one thousand acres of land was annexed. This made Chicago first in ownership of park territory nationwide.
47. *Annual Report of the South Park Commissioners, 1905* (Chicago: City of Chicago, 1906), 49, and Tippens, "Synthesis of Reform," 23.
48. Members of the Special Park Commission included Zueblin, nine aldermen, Dwight Perkins, O. C. Simonds, Graham Taylor, the president of the Art Institute of Chicago, a physician, and representatives of three regional park commissions; Zueblin and other members of Special Park Commission systematized methods of selecting and creating park sites. A. W. Beilfuss, "Municipal Playgrounds in Chicago," *Playgrounds* 2 (1908): 259–61.
49. Fred H. Matthews, *Quest for an American Sociology: Robert E. Park and the Chicago School of Sociology* (Montreal: McGill-Queens University Press, 1977), 93. See also Lester R. Kurtz, *Evaluating Chicago Sociology: A Guide to the Literature, with an Annotated Bibliography* (Chicago: University of Chicago Press, 1984), 11–59, for further discussion of the relation between scientific method, the sociology of knowledge, and urban reform.

50. Other reformers undertook studies to determine social needs in the city, like *Hull-House Maps and Papers,* ed. Jane Addams (New York: Crowell, 1895), and the City Home Association's *Tenement Conditions in Chicago* (Chicago: City Home Association, 1901), both focusing on the West Side. Charles J. Bushnell, "Some Social Aspects of the Chicago Stock Yards," part 2, *American Journal of Sociology* 7 (Nov. 1901): 289–330, provided data about the number of saloons in districts versus the number of playgrounds (the South Side Stockyards area had five hundred saloons and only twenty-six schoolyards).
51. City of Chicago, Special Park Commission, *Report on Sites and Needs, to the Honorable the South Park Commissioners* (Chicago: City of Chicago, 1902), 1–2.
52. City of Chicago, Special Park Commission, *Report on Conditions, to the Honorable the South Park Commissioners* (Chicago, 1904), 2, 5, 7.
53. Ibid., 5.
54. Perkins, *Report of the Special Park Commission* (1904), 56.
55. *Galesburg, Illinois Register,* July 27, 1903. South Park District Clipping Files, CPD.
56. Amalie Hofer Jerome, "The Playground as a Social Center," *Annals of the Academy of Political and Social Science* 35 (Mar. 1910): 132.
57. See Cranz, *Politics of Park Design,* 203–6.
58. Louise de Koven Bowen, *Safeguards for City Youth at Work and at Play* (New York: Macmillan, 1914), 1–7. For further discussion of the juvenile court in Chicago, see Victoria Lynn Getis, "A Disciplined Society: The Juvenile Court, Reform, and the Social Sciences in Chicago, 1890–1930" (Ph.D. diss., University of Michigan, 1994), and Michael Willrich, "City of Courts: Crime, Law, and Social Policy in Chicago, 1880–1930" (Ph.D. diss., University of Chicago, 1997).
59. Bowen, *Safeguards for City Youth,* 4.
60. Ibid., 46.
61. Ibid., 12–25.
62. Jane Addams, *The Spirit of Youth and the City Streets* (New York: Macmillan, 1909), 75.
63. In 1907 several revisions to the municipal code resulted from the investigations of the JPA. It became unlawful, for example, for places of commercial amusement to sell admission tickets to anyone under age fourteen not accompanied by an adult. Licensing for theaters also became more rigorous, and the City Club of Chicago proposed a committee on censorship to monitor the content of films. See "Extracts from Ordinance in the Municipal Code Regulating Five-Cent Theaters," Apr. 13, 1907, City Club papers, Chicago Historical Society, box 9, folder 5. For further studies that exposed poor conditions in working-class neighborhoods and encouraged municipal response, see especially Edith

Abbott, *The Tenements of Chicago, 1908–1935* (Chicago: University of Chicago Press, 1936); Sophonisba Breckinridge and Edith Abbott, *The Delinquent Child and the Home* (New York: United Charities Publication Committee, 1912); and Vice Commission of Chicago, *The Social Evil in Chicago: A Study of Existing Conditions with Recommendations of the Vice Commission of Chicago* (Chicago: Gunthorp-Warren, 1911).

64. Jane Addams, "Preface," in Bowen, *Safeguards for City Youth,* xii.

65. C. S. Sargent, "Playgrounds and Parks," *Garden and Forest* 7 (June 6, 1894): 221, quoted in Cranz, *Politics of Park Design,* 15.

66. *Chicago Record-Herald,* June 1, 1902, Lincoln Park Commission Newspaper Clippings, CPD.

67. Henry C. Foreman, *Recreation Needs of Chicago, Delivered on Labor Day, 1904, at Morgan Park* (Chicago: Cook County Board of Commissioners, 1904), 5, 9; quoted in McCarthy, "Politics and the Parks," 165.

68. J. Frank Foster, *An Article on Small Parks Read Before the Chicago Society for School Extension* (Chicago: Chicago Historical Society, 1902).

69. McArthur, "Parks, Playgrounds, and Progressivism," 11. See also Dominick Cavallo, *Muscles and Morals: Organized Playgrounds and Urban Reform, 1880–1920* (Philadelphia: University of Pennsylvania Press, 1981).

70. Quoted in Cavallo, *Muscles and Morals,* 75.

71. Breckinridge and Abbott, *Delinquent Child and the Home,* 157.

72. *Chicago Recreation Survey,* 4, 19. McArthur, "Chicago Playground Movement," 379.

73. Howard E. Wilson, *Mary McDowell, Neighbor* (Chicago: University of Chicago Press, 1928), 73; Graham Romeyn Taylor, "How They Played at Chicago," *Charities and the Commons,* Aug. 3, 1907, 1–8, esp. 4.

74. Luther Halsey Gulick, "Play and Democracy," *Charities and the Commons,* Aug. 3, 1907, 15–17, quotation on 15.

75. Charles Zueblin, *American Municipal Progress* (New York: Macmillan, 1916), 276.

76. Perkins, *Report of the Special Park Commission* (1901), 8.

77. Perkins, "Union of Playgrounds and Public Schools," *Charities and the Commons,* Aug. 3, 1907, 68–73, 69.

78. *Chicago Recreation Survey,* 19, and Halsey, *Development of Public Recreation,* 26.

79. McArthur, "Parks, Playgrounds, and Progressivism," 13. See also William A. Gleason, *The Leisure Ethic* (Stanford: Stanford University Press, 1999).

80. *Annual Report of the South Park Commissioners, 1909* (Chicago: City of Chicago, 1910), 37; Halsey, *Development of Public Recreation,* 31; and McCarthy, "Politics and the Parks, 164–65. For further discussion of Theodore Roosevelt, masculinity, and the strenuous life, see

Elliott Gorn, *The Manly Art: Bare Knuckle Prize Fighting in Victorian America* (Ithaca: Cornell University Press, 1986); Elizabeth H. Pleck and Joseph H. Pleck, eds., *The American Man* (Englewood Cliffs, N.J.: Prentice-Hall, 1980); and Arnaldo Testi, "The Gender of Reform Politics: Theodore Roosevelt and the Culture of Masculinity," *Journal of American History* 81 (Mar. 1995): 1509–33.

81. McArthur, "Parks, Playgrounds, and Progressivism," 13.
82. Henry S. Curtis, "Playground Progress and Tendencies of the Year," *Charities and the Commons,* Aug. 3, 1907, 26.
83. "Commercialized Recreation in the Metropolitan Community," adapted from Michael M. Davis, *The Exploitation of Pleasure: A Study of Commercial Recreations in New York City* (New York: Russell Sage Foundation, 1911), 3–24, Ernest Burgess Papers, box 31, folder 4, Special Collections Research Center, University of Chicago Library.
84. *Annual Report of the Special Park Commission, 1909* (Chicago: City of Chicago, 1910), 7.
85. *Chicago Recreation Survey 1937,* 22.
86. Perkins, *Report of the Special Park Commission* (1901), 7.
87. *Chicago Examiner,* Feb. 5, 1904, SPCNC.
88. *Chicago Record-Herald,* Feb. 14, 1904, SPCNC.
89. *Annual Report of the South Park Commissioners, 1903* (Chicago: City of Chicago, 1904), 6.
90. *Chicago Inter-Ocean,* Feb. 5, 1904, SPCNC. There were instances, however, when the location selection and spending practices of the park commissions were questioned. In 1904, attorney James R. Ward filed a motion attacking the right of the South Park Commission to condemn land in the interest of developing small parks. The defendants claimed that the 1901 act enabling the commission to "acquire, approve, and maintain additional small parks and pleasure grounds" was unconstitutional. The suit claimed that since the residents in the South Park District had not approved this act, it should be null and void. This action tied the commissioners' hands in acquiring land for several months, but eventually the suit was thrown out.
91. *Chicago Inter-Ocean,* Sept. 24, 1902; *Chicago Tribune,* Sept. 25, 1902.
92. *Chicago American,* Feb. 5, 1904, SPCNC.
93. "Address of Henry G. Foreman, President of the South Park Commissioners, on the Occasion of the Dedication of McKinley Park, June 13, 1903," CPD. For further discussion of McKinley Park, and Chicago parks in general, see Julia Sniderman Bachrach, *The City in a Garden* (Santa Fe: Center for American Places, 2001), 117.
94. The *Annual Report of the South Park Commissioners, 1904* (Chicago: City of Chicago, 1905), 7, discusses design plans for field houses and facilities.

95. Mary McDowell, "The Field Houses of Chicago and Their Possibilities," *Charities and the Commons,* Aug. 3, 1907, 65.

96. Ibid., 68.

97. Ranney, *Olmsted in Chicago,* 39. See also Bachrach, *City in a Garden,* 12–14.

98. *Annual Report of the South Park Commissioners, 1905,* 49; *Chicago Record-Herald,* May 14, 1905. See also Draper, "Park Planning," 10, Cranz, *Politics of Park Design,* 85–92, and William W. Tippens and Julia Sniderman, "The Planning and Design of Chicago's Neighborhood Parks," in *Breath of Fresh Air,* 21–24.

99. *Chicago Record-Herald,* May 14, 1905.

100. *Chicago Tribune,* May 14, 1905.

101. Tippens, "Synthesis of Reform," 31. Tippens highlights many of the variations. Russell Square (5.04 acres) and Cornell Square (8.72 acres) had sunken ball fields; Mark White Square (9.46 acres) had a small tree-lined grove and an irregularly shaped wading pool as a result of the angle of Poplar Avenue to the west. Armour Square was the most dramatic departure from the Davis Square model, with the line of symmetry moved to the diagonal and the field house in the northwest corner of the site; this allowed the Olmsteds to get out of a grid model for the park interior and create an oval ball field and walkways leading to it, thereby devoting more land to shrubbery and passive recreation. This design allowed for more differentiated views as one walked along the promenade, and introducing secondary paths created areas for picnicking, thus fitting square patterns into the Olmsteds' vision for formal design and altered perspectives, with field houses providing distant focal point while the ball field served as open expanse providing sweeping views. 34.

102. Quoted in Tippens, "Synthesis of Reform," 44. See also Joan Draper, *Edward H. Bennett, Architect and City Planner, 1874–1954* (Chicago: Art Institute of Chicago, 1982), for further discussion of Bennett's classical design ideal and his relation to the City Beautiful movement.

103. Henry Foreman, "Chicago's New Park Service," *Century Magazine* 69, no. 4 (1905): 613. Joan Draper argues that Bennett's off-white, rough-cast concrete buildings had a "decidedly public and official character, looking more like a library or city hall than a sports facility or neighborhood social hall." Indeed, this building style would reappear in his design for city hall in the 1909 *Plan of Chicago.* Draper, "Art and Science of Park Planning," 101.

104. "Chicago Parks and Their Landscape Architecture," *Architectural Record* 24 (July 1908): 26.

105. Everett B. Mero, ed., *American Playgrounds: Their Construction, Equipment, Maintenance and Utility* (New York: Baker and Taylor, 1909), 60–69.
106. Halsey, *Development of Public Recreation,* 33.
107. *Chicago Post,* May 3, 1906, SPCNC.
108. "Planning and Development of a City Park System," *Park and Cemetery* 17, no. 5 (July 1908): 376, CPD.
109. *Annual Report of the South Park Commissioners, 1905,* 48. See also *Annual Report of the Special Park Commission, 1909,* 26–28.
110. Theodore A. Gross, "Playgrounds and Bathing Beaches: Report of the Superintendent," *Annual Report of the Special Park Commission, 1910* (Chicago: City of Chicago, 1911), 28.
111. McDowell, " Field Houses of Chicago," 53.
112. Bowen, *Safeguards for City Youth,* 46–49.
113. *Annual Report of the South Park Commissioners, 1906* (Chicago: City of Chicago, 1907), and "A Year's Record of the New Small Parks in Chicago," *Park and Cemetery* 16, no. 6 (June 1906): 72. These figures include repeat users.
114. "Year's Record," 72.
115. *Annual Report of the South Park Commissioners, 1908* (Chicago: City of Chicago, 1909), 114. Similarly, a 1912 report observed that the number of poolrooms and dance halls diminished in neighborhoods where small parks were created, and infant mortality rates declined as well. *Annual Report of the South Park Commissioners, 1912* (Chicago: City of Chicago, 1913), 45.
116. *Chicago Chronicle,* Oct. 7, 1905, SPCNC.
117. *Chicago Post* and *Chicago Chronicle,* Nov. 16, 1905; *Chicago Journal,* Sept. 28, 1905; *Chicago Examiner,* Oct. 30, 1905; SPNC.
118. Henriette Greenebaum Frank and Amalie Hofer Jerome, *Annals of the Chicago Woman's Club for the First Forty Years of Its Organization, 1876–1916* (Chicago: Chicago Woman's Club, 1916), 248; also quoted in Maureen A. Flanagan, *Seeing with Their Hearts: Chicago Women and the Vision of the Good City, 1871–1933* (Princeton: Princeton University Press, 2002), 104, 106.
119. "Crime—Canaryville," MMP, box 2, folder 10.
120. Chicago Commission on Race Relations, *The Negro in Chicago: A Study of Race Relations and a Race Riot* (Chicago: University of Chicago Press, 1922), 278.
121. Ibid., 12–14, 288–95; and Allan H. Spear, *Black Chicago: The Making of a Negro Ghetto, 1890–1920* (Chicago: University of Chicago Press, 1970), 206.
122. *Annual Report of the Special Park Commission* (1909), 26.

123. Chicago Commission on Race Relations, *Negro in Chicago,* 272–73.

124. *Dziennik Zwiaskowy,* Jan. 8, 1918, in *Chicago Foreign Language Press Survey,* Chicago Public Library Omnibus Project (Chicago: The Project, 1942); *Englewood Times,* Sept. 8, 1905. See Dominic Pacyga, "Planning for the Poor: Chicago's Progressive-Era Parks and their Working-Class Constituents," paper in author's possession.

125. Kroll, "History of the University of Chicago Settlement."

126. Paul Cressy, "Article for the Handbook on the McKinley Park Community," Ernest Burgess Papers, box 129, folder 7, Special Collections Research Center, University of Chicago Library.

127. "A Study of Gaelic Park," Ernest Burgess Papers, box 129, folder 7, Special Collections Research Center, University of Chicago Library.

128. *Chicago Journal,* Aug. 25, 1904, SSPCNC.

129. *Denni Hlasatel,* Aug. 31, 1908, CFLPS.

130. *Denni Hlasatel,* July 31, 1911, CFLPS

131. *Denni Hlasatel,* Sept. 27, 1914, CFLPS.

132. *Denni Hlasatel,* Mar. 5, 1918, CFLPS.

133. Quoted in Mary McDowell, "A Quarter of a Century in the Stockyards District," MMP, box 1, folder 39.

134. Ibid.

135. *Chicago Chronicle,* May 29, 1902, SPCNC.

136. *Chicago Tribune,* Sept. 9, 1902, SPCNC.

137. *Chicago Record-Herald,* Nov. 5, 1905, SPCNC..

138. *Chicago American,* Nov. 5, 1905, SPCNC.

139. *Chicago American,* Nov. 4, 1905, SPCNC.

140. *Chicago Examiner,* Nov. 7, 1905, SPCNC.

141. Quoted in Rosenzweig, *Eight Hours for What We Will,* 135–36.

142. For further discussion of the links between civic organizations, labor, gender, and politics, see Nancy Schrom Dye, "Creating a Feminist Alliance: Sisterhood and Class Conflict in the New York Women's Trade Union League, 1903–1914," *Feminist Studies* 3 (Fall 1975): 111–25; Maureen A. Flanagan, "Gender and Urban Political Reform: The City Club and the Women's City Club of Chicago in the Progressive Era," *American Historical Review* 95 (October 1990): 1032–50; Flanagan, *Seeing with Their Hearts;* Joanne J. Meyerowitz, *Women Adrift: Independent Wage Earners in Chicago, 1880–1930* (Chicago: University of Chicago Press, 1988); Elizabeth Anne Payne, *Reform, Labor, and Feminism: Margaret Dreier Robins and the Women's Trade Union League* (Urbana: University of Illinois Press, 1988);

Mary P. Ryan, "The Power of Women's Networks: A Case Study of Female Moral Reform in Antebellum America," *Feminist Studies* 5 (Spring 1979): 66–85; Katherine Kish Sklar, "Two Political Cultures in the Progressive Era: The National Consumers' League and the American Association for Labor Legislation," in *U.S. History as Women's History: New Feminist Essays,* ed. Linda Kerber et al. (Chapel Hill: University of North Carolina Press, 1995), 36–62; and Christine Stansell, *City of Women: Sex and Class in New York, 1789–1860* (New York: Alfred A. Knopf, 1986).

143. Bluestone, *Constructing Chicago,* 30.
144. For further discussion of class, public space, and visibility, see especially Susan Davis, *Parades and Power: Street Theater in Nineteenth-Century Philadelphia* (Philadelphia: Temple University Press, 1986); Lawrence Levine, *Highbrow/Lowbrow: The Emergence of Cultural Hierarchy in America* (Cambridge: Harvard University Press, 1988); Mary P. Ryan, *Women in Public: Between Banners and Ballots, 1825–1880* (Baltimore: Johns Hopkins University Press, 1990); and Robert Slayton, *Back of the Yards: The Making of a Local Democracy* (Chicago: University of Chicago Press, 1986).

CHAPTER FOUR

1. Quoted in Charles Moore, *Daniel H. Burnham: Architect, Planner of Cities,* 2 vols. (Boston: Houghton Mifflin, 1921), 2:147. According to Burnham's later biographer, Thomas S. Hines, Burnham did not utter these famous words in exactly this way. Nonetheless, this quotation captures the essence and style of Burnham's ideas about the Chicago Plan and the City Beautiful. See Thomas S. Hines, *Burnham of Chicago: Architect and Planner* (Chicago: University of Chicago Press, 1979), 401, n. 8.
2. Daniel H. Burnham and Edward H. Bennett, *Plan of Chicago* (1909; New York: Princeton Architectural Press, 1993), 4.
3. Ibid., 2. For further discussion of progressivism and the Chicago Plan, see Daniel Bluestone, *Constructing Chicago* (New Haven: Yale University Press, 1991), 194–204; Paul Boyer, *Urban Masses and Moral Order in America, 1820–1920* (Cambridge: Harvard University Press, 1978), 261–76, which focuses on the moral overtones of city planning; Hines, *Burnham of Chicago,* 312–45; Helen Lefkowitz Horowitz, *Culture and the City: Cultural Philanthropy in Chicago from the 1880s to 1917* (Chicago: University of Chicago Press, 1976), 221–27; Kristen Schaffer, "Fabric of City Life: The Social Agenda in Burnham's Draft of the *Plan of Chicago,*" in Burnham and Bennett, *Plan of Chicago,* v–xvi; and William H. Wilson,

The City Beautiful Movement (Baltimore: Johns Hopkins University Press, 1989), 1–6. For discussions of the ambiguous relation between commercialism and park planning, see Michael P. McCarthy, "Chicago Businessmen and the Burnham Plan," *Journal of the Illinois State Historical Society* 63 (Autumn 1970): 228–56; Roy Rosenzweig and Elizabeth Blackmar, *The Park and the People: A History of Central Park* (Ithaca: Cornell University Press, 1992), 150–79; and David M. Scobey, *Empire City: The Making and Meaning of the New York City Landscape* (Philadelphia: Temple University Press, 2002).

4. Daniel H. Burnham, "The Commercial Value of Beauty," reprinted in Moore, *Daniel H. Burnham*, 2:101–2.
5. Ibid.
6. M. Christine Boyer, *Dreaming the Rational City: The Myth of American City Planning* (Cambridge: MIT Press, 1983), 7.
7. *Plan of Chicago*, 6.
8. Ibid., 50.
9. Bluestone, *Constructing Chicago*, 194.
10. According to Benjamin F. Ayer, who discussed the history of lakefront questions before the Chicago Literary Club in 1888, "Nothing in the history of our local jurisprudence is more remarkable than the variety of novel and interesting questions which have arisen for adjudication affecting titles to real property along the border of the lake for some distance south of the mouth of the Chicago river." Benjamin F. Ayer, *Lake-Front Questions, Read Before the Chicago Literary Club, May 28, 1888* (Chicago: Barnard and Miller, 1888), 1.
11. Quoted in Lois Wille, *Forever Open, Clear, and Free: The Struggle for Chicago's Lakefront* (Chicago: University of Chicago Press, 1972), 22.
12. Ayer, *Lake-Front Questions*, 12. See also Rand McNally, *Map of Chicago Boulevards and Park Systems* (1889), Newberry Library, Special Collections.
13. Harold M. Mayer and Richard C. Wade, *Chicago: Growth of a Metropolis* (Chicago: University of Chicago Press, 1969), 12–20; Wille, *Forever Open, Clear, and Free*, 14, 24–25.
14. Ayer, *Lake-Front Questions*, 10–12; Wille, *Forever Open, Clear, and Free*, 36.
15. Ayer, *Lake-Front Questions*, 11. For further discussion of the early history of the lakefront, see Dennis H. Cremin, "Building Chicago's Front Yard, 1836–1936" (Ph.D. diss., Loyola University of Chicago, 1999), chap. 2.
16. M. A. Lane, "The Lake Front, Chicago," *Harper's Weekly*, Nov. 12, 1892, 1091.
17. Ibid.
18. *City of Chicago vs. A. Montgomery Ward and George R. Thorne, Abstract of Record* (Chicago: Fergus, 1896), 3. See also Wille, *Forever Open, Clear, and Free*, 71–74.

19. South Park Commissioners, *Statutes and Ordinances* (Chicago: Gunthrop Warren, 1908), 33. See also Walter L. Fisher, "Legal Aspects of the Plan of Chicago," in Burnham and Bennett, *Plan of Chicago,* 127–56, 137–38; *Chicago Tribune,* Nov. 10, 1902; Mayer and Wade, *Chicago,* 295; and Wille, *Forever Open, Clear, and Free,* 76–77.
20. *City of Chicago vs. Ward,* 2.
21. *Chicago Times-Herald,* Nov. 11, 1896.
22. *Chicago Inter-Ocean,* Nov. 25, 1896; *Chicago Times-Herald,* Nov. 24, 1896; *Chicago Journal,* Nov. 23, 1896.
23. "As to the Situation at Fifty-first Street," in *Joint Preliminary Report of the Committee on Bathing Beaches and Recreation Piers and the Lake Shore Reclamation Commission to Mayor Busse and the City Council, December 1910* (Chicago: Henry O. Shepard, 1910), 17; hereafter cited as *Bathing Beaches Report.*
24. Burnham to editor of *American Architect and Building News,* Oct. 26, 1896. Daniel H. Burnham Collection, Burnham Library, Art Institute of Chicago, box 61, folder 1.
25. *Report of the South Park Commissioners to the Board of County Commissioners* (Chicago: City of Chicago, 1903–4), 32. Dennis Cremin includes a table that illustrates the acres of land added to the park as a result of infill. See Cremin, "Building Chicago's Front Yard," 249.
26. *Bathing Beaches Report,* 6.
27. See *Bathing Beaches Report,* 11, 15, 27, 29. See also "Report of the Committee of the City Club of Chicago on Harbors, Wharves, and Bridges, Feb. 14, 1906," City Club of Chicago Collection, Chicago Historical Society, Special Collections, box 9, folder 5.
28. Woman's City Club, *Bulletin,* November 1916, 7–8, quoted in Maureen A. Flanagan, *Seeing with Their Hearts: Chicago Women and the Vision of the Good City, 1871–1933* (Princeton: Princeton University Press, 2002), 107. The Commission dropped its plans for the recreational pier at Seventy-fifth Street.
29. *Annual Report of the Special Park Commission, 1910* (Chicago: City of Chicago, 1911), 29.
30. *Chicago Record-Herald,* Mar. 18, 1903; *Park and Cemetery* 16 (July 1906): 5 and 19 (Feb. 1910): 12; South Park Commission Collection (hereafter cited as SPCC), Chicago Park District, Special Collections; Wille, *Forever Open, Clear, and Free,* 77.
31. The Crerar Library opened in 1897 in an annex of Marshall Field's department store at Washington and Wabash. John Crerar left a large portion of his estate for the "erection, creation, maintenance and endowment of a free public library." The trustees of the estate stipulated that the building be in Grant Park, in line with the Art Institute Building. See *Report of the South Park Commissioners to the Board of County Commissioners of Cook County* (1903–4), 11.

32. *Report of the South Park Commissioners for a Period of Fifteen Months from Dec. 1, 1906 to Feb. 29, 1908* (Chicago: City of Chicago, 1908). See also South Park Commissioners, Olmsted Brothers, landscape architects, "Preliminary Plan for Grant Park, July 27, 1903," Chicago Park District, Special Collections.
33. *Chicago Record-Herald,* May 8, 1903.
34. *Chicago Tribune,* Nov. 28, 1903.
35. *Chicago Tribune,* June 24, 1906.
36. *Chicago Magazine,* 21 (Apr. 1911), 2, SPCC.
37. *Chicago Post,* Jan. 28, 1907, South Park Commission Newspaper Clippings (hereafter cited as SPCNC), Chicago Park District, Special Collections.
38. *Chicago Tribune,* Nov. 11, 1903.
39. *Chicago American,* May 6, 1903, SPCNC.
40. Quoted in Wille, *Forever Open, Clear, and Free,* 79.
41. Ibid.; and *Chicago Tribune,* June 24, 1906.
42. Quoted in Wille, *Forever Open, Clear, and Free,* 80.
43. *Chicago American,* May 6, 1903, SPCNC.
44. See Wille, *Forever Open, Clear, and Free,* 80–81.
45. *Chicago Chronicle,* Apr. 26, 1903, SPCNC.
46. *South Park Improvement Association, Amended By-Laws* (Feb. 15, 1909), Hyde Park Historical Society Collection, box 4, folder 6, Special Collections Research Center, University of Chicago Library.
47. Ibid.; *Chicago Tribune,* Mar. 30, 1902; and Jean Block, *Hyde Park Houses: An Informal History, 1865–1910* (Chicago: University of Chicago Press, 1978), 70.
48. *Chicago Record-Herald,* Apr. 27, 1902.
49. *Chicago Journal,* Nov. 27, 1902, SPCNC.
50. *Chicago Chronicle,* Apr. 30, 1902, SPCNC, and Horowitz, *Culture and the City,* 211, 219.
51. *Chicago Record-Herald,* Oct. 20, 1905, SPCNC.
52. *Chicago Chronicle,* Apr. 11, 1903; *Chicago News,* Aug. 2, 1901, SPCNC; and Horowitz, *Culture and the City,* 219.
53. *Chicago Tribune,* Nov. 14, 1901.
54. *Chicago Journal,* July 24, 1901, SPCNC.
55. Ibid.
56. *Chicago American,* Aug. 5, 1901, SPCNC.
57. *Chicago Examiner,* Aug. 20, 1904, SPCNC.
58. *Chicago Post,* Nov. 11, 1901, SPCNC.

59. *Chicago Post,* Nov. 5, 1901, SPCNC.
60. *Chicago Tribune, Chicago Inter-Ocean,* and *Chicago Post,* Feb. 15, 1903, SPCNC.
61. Burnham and Bennett, *Plan of Chicago,* 50.
62. Joan E. Draper, "Paris By the Lake: Sources of Burnham's Plan of Chicago," in *Chicago Architecture, 1872–1922: Birth of a Metropolis,* ed. John Zukowksy (Munich: Prestel-Verlag, 1987), 107–19, esp. 115; and Horowitz, *Culture and the City,* 222–23. See also David P. Jordon, *Transforming Paris: The Life and Labors of Baron Haussmann* (New York: Free Press, 1995), 247.
63. Burnham and Bennett, *Plan of Chicago,* 14.
64. Ibid., 111.
65. Ibid., 112.
66. Walter D. Moody, *Wacker's Manual of the Plan of Chicago: Municipal Economy* (Chicago: Chicago Plan Commission, 1912), i, ii.
67. The female organizers of the first national conference on American city planning in 1909 shared a vision about the intimate connection between city building and community building. Settlement house workers Mary Simkovitch, Florence Kelley, and Lillian Wald linked shaping urban growth directly with forging tightly knit urban communities. They tied the improvement and beautification of urban space to the eradication of larger social problems. They affirmed, "City planning for social and economic ends will logically result in a genuinely and completely beautiful city." Quoted in Richard E. Fogelsong, *Planning the Capitalist City: The Colonial Era to the 1920s* (Princeton: Princeton University Press, 1986), 202–3. Yet this connection between social reform and urban beautification quickly broke down as planning became more professionalized. For further discussion of female reformers' part in early planning ideas, see Susan Marie Wirka, "The City Social Movement: Progressive Women Reformers and Early Social Planning," in *Planning the Twentieth-Century American City,* ed. Mary Corbin Sies and Christopher Silver (Baltimore: Johns Hopkins University Press, 1996), 55–75. See also *Proceedings of the First National Conference on City Planning, 1909,* republished as 61st Cong., 2d sess., S. Doc. 422 (Washington, D.C.: Government Printing Office, 1910).
68. *Chicago Record-Herald,* Nov. 3, 1909.
69. Ibid., July 5, 1909. See also *Chicago Tribune, Chicago Examiner, Chicago Chronicle,* and *Chicago Post,* July 5, 1909.
70. Moody, *Wacker's Manual,* ii.
71. Ibid., 81.
72. Hines, *Burnham of Chicago,* 324, 332.

73. Letter from the Board of the University of Chicago Settlement to the Chicago Plan Commission, Oct. 5, 1910, University of Chicago Settlement Board Meeting Minutes, Feb. 1896–Oct. 1910, Mary McDowell Papers, Chicago Historical Society, Special Collections.

74. For further discussion of John Fitzpatrick's objections to the Chicago Plan, see *Chicago Record-Herald* and *Chicago Tribune,* Nov. 5, 1909. For his part in the campaign for municipal charter reform, see *Chicago Federation of Labor Minutes,* July 21, 1907, Chicago Historical Society; Maureen A. Flanagan, *Charter Reform in Chicago* (Carbondale: Southern Illinois University Press, 1987), 117–40; and Georg Leidenberger, "Working-Class Progressivism and the Politics of Transportation in Chicago, 1895–1907" (Ph.D. diss., University of North Carolina, 1995), 40–50.

75. *Chicago Record-Herald,* Nov. 5, 1909.

76. For further discussion of the competing responses to the Burnham Plan, see Bluestone, *Constructing Chicago,* 198–204; *Boyer, Urban Masses,* 274–76; Hines, *Burnham of Chicago,* 332–34; Horowitz, *Culture and the City,* 221–27; McCarthy, "Chicago Businessmen," 254–56; and Schaffer, "Fabric of City Life," xi–xiii.

CHAPTER FIVE

1. *Chicago Tribune,* Mar. 18, 1910, and *Chicago Record-Herald,* Mar. 18, 1910. For further discussion of the building of Comiskey Park, see Michael Benson, *Ballparks of North America: A Comprehensive Historical Reference to Baseball Grounds, Yards, and Stadiums, 1845 to Present* (Jefferson, N.C.: McFarland, 1989), 88–93; Frank Budreck, *Goodbye Old Friend: A Pictorial Essay on the Final Season at Old Comiskey Park* (Lyons, Ill.: Aland, 1992), 14; Douglas Bukowski, *Baseball Palace of the World: The Last Year of Comiskey Park* (Chicago: Lyceum Books, 1992), 24–25; Richard Lindberg, "Through the Years: A Journey through Comiskey Park's Colorful History from 1910 to 1990," in *Through the Years* (Chicago: Sherman Media, 1990), 4–5; Philip Lowry, *Green Cathedrals: The Ultimate Celebration of 271 Major League and Negro League Ballparks Past and Present* (Reading, Mass.: Addison-Wesley, 1992), 128–31; Lowell Reidenbaugh, *Take Me out to the Ball Park* (St. Louis: Sporting News, 1987); and Lawrence S. Ritter, *Lost Ballparks: A Celebration of Baseball's Legendary Fields* (New York: Penguin Books, 1992), 29–30.

2. For further discussion of the relation between mass amusement and working-class culture, see Paul Boyer, *Urban Masses and Moral Order in America, 1820–1920* (Cambridge: Harvard University Press, 1978); John F. Kasson, *Amusing the Million: Coney Island at the Turn*

of the Century (New York: Hill and Wang, 1978); Kasson, *Rudeness and Civility: Manners in Nineteenth Century Urban America* (New York: W. W. Norton, 1990); and Lawrence Levine, *Highbrow/Lowbrow: The Emergence of Cultural Hierarchy in America* (Cambridge: Harvard University Press, 1988).

3. David Nasaw, *Going Out: The Rise and Fall of Public Amusements* (New York: Basic Books, 1993); Kathy Peiss, *Cheap Amusements: Working Women and Leisure in Turn-of-the Century New York* (Philadelphia: Temple University Press, 1986), 6; and Roy Rosenzweig, *Eight Hours for What We Will: Workers and Leisure in an Industrial City, 1870–1920* (Cambridge: Cambridge University Press, 1983). See also Lewis Erenberg, *Steppin' Out: New York Nightlife and the Transformation of American Culture, 1890–1930* (Westport, Conn.: Greenwood Press, 1981).

4. As several cultural historians have argued, mass culture helped European immigrants overcome ethnic differences and, in the space of the theater, amusement park, and baseball park, created a shared culture of "whiteness." See Shelley Fisher Fishkin, "Interrogating 'Whiteness,' Complicating 'Blackness': Remapping American Culture," *American Quarterly* 47 (Sept. 1995): 428–66; George Lipsitz, "The Possessive Investment in Whiteness: Racialized Social Democracy and the 'White' Problem in American Studies," *American Quarterly* 47 (Sept. 1995): 369–87; Eric Lott, *Love and Theft: Blackface Minstrelsy and the American Working Class* (New York: Oxford University Press, 1993); Nasaw, *Going Out*, especially 47–61; and Michael Rogin, *Blackface, White Noise: Jewish Immigrants in the Hollywood Melting Pot* (Berkeley: University of California Press, 1996). David R. Roediger discusses the role of labor in racializing European ethnics as "white" in *The Wages of Whiteness: Race and the Making of the American Working Class* (London: Verso, 1991).

5. See Louise de Koven Bowen, *Safeguards for City Youth at Work and at Play* (New York: Macmillan, 1914), 4.

6. Vice Commission of Chicago, *The Social Evil in Chicago: A Study of Existing Conditions with Recommendations of the Vice Commission of Chicago* (Chicago: Gunthorp-Warren, 1911), 202, 204.

7. Theodore Dreiser, *Sister Carrie* (1900; New York: Dell, 1959). For further discussion of working-class women's culture in the city, see Edith Abbott, *Women in Industry* (New York; D. Appleton, 1910); Susan Porter Benson, *Counter Cultures: Saleswomen, Managers, and Customers in American Department Stores, 1890–1940* (Urbana: University of Illinois Press, 1986); Angel Kwolek-Folland, *Engendering Business: Men and Women in the Corporate Office, 1870–1930* (Baltimore: Johns Hopkins University Press, 1994); William Leach, *Land of Desire: Merchants, Power, and the Rise of a New American Culture* (New York: Vintage Books, 1993) 91–11; Joanne J. Meyerowitz, *Women Adrift: Independent Wage Earners in Chicago, 1880–1930* (Chicago: University of Chicago Press, 1988); and Peiss, *Cheap Amusements.*

8. Bowen, *Safeguards for City Youth*, 45.

9. Kathy Peiss argues that working women carefully negotiated their public roles and opened up a range of exchanges between themselves and male suitors. In the process, they reshaped ideas about female sexuality and its place in the public life of the city. See Peiss, *Cheap Amusements,* 3–10.
10. Jane Addams, *The Spirit of Youth and the City Streets* (New York: Macmillan, 1909), 95–96.
11. Benjamin McArthur, "Parks, Playgrounds, and Progressivism," in *A Breath of Fresh Air: Chicago's Neighborhood Parks of the Progressive Reform Era, 1900–1925* (Chicago: Chicago Park District, 1989), 13. For more on the play movement, see Boyer, *Urban Masses;* Dominick Cavallo, *Muscles and Morals: Organized Playgrounds and Urban Reform, 1880–1920* (Philadelphia: University of Pennsylvania Press, 1981); Cary Goodman, *Choosing Sides: Playground and Street Life on the Lower East Side* (New York: Schocken Books, 1979); Elizabeth Halsey, *Development of Public Recreation in Metropolitan Chicago* (Chicago: Chicago Recreation Commission, 1940), 8, 115; and Steven A. Riess, *City Games: The Evolution of American Urban Society and the Rise of Sports* (Urbana: University of Illinois Press, 1989), 132–68. See also Benjamin McArthur, "The Chicago Playground Movement: A Neglected Feature of Social Justice," *Social Science Review* 49 (Sept. 1975): 376–95, esp. 379.
12. Daniel T. Rodgers, *The Work Ethic in Industrial America, 1850–1920* (Chicago: University of Chicago Press, 1978), 102.
13. Theodore Roosevelt, "The Value of an Athletic Training," *Harper's Weekly* 27 (Dec. 23, 1893): 35–68.
14. See Morris Cohen, "Baseball," *Dial,* July 26, 1919, 57, for a discussion of William James's ideas on the "moral equivalent of war" and their relation to sports.
15. Addams, *Spirit of Youth,* 147.
16. See Cavallo's discussion of progressive theories of play in *Muscles and Morals,* 9, 55–70. Allen Guttmann supports Cavallo's contention that supervised play was not merely an example of bourgeois social control and takes issue with Cary Goodman's argument that the playground movement reflected the hegemony of middle-class aspirations. See Allen Guttmann, *A Whole New Ball Game: An Interpretation of American Sports* (Chapel Hill: University of North Carolina Press, 1988), 88–89. See also David A. Karp, Gregory P. Stone, and William C. Yoels, *Being Urban: A Sociology of City Life* (New York: Praeger, 1991), 200, for a discussion of the play movement as a contest for the urban space and leisure time of immigrant children.
17. Shailer Matthews, quoted in John S. Watterson, "Chicago's City Championship: Northwestern University versus the University of Chicago, 1892–1905," *Chicago History* 11, no. 3 (Fall–Winter 1982): 161–74, quotation on 172.

18. Quoted in Steven A. Riess, *Touching Base: Professional Baseball and American Culture in the Progressive Era* (Westport, CT: Greenwood Press, 1980), 25.
19. Henry Curtis, *The Practical Conduct of Play* (New York: Macmillan, 1915), 212.
20. For further discussion of ethnic athletic clubs and their role in creating a "bachelor subculture," see Melvin L. Adelman, *A Sporting Time: New York City and the Rise of Modern Athletics, 1820–1870* (Urbana: University of Illinois Press, 1990), 224; Gerald R. Gems, *Windy City Wars: Labor, Leisure and Sport in the Making of Chicago* (Lanham, Md.: Scarecrow Press, 1997), 25–30; Elliot J. Gorn and Warren Goldstein, *A Brief History of American Sports* (New York: Hill and Wang, 1993), 14, 70–72; Benjamin G. Roder, *American Sports: From the Age of Folk Games to the Age of Spectators* (Englewood Cliffs, N.J.: Prentice-Hall, 1983), 97–98; Benjamin G. Rader, "The Quest for Subcommunities and the Rise of American Sport," in *The Sporting Image: Readings in American Sport History,* ed. Paul J. Zingg (Lanham, Md.: University Press of America, 1988); and Riess, *City Games,* 16, 22–25. My discussion of changing views of "manliness" is largely informed by Gorn and Goldstein, *Brief History,* 80. See also Mary Ann Clawson, *Constructing Brotherhood: Class, Gender, and Fraternalism* (Princeton: Princeton University Press, 1989), chap. 4.
21. For further discussion of gender and athletics, see Susan K. Cahn, *Coming on Strong: Gender and Sexuality in Twentieth-Century Women's Sport* (New York: Free Press, 1994), esp. chaps 1–3; George Eisen, "Sport, Recreation and Gender: Jewish Immigrant Women in Turn-of-the-Century America (1880–1920)," *Journal of Sport History* 18 (Spring 1991): 103–20; Allen Guttmann, *Women's Sports: A History* (New York: Columbia University Press, 1991); Helen Lenskyj, *Out of Bounds: Women, Sport, and Sexuality* (Toronto: Women's Press, 1986); Michael Messner and Don Sabo, eds., *Sport, Men, and the Gender Order: Critical Feminist Perspectives* (Champaign, Ill.: Human Kinetics, 1990); Gregory Kent Stanley, *The Rise and Fall of the Sportswoman: Women's Health, Fitness, and Athletics, 1860–1940* (New York: Peter Lang, 1996); Stephanie L. Twin, *Out of the Bleachers: Writing on Women and Sport* (Old Westbury, N.Y.: Feminist Press, 1979); Stephanie L. Twin, "Women and Sport," in *Sport in America: New Historical Perspectives,* ed. Donald Spivey (Westport, Conn.: Greenwood Press, 1985), 193–217; and Patricia A. Vertinsky, *The Eternally Wounded Woman: Women, Doctors, and Exercise in the Late Nineteenth Century* (Manchester: Manchester University Press, 1990).
22. For general histories of professional baseball, see Adelman, *Sporting Time;* Charles C. Alexander, *Our Game: An American Baseball History* (New York: Henry Holt, 1991); Warren Goldstein, *Playing for Keeps: A History of Early Baseball* (Ithaca: Cornell University Press, 1989); Allen Guttmann, *From Ritual to Record: The Nature of Modern Sports* (New York: Columbia University Press, 1978); Donald Honig, *Baseball America: The Heroes of the Game and*

the Times of Their Glory (New York: Macmillan, 1985); Riess, *Touching Base;* Harold Seymour, *Baseball* vol. 1, *The Early Years* (New York: Oxford University Press, 1960), and Harold Seymour, *Baseball,* vol. 2, *The Golden Age* (New York: Oxford University Press, 1971); David Q. Voigt, *American Baseball,* vol. 1, *From Gentlemen's Sport to the Commissioner System* (Norman: University of Oklahoma Press, 1966), and David Q. Voigt, *American Baseball,* vol. 2, *From the Commissioners to the Continental Expansion* (Norman: University of Oklahoma Press, 1970); G. Edward White, *Creating the National Pastime: Baseball Transforms Itself* (Princeton: Princeton University Press, 1996); and Joel Zoss and John Bowman, *Diamonds in the Rough: The Untold History of Baseball* (New York: Contemporary Books, 1996).

23. As Allen Guttmann points out, baseball's attraction "lies in its primitive-pastoral elements and simultaneously in its extraordinary modernity, in its closeness to the seasonal rhythms of nature and, at the same time, in the rarefied realm of numbers." Guttmann, *From Ritual to Record,* 113–14. For further discussion of industrial work culture, see Herbert G. Gutman, *Work, Culture, and Society in Industrializing America* (New York: Vintage Books, 1976); David Montgomery, "The New Unionism and the Transformation of Workers' Consciousness in America: 1909–1922," *Journal of Social History* 7 (Summer 1974): 511; and E. P. Thompson, "Time, Work-Discipline, and Industrial Capitalism," *Past and Present* 38 (Dec. 1967): 56–97. Warren Goldstein argues that baseball has followed two paths throughout its history. Baseball's relationship with money shapes what Goldstein refers to as the "linear" history of the game, while its emotional and mythic element lends itself to a cyclical history, defined by attempts to recreate a "golden age." I agree with this assessment but would go further and argue that these two elements of baseball history are integrally related. During periods when labor and money issues became more prominent, baseball proponents were more likely to construct baseball as a pastoral, preindustrial activity removed from the world of the marketplace. See Goldstein, *Playing for Keeps,* 70.

24. Quoted in Goldstein, *Playing for Keeps,* 11.

25. Ibid. The Doubleday story is myth. In 1839 Doubleday was about twenty years old and was attending West Point, a long way from Cooperstown. Most scholars agree that baseball evolved from other games that were British in origin, including cricket, rounders, and town ball. Until recently most scholars also agreed that the first organized baseball game took place in 1846 at the Elysian Fields in Hoboken, New Jersey, and was played not by farmers but by small shopkeepers and clerks.

In 2001, a librarian at New York University came across two newspaper references to organized baseball from an even earlier period. Both articles appeared in New York City newspapers in 1823; an article in the *National Advocate* talked about a game being played in what is today Greenwich Village. The writer stated, "Any person fond of witnessing this game may avail himself of seeing it played with consummate skill and wonderful dexterity. . . . it is innocent amusement, and healthy exercise, attended with but little expense, and has no demoralizing tendency." The article, along with another like it, suggests that baseball was familiar to many New Yorkers as early as the 1820s. See *New York Times,* July 8, 2001.

26. Peter Levine, *A. G. Spalding and the Rise of Baseball: The Promise of American Sport* (New York: Oxford University Press, 1985), xiv, 14. Levine compares Spalding to John D. Rockefeller and Frederick Winslow Taylor.

27. *Spalding's Handbook of Sporting Rules and Training, Containing Full and Authentic Codes of Rules Governing All Popular Games and Sports* (New York: A. G. Spalding, 1886).

28. *Constitution and Playing Rules of the National League of Professional Base Ball Clubs* (1876; Chicago: A. G. Spalding, 1886), 2–3, 6–8, 13–18. See also Honig, *Baseball America,* 10–11; Levine, *Spalding,* 21; Riess, *City Games,* 194–96; Seymour, *Baseball: The Early Years,* chap. 7; and Voigt, *American Baseball,* vol. 1, chap. 1.

29. For further discussion of the relation between spatial arrangements, the division of labor, and the workplace, see Harry Braverman, *Labor and Monopoly Capital: The Degradation of Work in the Twentieth Century* (New York: Monthly Review Press, 1974), 304–10; Alfred D. Chandler Jr., *The Visible Hand: The Managerial Revolution in American Business* (Cambridge, Mass.: Belknap Press, 1977), 6–12, 274–81; David M. Gordon et al., *Segmented Work, Divided Workers: The Historical Transformation of Labor in the United States* (Cambridge: Cambridge University Press, 1982), 151–52; Gutman, *Work, Culture, and Society,* esp. chap. 1; Angel Kwollek-Folland, *Engendering Business: Men and Women in the Corporate Office, 1870–1930* (Baltimore: Johns Hopkins University Press, 1994), 94–128; David Montgomery, *Workers' Control in America: Studies in the History of Work, Technology, and Labor Struggles* (Cambridge: Cambridge University Press, 1979), 44–46; David F. Noble, *America by Design: Science, Technology, and the Rise of Corporate Capitalism* (New York: Alfred A. Knopf, 1979), 264–320; Sharon Hartman Strom, *Beyond the Typewriter: Gender, Class, and the Origins of Modern American Office Work, 1900–1930* (Urbana: University of Illinois Press, 1992), 235; Thompson, "Time, Work-Discipline, and Industrial Capitalism"; and Alan Trachtenberg, *The Incorporation of America: Culture and Society in the Gilded Age* (New York: Hill and Wang, 1982).

30. *Constitution and Playing Rules,* 8–13. See also Burton J. Bledstein, *The Culture of Professionalism: The Middle Class and the Development of Higher Education in America* (New York: W. W. Norton, 1976), 81–85.

31. Nominating Committee, National Association of Base Ball Players (1867), quoted in Robert Peterson, *Only the Ball Was White: A History of Legendary Black Players and All-Black Professional Teams before Black Men Played in the Major Leagues* (New York: McGraw-Hill, 1984), 16.
32. For further discussion of African Americans in baseball, see Phil Dixon with Patrick J. Hannigan, *The Negro Baseball Leagues, 1867–1955: A Photographic History* (Mattituck, N.Y.: Amereon House, 1992); David Falkner, *Great Time Coming: The Life of Jackie Robinson from Baseball to Birmingham* (New York: Simon and Schuster, 1995); John B. Holway, *Blackball Stars: Negro League Pioneers* (Westport, Conn.: Meckler Books, 1988); John B. Holway, *Black Diamonds: Life in the Negro Leagues from the Men Who Lived It* (Westport, Conn.: Meckler Books, 1989); Peterson, *Only the Ball;* Mark Ribowsky, *A Complete History of the Negro Leagues, 1884–1955* (Secaucus, N.J.: Carol, 1995); Mark Ribowsky, *The Power and the Darkness: The Life of Josh Gibson in the Shadows of the Game* (New York: Simon and Schuster, 1996); Harold Seymour, *Baseball: The People's Game* (New York: Oxford University Press, 1990), 531–94; Sol White, *Sol White's History of Colored Base Ball, with Other Documents of the Early Black Game, 1886–1936* (Lincoln: University of Nebraska Press, 1995); and Jules Tygiel, *Baseball's Great Experiment: Jackie Robinson and His Legacy* (New York: Oxford University Press, 1983).
33. *Brooklyn Daily Union,* Oct. 1867, quoted in Peterson, *Only the Ball,* 17.
34. For further discussion of the role of sport in African American communities, see James R. Grossman, *Land of Hope: Chicago, Black Southerners, and the Great Migration* (Chicago: University of Chicago Press, 1989), 86–90; Earl Lewis, *In Their Own Interests: Race, Class, and Power in Twentieth-Century Norfolk, Virginia* (Berkeley: University of California Press, 1991), 90–96; and Rob Ruck, *Sandlot Seasons: Sport in Black Pittsburgh* (Urbana: University of Illinois Press, 1987), esp. 37.
35. Henry Chadwick, *The Game of Baseball: How to Learn It, How to Play It, and How to Teach It* (New York: George Munro, 1868), quoted in Levine, *Spalding,* 82.
36. *Constitution and Playing Rules,* 16, sec. 39; Gorn and Goldstein, *Brief History,* 209; Goldstein, *Playing for Keeps,* 35; Riess, *Touching Base,* 122; Seymour, *Baseball: The Early Years,* 35–59; and Voigt, *American Baseball,* 1:3–34.
37. *Sporting News,* Jan. 22, 1887, quoted in Levine, *Spalding,* 43.
38. Spalding, quoted in Levine, *Spalding,* 42.
39. Riess, *City Games,* 196.
40. *Constitution and Playing Rules,* 8–13; Paul Douglas, *Real Wages in the United States, 1890–1926* (Boston: Houghton-Mifflin, 1930), 112–14; Clarence D. Long, *Wages and Earnings in the United States, 1860–1890* (Princeton: Princeton University Press, 1960), 4; and Riess, *Touching Base,* 33.

41. Riess, *City Games,* 70, 196; Riess, *Touching Base,* 31–34; Seymour, *Baseball: The Early Years,* chap. 13; and Voigt, *American Baseball,* 1:121–30.
42. Seymour, *Baseball: The Early Years,* chap. 13.
43. Warren Brown, *The Chicago White Sox* (New York: G. P. Putnam's Sons, 1952), 1. See also G. W. Axelson, *"Commy": The Life Story of Charles A. Comiskey* (Chicago: Reilly and Lee, 1919), 33–35; and Judith Helm, "Comiskey Family Album," in *Through the Years,* 25–30, 26. See also Richard C. Lindberg, *The White Sox Encyclopedia* (Philadelphia: Temple University Press, 1997).
44. Brown, *Chicago White Sox,* 2.
45. Axelson, *"Commy,"* 73; Brown, *Chicago White Sox,* 7–11; Helm, "Comiskey Family Album," 26; and Riess, *Touching Base,* 156–57.
46. John Montgomery Ward, "The Brotherhood of Professional Base Ball Players' Manifesto" (1889), quoted in Anthony J. Connor, *Baseball for the Love of It: Hall of Famers Tell It Like It Was* (New York: Macmillan, 1982), 216.
47. Riess, *Touching Base,* 156–57; Seymour, *Baseball: The Early Years,* 267–70; and Voigt, *American Baseball,* 1:233–34. The difficulty of challenging the myth of baseball was made clear in 1915, when the Federal League sued the National and American Leagues for violating the Sherman Anti-Trust Act. Owners of Federal League teams initiated the lawsuit after they were unable to compete effectively for players against the two big leagues. They argued that the reserve clause barred fair competition in the marketplace. Judge Kenesaw Mountain Landis presided over the hearing but never issued a verdict because he felt it would forever alter the history of baseball. When the case reached the Supreme Court, Justice Oliver Wendell Holmes argued that baseball leagues were not sources of interstate commerce and therefore could not have violated antitrust laws. See Robert F. Burk, *Never Just a Game: Players, Owners, and American Baseball to 1920* (Chapel Hill: University of North Carolina Press, 1994), 207–9; Guttmann, *Whole New Ball Game,* 65–69; Lee Lowenfish, *Imperfect Diamond: The Story of Baseball's Reserve System and the Men Who Fought to Change It* (New York: Stein and Day, 1980), 88–90; Seymour, *Baseball: The Golden Age,* 212, 230–34; and Voigt, *American Baseball,* 2:21, 81.
48. For licensing fees and taxes on ballparks, see *Proceedings of the Chicago City Council,* Apr. 2, 1919, 1947; Dec. 29, 1919, 1689; and Jan. 4, 1920, 1897. Comiskey claimed that he paid all the police officers working in the park. See *Chicago Daily News,* Oct. 4, 1919. See also Riess, *City Games,* 199, and Riess, *Touching Base,* 59–61, 73–75. Levine points out that Spalding initiated these connections between ball club owners in Chicago and local politicians. Spalding offered free passes to local politicians, negotiated streetcar schedules with the West Division Rail Company, and encouraged White Stockings investor

John R. Walsh, owner of the *Chicago Herald,* to use press coverage to attract fans to the game. See Levine, *Spalding,* 44. Of course the Brooklyn National League team was the most famous for these types of arrangements. The team was owned by a traction magnate who moved his team to Brownsville, an area served by his trolley line. When Charles Ebbets bought the team in 1898, he moved the team back to Brooklyn with the help of other local traction firms. Ebbets Field's location at the crossing of numerous trolley lines earned Brooklyn fans the moniker "trolley dodgers," hence the team name "the Dodgers." See Robert F. Bluthardt, "Fenway Park and the Golden Age of the Baseball Park, 1909–1915," *Journal of Popular Culture* 21 (Summer 1987): 43–52, esp. 43; Michael Gershman, *Diamonds: The Evolution of the Ballpark* (Boston: Houghton Mifflin, 1993), 110–15; Riess, *City Games,* 208–16; and Riess, *Touching Base,* 70–71, 80. For a discussion of the politics and business of baseball in Philadelphia, see Bruce Kuklick, *To Every Thing a Season: Shibe Park and Urban Philadelphia, 1909–1976* (Princeton: Princeton University Press, 1991), 13–22, 95–111.

49. Riess, *City Games,* 197; Riess, *Touching Base,* 69–70; Seymour, *Baseball: The Middle Years,* 68–72; and Voigt, *American Baseball,* 2:108–9.
50. Quoted in Axelson, *"Commy,"* 315, 318. I thank Dan Nathan for bringing this quotation to my attention.
51. For further discussion of early Chicago ballparks, see Benson, *Ballparks,* 79–88; *Chicago Tribune,* June 25, 1884; "The Chicago Base-Ball Grounds," *Harper's Weekly* 27 (May 12, 1883): 200; Gershman, *Diamonds,* 19–34, 45, 54; Levine, *Spalding,* 37–47; Lowry, *Green Cathedrals,* 126–31; Riess, *City Games,* 217; Riess, *Touching Base,* 86; and *Sporting News,* Jan. 9, 1892.
52. Axelson, *"Commy,"* 149.
53. Everett Julian Allgood, "The Development of Baseball Architecture in Twentieth Century America" (M.A. thesis, Emory University, 1989), 6–7; Benson, *Ballparks,* 84; and Bill Shannon and George Kalinsky, *The Ballparks* (New York: Hawthorn Books, 1975), 11.
54. Tommy Leach, in Lawrence S. Ritter, *The Glory of Their Times: The Story of the Early Days of Baseball Told by the Men Who Played It* (New York: Macmillan, 1966), 26–27.
55. Edward Brundage, *The Chicago Code of 1911* (Chicago: Callahan, 1911), 7–10; *Chicago Tribune,* Dec. 24, 1910; Riess, *City Games,* 217; and Riess, *Touching Base,* 95–96.
56. Barney Dreyfuss, quoted in Bluthardt, "Fenway Park," 44.
57. Bluthardt, "Fenway Park," 44–45; Gershman, *Diamonds,* 85–104; Kuklick, *To Every Thing a Season,* 19–29.
58. "Ancient Permit File Index," Department of Inspectional Services, Permit B3833, Feb. 9, 1950, book 61, 79, City Hall, Chicago, Illinois; *Chicago Tribune,* July 2, 1910; *Chicago Record-*

Herald, July 2, 1910: George W. Hilton, "Comiskey Park," *Baseball Historical Review,* 1981, 1–8, esp. 1; and Lindberg, "Through the Years," 5–11.

59. In a similar move of fiscal conservatism, Comiskey decided to incorporate support pillars into the grandstand design, producing seats with obstructed views. Vitzhum's plan to produce a cantilevered grandstand free of posts could have added as much as $350,000 to the cost of the park. For further discussion of the design of Comiskey, see Budreck, *Goodbye Old Friend,* 14, 19, 30; Bukowski, *Baseball Palace,* 24–25, 152, 163; Wayne Guskind, "The Stadium as Civic Architecture" (M.A. thesis, Georgia Institute of Technology, 1984), 20–24; Hilton, "Comiskey Park," 2; Brian James Nielson, "Dialogue with the City: The Evolution of Baseball Parks," *Landscape* 29 (1986): 39–47 45; John Pastier, "The Business of Baseball," *Inland Architect* (Jan.–Feb. 1989), 56–62, 59; and Ritter, *Lost Ballparks,* 30.

60. Bukowski, *Baseball Palace,* 158; *Rascher's Atlas of North Half of Hyde Park* (1890), Chicago Historical Society Library; Riess, *Touching Base,* 97; *Sanborn Fire Insurance Atlas* (1895, corrected to 1909), Chicago Historical Society Library.

61. Homer Hoyt, *One Hundred Years of Land Values in Chicago, 1830–1930* (Chicago: University of Chicago Press, 1933), 148–49, 206, 231, 247, 301; *Olcott's Land Values Blue Book of Chicago, 1909–1930* (Chicago: G. C. Olcott, 1909–1930), 101; and Riess, *Touching Base,* 98.

62. Benson, *Ballparks,* 88; Bukowski, *Baseball Palace,* 17; Lindberg, "Through the Years," 3; and Ritter, *Lost Ballparks,* 30–31.

63. Ibid.

64. *Chicago Record-Herald,* July 2, 1910.

65. *Chicago Tribune,* July 2, 1910.

66. *Chicago Record-Herald,* July 2, 1910. See also Bluthardt, "Fenway Park," 48, and Riess, *City Games,* 223 for further discussion of crowd control.

67. Hilton, "Comiskey Park," 3.

68. Riess, *City Games,* 223.

69. *Chicago Defender,* June 17, 1911.

70. Brown, *Chicago White Sox,* 102–3; Jerry Klinkowitz, ed., *Writing Baseball* (Urbana: University of Illinois Press, 1991); Ring Lardner, *You Know Me Al* (1914; New York: Charles Scribner's Sons, 1960); and Lindberg, "Through the Years," 6.

71. James T. Farrell, *My Baseball Diary* (New York: A. S. Barnes, 1957), 8.

72. Ibid., 60.

73. Edward B. Moss, "The Fan and His Ways," *Harper's Weekly* 54 (June 11, 1910): 13. Also quoted in Riess, *Touching Base,* 24. Yet this public space was mediated by owners seeking

to promote a particular vision of baseball that reflected their conception of what would sell. As Warren Goldstein points out, "The democracy of the national pastime could be celebrated only by those who did not play the game and therefore *could* experience the ballpark exclusively as an arena of play." Goldstein, *Playing for Keeps,* 149.

74. *Denni Hlasatel,* Sept. 16, 1911; and *Svornost,* Apr. 8, 1890, in *Chicago Foreign Language Press Survey,* Chicago Public Library Omnibus Project (Chicago: The Project, 1942). See also Steven S. Riess, "Ethnic Sports," in *Ethnic Chicago: A Multicultural Reader,* ed. Melvin G. Holli and Peter d'A. Jones (Grand Rapids, Mich.: William B. Eerdmans, 1995), 529–56, 539–43, and Riess, *Touching Base,* 36–37, 189–91.
75. Riess, *Touching Base,* 189–91; and Nicholas Dawidoff, *The Catcher Was a Spy: The Mysterious Life of Moe Berg* (New York: Vintage Books, 1994), 61.
76. Farrell, *Baseball Diary,* 47.
77. From Charles S. Johnson, "Chicago Study, Migration Interviews," quoted in Grossman, *Land of Hope,* 89.
78. Donald Spivey, *Union and the Black Musician: the Narrative of William Everett Samuels and Chicago Local 208* (Boston: University Press of America, 1984), 21–22.
79. St. Clair Drake and Horace R. Cayton, *Black Metropolis: A Study of Negro Life in a Northern City,* vol. 1 (New York: Harcourt, Brace, 1945), 102. See also *Chicago Defender,* July 2, 1910; May 20, 1911; Aug. 5, 1911.
80. For further discussion of baseball and the construction of whiteness, see Nasaw, *Going Out,* 100; Peterson, *Only the Ball,* 14–15; and Riess, *City Games,* 103.
81. In *Saying It's So: A Cultural History of the Black Sox Scandal* (Urbana: University of Illinois Press, 2003), 23–28, historian Daniel A. Nathan discusses the origins of the expression "Black Sox." One of the first times it appeared in print was in a headline in the *Chicago Herald and Examiner* on October 1, 1920: "Here's Hope for Black Sox Let 'Em Grow Beards and Change Names." By 1921, newspapers throughout the nation employed the phrase when referring to the scandal. Nathan points out that the use of blackness as a metaphor for the scandal drew on pejorative connotations of the word "black" as well as notions of contamination and dirtiness.
82. For further discussion of the Black Sox scandal, see Eliot Asinof, *Eight Men Out: The Black Sox and the 1919 World Series* (New York: Henry Holt, 1963); Burk, *Never Just a Game,* 232–35; Harvey Frommer, *Shoeless Joe and Ragtime Baseball* (Dallas: Taylor, 1992), Robert I. Goler, "Black Sox," *Chicago History* 17 (Fall and Winter 1988–89): 42–69; Nathan, *Saying It's So;* Riess, *Touching Base,* 67–73; and Harold Seymour, *Baseball: The Golden Years,* 294–339.

83. Recent films, including *Eight Men Out* (based on the Asinoff book) and *Field of Dreams,* offer more sympathetic accounts of the role of the players in the Black Sox scandal. It is striking how often the story of the scandal has been retold in American popular culture. John Sayles's *Eight Men Out* also explores how labor issues shaped the unfolding scandal. Daniel Nathan analyzes cultural representations of the scandal—in newspapers, novels, and film—and suggests how its reappearance and shifting mythology reflect broader changes in American ideas of innocence and nostalgia. See Nathan, *Saying It's So.*
84. See Farrell, *My Baseball Diary,* 106, for a slightly different version of the story.
85. Morris Cohen, "Baseball," *Dial,* July 26, 1919, 57.
86. *New York Times,* Oct. 9, 1919.
87. Cohen, "Baseball," 57.
88. Joe Jackson went to work for a subsidiary of Bethlehem Steel and played on the company team. Burk, *Never Just a Game,* 219; Frommer, *Shoeless Joe,* 68–69, 79–84; Rob Ruck, *Sandlot Seasons: Sport in Black Pittsburgh* (Urbana: University of Illinois Press, 1987), 42; and Seymour, *Golden Age,* 244–47.
89. See Burk, *Never Just a Game,* 220–21; Lowenfish, *Imperfect Diamond,* 96; and Seymour, *Baseball: The Golden Age,* 251–52.
90. Joe Jackson earned $6,000 a year, while Buck Weaver, Chick Gandil, and Happy Felsch each earned $4,000. Eddie Cicotte, the White Sox star pitcher, earned $5,500 even though many believed he was the best pitcher in the league after Walter Johnson. In 1917, when the White Sox won the World Series, Charles Comiskey promised Cicotte a $10,000 bonus if he won thirty games. When Cicotte was close to achieving that mark, Comiskey benched him so he came up short. See Asinof, *Eight Men Out,* 15–20; Burk, *Never Just a Game,* 233; Frommer, *Shoeless Joe,* 86; and Lowenfish, *Imperfect Diamond,* 98–99. Frommer follows Asinof's lead by suggesting that the White Sox were one of the lowest-paid teams in 1919. Burk's appendix for player salaries, however, illustrates that the White Sox in general were earning salaries commensurate with those paid other teams, though the other teams did not have the same earning power in gate receipts. See Burk, *Never Just a Game,* appendix figs. 1 and 5, 243, 247.
91. The *Chicago Daily News* reported, "Before the World Series it was not thought possible the Cincinnati Reds could win from the Chicago White Sox. . . . The Reds were not given a ghost of a chance, because it was thought they won in an inferior league and therefore were greatly inferior to the tribe piloted by Manager Kid Gleason. Some even said it was a crime to pit the Reds against the South Siders." *Chicago Daily News,* Oct. 10, 1919.

92. An editorial in *Baseball Magazine* argued, "If a man really knows so little about baseball that he believes the game is or can be fixed, he should keep his mouth shut in the presence of intelligent people." *Baseball Magazine,* Nov. 1919, quoted in Frommer, *Shoeless Joe,* 119.
93. *Chicago Daily News,* Oct. 11, 1919. The Reds were quick to point to the legitimacy of their title, too. Reds manager Pat Moran argued, "The best team won the series, and don't you forget it." *Chicago Herald Examiner,* Oct. 1, 1920.
94. See *Chicago Tribune, Chicago Herald and Examiner,* and *New York Times,* Sept. 8, 1920. See also Asinof, *Eight Men Out,* 149–60; Burk, *Never Just a Game,* 231–33; Frommer, *Shoeless Joe,* 130–34; and Seymour, *Baseball: The Golden Age,* 300–305, 384–85.
95. See above, as well as the *Chicago Tribune, Chicago Herald and Examiner, Chicago Record-Herald,* and *New York Times,* Sept. 29, 1920.
96. "The Baseball Scandal," *Nation,* Oct. 13, 1920, 395.
97. Walter Camp, "The Truth about Baseball," *North American Review* 213 (Apr. 1921): 483.
98. Camp, "Truth," 487; Hugh Fullerton, "Baseball—the Sport and the Business," *American Review of Reviews* 61 (Apr. 6, 1920): 420.
99. *Philadelphia Bulletin,* quoted in Frommer, *Shoeless Joe,* 154.
100. *Chicago Tribune, Chicago Daily News,* and *New York Times,* Oct. 1, 1920. Actually, Comiskey did not divide the whole difference among the ten players, for he kept close to $500 for himself. Moreover, the total players' share of the receipts from the 1919 series was $260,249.66, while the owners' share was $389,822.94. See *New York Times,* Oct. 10, 1919. Comiskey also offered large bonuses and salaries to the suspected players before the 1920 season, suggesting that he was more concerned with fielding a winning team than with punishing his "disloyal" players. See Chicago White Sox Contracts, White Sox Collection, Chicago Historical Society, Special Collections.
101. See the grand jury testimony of Joe Jackson, Sept. 28, 1920, Joe Jackson Papers, Chicago Historical Society, Special Collections; *Chicago Tribune* and *New York Times,* Aug. 3, 1920; Asinof, *Eight Men Out,* 22–31; Burk, *Never Just a Game,* 232; Frommer, *Shoeless Joe,* 168–70; and Goler, *Black Sox,* 60.
102. See *Chicago Tribune* and *New York Times,* Oct. 2, 1920; Asinof, *Eight Men Out,* 240–41; and Frommer, *Shoeless Joe,* 159–70.
103. "The Gamblers and the Ballplayers," *Outlook* 126 (Oct. 13, 1920): 267. The article also argues that if baseball is to be "kept clean" in the future, it must be run by those "interested in baseball as a sport, and not in a business way." It is the taint of commercialism associated with the game that needs to be lessened if baseball is to recover and regain its purity in the minds of fans.

104. *Grand Rapids Herald* article, cited in "The Flaw in the Diamond," *Literary Digest* 67 (Oct. 9, 1920): 13.
105. J. G. Taylor Spink, *Sporting News,* Oct. 1919; *Dearborn Independent,* Aug. 3, 1921; *Sporting News,* Aug. 1921, all cited in Asinof, *Eight Men Out,* 136.
106. *New York Times,* Aug. 3, 1921.
107. The *Kansas City Times* quotation is cited in "The Flaw in the Diamond," *Literary Digest* 67 (Oct. 9, 1920): 12–13.
108. *New York Times,* Nov. 7, 1920.
109. See "Making the Black Sox White Again," *Literary Digest* 70 (Aug. 20, 1921), 13–14; "The Flaw in the Diamond," *Literary Digest* 67 (Oct. 9, 1920): 12–13; "The Baseball Scandal," *Nation,* Oct. 13, 1920, 395; and "For Honest Baseball," *Outlook* 126 (Oct. 6, 1920): 219–20.
110. *Chicago Tribune, Herald and Examiner,* and *New York Times,* Oct. 2, 1920. Coincidentally, Judge Landis, who was appointed to "clean up baseball," was the same judge who presided over the trial of IWW leader "Big Bill" Haywood during World War I, when he sentenced Haywood and ninety-two other union members to prison for sedition and alleged obstruction of the nation's war preparations. See Melvyn Dubofsky, *"Big Bill" Haywood* (New York: St. Martin's Press, 1987).
111. "Judge Landis, the New Czar of Baseballdom," *Literary Digest* 67 (Dec. 4, 1920): 46–48. See also Burk, *Never Just a Game,* 235–240.
112. *New York World,* quoted in Frommer, *Shoeless Joe,* 170; *Literary Digest* 70 (Aug. 20, 1921): 13–14; *New York Evening Post,* Jan. 28, 1927; and "Judge Landis, the New Czar," *Literary Digest* 67 (Dec. 4, 1930): 46–48.
113. See Lizabeth Cohen, *Making a New Deal: Industrial Workers in Chicago, 1919–1939* (Cambridge: Cambridge University Press, 1990), 144–45; Peiss, *Cheap Amusements;* and Rosenzweig, *Eight Hours,* 172. See also Kathryn J. Oberdeck's article "Religion, Culture, and the Politics of Class: Alexander Irvine's Mission to Turn-of-the Century New Haven," *American Quarterly* 47 (June 1995): 236–79.

CHAPTER SIX

1. Langston Hughes, *The Big Sea: An Autobiography* (New York: Alfred A. Knopf, 1945), 33.
2. *Chicago Defender,* June 18, 1910; Apr. 9, 1910.
3. Donald Spivey, *Union and the Black Musician: The Narrative of William Everett Samuels and Chicago Local 208* (Boston: University Press of America, 1984), 38–39.

4. For further discussion of the race riot, see Chicago Commission on Race Relations (hereafter cited as CCRR), *The Negro in Chicago* (Chicago: University of Chicago Press, 1922); St. Clair Drake and Horace R. Cayton, *Black Metropolis: A Study of Negro Life in a Northern City,* 2 vols. (New York: Harcourt, Brace, 1945), 65–73; James R. Grossman, *Land of Hope: Chicago, Black Southerners, and the Great Migration* (Chicago: University of Chicago Press, 1989), 178–80; Arnold R. Hirsch, *Making the Second Ghetto: Race and Housing in Chicago, 1940–1960* (Cambridge: Cambridge University Press, 1983), 40–45, 68–69; Allan H. Spear, *Black Chicago: The Making of a Negro Ghetto* (Chicago: University of Chicago Press, 1967); and William M. Tuttle Jr., *Race Riot: Chicago in the Red Summer of 1919* (New York: Atheneum, 1970).
5. Previous accounts of the riot focus on both housing and workplace tensions as its cause. While racial animosity in both arenas certainly provided the tinder, the issue of access to public leisure space sparked the violence. See Spear, *Black Chicago,* for an account of the riot that stresses housing, and Tuttle, *Race Riot,* for a focus on workplace tensions.
6. See Kevin J. Mumford, *Interzones: Black / White Sex Districts in Chicago and New York in the Early Twentieth Century* (New York: Columbia University Press, 1997), 27, for further discussion of racial segregation and "vice" reform.
7. Drake and Cayton, *Black Metropolis,* 1:178–211; Otis D. Duncan and Beverly Duncan, *The Negro Population of Chicago* (Chicago: University of Chicago Press, 1957), 89; Spear, *Black Chicago,* 20–21.
8. CCRR, *Negro in Chicago,* 117.
9. Grossman, *Land of Hope,* 135.
10. Announcement of Hyde Park–Kenwood Property Owners' Association meeting, quoted in CCRR, *Negro in Chicago,* 118.
11. *Property Owners' Journal,* Dec. 13, 1919, Jan. 1, 1920, quoted in CCRR, *Negro in Chicago,* 121.
12. CCRR, *Negro in Chicago,* 123.
13. Ibid., 124.
14. *Chicago Defender,* Nov. 5, 1910. For further discussion of Binga's background, see Drake and Cayton, *Black Metropolis,* 82; and Christopher Robert Reed, *The Chicago NAACP and the Rise of Professional Black Leadership, 1910–1966* (Bloomington: Indiana University Press, 1997), 59–60.
15. CCRR, *Negro in Chicago,* 125–26.
16. "Chicago Commission on Race Relations—Housing," Victor Lawson Papers, Newberry Library.
17. For further discussion of definitions of "vice" and its relation to an "informal" economy,

see Cynthia Blair, "Vicious Commerce: African American Women's Sex Work and the Transformation of Urban Space in Chicago, 1850–1915" (Ph.D. diss., Harvard University, 1999), 182–86; Timothy Gilfoyle, *City of Eros: New York City, Prostitution, and the Commercialization of Sex* (New York: W. W. Norton, 1992); and Victoria W. Wolcott, *Remaking Respectability: African American Women in Interwar Detroit* (Chapel Hill: University of North Carolina Press, 2001), esp. chap. 3.

18. Herbert Asbury, *The Gem of the Prairie: An Informal History of the Chicago Underworld* (De Kalb: Northern Illinois University, 1941), 102. See also Clifton R. Wooldridge, *Hands Up! In the World of Crime* (Chicago: Police Publishing Company, 1901), 60.

19. Walter Reckless, *Vice in Chicago* (Chicago: University of Chicago Press, 1933); William T. Stead, *If Christ Came to Chicago! A Plea for the Union of All Who Love in the Service of All Who Suffer* (Chicago: Laird and Lee, 1894).

20. Stead, *If Christ Came to Chicago!* 249–52.

21. Wooldridge, *Hands Up!* 482–83.

22. Blair, "Vicious Commerce," 239–40.

23. See Asbury, *Gem of the Prairie,* chap. 4; Mumford, *Interzones,* chap. 1; Walter C. Reckless, "The Natural History of Vice Areas in Chicago" (Ph.D. diss.: University of Chicago, 1925), 12. For further discussion of urban space and homosexuality, see George Chauncey, *Gay New York: Gender, Urban Culture, and the Making of the Gay Male World, 1890–1940* (New York: Basic Books, 1994); Elizabeth Lapovsky Kennedy and Madeline D. Davis, *Boots of Leather, Slippers of Gold: The History of a Lesbian Community* (New York: Routledge, 1993); Esther Newton, *Cherry Grove, Fire Island: Sixty Years in America's First Gay and Lesbian Town* (Boston: Beacon, 1993); and Marc Stein, *City of Sisterly and Brotherly Loves: Lesbian and Gay Philadelphia, 1945–1972* (Chicago: University of Chicago Press, 2000).

24. Carter H. *Harrison, Stormy Years: The Autobiography of Carter H. Harrison, Five Times Mayor of Chicago* (New York: Bobbs-Merrill, 1935), 311.

25. *Chicago Record-Herald,* May 31, 1905. Historian Peter Baldwin argues that these efforts at segregating vice grew out of reformers' failure to completely eradicate it. Segregation, then, was a compromise between reformers and the political officials and owners of illicit businesses to address the problem of vice in the city. See Peter C. Baldwin, *Domesticating the Street: The Reform of Public Space in Hartford, 1850–1930* (Columbus: Ohio State University Press, 1999).

26. Chicago Vice Commission, *The Social Evil in Chicago* (Chicago: Chicago Vice Commission, 1913), 7–10.

27. For further discussion of the relation between vice, interracial sex districts, and reform,

see Blair, "Vicious Commerce," chap. 5; Mumford, *Interzones,* 18–35; Gilfoyle, *City of Eros,* 209–15; and Wolcott, *Remaking Respectability,* 93-113.

28. Chicago Vice Commission, *Social Evil in Chicago,* 77.
29. Ibid., 82, 34.
30. Ibid., 34.
31. Ibid., 35.
32. Ibid., 45. For further discussion of women's reform efforts to counter prostitution, see Joanne Meyerowitz, *Women Adrift: Independent Wage-Earning Women in Chicago, 1880–1930* (Chicago: University of Chicago Press, 1988); Kathy Peiss, *Cheap Amusements: Working Women and Leisure in Turn-of-the-Century New York* (Philadelphia: Temple University Press, 1988); Ruth Rosen, *The Lost Sisterhood: Prostitution in the Progressive Era* (Chicago: University of Chicago Press, 1982); and Christine Stansell, *City of Women: Sex and Class in New York, 1789–1860* (Urbana: University of Illinois Press, 1987).
33. *Chicago Defender,* Oct. 12, 1912.
34. Chicago Vice Commission, *Social Evil in Chicago,* 38.
35. Louise de Koven Bowen, *The Colored People of Chicago* (Chicago: University of Chicago Press, 1913), 11; E. Franklin Frazier, *The Negro Family in Chicago* (Chicago: University of Chicago Press, 1930).
36. Chicago League on Urban Conditions among Negroes, "Suggestions for Block Visitors," Arthur Aldis Papers, Special Collections, University of Illinois at Chicago, folder 6 (1917).
37. For further discussion of gender, race, and reform, see Evelyn Brooks Higginbotham, *Righteous Discontent: The Women's Movement in the Black Baptist Church, 1880–1920* (Cambridge: Harvard University Press, 1993), 185–229; Anne Meis Knupfer, *Toward a Tenderer Humanity and a Nobler Womanhood; Africa-American Women's Clubs in Turn-of-the-Century Chicago* (New York: New York University Press, 1996); Elizabeth Lasch-Quinn, *Black Neighbors: Race and the Limits of the American Settlement House Movement, 1890–1945* (Chapel Hill: University of North Carolina Press, 1993); Stephanie Shaw, *What a Woman Ought to Be and to Do: Black Professional Women Workers during the Jim Crow Era* (Chicago: University of Chicago Press, 1996); Daphne Spain, *How Women Saved the City* (Minneapolis: University of Minnesota Press, 2001), esp. 118–22; and Wolcott, *Remaking Respectability,* esp. chap. 2.
38. *Broad Ax,* July 20, 1913. For further discussion of Ida B. Wells-Barnett, see Ida B. Wells, *Crusade for Justice: The Autobiography of Ida B. Wells,* ed. Alfreda M. Duster (Chicago: University of Chicago Press, 1970); Linda O. McMurray, *To Keep the Waters Troubled: The Life of Ida B. Wells* (New York: Oxford University Press, 1998); and Patricia A. Schechter, *Ida B.*

Wells-Barnett and American Reform, 1880–1930 (Chapel Hill: University of North Carolina Press, 2001).

39. "Ida B. Wells—the Mother of Clubs," Ida B. Wells Papers, box 10, folder 10, Special Collections Research Center, University of Chicago Library.

40. Schecter, *Ida B. Wells-Barnett*, 181.

41. *Chicago Defender*, Feb. 28, 1920.

42. Quoted in Grossman, *Land of Hope*, 140–41.

43. Higginbotham, *Righteous Discontent*, 214; Daphne Spain, "Black Women as City Builders: Redemptive Places and the Legacy of Nannie Helen Burroughs," in *Gendering the City: Women, Boundaries, and Visions of Urban Life*, ed. Kristine B. Miranne and Alma H. Young (Lanham, Md.: Rowman and Littlefield, 2000), 105–18; and Victoria W. Wolcott, "'Bible, Bath, and Broom': Nannie Helen Burroughs's National Training School and African-American Racial Uplift," *Journal of Women's History* 9 (Spring 1997): 89–110. Wolcott points out that of the dozens of letters requesting information about the National Training School, none asks for information about domestic science courses, suggesting that many women preferred commercial and business training to escape the drudgery and low status of domestic work. See Wolcott, *Remaking Respectability*, 253, n. 58.

44. See Knupfer, *Toward a Tenderer Humanity*, 8, and Elizabeth Lindsay Davis, *Lifting as They Climb* (New York: G. K. Hall, 1996).

45. See Grossman, *Land of Hope*, 229.

46. Victor F. Lawson to Ida B. Wells-Barnett, June 10, 1910, in Victor Lawson Papers, Newberry Library. See also Schechter, *Ida B. Wells-Barnett*, 189.

47. *Chicago Defender*, Jan. 7, 1911; Oct. 11, 1911: Aug. 26, 1911.

48. Commission on Chicago Landmarks, *Black Metropolis Historic District*, (Chicago: Commission on Chicago Landmarks, 1994), 16. For further discussion of YMCA architecture, see Paula Lupkin, "YMCA Architecture: Building Character in the American City, 1869–1930" (Ph.D. diss., University of Pennsylvania, 1997).

49. *Chicago Defender*, Aug. 26, 1911.

50. Wells, *Crusade for Justice*, 332. See also Grossman, *Land of Hope*, 141. James Grossman points out that the Wabash YMCA became a vehicle for promoting antiunion sentiment, with Swift, Armour, and other packinghouse employers buying company memberships for their workers and sponsoring talks on discipline, industriousness, and worker loyalty. In addition, many of the YMCA's recreational programs were sponsored by packing companies and tried to cement worker loyalty to the company. See Grossman, *Land of Hope*, 228.

51. Quoted in Grossman, *Land of Hope*, 142.
52. Reed, *Chicago NAACP*, 46. Newspapers like the *Chicago Defender* celebrated the success of both the Wabash YMCA and the Urban League and their roles in aiding new migrants both through finding them housing and employment and in promoting uplift and respectability. Yet these two institutions also diverted money from neighborhood-based black civic institutions like Wells-Barnett's Negro Fellowship League. See Schechter, *Ida B. Wells-Barnett*, 189–90.
53. *Chicago Defender*, Aug. 17, 1918.
54. *Chicago Defender*, May 21, 1910; July 2, 1910; Aug. 5, 1911; Sept. 23, 1911; Robert Peterson, *Only the Ball Was White: A History of Legendary Black Players and All-Black Professional Teams before Black Men Played in the Major Leagues* (New York: McGraw-Hill, 1984), 63–64; and Harold Seymour, *Baseball: The People's Game* (New York: Oxford University Press, 1990), 262. For further discussion of African Americans in baseball, see Phil Dixon with Patrick J. Hannigan, *The Negro Baseball Leagues, 1867–1955: A Photographic History* (Mattituck, N.Y.: Amereon House, 1992); David Falkner, *Great Time Coming: The Life of Jackie Robinson from Baseball to Birmingham* (New York: Simon and Schuster, 1995); John B. Holway, *Blackball Stars: Negro League Pioneers* (Westport, Conn.: Meckler Books, 1988); Holway, *Black Diamonds: Life in the Negro Leagues from the Men Who Lived It* (Westport, Conn.: Meckler Books, 1989); Mark Ribowsky, *A Complete History of the Negro Leagues, 1884–1955* (Secaucus, N.J.: Carol, 1995); Ribowsky, *The Power and the Darkness: The Life of Josh Gibson in the Shadows of the Game* (New York: Simon and Schuster, 1996); *Sol White's History of Colored Base Ball, with Other Documents of the Early Black Game, 1886–1936* (Lincoln: University of Nebraska Press, 1995); and Jules Tygiel, *Baseball's Great Experiment: Jackie Robinson and His Legacy* (New York: Oxford University Press, 1983).
55. *Broad Ax*, Nov. 2, 1907; *Chicago Defender*, July 2, 1910; Michael E. Lomax, "Black Entrepreneurship in the National Pastime: The Rise of Semiprofessional Baseball in Black Chicago, 1890–1915," *Journal of Sport History* 25, 1 (Spring 1998): 43–64, esp. 50; Peterson, *Only the Ball*, 104–8; Steven Riess, *City Games: The Evolution of American Urban Society and the Rise of Sports* (Urbana: University of Illinois Press, 1989), 118; *Sol White's History*, 143–45; Spear, *Black Chicago*, 116–18; and Linda Ziemer, "Chicago's Negro Leagues," *Chicago History* 22 (Fall–Winter 1994–95): 37–51, 37.
56. *Chicago Defender*, May 14, 1910.
57. *Chicago Defender*, June 25, 1910. The team left its other site, Auburn Park, because the grounds were being sold and the city planned to subdivide the lot.
58. *Chicago Defender*, advertisement for Leland Giants, in multiple issues after June 1910.

59. *Chicago Defender,* June 18, 1910. There actually were four black professional teams in Chicago in 1911: the American Giants, the Leland Giants, the Chicago Giants, and the Union Giants. See Lomax, "Black Entrepreneurship," 56.

60. Leland Giants advertisement in the *Chicago Defender,* May 27, 1911.

61. *Chicago Defender,* Aug. 5, 1911; Peterson, *Only the Ball,* 112–15; Ribowsky, *Complete History,* chaps. 1–2; and *Sol White's History,* xxiv, xliv, 147, 152.

62. Advertisement in *Chicago Defender,* Apr. 23, 1910.

63. *Chicago Defender,* Aug. 17, 1910. See also Lomax, "Black Entrepreneurship," 51.

64. *Chicago Defender,* May 21, 1910.

65. *Chicago Defender,* May 21, 1910; June 7, 1910. See also Apr. 28, 1910 and July 2, 1910.

66. *Chicago Defender,* Dec. 3, 1910.

67. *Chicago Defender,* July 13, 1912.

68. Jack Johnson, *The Autobiography of Jack Johnson: In the Ring and Out* (Chicago: National Sports Press, 1927), 66.

69. Dempsey J. Travis, *An Autobiography of Black Jazz* (Chicago: Urban Research Institute, 1983), 69.

70. *Chicago Defender,* July 13, 1912.

71. Randy Roberts, *Papa Jack: Jack Johnson and the Era of White Hopes* (New York: Free Press, 1983), 138. See also Blair, "Vicious Commerce," 359.

72. *Chicago Defender,* June 11, 1910.

73. *Chicago Inter-Ocean,* May 12, 1901.

74. Quoted in Travis, *Black Jazz,* 26.

75. For further discussion of policy in Chicago, and its relation to black business and politics, see Mark H. Haller, "Policy Gambling, Entertainment, and the Emergence of Black Politics: Chicago from 1900–1940," *Journal of Social History* 24, no. 4 (Summer 1991): 719–39. See also Drake and Cayton, *Black Metropolis,* 490–94.

76. *Chicago Defender,* Feb. 24, 1912.

77. *Broad Ax,* Feb. 3, 1906; July 9, 1910. For further discussion of the origins of the Pekin, see William Howland Kenney, *Chicago Jazz: A Cultural History* (New York: Oxford University Press, 1993), 5–8.

78. Wells, *Crusade for Justice,* 290.

79. *Chicago Defender,* May 12, 1906.

80. Wells, *Crusade for Justice,* 289–95; Knupfer, *Toward a Tenderer Humanity,* 126; and Schechter, *Ida B. Wells-Barnett,* 185–86. Jane Addams jumped in with help after the theatrical troop canceled, providing performers from the Hull House School of Dramatic Art.

81. *Broad Ax,* May 5, 1906.

82. Robert E. Weems, *Black Business in the Black Metropolis: The Chicago Metropolitan Assurance Company, 1925–1985* (Bloomington: Indiana University Press, 1996), 1–5. Robert A. Cole, who took over the funeral association, would use his money to support the American Giants, keeping the team in black hands after the death of Rube Foster in 1930. Weems, *Black Business,* 63.

83. *Chicago Defender,* Mar. 16, 1912.

84. *Crisis* 4, no. 5 (Sept. 1912): 217.

85. *Chicago Daily News,* Dec. 14, 1916.

86. Alberta Hunter, quoted in *Hear Me Talkin' to Ya: The Story of Jazz as Told by the Men Who Made It,* ed. Nat Shapiro and Nat Hentoff (New York: Dover, 1966), 88.

87. Frederic Ramsey Jr., "Going down State Street: Lincoln Gardens and Friar's Inn Set the Stage for Chicago Jazz," in *Jazzways,* ed. George S. Rosenthal and Frank Zachary (New York: Greenberg, 1947), 22–33, esp. 24–26.

88. Burton W. Peretti, *The Creation of Jazz: Music, Race, and Culture in Urban America* (Urbana: University of Illinois Press, 1994), 52. For a discussion of leisure sites in structuring black communal life, see Farah Jasmine Griffin, *"Who Set You Flowin'?": The African-American Migration Narrative* (New York: Oxford University Press, 1995). For further discussion of jazz clubs and their role in urban nightlife see Lewis Erenberg, *Steppin' Out: New York Nightlife and the Transformation of American Culture, 1890–1930* (Westport, Conn.: Greenwood Press, 1981), 129–30. There are two Web sites that are particularly useful for tracing the locations of dance halls and theaters in the Black Belt. They are the Chicago Jazz Archive site, which can be found through the University of Chicago's library site at www.lib.uchicaqo.edu/e/su/cja, and the Jazz Age Chicago site, created by Scott A. Newman, at www.suba.com~scottn/explore/mainmenu/htm.

89. *Chicago Defender* Jan. 23, 1915. See also Kenney, *Chicago Jazz,* 10.

90. Stanley Dance, *The World of Earl Hines* (New York: Scribner, 1977), 36.

91. Ibid.

92. *Chicago Defender,* quoted in Rosenthal and Zachary, *Jazzways,* 27.

93. Kenney, *Chicago Jazz,* 24.

94. *Chicago Defender,* July 27, 1920.

95. CCRR, *Negro in Chicago,* 323.

96. Louise de Koven Bowen, *The Public Dance Halls of Chicago* (Chicago: Juvenile Protective Association, 1917), 4.

97. Alberta Hunter, quoted in *Hear Me Talkin' to Ya,* 87.

98. Earl Hines, quoted in Dance, *World of Earl Hines,* 36; Scoville Brown, quoted in Peretti, *Creation of Jazz,* 138. In addition, Dan Jackson ran a policy wheel in a gambling house above the Dreamland Café. See Haller, "Policy Gambling," 725.

99. Alberta Hunter, quoted in Peretti, *Creation of Jazz,* 68.

100. *Chicago Defender,* May 23, 1914.

101. "Chicago Jazz Spots, 1914–1928," in Paul Eduard Miller, *Esquire Magazine's 1946 Jazz Book* (New York: A. S. Barnes, 1946). The map appears in a foldout at the back of the book.

102. See Drake and Cayton, *Black Metropolis,* 360–67; Harold F. Gosnell, *Negro Politicians: The Rise of Negro Politics in Chicago* (Chicago: University of Chicago Press, 1967), chap. 3; and Haller, "Policy Gambling," 724–25.

103. *Chicago Defender,* Sept. 18, 1915, quoted in Tuttle, *Race Riot,* 190–91.

104. For further discussion of black support for Thompson, see Douglas Bukowski, *Big Bill Thompson, Chicago, and the Politics of Image* (Urbana: University of Illinois Press, 1998), chap. 4; Gosnell, *Negro Politicians,* chap. 3; Mark Haller, "Urban Vice and Civic Reform: Chicago in the Early Twentieth Century," in *Cities in American History,* ed. Kenneth T. Jackson and Stanley K. Schultz (New York: Alfred A. Knopf, 1971), 290–305; and Spear, *Black Chicago,* 187–91.

105. See Wells, *Crusade for Justice,* 348–50, and Schechter, *Ida B. Wells-Barnett,* 205–6.

106. Quoted in Drake and Cayton, *Black Metropolis,* 365.

107. Claude A. Barnett, "We Win a Place in Industry," *Opportunity,* March 1929, reprinted in *African Americans in the Industrial Age: A Documentary History, 1915–1945,* ed. Joe W, Trotter and Earl Lewis (Boston: Northeastern University Press, 1996), 126–35, 128–29.

108. For general discussions of organizing during the postwar period, see Foster Rhea Dulles and Melvyn Dubofsky, *Labor in America: A History* (New York: Harlan Davidson, 1984), especially chaps. 11 and 12; James R. Green, *The World of the Worker: Labor in Twentieth Century America* (New York: Hill and Wang, 1980); and David Montgomery, *The Fall of the House of Labor: The Workplace, the State, and American Labor Activism, 1865–1925* (Cambridge: Cambridge University Press, 1987).

109. For further discussion of the links between Americanism, class, and whiteness, see James R. Barrett, "Americanization from the Bottom Up: Immigration and the Remaking of the Working Class in United States, 1880–1930," *Journal of* American *History* 79 (December 1992): 996-1020; David R. Roediger, "Whiteness and Ethnicity in the History of 'White Ethnics' in the United States, in *Towards the Abolition of Whiteness: Essays on Race,*

Politics, and Working Class History, ed. David R. Roediger (London: Verso, 1994), 181–98; and David R. Roediger, *The Wages of Whiteness: Race and the Making of the American Working Class* (London: Verso, 1991), esp. chap. 6.

110. James R. Barrett, *Work and Community in the Jungle: Chicago's Packinghouse Workers, 1894–1922* (Urbana: University of Illinois Press, 1987), 189–228, and Robert A. Slayton, *Back of the Yards: The Making of a Local Democracy* (Chicago: University of Chicago Press, 1986), 94–95.

111. *Sunday Jewish Courier,* June 8, 1919, quoted in Tuttle, *Race Riot,* 134. See also Barrett, *Work and Community,* 194–95; CCRR, *Negro in Chicago;* Alma Herbst, *The Negro in the Slaughtering and Meat Packing Industry in Chicago* (New York: Houghton, Mifflin, 1932), 32–35; Spear, *Black Chicago,* 161; and Tuttle, *Race Riot,* 124–25.

112. *Chicago Whip,* July 19, 1919, quoted in Spear, *Black Chicago,* 161.

113. *Chicago Defender,* Feb. 23, 1918. See also Barrett, *Work and Community,* 195, and Grossman, *Land of Hope,* 208–21.

114. *New Majority,* Nov. 22, 1919, quoted in Barrett, *Work and Community,* 200, and Tuttle, *Race Riot,* 126–27. See also Eleanor Kroll, "The History of the University of Chicago Settlement," Mary McDowell Papers, box 1, folder 3a, Chicago Historical Society, Special Collections.

115. Bureau of Labor Statistics, *Retail Prices 1913 to December 1919* (Washington, D.C.: Government Printing Office, 1921), 130–35.

116. See Ray Stannard Baker, *The New Industrial Unrest* (Garden City, N.Y.: Doubleday, Page, 1920), 112; Nell Irvin Painter, *Standing at Armageddon: The United States, 1877–1919* (New York: W. W. Norton, 1987), 358–62; and Tuttle, *Race Riot,* 141.

117. Robert Parker advertisement for the American Unity Welfare Labor League, quoted in Barrett, *Work and Community,* 218. See also CCRR, *Negro in Chicago,* 422–23; Grossman, *Land of Hope,* 227; Paul Street, "Packinghouse Blues," *Chicago History* 18 (Fall 1989): 69–85, esp. 72–73; and Tuttle, *Race Riot,* 152.

118. Barrett, *Work and Community,* 218.

119. See David Brody, *Steelworkers in America: The Non-union Era* (Cambridge: Harvard University Press, 1960), and Lizabeth Cohen, *Making a New Deal: Industrial Workers in Chicago, 1919–1939* (Cambridge: Cambridge University Press, 1990), 38–34.

120. "Steel Trust Spy Chiefs Try to Start Race Riot," *New Majority,* Oct. 11, 1919, also quoted in Cohen, *Making a New Deal,* 41.

121. William Z. Foster, *The Great Steel Strike and Its Lessons* (New York: B. W. Huebsch, 1920), 198, also quoted in Cohen, *Making a New Deal,* 41.

122. See Brody, *Steelworkers in America,* 224–25; CCRR, *Negro in Chicago,* 430; Foster, *Great Steel Strike,* 205–7; Grossman, *Land of Hope,* 211; and Spear, *Black Chicago,* 163–64.

123. For further discussion of the steel strike, see David Brody, *Labor in Crisis: The Steel Strike of 1919* (Philadelphia: J. B. Lippincott, 1965); Brody, *Steelworkers in America;* Cohen, *Making a New Deal,* esp. 38–43; Commission of Inquiry, Interchurch World Movement, *Report on the Steel Strike of 1919* (1920; New York: Da Capo Press, 1970); Melvin Dubofsky, *We Shall Be All: A History of the Industrial Workers of the World* (Urbana: University of Illinois Press, 1988); David Montgomery, *The Fall of the House of Labor: The Workplace, the State, and American Labor Activism* (Cambridge: Cambridge University Press, 1987); and Colston E. Warne, ed., *The Steel Strike of 1919* (Boston: D. C. Heath, 1963).

124. *Chicago Defender,* July 12, 1919.

125. CCRR, *Negro in Chicago,* 5–8; Carl Sandberg, *The Chicago Race Riots, July, 1919* (1919; New York: Harcourt, Brace and World, 1969) 5.

126. *Chicago Defender,* Aug. 2, 1919, cited in CCRR, *Negro in Chicago,* 31.

127. *Chicago Daily News,* July 30, 1919, cited in CCRR, *Negro in Chicago,* 31.

128. In addition, one account of the very beginnings of the riot claimed it stemmed from a disagreement between black and white gamblers over a craps game on the shore that was "virtually under the protection of the police officer on the beat." According to this account, the police officer was so immersed in the crap game that he failed to arrest the white youth responsible for Williams's murder, thereby precipitating the riot. CCRR, *Negro in Chicago,* 5.

129. Mary McDowell, "Prejudice," in *Mary McDowell and Municipal Housekeeping,* ed. Caroline Hill (Chicago: University of Chicago Press, 1938), 32. See also Sandberg, *Chicago Race Riots,* 5.

130. CCRR, *Negro in Chicago,* 9, 11.

131. *Chicago Daily Tribune,* July 29, 1919.

132. "For White Union Men to Read," *New Majority,* quoted in CCRR, *Negro in Chicago,* 45.

133. Quoted in CCRR, *Negro in Chicago,* 46.

134. *New York Times,* Oct. 3, 1919; Oct. 5, 1919; Oct. 1, 1919.

135. For further discussion of the Palmer Raids, see Green, *World of the Worker,* 90–95; John Higham, *Strangers in the Land: Patterns of American Nativism, 1860–1925* (New York: Atheneum, 1963), 226–33; Painter, *Standing at Armageddon,* 367–80; and Tuttle, *Race Riot,* 17–20.

136. *Chicago Defender,* Feb. 7, 1920.

137. Robert E. Parker to Warren G. Harding, Mar. 11, 1921, Record Group 280, Federal Mediation and Conciliation Service, Washington National Records Center. I thank James R. Grossman for providing me with a copy of this letter.

138. *Chicago Defender,* July 12, 1919.

139. Drake and Cayton, *Black Metropolis,* 57.

140. For further discussion of race, labor, and the creation of whiteness, see George Lipsitz, "The Possessive Investment in Whiteness: Racialized Social Democracy and the 'White' Problem in American Studies," *American Quarterly* 47, no. 3 (Sept. 1995): 369–87; Roediger, "Whiteness and Ethnicity," 181–98; and Roediger, *Wages of Whiteness,* esp. chap. 6.

141. For further discussion of white jazz, see Lewis A. Erenberg, *Swinging the Dream: Big Band Jazz and the Rebirth of American Culture* (Chicago: University of Chicago Press, 1998); Kenney, Chicago Jazz, chaps. 3 and 4; and Peretti, *Creation of Jazz.*

CONCLUSION

1. Richard Hofstadter's classic text *The Age of Reform* (New York: Vintage Books, 1955) was the first of several accounts to show how progressivism as well as populism ultimately resulted in state-centered reform.

2. John Higham, "Integrating America: The Problem of Assimilation in the Nineteenth Century," *Journal of American Ethnic History* 1, no. 1 (Fall 1981): 7–25, esp. 7.

3. For further discussion of the Chicago school's "race relations cycle," see Robert E. L. Faris, *Chicago Sociology, 1920–1932* (Chicago: University of Chicago Press, 1967), 57; Lester R. Kurtz, *Evaluating Chicago Sociology: A Guide to the Literature, with an Annotated Bibliography* (Chicago: University of Chicago Press, 1984), 70–72; and Stow Persons, *Ethnic Studies at Chicago, 1905–45* (Urbana: University of Illinois Press, 1987), 602. For a thoughtful evaluation of the historiography of assimilation, see Russell A. Kazal, "Revisiting Assimilation: The Rise, Fall, and Reappraisal of a Concept in American Ethnic History," *American Historical Review* 100 (April 1995): 347–471.

4. Ernest W. Burgess, "Can Neighborhood Work Have a Scientific Basis?" in *The City,* ed. Robert E. Park, Ernest W. Burgess, and Roderick D. McKenzie (1925; Chicago: University of Chicago Press, 1967), 143.

5. Ernest W. Burgess and Donald J. Bogue, *Contributions to Urban Sociology* (Chicago: University of Chicago Press, 1964), 488. See also Charles Horton Cooley, *Social Organization: A Study of the Larger Mind* (New York: Scribner, 1909), 342–53, for further discussion of social ecology based on themes of disorganization.

6. Ernest W. Burgess, "The Growth of the City: An Introduction to a Research Project," in *The City,* ed. Robert E. Park, Ernest W. Burgess, and Roderick D. McKenzie (1925; Chicago: University of Chicago Press, 1967), 57. See Faris, *Chicago Sociology,* 49; and Per-

sons, *Ethnic Studies at Chicago*, 60–63, for a discussion of Park's understanding of this pattern.

7. For a discussion of these critiques of the Chicago School, see Kurtz, *Evaluating Chicago Sociology*, 71–72.
8. See W. E. B. Du Bois, *The Souls of Black Folk* (Chicago: A. C. McClurg, 1906), quoted in David Levering Lewis, *W. E. B. Du Bois: Biography of a Race, 1868–1919* (New York: Henry Holt, 1993), 281. Lewis argues that Du Bois's theory of double consciousness transcended the dialectic of African American assimilation verses separateness by "affirming them in permanent tension."
9. Robert E. Park, "Human Migration and the Marginal Man," *American Journal of Sociology* 33 (May 1928): 339–44. See also Kurtz, *Evaluating Chicago Sociology*, 54–55.
10. While Park emphasized the importance of neutral scientific observation, he also played a leading role in local civic activities, especially in his capacity as first president of the Chicago Urban League.
11. W. E. B. Du Bois, *The Philadelphia Negro* (Philadelphia: University of Pennsylvania, 1899). For further discussion of some of the tensions within Du Bois's work, see "Introduction," in *W. E. B. Du Bois, Race, and the City: The Philadelphia Negro and Its Legacy*, ed. Michael B. Katz and Thomas J. Sugrue (Philadelphia: University of Pennsylvania Press, 1998), 1–37.
12. Chicago Commission on Race Relations, *The Negro in Chicago* (Chicago: University of Chicago Press, 1922), 652–53.
13. Ibid., 645.
14. Charles Edward Merriam, *Chicago: A More Intimate View of Urban Politics* (New York: Macmillan, 1929), 26.
15. Ibid., chap. 7.
16. See Edward R. Kantowicz, *Polish-American Politics in Chicago, 1888–1940* (Chicago: University of Chicago Press, 1979), 135–38, for further discussion of Sweitzer. Kantowicz explains that while Sweitzer's father was Irish American, he died when Robert was young. Robert's mother later married Sweitzer, who adopted Robert and gave him his name.
17. *Dziennik Zwiazkowy*, Apr. 5, 1915, in *Chicago Foreign Language Press Survey*, Chicago Public Library Omnibus Project (Chicago: The Project, 1942).
18. *Chicago Tribune*, Apr. 6, 1915.
19. For further discussion of Thompson's wartime coalitions and his relationship with African American voters, see John M. Allswang, *A House for All Peoples: Ethnic Politics in Chicago, 1890–1936* (Lexington: University of Kentucky Press, 1971), 34–36; St. Clair Drake

and Horace R. Cayton, *Black Metropolis: A Study of Negro Life in a Northern City* (New York: Harcourt, Brace, 1945), 24, 108–11, 372; Harold F. Gosnell, *Negro Politicians: The Rise of Negro Politics in Chicago* (Chicago: University of Chicago Press, 1935), 40–51; William J. Grimshaw, *Bitter Fruit: Black Politics and the Chicago Machine, 1931–1991* (Chicago: University of Chicago Press, 1992), 3–25; Allan H. Spear, *Black Chicago: The Making of a Negro Ghetto* (Chicago: University of Chicago Press, 1967), 186–92; William M. Tuttle Jr., *Race Riot: Chicago in the Red Summer of 1919* (New York: Atheneum, 1970), 184–207; and Lloyd Wendt and Herman Kogan, *Big Bill of Chicago* (Indianapolis: Bobbs-Merrill, 1953), 94–96, 112–14.

20. Quoted in Tuttle, *Race Riot,* 201. See also *Chicago Daily News,* Apr. 1, 1919; Gosnell, *Negro Politicians,* 369; and Wendt and Kogan, *Big Bill,* 167–68.

21. See James R. Grossman, *Land of Hope: Chicago, Black Southerners, and the Great Migration* (Chicago: University of Chicago Press, 1989), 177.

22. *New York Times,* Apr. 2, 1919.

23. The election totals were as follows: Thompson (Republican), 259,828; Sweitzer (Democrat), 238,206; Hoyne (Independent), 110,851; Fitzpatrick (Labor), 55,900; and Collins (Socialist), 24,079. See *Chicago Daily News, Chicago Defender,* and *Chicago Tribune,* Apr. 2, 1919; Allswang, *House for All Peoples,* 41–46; Gosnell, *Negro Politicians,* 38–41; Kantowicz, *Polish-American Politics,* 143; and Merriam, *Chicago,* 189. Thompson got only 13 percent of the Polish vote and did poorly among the Czechs, Lithuanians, Yugoslavians, and Italians, most of whom voted Democratic. He successfully captured the German and Swedish votes, however, along with the Jewish and African American vote. See Allswang, *House for All Peoples,* 40.

24. Drake and Cayton, *Black Metropolis,* 24.

25. *Chicago Tribune,* 1931, quoted in Mark Norman, *Mayors, Madams, and Madmen* (Chicago: Chicago Review Press, 1979), 65.

26. Gosnell, *Negro Politicians,* 372.

27. Merriam, *Chicago,* 303.

28. Some of the central texts in the historiography of progressivism include Richard T. Hofstadter, *The Age of Reform: From Bryan to F.D.R.* (New York: Vintage Books, 1955), and Robert H. Wiebe, *The Search for Order, 1877–1920* (New York: Hill and Wang, 1967). Neo-Marxist views of progressivism include Samuel P. Hays, "The Politics of Reform in Municipal Government in the Progressive Era," *Pacific Northwest Quarterly* 55 (October 1964): 157–69; Gabriel Kolko, *The Triumph of Conservatism: A Reinterpretation of American History* (New York: Alfred A. Knopf, 1963); and James Weinstein, *The Corporate Ideal in the Liberal State, 1900–1918* (Boston: Beacon Press, 1968). Accounts that emphasize progres-

sivism's role in creating technocracy and an "organizational synthesis" include Louis Galambos, "Technology, Political Economy, and Professionalization: Central Themes of the Organizational Synthesis," *Business History Review* 57 (Winter 1983): 471–93; Eric Nordlinger, "Taking the State Seriously," in *Understanding Political Development,* ed. Myron Weiner and Samuel P. Huntington (Boston: Little, Brown, 1987), 353–390; and Stephen Skowronek, *Building the New American State: The Expansion of National Administrative Capacities, 1877–1920* (Cambridge: Cambridge University Press, 1982).

29. For further discussion of progressivism and the changing understanding of reform, see Blaine A. Brownell, "Interpretations of Twentieth-Century Urban Progressive Reform," in *Reform and Reformers in the Progressive Era,* ed. David R. Colburn and George E. Pozzetta (Westport, Conn.: Greenwood Press, 1983), 5–7; Eldon J. Eisenach, *The Lost Promise of Progressivism* (Lawrence: University of Kansas Press, 1994), 221; Arthur A. Ekirch Jr., *Progressivism in America: A Study of the Era from Theodore Roosevelt to Woodrow Wilson* (New York: New Viewpoints, 1974) 94–95; Maureen A. Flanagan, *Charter Reform in Chicago* (Carbondale: Southern Illinois University Press, 1987), x; Georg Leidenberger, "Working-Class Progressivism and the Politics of Transportation in Chicago, 1895–1907" (Ph.D. diss., University of North Carolina, 1995), 230; and Daniel T. Rodgers, "In Search of Progressivism," *Reviews in American History* 10, no. 4 (December 1982): 113–32. For examinations of progressivism that focus on the state's ability to structure and constitute civil society, see Philip J. Ethington, *The Public City: The Political Construction of Urban Life in San Francisco, 1850–1900* (Cambridge: Cambridge University Press, 1994); Gary Gerstle, "The Protean Character of American Liberalism," *American Historical Review* 99 (October 1994): 1043–73; Stephen D. Krasner, "Approaches to the State: Alternative Conceptions and Historical Dynamics," *Comparative Politics* 16 (January 1984): 223–46; Terrence J. McDonald, "The Burdens of Urban History: The Theory of the State in Recent American Social History," in *Studies in American Political Development: An Annual,* vol. 3 (New Haven: Yale University Press, 1989), 3–55; Terrence J. McDonald, *The Parameters of Urban Fiscal Policy: Socioeconomic Change in San Francisco, 1860–1906* (Berkeley: University of California Press, 1986), 1–18; and Theda Skocpol, "Bringing the State Back In: Strategies of Analysis in Current Research," in *Bringing the State Back In,* ed. Peter Evans, Dietrich Rueschmeyer, and Theda Skocpol (Cambridge: Cambridge University Press, 1985), 3–37.

INDEX